Civil War, Civil Peace

Edited by Helen Yanacopulos and Joseph Hanlon

The Open University
Milton Keynes, United Kingdom

in association with

James Currey
Oxford, United Kingdom

Ohio University Research in International Studies
Global and Comparative Studies Series No. 5
Ohio University Press
Athens

James Currey, 73 Botley Road, Oxford OX2 0BS, United Kingdom
www.jamescurrey.co.uk

Ohio University Press, Athens, OH 45701-2979, USA

The Open University, Walton Hall, Milton Keynes MK7 6AA, United Kingdom

Edited, designed and typeset by The Open University.

Printed and bound in the United Kingdom by Bath Press

Details of Open University courses can be obtained from the Student Registration and Enquiry Service, The Open University, PO Box 197, Milton Keynes, MK7 6BJ, United Kingdom: tel. +44 (0)870 333 4340, email general-enquiries@open.ac.uk

http://www.open.ac.uk

British Library Cataloguing in Publication Data available on request.

Library of Congress Cataloging in Publication Data available on request.

ISBN-10: 0-85255-895-3 (James Currey paper)

ISBN-13: 978-085255-895-9 (James Currey paper)

ISBN: 0-89680-249-3 (Ohio)

Contents

Introduction

Joseph Hanlon and Helen Yanacopulos

More than 200 wars have been fought in the past half-century. Nearly all have been civil wars – wars within a single country. At the beginning of the twenty-first century, more than 30 civil wars were taking place; when fighting stopped in one place, new violence broke out somewhere else, and half of all civil wars started again.

Civil wars are angry and brutal as neighbours and former colleagues fight each other. Millions are killed and maimed; physical destruction sets development back decades; anger and distrust poisons the atmosphere. The 'rules' of interstate war do not apply; each atrocity provokes retribution and civil war takes on a horrible dynamic of its own.

The special brutality and bitterness of civil wars promotes a deep-seated mistrust of the other side. Both leaders and participants argue that the other side killed, raped and maimed and cannot be trusted; 'they' still want to kill 'us' and want to gain through peace talks and postwar rebuilding what 'they' could not gain during war. 'They' always have a hidden agenda to do 'us' down. Frequently, it requires outsiders who are seen as independent of the warring parties to create the climate of security and fairness from which some degree of trust can grow. The warring parties often recognise the need and invite international interveners to play a special role in helping to halt the civil war, helping to guarantee the ceasefire, and helping to rebuild both the physical infrastructure and the social and governmental structure necessary to prevent a return to war.

The United Nations, government aid agencies and non-government organisations (NGOs) have all played critical roles in helping to end civil wars and build a just and stable peace. UN soldiers, whether in their blue helmets or their national uniforms, have kept the warring parties apart and created a climate of confidence which encourages the fighters to disarm. UN agencies, bilateral donors and NGOs have played key roles in providing food and health care to devastated countries and in helping to rebuild schools, roads and even governments.

Outsiders may go to a civil war country and intervene directly in the life of that country; it seems a natural human desire to want to help those who are suffering, and it is clear that many people in those countries are hugely grateful, knowing that the end of the war and their personal survival resulted from outsiders willing to make sacrifices and intervene in someone else's war. But we also know that the results of outside intervention have been decidedly mixed. There have been successes, but there are also many examples where outside interveners have failed to help, or even made matters worse. First, outsiders can only be effective if their intervention is genuinely welcome; if most people want the war to end and if the interveners respond to local needs. The record of forcible intervention has not been good. Second, many past failures result, at least in part, from outsiders who are desperate to 'do something' making simplistic assumptions and acting in ways which prove useless or counterproductive.

Fairness rather than strict neutrality and impartiality seems to be one key to acceptance. For example, if peacekeeping troops are deployed after a peace agreement and one side then breaks that agreement, the peacekeepers cannot stand by and watch – they cannot be neutral between aggressor and victim. People accept and support the peacekeepers because they provide a degree of security for everyone.

Similarly, civil wars often start because one group feels it is being discriminated against and has no other redress. Aid agencies sometimes put a stress on rebuilding which restores what was there before. But that may be seen as restoring serious discrimination or inequity. Fairness means rebuilding in a new way. And rebuilding is as much about institutions as about infrastructure.

Finally, wars change the political and social landscape permanently and irreparably; if leaders of warring groups have gained power they will be reluctant to give it up, while at the base, women, young people or specific regional or social groups may have been empowered by the war. These changes, too, must be dealt with subtly by outsiders trying to balance new power against old, changes in power that some will see as unfair, and the trade-offs which may be unfair but are necessary to end the killing.

It is simpler to be neutral – to bind the wounds and treat all sides of the war equally. But a just and stable peace is not created by simply restoring the conditions that caused the civil war in the first place. The failure to redress the underlying problems is one reason why half of all civil wars start again. This book is written in the belief that outside intervention can be peacebuilding – not simply *re*building but, rather, outsiders working with local people at all levels to support change and build a fair and just peace.

'Building the peace' involves creating conditions that reduce the chances of the war recurring. It is the implicit assumption of peacebuilding and some types of development assistance that we do have influence over the causes of the violence and might be able to reduce suffering by tackling those causes. Peacebuilding actions will address the underlying grievances and inequalities that caused the war; these features can also be seen as part of developmental processes. However, in the past, development interventions have been seen as the answer. There is a contradiction here – development can be peacebuilding but development interventions can change situations and have a destabilising effect. What are needed are development processes which establish institutions that deal with inequalities within a society and with ways of dealing with conflict within societies before violence becomes a reasonable solution. Peacebuilding is a form of specialised development intervention, that is sensitised to the issues in the conflict (and identified through a conflict analysis) that seeks to build new institutions and relations that address original grievances and reconfigure relationships. These peacebuilding and development themes are discussed by the various contributors to this book.

Increasingly we find that there are limits to what outsiders can do in peacebuilding. A study commissioned by the European Union High Representative for Foreign Policy makes the point that:

> International interventions can never be more than 'enabling'. What they can achieve depends on the consent of most of the population. There is a tendency among 'internationals' to assume that they know best. Conventional attitudes have too often been to 'do it for them' or to work with weak or criminalised 'leaders'. Institution building is bound to fail when it excludes those for whom the institutions are built.
>
> (Study Group, 2004)

Yet, in an attempt not to be arrogant and seem to 'know best' and in trying to gain the consent of the population or at least its presumed leaders, outsiders often accept what they call 'traditional' practices and discriminations – despite the fact that the civil war may have come about because a group no longer was willing to put up with being discriminated against in the 'traditional' way. Outsiders are important for peacebuilding precisely because they bring with them approaches and new ideas about democracy, human rights, fairness and justice. The very independence of international interveners is one of their strengths – they can stand between the warring parties and provide security; they can identify past discrimination and point to ways forward.

Like a good juggler, an international intervener can only be successful by keeping several balls in the air at once. The intervener needs an outsider's perspective, needs to understand the civil war well enough to promote actions which increase fairness and redress grievances, needs to carry with them the bulk of the population in the development of peacebuilding changes, and needs to know when to 'do' and when to 'enable'.

In its 1994 manual *Humanitarian Principles and Operational Dilemmas in War Zones*, the United Nations Development Programme (UNDP) Disaster Management Programme warns:

> The motto of most humanitarian organizations and personnel confronted by life-threatening emergencies is the familiar 'Don't just stand there. Do something!' In the light of the complexities of humanitarian action described above, a more helpful directive might be the reverse: 'Don't just do something. Stand there!' Rushing into action pre-empts adequate consideration of the wide-ranging, negative and positive effects that external organizations may trigger.

This book is about understanding civil wars and their roots and participants. It is about what you do when you stand there contemplating, before trying to 'do something'. It is a cliché to say that every war is different, but that does not make it any less true or less central to analysis. Indeed, we argue that only by understanding the specificities of the civil war and the country and the various stakeholders can interveners be peacebuilding, fair, enabling and acceptable – all at the same time.

There is no rule book and no best practice handbook; what interveners learned in one war is often not applicable in the next. The reasons that neighbour was willing to be cruel to neighbour, the explanation of why the brutality continued long after it could be justified, the reasons why people want to stop fighting now, and what needs to be done to prevent the war from starting again will be different in each civil war – international interventions must be tailored to individual wars. This requires a degree of understanding and analysis that is more fundamental and more time consuming than is customary for those who rush in to help. Some will take time to think and study. For many, the motto will remain 'Do something quickly', but even they should be able to analyse the war as they work, trying to modify their actions and programme to reflect their growing understanding of the civil war and its actors.

Hundreds of books, academic papers, and articles have been written about civil war and intervention. Nearly all have a narrow view or line which the authors use to explain most civil wars. In part, this is because civil wars have rarely been a specific area of study; most people who write about civil wars come from disciplines, including economics, development studies, area studies, international relations, conflict resolution, anthropology and environment. This brings a richness to the study of civil wars. But it also brings serious problems. Scholars from the different backgrounds often do not talk to each other. Research and data analysis methods vary widely. And there is no agreed language and even few agreed 'facts'.

Incredibly, there is no agreement on what constitutes a war or a civil war, or even how many wars there are or have been. There is a broad consensus that since the end of the Second World War in 1945, there have been more than 200 wars. There is also broad agreement that the number of wars increased steadily during the Cold War period (1947–89). But there is heated disagreement as to whether the number of wars increased or decreased after that, and whether they became more or less intense.

Some writers have argued that the end of the Cold War brought a change in the nature of civil wars, but instead we see the wars of the 1990s being very similar to the civil wars which came before. What is agreed, however, is that the end of the Cold War removed a straitjacket from international affairs and this allowed outside interveners to play a larger role. In particular, the role of the United Nations has been sharply increased. From its foundation in 1945, until 1988, the UN agreed only 13 peacekeeping missions, while in the next 15 years 43 were approved. There was also a switch as UN and bilateral development agencies and NGOs moved from a concentration on development and on natural disasters to dealing with war. This book is about making civil-war-linked interventions more effective in their peacebuilding role.

But when there is not even agreement on whether or not the problem of civil wars is getting worse, we cannot expect agreement on much of anything relating to civil wars. Instead of trying to choose between interpretations, we argue here that the rich and varied approaches to civil war represent different understandings of a very complex process and most are, to at least some extent, valid. A genuine understanding of civil war requires multiple approaches, and this book sets out many of the different ways of thinking about civil war and intervention.

So our overstretched international intervener has to be a juggler many times over – not only juggling perspective, fairness, acceptance and enabling – but also juggling the different ways to look at the war. But successful jugglers can keep balls and bottles in the air at the same time, and successful interveners can juggle interventions and understandings. We all drop the ball sometimes, but a successful international intervener will have gained sufficient local acceptance and trust to ensure that dropped balls can be picked up – mistakes can be discussed and approaches changed.

In summary, this book has three themes:

- Every war is different. Wars have multiple causes and multiple stakeholders. The causes of the war must be addressed.
- Peacebuilding is not easy; it necessarily involves change and fairness. International interveners must balance the need to maintain an outsider's independent perspective with the need to gain acceptance of a large part of the population.
- There are no right answers; there are only hard choices. But understanding the roots of the war and the interests of the stakeholders makes it more likely that better choices will be made.

The first part of this book pulls together the disparate writing and thinking on civil wars. We start by simply trying to set some definitions. Most people think they know what a 'war' is, but asked to write down a definition many will have different definitions, and when asked to apply that definition to violence in India or Spain, they will discover major disagreements as to whether a particular fight should be called a war. Many analysts, for example, do not consider the 1994 Rwanda genocide to have been a 'war', even though hundreds of thousands of people were killed. It is this confusion over definitions which means that in the early twenty-first century researchers even disagreed about whether the number of wars was increasing or decreasing, leading to conflicting generalisations: 'it's getting worse' versus 'it's getting better'. There is, however, consensus that there are still a lot of civil wars out there, with at least 30 ongoing at the start of the millennium.

An important conceptual and definitional issue relates to the word 'conflict'. For many writers and practitioners, 'conflict' is something nasty and irrational which must be stopped and prevented. The authors of this book take a very different view, namely that conflict is normal and natural in any society and is directly linked to processes of change and development. Societies develop ways to resolve and mediate conflict; negotiation, transparency and democratic processes can play positive roles. But conflicts can become violent, and if still unresolved, groups may begin killing each other as the conflict escalates to civil war. A central goal of international interveners is promoting a just and stable peace by helping to end the war and creating the conditions that reduce the likelihood of the war starting again. That is 'peacebuilding' and is the primary focus of this book.

Outsiders are essential for peacebuilding, but they often get it wrong and have been accused of unintentionally promoting war instead of peace. Florence Nightingale, known for her contribution to the development of nursing in Britain, opposed the creation of the Red Cross on the grounds that it would 'render war more easy'. Many writers argue that actions by the international community had the effect of promoting rather than blocking the Rwanda genocide. Mary B. Anderson in the 1990s recognised the damage sometimes done by aid workers, and developed the concept of 'do no harm' (Anderson, 1999) where 'humanitarianism' is an important impulse that can sometimes do more harm than good.

The second chapter looks at who intervenes and the critical question of acting when not everyone in a country accepts the intervention. Should the international community have intervened to stop the Rwanda genocide? If so, what rules apply? The angry and polarised debate over the Iraq intervention in 2003 shows how little agreement there is. How do we balance self-interest and the interests of the country subject to the intervention; how do we ensure that the intervention really will be peacebuilding?

That sets the agenda for the rest of the book, which is designed to provide the understanding and analysis tools to increase the chances that outside interventions will have a positive impact. Our starting point is that it is essential to understand the roots of the civil war – why and how the war began, and how it continued. The literature on this subject is littered with technical terms about conditions, triggers and so on, with writers trying to unpack the process of the onset of civil wars. We do not feel that these distinctions are useful for those trying to understand the roots of the war well enough to improve the quality of interventions. Rather, we think it good enough for interveners to understand the various causes of the war.

For ease of discussion, we look at three aspects of war, but we stress they are not distinct and overlap in practice. The first is the conditions which make war more likely – conditions which make it hard for a country to successfully resolve conflicts and prevent the escalation to violence and war. Civil war states tend to be young, having been formed out of decolonisation processes and empire break-ups in the twentieth century. They also tend to be weak, and Chapter 3 looks at how both the Cold War and the processes linked to economic globalisation have weakened some states.

The second aspect is the actual roots of violence and war, discussed in more detail below. The third aspect is those factors which allow the war to continue and may even make it hard to end. These are often the same as the roots of the war, but their importance may be different once the civil war is under way. Particularly important in this period are resources to pay for food and weapons and to keep fighters satisfied and on side.

In Chapters 4 and 5 we look in some detail at the conventional explanations of the roots of civil war. Civil wars are between groups or between a group and the government. Ethnicity and religion are two common identifiers of groups, which has led to a long tradition of seeing civil wars as being ethnic, tribal, racial or religious wars. In particular, separatist wars often have ethnic labels – Tamils or Croatians or Basques demanding autonomy or independence or at least a fair share of wealth and power. But how important and how fundamental are these labels? 'Primordialists' view ethnicity as a permanent identity linked to ancient differences and hatreds, and view as ethnic some civil wars where the participants themselves do not prioritise identity. 'Constructivists' see ethnicity as a malleable and changing identity, which can be used to mobilise for war but is not a root of the war. This remains a highly contentious area, with contradictory implications – a primordial view would suggest that interveners should work to keep warring ethnic groups apart, while a constructivist view would put the emphasis on other factors and interventions to eliminate the impacts of past discrimination. It is also not explanatory, at least in isolation, since most countries with different ethnic groups are not involved in civil wars.

Democracy is often promoted as an antidote to civil war, but research has shown that the transition to democracy is destabilising, particularly because it allows mobilisation around identity. Shortages of land and water and other forms of environmental factors have led to a neo-Malthusian explanation of civil wars, with people fighting over scarce resources. So far, however, this is not proving to be a key root of civil war, with resource conflicts normally being resolved amicably.

International factors play an underrated role in civil wars. Neighbouring states can interfere and even support break-away factions, as India did in backing the creation of Bangladesh. The Cold War saw many examples, with the West backing and even creating opposition groups waging civil war in Angola, Nicaragua and elsewhere. Economic factors from falling commodity prices to curbs in government spending imposed under structural adjustment have weakened states to the point where they cannot resolve violent conflicts, which then descend into war.

The importance given to any of these factors will have a direct impact on decisions about interventions, so we have included 'intervention implications' in these chapters. We also note that the suggested causes of war can be loosely grouped into whether we put the blame on individuals or on social pressure. We characterise the former approach as the 'big bad men' view of the world, with civil war being attributed to local leaders, often described as 'warlords', or to international leaders such as the President of the United States or the head of the World Bank. We characterise the latter view as 'people under pressure' who can find no other way to resolve their problems than to go to war.

These explanations for the roots of war come from anthropologists, environmentalists and international relations analysts trying to apply their expertise to the complexities of civil war. It was not until the mid 1990s that economists took a serious look at civil wars, and their explanations are the focus of Chapters 6 and 7.

One approach developed at WIDER at the United Nations University in Helsinki, was based on two interconnected concepts: group inequality and social contract. Frances Stewart developed the theory that civil wars are based on relative inequality in wealth or power between self-defined groups. These groups can be ethnic, religious, language or clan based, but they can also be class or region based. Often tension increases when government policy, particularly relating to education or jobs, favours one group over another. The key for Stewart is that it is the inequality, and not the group identifier, that causes the war. But why? After all, the world is full of group inequalities which do not lead to war.

The other half of the WIDER package tries to answer that question. It returns to the concept of social contract, first developed by the eighteenth-century philosopher Jean-Jacques Rousseau. This argues that society operates by an agreed set of rules and that the citizens of a country have reached an informal understanding, the 'social contract', with the state under which the citizens give up some of their freedom of action and the state provides security, dispute resolution and other benefits. When the social contract functions well, society and the state are able to resolve conflicts. Any society has many group inequalities, but they become an issue only when they are felt and then become politicised. Working-class pressure for the vote, higher wages, and social security in the early twentieth century was resolved peacefully in some countries but led to civil war in others. Similar things happened with decolonisation and reducing discrimination against minorities. The WIDER argument is that civil war occurs when there is a perceived group inequality and when the social contract has broken down to the extent that the state is unable to resolve the intergroup conflict. This can lead to war in three ways: two groups may fight, one group goes to war against a government which is seen to represent the other group, or a government represses an increasingly militant group.

Key individuals play a role on both sides. First, civil war often comes about when a dictatorial government leader suppresses a group making what it sees as legitimate claims against an intergroup inequality, and second, rebelling groups need leaders. But in the terms we set out above, the WIDER view can be mainly characterised as 'people under pressure'. A totally different 'big bad men' approach was taken by Paul Collier and World Bank economists, and is known by Collier's characterisation of 'greed or grievance'. By 1999 Collier was arguing that there was no evidence that grievance causes civil war, and that the main driving force was greed by leaders, both opposition leaders typically called 'warlords', and those in power in government. Thus lootable resources such as diamonds or timber, or resources that could be sold by government, such as oil, were the main factors driving civil wars. Collier, therefore, totally rejected the WIDER approach and the concept of group inequalities.

By 2003, however, Collier and the World Bank had backed down substantially, and 'argued against a greed-based interpretation of rebellion'. Although they still continued with the 'big bad men' approach, they accepted that some leaders of rebellions really did start with political objectives. Leaders have to fund the rebellion, which is easier when there are lootable resources, and leaders often lose their way and become greedy criminals. So greed no longer drives the original rebellion, but it does drive the continuation of the civil war. This more nuanced view received much less publicity than the original version, so many people still say that civil wars are caused by greed and not grievance.

Understanding the specific roots and stakeholders of each civil war is essential for effective outside intervention, and that leads on to the second part of the book which provides tools for intervention. The previous part gave our intervening juggler the balls of the war to keep in the air; this part gives the bottles of intervention which have to be kept in the air as well. Peacebuilding requires change and outside interveners can enable local actors to understand the changes that need to be made and to develop and carry forward appropriate actions. Outsiders bring new perceptions and understandings as well as skills and, most importantly, resources that can assist and support local people.

In Part 2 of the book we start with looking more closely at the concept of development and how it relates both to war and to peacebuilding. 'Development' has come to be seen as specific actions to ameliorate poverty, often those done by aid workers to or for poor people in order to reach precise goals, for example statistical targets such as the number of children in school. In Chapter 8, Alan Thomas sees development much more broadly, and argues that it has three components. Development can be a vision of a desirable society, it can be an historical change process, and it can be deliberate efforts at improvement (which should be more than simple projects). Thomas notes that development can cause war, for example when a government fails to manage change equitably and only one group benefits. Also, the Sierra Leone civil war could be seen as having been caused by a vision of development, when youth rebelled against 'old men' they saw as blocking their access to education and jobs. But development is also an essential part of peacebuilding; change is necessary and the postwar change process needs vision and goals, as well as a huge range of deliberate efforts at improvement. But the lesson of many decades of aid is that people cannot 'be developed' by others doing things to or for them. Instead intervention involves thinking about values and visions and supporting people's own quest to build a more just and equitable society that will not return to war.

Local people may recognise that outside intervention is essential to provide security, new ways of thinking and resources for reconstruction. And they will recognise that change is essential to remove the causes of the war. But they will also be fearful that they will lose what little they have and that powerful outsiders will impose unacceptable change. To navigate this social and political minefield, interveners need a good perception of people's own understanding of power, identity and agency. Power relations at the root of the war can and must be changed; in Chapter 9 Judy El-Bushra points out that power is often exercised in subtle ways which are hard for the outsider to recognise. Changing power relations involves changing the way people think about themselves and about their social relations. People often accept the stereotypes about their roles, and violence sometimes arises from the gap between reality and unrealistic expectations. Research on the concept of 'agency', an individual's capacity to act in furtherance of personal and group goals, shows that people have huge power to transform their lives and situations. This leads to the development of a 'social relations framework' to guide the essential changes in roles, identities, relations and institutions. This inevitably results in the transformation of political institutions and of the state itself.

Clearly a society in which neighbours were prepared to butcher neighbours requires major postwar transformation of institutions and power relations; outside interveners can play a major role in supporting these internal changes. But the history of outside intervention shows that outsiders can make matters substantially worse, by promoting or supporting changes which reinforce rather than transform power relations. And interveners will be ineffective if they work against the grain of the society. The goal of Judy El-Bushra's Chapter 10 is to help interveners work toward progressive and peacebuilding change.

We end the book with two chapters by Jonathan Goodhand on the actual mechanics of intervention for peacebuilding: How does one promote positive change? He calls on interveners to think of themselves less as managers of projects and more as change agents, capacity builders and advocates. He develops what he calls a 'conflict sensitive' approach to development. He distinguishes three approaches to war. The first is of working 'around' war, which tries to ignore the war or just treat it as an impediment to development. This is the keeping-your-head-down-and-getting-on-with-the-job approach, and can often reinforce the unresolved conflicts that led to the war. The second is of working 'in' war, which tends to involve risk reduction and a do-no-harm approach. The third is working 'on' war, in which agencies focus on war prevention and conflict management and resolution. This approach is most needed and least common. Goodhand then looks at a way of preparing for intervention in a war or postwar context, so that actions can be smarter and more tailored for peacebuilding. There is no 'best practice' that can be applied everywhere, but there is a 'better practice' which can be developed in the specific context, he concludes.

Outside interveners are important facilitators in the essential transformations required after a civil war. But it is not an easy task. Sometimes outsiders are welcome, but all too often their very presence becomes a mark of past failure and the welcome can become very grudging. And history shows how easy it is for interveners to make mistakes. We have talked in this introduction about the need for interveners to be jugglers, juggling the different explanations for the roots of war, perspective, fairness, acceptance and enabling all at once. We hope this book provides a small contribution to these skills and thus to peacebuilding and a reduction in civil wars.

References

Anderson, M.B. (1999) *Do No Harm: How Aid Can Support Peace – or War*. Boulder, CO, Lynne Reinner.

Study Group on Europe's Security Capabilities (2004) *A Human Security Doctrine for Europe*, known as the Barcelona Report to EU High Representative for Common Foreign and Security Policy Javier Solana, Barcelona, 15 September 2004, (Mary Kaldor convenor), www.lse.ac.uk/Depts/global (accessed November 2004).

UNDP (1994) *Humanitarian Principles and Operational Dilemmas in War Zones*, New York, United Nations Development Programme Disaster Management Programme.

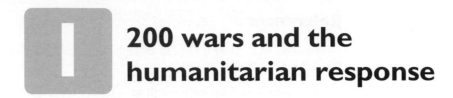

200 wars and the humanitarian response

Joseph Hanlon

1.1   Introduction

The First International Peace Conference was convened in 1899 in The Hague at the invitation of Queen Wilhelmina of the Netherlands and Czar Nicholas II of Russia. Representatives of 25 governments agreed a Convention for the Peaceful Adjustment of International Differences. Despite their hopes, the subsequent century proved to be the bloodiest and most violent in world history, with at least 110 million war-related deaths, half in the Second World War. There have been more than 200 wars in the past 50 years, killing tens of millions of people, forcing tens of millions of others to flee their homes, and causing inestimable damage. Taking history as a guide, as you read this at least 20 wars are being waged. Nearly all these wars are 'civil wars', inside one country, although often with significant stirring of the pot by other countries. Some, such as civil wars in Israel, Colombia and Sudan and the fight between India and Pakistan in Kashmir have been going on since the 1960s.

In the second half of the twentieth century there were major international wars – in Korea 1950–53, in Vietnam 1965–75, and between Iran and Iraq 1980–88. But nearly all wars in the past 50 years have been 'civil wars', and some have been horrific. In 1967–70 Biafra failed to break away from Nigeria, and a year later Bangladesh successfully broke away from Pakistan, but in each war more than a million people died. In Cambodia more than a million people died in civil war in the late 1970s. In 1975 Mozambique won a liberation war against the Portuguese colonisers, only to be plunged into a new war linked to the Cold War, with apartheid South Africa and the United States backing the insurgents and the Soviet Union backing the government; the war finally ended in 1992, with more than a million dead. Civil war and genocide in Rwanda in 1994–95 led to more than 600,000 deaths. Civil war in the Democratic Republic of the Congo was still continuing in 2004 and had already cost more than two million lives.

Of course bloody civil wars are not new. But the last part of the twentieth century saw a sharp increase in the number of civil wars. In the late 1940s and 1950s the number of wars remained under 20, but then the number rose steadily through the Cold War era. The 15 years after the end of the Cold War saw many wars settled, including long-running civil wars in Britain (Northern Ireland), Mozambique, Angola and Sri Lanka. But others continued, including 'small wars' and ongoing insurgencies in Burma/ Myanmar, India, Indonesia, Peru and Chad which were rarely reported in

The First International Peace Conference, 1899, The Hague, Netherlands.

the mainstream media. And some new wars started (or old wars restarted), such as those in the former Yugoslavia, Burundi, Nepal and Liberia.

Civil wars have a special brutality and ferocity. Several factors contribute to this. First, violence is often more extreme, in part because the fighting is between families, neighbours and co-workers and because civilians do much of the killing and dying. In a conventional interstate war, the enemy belongs to the other country and thus has a different identity. In a civil war the enemy is similar, so it becomes increasingly important to dehumanise and demonise the enemy in order to turn the former neighbour into an evil 'other' who no longer deserves trust and respect. Rape and mutilation are used to dehumanise the opposition, but this is then used by the victims to argue that the other side are terrorists. If 'they' do horrible things to 'us', then 'they' can no longer be trusted and to defend ourselves 'we' must do horrible things to 'them'. Rules of war defined for conventional interstate wars by the Geneva Conventions often are not applied. For example, prisoners of war are tortured and executed. The war takes on a very personal character, and social accountability collapses, especially within poorly trained militias and guerrilla forces. In addition, civil war killing tends to be much more personal; it is done with handguns or knives, rather than at a distance with aircraft; the killer and victim actually see each other. As Mary Anderson (1999, pp. 11, 16) notes, people commit atrocities against former friends or colleagues, or do nothing to stop someone being attacked, and feel very strong guilt at committing violence against someone they know; they can only assuage the guilt and justify the action by believing that the former friend is now – perhaps always was – evil and out to destroy them.

The other factor is that civil wars tend to be 'here' rather than somewhere else. Mary Anderson notes that :

> civilian-based civil wars are fought in everyday living spaces. The outdoor café, the intervillage bus, the weekend marketplace become battlegrounds, targeted because they are places in which civilians live and work.

This also means that the opponent can actually be unidentified within our midst – the spy or potential terrorist can be anywhere. This creates a level of fear and distrust which is seen to justify a degree of repression and loss of civil liberties that would not be allowed in 'normal' times. Criminal acts and interpersonal violence are easier because they can be done under the cloak of the civil war. If the war continues long enough, violence and distrust can become the norm.

The necessity to justify brutal acts against former friends and neighbours who were once trusted creates a spiral of violence and hatred that can last for generations, and makes peacebuilding very difficult when the war is over. The United States civil war of 1861–65, an unsuccessful breakaway of the southern states, cost 600,000 lives and continues, nearly 150 years later, to have an impact on US politics. Finland remains divided after a brief but brutal civil war in 1918 in which 30,000 people died; probably more were executed than killed in battle. At least 500,000 people died in the Spanish civil war of 1936–39 which left a nation traumatised; only after 60 years did elderly survivors begin to identify mass graves of those who had been executed during the war, and a programme was begun to exhume the bodies. It was 55 years after the Greek civil war of 1946–49 that those who left the country as children, when they were evacuated to avoid the fighting, were allowed to re-enter Greece – but only to visit (*Guardian*, 17 October 2003).

In this chapter we look at interventions in response to civil war, from the immediate humanitarian response of reducing suffering to more complex responses around peacekeeping and peacebuilding. These involve intervention in the civil war and in postwar peace support by people within the country and by a whole range of international actors. Usually called the 'aid agencies', the 'aid community', or even the 'aid industry', these include:

- international non-government organisations (NGOs or INGOs), ranging from small faith-based groups to major international coalitions such as World Vision International with budgets of over US$1 billion per year. Most provide humanitarian and development aid, but some are pressure groups like Amnesty International
- the Red Cross, which consists of the oldest of the humanitarian agencies, the International Committee of the Red Cross, and the International Federation of Red Cross and Red Crescent Societies which is a federation of national bodies
- government aid agencies such as USAID (United States Agency for International Development) and Britain's DfID (Department for International Development)

- United Nations agencies, including UNICEF (the children's fund), the United Nations Development Programme (UNDP), and the United Nations High Commissioner for Refugees (UNHCR).

The end of most civil wars involves some international military and police involvement, sometimes just as observers and sometimes in more active roles to maintain security. Intervening forces can be from one or a few countries, from a regional body, or from the United Nations. Finally, there will normally be diplomatic intervention from embassies in the country, mediating statespeople, and regional and UN bodies.

It quickly becomes clear that the complexity of civil wars and the wide range of mandates of the interveners means there is little agreement on what kind of interventions are appropriate. Organisations and individuals face hard choices fuelled by competing goals (for example, patching up the injured versus trying to prevent future fighting) and by different ethical positions (for example, neutrality between the sides in the war versus opposition to a side which commits atrocities). These are real dilemmas, made more acute by the knowledge that the wrong decision can cause serious harm and perhaps contribute to a renewal of the war. Honest disagreements start at the very beginning, with what we mean by the terms we use, and we start with that problem.

1.2   Definitions and the Humpty Dumpty problem

Answering the obvious and apparently simple question: 'Did the number of wars increase or decrease during the 1990s?' turns out to be neither simple nor obvious. Researchers disagree over the number of wars and whether or not it has fallen since the end of the Cold War because there are fundamental disagreements as to what is a 'war'. Not only is there no agreement on the word 'war', but, remarkably, there is no broad agreement on the definitions of many of the key words used in this book.

One problem is that, traditionally, an armed conflict was only a 'war' if it was between two states and was formally declared. For example, Article I of the United States Constitution gives Congress 'the power ... to declare war'. In recent years, very few wars have been formally declared, so we must decide when violence becomes a 'war'. The other problem is about what constitutes a 'civil' war. For example, some researchers require that a government army be involved for the violence to count as a 'civil war' which means some exclude the Rwanda genocide from lists of 'civil wars' on the grounds that the government's army was not involved.

We call this the Humpty Dumpty problem. In *Through the Looking Glass* by Lewis Carroll (Chapter 6, 'Humpty Dumpty'), Alice meets the egg Humpty Dumpty sitting on his wall. The story continues:

> 'When *I* use a word,' Humpty Dumpty said, in rather a scornful tone, 'it means just what I choose it to mean – neither more nor less.'

In a similar way, politicians, diplomats and academic researchers twist the definitions of words to what they choose them to mean. It is hardly surprising, then, that academic researchers often find totally contradictory results.

In this book, we will sometimes return to the Humpty Dumpty problem as we try to clarify what we and others mean by various words and terms. The confusion is so great that we feel it important to lay down some basic definitions here at the start.

1.2.1 'War' and 'civil war'

In the 1998 BBC Reith Lectures Sir John Keegan, an eminent military historian, gave a simple definition which we will also adopt (Keegan, 1999):

> War is collective killing for some collective purpose.

For a set of events to be a war, people need to be killed in some organised way, which excludes simple crime and banditry. Furthermore, including 'collective purpose' in the definition means that some group of people approves of the killing and feels it justified for some legitimate purpose.

For civil war, the main topic of this book, we will expand Keegan's definition:

> Civil war is collective killing for some collective purpose, mainly within one country, and where the fighting is primarily between people of that country.

Thus the Iraq war of 2003 is not a civil war because, although the fighting was mainly within one country, it was an invasion of forces of a US-led coalition intended to change the Iraqi Government. Civil wars, however, can have large external components and even be externally driven, as Box 1.1 on Angola shows. There is even a problem with the phrase 'within one country' because many wars take on a separatist character, with a group or part of a country believing it can only achieve its aims if it becomes self-governing. The violent breakup of the former Yugoslavia in the 1990s shows this clearly. We will use the word 'country' loosely, but in practice a breakaway war is still within a larger single country.

Box 1.1   Four wars in Angola

Angola, an ex-Portuguese colony in south-west Africa, suffered four different wars in the last part of the twentieth century. The Popular Movement for the Liberation of Angola (MPLA) began an independence war in 1961. Three other movements also took up arms, the Front for the National Liberation of Angola (FNLA) and the National Union for the Total Independence of Angola

(UNITA), plus the Cabinda Liberation Front (FLEC) which was fighting in the tiny enclave of Cabinda, which is separated from the rest of Angola. Portugal was then ruled by a dictator, and independence wars in the colonies were linked to an anti-fascist movement in Portugal. On 25 April 1974, a coup in Portugal led by veterans of the colonial wars overthrew the dictator, Marcelo Caetano. The new government offered independence to the colonies and an agreement was reached in January 1975 ending the first Angola war.

During the liberation war, the MPLA had a Marxist orientation and drew support from the then USSR and socialist bloc. UNITA gained support from China. Both UNITA and the FNLA gained covert support from the US and even from the Portuguese security services, who hoped they would direct their fire on the opposition MPLA rather than on Portugal. The three main liberation movements could not reach agreement and began to squabble, immediately drawing in the big powers. This was the era of the Cold War, and oil-rich Angola became a Cold War battlefield.

The MPLA was the main liberation movement and it controlled the capital, Luanda. To prevent what they saw as a Marxist takeover, the US threw its weight behind UNITA and the white minority 'apartheid' government in South Africa invaded the south of Angola. When South African troops had nearly reached Luanda, the MPLA gained support from Cuba and the South Africans were expelled. The US congress banned aid to UNITA at the end of 1975. Although UNITA and the FNLA continued to occupy parts of Angola and low-level fighting continued, the international community recognised the MPLA as the legitimate government. By the late 1970s South Africa was again attacking Angola and both South Africa and the US were giving support to UNITA, and the war intensified. Over the next decade more than 500,000 people died in the war between the Cuban- and Soviet-backed government and US-based UNITA and South African forces. By the end of the 1980s there were Cold-War-linked wars going on in four southern African countries – Namibia, Angola, Mozambique and South Africa, but with the end of the Cold War all were resolved. Movements which had been opposed by the West won elections in all four countries.

In Angola there was a ceasefire in 1988 which also included the departure of Cuban troops. The UN Security Council created the United Nations Angolan Verification Mission (UNAVEM) to supervise the Cuban withdrawal. There was a formal peace deal involving the continued presence of the UN, leading to elections in 1992. There was supposed to be a new joint army, but this was never created. Elections on 29–30 September 1992 were praised as generally free and fair by international observers. With a 92 per cent turnout, the MPLA won 54 per cent of votes for parliament and the MPLA's presidential candidate, Jose Eduardo dos Santos, won 49.6 per cent of votes compared with 40.7 per cent for UNITA's Jonas Savimbi. Western backers of Savimbi believed their own propaganda; they believed Savimbi would win and convinced him to accept the peace deal because he would become president. Savimbi was allowed to violate the peace accord and not demobilise his army because the

West assumed he would win and his army would become the government army. Instead, a shocked Savimbi rejected the election and immediately went back to war, starting the third Angola war. UNAVEM was powerless to prevent the war from starting again, and the US was not prepared to intervene against its old ally.

UNITA quickly gained control of the diamond mining areas of eastern Angola, and despite the lack of international support for this third war, Savimbi was able to sell enough diamonds to fund his own war. Oil production had expanded and the MPLA government used it to pay for its arms. Leaders of both sides used their diamond and oil earnings to amass substantial personal wealth. The brutal war killed another 500,000 people and only ended when Savimbi was assassinated in 2002.

Meanwhile, oil had been found in Cabinda and in the 1990s FLEC resumed its separatist war; as it had a small population and large amounts of oil, FLEC leaders believed their tiny territory could be rich if it separated from Angola.

Thus Angola has really had four different wars – a liberation war in the 1960s, a Cold War proxy war in the 1980s, and two wars largely driven by greed and power in the 1990s. Note that we consider all of these wars to be 'civil wars' even though each has substantial outside involvement. The first, liberation, war was against a foreign occupying power. (Portugal defined Angola as a province of Portugal, which means to the Portuguese Government it was still a civil war, but within Portugal. This applies to any breakaway or independence movement.) The Cold War proxy war was between Angolans, but was largely driven by external factors. The other two are mainly internal, but were dependent on international actors buying the diamonds and oil in order to provide the finances for the war.

Most wars of the second half of the twentieth century were not conventional ones fought by armies and heavy weapons. Rather, in most wars at least one side has been weak and has been forced to use guerrilla tactics and various forms of unconventional warfare, including suicide bombings and attacks with light weapons or even just machetes or knives. Especially when confronting a strong government, a group's command structures may be very decentralised and actions disparate. Some kinds of crime, such as bank robberies, can even become a weapon of war. In the 1980s, the African National Congress (ANC) fought its war inside South Africa against the white apartheid government by explicitly trying to make the country ungovernable – chaos was a weapon of war. So the phrases 'collective action' and 'collective purpose' are often subject to dispute. How far can we push this definition? The United States talks of a 'war on drugs' while some people accuse it of using drugs to wage a war on its own citizens (see Box 1.3 later). Are the Mafia and the Italian state fighting a war? Also, wars change and have different characters at different times, as we saw in Angola.

Box 1.2   Was there a civil war in Los Angeles?

In the 1980s, there was an explosion of cocaine use in the predominantly black neighbourhoods of the South-Central area in Los Angeles. Drug deaths topped 500 a year and the *Los Angeles Times* (18 December 1994) reported that hundreds of people a year were killed in drug-related murders and more than 50,000 people a year were arrested for narcotics offences. Hundreds of millions of dollars were spent on expansion of the prisons.

Black militants accused the government of flooding South-Central with drugs to wage 'war' on the black community. At first, the idea seemed absurd. But then in 1989 a US Senate Subcommittee on Terrorism, Narcotics and International Operations, headed by John Kerry, reported that the United States had knowledge of and tolerated drug smuggling from central America under the guise of 'national security'. In 1979 the Sandinista Front in Nicaragua had overthrown the US-backed dictator Anastasio Samoza. The US responded by setting up an opposition military force, the Contras, which invaded Nicaragua from neighbouring states. The Kerry committee found that profits from illegal drugs sales were being used to fund the Contras.

Then in 1996 the *San Jose Mercury News*, a newspaper in the Los Angeles area, ran a series of investigative articles alleging that with the knowledge and support of the US Central Intelligence Agency, drug dealers had poured more than 50 tonnes of cocaine into Los Angeles and funnelled tens of millions of dollars to the Contras. Although the US Government disputed much of the story of CIA involvement, there seemed no question that the cocaine explosion in South-Central was fuelled as part of funding the Contras and that, at the very least, US security and law enforcement officials looked the other way (Kornbluh, 1997).

That raises two questions. Civil wars often spill over their borders, and the first question is whether events in Los Angeles should be treated as part of the 'civil war' in Nicaragua. But the second question is more complex. Even if the main purpose was to raise funding for a civil war in Nicaragua, what were the implications of selling cocaine specifically in predominantly black neighbourhoods at prices which were so cheap that even poor people could buy it, leading to the deaths of thousands and the imprisonment of tens of thousands? Cynthia Tucker (1996) of the newspaper *The Atlanta Journal-Constitution* accused the US Government of waging a racist 'war on the vulnerable black and brown poor'. On radio talk shows in black areas of the US, many people claimed that cocaine was being used by the government to deliberately wage war on the African-American minority.

Los Angeles does not figure in any of the lists of civil wars; although the number of dead is large enough, they are normally treated as victims of criminal actions and drug abuse. But if prominent people within a community claim they are victims of a civil war, should that be accepted? Los Angeles shows just how hard it is to find an agreed definition of what constitutes a 'civil war'. The cocaine victims may not have been shot by an army, but some commentators argue that they were collectively and purposefully killed, which would make it a civil war by our definition.

In Box 1.3 (opposite) we list the definitions of four different research groups and note that while all agree that there is a significant number of ongoing civil wars, three groups say the number of wars has decreased since the end of the Cold War while one says it has increased.

Figure 1.1 is a graph based on data from one of the groups in Box 1.3, a joint team from Uppsala University in Sweden and International Peace Research Institute (PRIO) in Oslo, Norway. The data is from the Armed Conflict Data Set of the Department of Peace and Conflict Studies, Uppsala, and the Centre for the Study of Civil War at PRIO – usually known as the Uppsala data set. It combines three subsets of armed conflict: *war*, with at least 1000 battle-related deaths per year; *intermediate armed conflict*, with at least 25 battled-related deaths per year and an accumulated total of at least 1000 deaths, but fewer than 1000 in one year; and *minor armed conflict*, with at least 25 battled-related deaths per year and an accumulated total of fewer than 1000 deaths in the course of the conflict. (Note the Humpty Dumpty issue; in this book we define all of these as 'wars'.) The figure shows a decline, from 49 civil wars in 1992 to 27 in 2003. But another research team, at the Université Catholique de Louvain in Belgium, says that between 1992 and 2001 the number of wars rose from 45 to 54.

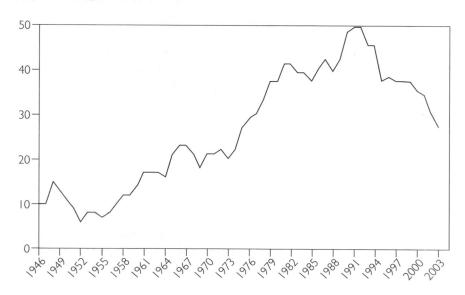

Figure 1.1 Number of internal armed conflicts (data from Uppsala University and PRIO, Oslo). Source: Eriksson et al. (2003); Eriksson and Wallensteen (2003) and Hegre (2005).

Defining when violence is a 'war' can be politically very sensitive. Governments facing insurgencies tend to dismiss the violence as being merely caused by criminals or 'armed bandits' or 'mindless terrorists', and surely not a war. One example of the difficulty in definition was KwaZulu-Natal province in South Africa, where several thousand people lost their lives in political violence in the second half of the 1990s – two treat KwaZulu-Natal as a war and two do not. Box 1.2 looks at the same question with respect to violence in Los Angeles in the United States. So we cannot in any rigorous way establish if the number and intensity of wars now are lessening, as some argue, or are similar to that of a decade ago, as others say. But what is unquestionably clear is that many wars remain, with huge levels of violence and suffering. Furthermore, although some wars are being resolved, others are restarting and still others are beginning.

Box 1.3   Different definitions of war

- *Hamburg.* The Study Group on the Causes of War, at Hamburg University, uses the simplest definition: the regular armed forces of a government must be involved. This tends to leave out civil wars between different non-government bodies, and wars where only the police are involved.

- *Uppsala.* A joint team from the Department of Peace and Conflict Research at Uppsala University in Sweden and the International Peace Research Institute (PRIO) in Oslo, Norway, uses a three-tier structure – a 'war' has more than 1000 battle-related deaths per year, an 'intermediate armed conflict' has 1000 battle related deaths over the course of the conflict, but not in a single year, and a 'minor armed conflict' has at least 25 battle-related deaths a year but fewer than 1000 battle-related deaths overall. (In discussing this team, we lump all three categories into 'war'.)

- *Louvain.* The OFDA/CRED International Disaster Database of Université Catholique de Louvain in Belgium uses a mix of the other two – the military force of a government must be involved, resulting in at least 10 battle-related deaths or 100 people affected in one year.

- *Waterloo.* Project Ploughshares in Waterloo, Canada, part of the Canadian Council of Churches, says 'an armed conflict is defined as a political conflict in which armed combat involved the armed forces of at least one state or one or more armed factions seeking to gain control of all or part of a state and in which at least 1000 people have been killed by the fighting.'

There is a reasonable correlation between the four during the Cold War, but since then the Louvain database has identified many more small wars. In particular, it has a higher total number of wars because it divides the wars in more countries. In 2001, for example, Hamburg gives the smallest number of wars, but for the most part the lists are similar. The following table gives a few countries considered by some as wars but not others.

	Hamburg	Uppsala	Louvain	Waterloo (Canada)
Individual wars in 2001				
Somalia	✓		✓	✓
Turkey		✓	✓	✓
Central African Republic		✓		
More than one war in 2001				
Indonesia	1 war	1 war	4 wars	5 wars
India	5 wars	5 wars	3 wars	3 wars
Iran	no wars	1 war	3 wars	1 war
Total number of wars				
1992	55	54	45	42
2001	31	34	54	37

These characterisations can be indefinitely varied. For example, the Interdisciplinary Research Programme on Causes of Human Rights Violations (PIOOM) at Leyden University in the Netherlands defined something called 'low intensity conflict' which is an armed conflict between two groups that caused between 100 and 1000 deaths (not necessarily battle-related) during a year. In 2000 it found 78 low-intensity conflicts, including 14 in India alone.

Many definitions of war depend on a body count – how many people are killed. But there does not seem to be any objective way of measuring casualties, and it is extremely hard to estimate how many die in a war. Both the Uppsala and Louvain groups use a figure of 'battle-related deaths', but even this is hard to estimate. A US librarian, Matthew White, set out to establish, from published figures, how many people were killed in various wars, and found huge variations even in apparently 'official' figures. For example, he found that estimates of deaths in both the Korean and Vietnam wars range from one million to over three million. Estimates of deaths in the 1971 Bangladesh war range from 300,000 to 3 million (White, 2004).

This problem of counting the dead has increased as civil wars have had more impact on civilians than combatants. Most civilians do not die in battle, but from hunger and disease, often because they do not have access to food or medical care which would have been available before the war.

Estimates of civilian deaths are often made by statistical means. UNICEF estimated one million additional deaths during the Mozambique civil war of 1982–92 – that is, one million more people, mainly children, died in that decade than if there had been no war. But the first census after the war showed a shortfall of two million people – one can only guess as to what portion are children who died compared with children not born and people who fled the country and did not return after the war. And whatever figure comes to be accepted, the war victims can never be identified, because many children would have died of disease anyway.

Civilian casualties are rarely counted. Families mourn those lost during the war, but no one keeps a running total, so estimates of the number of dead can only be guesses. An exception was the war in Iraq, which began in March 2003. Although the US-led forces did not keep a record of civilian casualties, two independent studies were done to estimate the number of civilians who died in the first 18 months of the war. A sample survey undertaken in Iraq and published in *The Lancet* estimated 100,000 civilians had died (Roberts et al., 2004). A London-based project called the Iraq Body Count (2005) tabulated all credible mainstream media reports of civilian deaths due to military action, and reported at least 16,000 dead by early 2005. During the same period, US-led forces said 1700 of their troops had been killed.

1.2.2 'Terrorism'

In a typical civil war, insurgents, often based in rural areas, try to control populations and deny access to government forces. Both sides try to win the 'hearts and minds' of the population, but often resort to force and terror. Although it has become increasingly easy to obtain small arms, insurgent fighters in civil wars are often poorly armed and equipped. They have no air force or artillery, and are forced into direct contact, often armed only with knives or machetes.

Terrorism, as the word suggests, is aimed at terrorising, frightening and intimidating the opposition so much that they do not resist. Terrorism is often the poor man's weapon, and often involves the use of arbitrary violence. People are forced to watch atrocities being committed and are warned to behave or meet a similar fate. The organisation Human Rights Watch writing about Sierra Leone noted that 'the rebel forces used sexual violence as a weapon to terrorise, humiliate and punish, and to force the civilian population into submission.' Very public sexual acts were intended to violate not only the victim, but also the wider society.

But powerful forces also try to target civilians in an effort to frighten the opposition into conceding quickly. The Nazi Blitzkrieg – Lightning War – of 1939–40 used air power and concentrations of tanks to smash through enemy lines and into the enemy's rear, destroying supplies and artillery positions and breaking the enemy's will to resist. In the first Gulf War (1990–91) and in attacks in the former Yugoslavia, the US and its allies developed the concept of 'effects-based operations' with its stress on the effect you want to achieve– for the enemy to give up quickly – rather than on simply destroying physical targets. It is a psychological and information war which includes the use of coordinated and precisely targeted military force to convince the general public to stop supporting their leaders. This turned into what was called 'shock and awe' tactics against Iraq in 2003. All these were intended to be 'brutal levels of power and force' that are 'sufficiently intimidating' so the opponents give up, according to the inventor of 'shock and awe', Oliver Burkeman. Indeed, Burkeman actually cites with approval a precursor in which Sun Tzu, the warrior-philosopher of ancient China, cut off the head of one of the emperor's concubines in order to command obedience of the others (*Guardian*, 25 March 2003). That sounds quite similar to the insurgents in many civil wars 25 centuries later.

As wars increasingly involve civilians, both sides hope to frighten or terrorise the other side into capitulation. Terror is a tactic and weapon of war, and must be recognised as such. Politicians have given 'terrorist' a pejorative meaning – 'their' side are 'terrorists' and 'our' side are 'freedom fighters' or 'resistance fighters'. It might be better to use a more neutral word like guerrilla, insurgent, or saboteur.

Finally, it is worth noting that two men who came to lead their countries and win Nobel Peace Prizes had both been guerrillas and, in the modern usage, terrorists. After the African National Congress was banned by the apartheid state in South Africa, Nelson Mandela set up its armed wing, Umkhonto we Sizwe. He was jailed as a terrorist for 27 years, finally being released in 1990 to negotiate a handover of power to the ANC. In 1993 he won the Nobel Peace Prize, and the following year was overwhelmingly elected president. In the British-mandated Palestine, Menachem Begin assumed command of Irgun Zvati Leumi (National Military Organization), which in 1946 bombed the King David Hotel in Jerusalem, then the site of the British military command, leaving 90 dead and 45 wounded. Begin and his forces won the war, and founded Israel. Begin was Prime Minister from 1977 to 1983 and won the Nobel Peace Prize in 1978.

1.2.3 'Conflict'

Many writers use the word 'conflict' when we would use the word 'war'. We take the following definition:

> 'conflict' means any struggle or confrontation between groups or individuals over resources or power.

Conflict is a natural process in any society and is especially linked to processes of change. Conflicts are often over economic or political power or over resources such as land.

Groups can be defined in many ways, by age, gender, income, location, religion, ethnicity, etc. Societies and nations have mechanisms for resolving conflicts in ways which are at least acceptable to the parties. Democracy is often seen as a good way of publicly resolving conflicts, but it can also lead to discrimination against minority groups.

If conflicts are not resolved, they may become violent. Peaceful protest can lead to 'violent conflict' such as land invasions or attacks on the other party in the conflict. Violent conflict can shade into criminal violence. When a conflict becomes violent, a society or country usually intervenes to end the violence and normally tries to at least partly redress the grievance that underlies the conflict.

If a conflict becomes violent and remains unresolved, one or both parties may take up arms, and we call this 'armed conflict'. This may further escalate into a war; we no longer label a 'war' as a 'conflict'.

Conflict is an inevitable part of change and of development, which shifts power relations and sometimes benefits some groups more than others. The need is to manage and eventually resolve those conflicts. The political process often requires the aggrieved or disadvantaged group to organise themselves in order to bring about political pressure; sometimes this involves major demonstrations and even riots and small-scale violence. If the conflict still cannot be resolved, the violence may escalate into war, and such an escalation reflects a breakdown in the 'social contract' between members of society (explored further in Chapter 6). Wars start when one group feels it has no other choice but to resort to violence. Countries such as India and Zimbabwe celebrate their independence wars; the people of South Africa feel their long war against apartheid (white minority rule) was justified. But the cost of civil war can be high and long lasting.

We give just one example of a very different use of the word 'conflict', Mary Anderson, in her book *Do No Harm* (1999, p. 7), writes:

> [T]he conflict we challenge is violent, destructive conflict. Some people use the word conflict to refer to healthy disagreements and struggles. For ease of discourse we use the term to mean negative, unhealthy usually violent interactions.

This is almost the opposite of how we use the word. We argue that conflict can be either constructive or destructive disagreements and struggles, and use war to mean the violent destructive conflicts. We consider conflict to be normal; our concern is with violent conflict and war, and our attention is to the prevention or ending of war. Indeed, a primary purpose of the contributing authors to this book is to provide the tools to better understand the conflicts which underlie the war.

1.2.4   'Peacebuilding'

The bitterness and mutual distrust generated by civil wars makes them difficult to stop, and even when peace is achieved, half of all civil wars restart within a decade (Collier et al., 2003, p. 7). Outsiders can play a key role in guaranteeing security and bridging the differences between the two sides. We make the following definition:

'Peacebuilding' is promoting a just and stable peace by helping to end the war and by helping to create the conditions that reduce the likelihood of the war starting again.

A similar definition has been used by UN Secretary-General Kofi Annan (Box 1.4).

Box 1.4   Peacebuilding

UN Secretary-General Kofi Annan, in a 1998 report to the Security Council on *The Causes of Conflict and the Promotion of Durable Peace and Sustainable Development in Africa*, said:

> 'By post-conflict peace-building, I mean actions undertaken at the end of a conflict to consolidate peace and prevent a recurrence of armed confrontation.'

> 'Peace-building does not replace ongoing humanitarian and development activities in countries that are emerging from crisis. Rather it aims to build on, add to, or reorient such activities in ways that are designed to reduce the risk of a resumption of conflict and contribute to creating conditions most conducive to reconciliation, reconstruction and recovery.'

Note where Kofi Annan talks of 'conflict', we would use the word 'war'.

Peacebuilding will include social actions like reconciliation and mediation. But the main peacebuilding actions will be ones addressing the underlying grievances and inequalities that caused the war, which can also be seen as a developmental process. This can involve significant changes to power relations, so that grievances can be addressed more effectively and conflicts resolved rather than escalating into war. It may involve job creation and increased access to schools, to try to respond to the demands of a disaffected youth. It might mean road building and other preferential support for remote areas that feel marginalised.

This book is written with two explicit assumptions. The first is that outsiders who intervene in wars – in peace-support operations, military or civilian, with humanitarian agencies or NGOs, or in any other way – want their interventions to encourage peacebuilding. The second assumption is that every war really is different and must be analysed in order to be understood. An understanding of the war is necessary to choose the most effective actions and to analyse their peacebuilding impact.

1.3   Humanitarianism

There is a strong humanitarian impulse to help the victims of war. The Red Cross was started in the 1860s to care for wounded soldiers and later began to support prisoners of war. It accepted the existence of war, but argued that once soldiers were out of the fighting they should be treated humanely. The first of the modern NGOs was Save the Children, which was founded in London in 1919, just after the First World War, to campaign against a blockade being imposed on the defeated Germany in an attempt to force it to accept the terms of peace demanded by the victorious allies. The new organisation claimed that children were dying in the street due to a lack of food, clothing and medicine, and organised a collection to raise money to break the blockade. The Oxford Committee for Famine Relief (now Oxfam) was founded in 1942, during the Second World War, to campaign against the allied blockade of Nazi-occupied Greece, which was blocking shipments of food. It then began to collect money for the Greek Red Cross. Eventually, the International Committee for the Red Cross (ICRC) successfully negotiated with Britain to gain access for food shipments to Greece. One of the other older and well known NGOs, CARE, was founded in 1945 to send 'CARE packages' to hungry people in postwar Europe; initially these were US army food packages intended for the invasion of Japan which became surplus when Japan surrendered.

The two United Nations agencies most linked with humanitarian actions grew out of the Second World War – as did the UN itself. UNICEF, the United Nations Children's Fund, was created in 1946 to provide food, clothing and health care to children in Europe. UNHCR, the UN High Commissioner for Refugees, has a more complex history, going back to the end of the First World War when the new League of Nations established a High Commissioner for refugees in 1921 and adopted a convention on refugees in 1933. After the Second World War, the UN Relief and Rehabilitation Agency and the International Refugee Organization were set up to deal with the millions of refugees. But by 1950, there were still one million refugees who had not been resettled; also the Cold War had begun in earnest and the West wanted to encourage people to leave the communist states of Eastern Europe. In 1950 the office of the UNHCR was created, and the following year a new Refugee Convention was agreed, promising refuge to those fleeing because of a 'well-founded fear of persecution' – but initially only 'as a result of events occurring before 1 January 1951'. The limitation was later removed, and UNHCR has helped more than 50 million refugees since its founding.

By the 1960s aid was increasingly focused on 'development'. This reflected the needs of the newly independent countries and the poor countries which by now made up a majority of the members of the United Nations, and it also reflected Cold War politics in which East and West wanted to support loyal allies in the developing world. The World Bank, also called the International Bank for Reconstruction and Development, was established for the purpose of providing funds to rebuild Europe after the Second World War, and directed increasing amounts of its money to the South.

But the growth of civil wars demanded more humanitarian and emergency aid. As Figures 1.2 and 1.3 show, a huge jump in emergency aid (for wars and disasters) began after the end of the Cold War. Official emergency aid flows grew both in volume, from US$738 million in 1990 to $3.6 bn just a decade later, and as a portion of total aid, from 1.4% to 6.8% of the official aid flows.

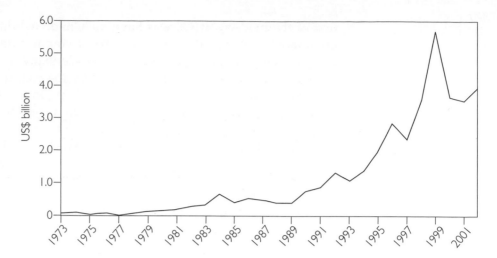

Figure 1.2   Emergency assistance by individual countries and by multinational organisations. 'Emergencies' include natural disasters, but most emergency aid is related to war. Source: Organisation for Economic Cooperation and Development, Development Assistance Committee (OECD DAC).

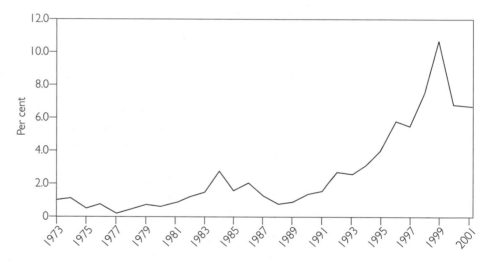

Figure 1.3   Percentage of aid spent on emergency. The portion of total aid of individual countries and multinational organisations spent on 'emergencies'. Source: Organisation for Economic Cooperation and Development, Development Assistance Committee (OECD DAC).

1.3.1   Impartial, neutral, independent

An army would clearly gain if its wounded were patched up by someone else and would be disadvantaged if the wounded of the other side were similarly helped. Thus over time the Red Cross movement developed a de facto deal with warring parties in which humanitarian agencies are allowed to operate in exchange for not interfering in the war itself. In 1965 this was eventually codified into the seven 'Fundamental Principles of the Red Cross' (Pictet, 1979):

- Humanity. 'To prevent and alleviate human suffering wherever it may be found.'
- Impartiality. To relieve suffering, priority is given to the most urgent cases. There can be no discrimination on the basis of nationality, race, religion, class or politics.
- Neutrality. '[T]he Red Cross may not take sides in hostilities or engage at any time in controversies of a political, racial, religious or ideological nature.'
- Independence. National Red Cross societies must remain independent of government.
- Voluntary. 'The Red Cross is a voluntary relief organisation.'
- Unity. There can be only one Red Cross society in a country.
- Universality. The Red Cross is worldwide and all member societies are equal.

The three concepts of impartiality, neutrality, and independence have been adopted by many other agencies in some form as the 'humanitarian principles'. Humanitarian agencies have been given a partial right of access to civilians in civil wars under the Geneva Conventions, which actually use the words 'humanitarian and impartial' (Box 1.5).

Box 1.5   The Geneva Conventions and civil war

Henry Dunant was a Swiss businessman who visited Napoleon III's headquarters near the northern Italian town of Solferino in 1859. He was stunned by the many thousands of wounded soldiers left on the battlefield to die, without receiving even the most basic medical attention that might have saved them. He later campaigned for the foundation of the Red Cross and for an international covenant to protect the wounded on the battlefield. This became the first 'Geneva Convention'.

International law does not ban war, nor does it ban combatants killing each other. What has evolved from the First Geneva Convention is a series of rules for war which reduce the suffering of non-combatants – wounded and captured soldiers and later civilians. There are now four Geneva Conventions, which are all in force:

- First Convention (1864): on the care of the wounded and sick members of armed forces in the field
- Second Convention (1906): on the care of the wounded, sick and shipwrecked members of armed forces at sea
- Third Convention (1929): on the treatment of prisoners of war
- Fourth Convention (1949): on the protection of civilian persons in time of war.

The Fourth Convention is quite restricted in that it does not protect civilian populations from the direct effect of hostilities. But it does require that 'If the whole or part of the population of an occupied territory is inadequately supplied', then both the occupying forces and their opponents must allow 'impartial humanitarian organizations' to bring in food, clothing and medicines (Article 59). But the obligation to allow the free passage is subject to the condition that the belligerent party 'is satisfied that there are no serious reasons for fearing:

(a) that the consignments may be diverted from their destination,

(b) that the control may not be effective, or

(c) that a definite advantage may accrue to the military efforts or economy of the enemy' through the supply of these goods (Article 23).

All Geneva Conventions were restricted to 'international armed conflicts'. Recognising this, two additional protocols to the Fourth Convention were adopted in 1977. Protocol 1 extends the protection of civilians, and also incorporates 'armed conflicts in which people are fighting against colonial domination and alien occupation and against racist regimes in the exercise of their right to self-determination'. Protocol 2 is specifically about the 'Protection of Victims of Non-International Armed Conflicts' (that is, civil wars). It says it includes 'all armed conflicts which are not covered' elsewhere, but puts its emphasis on wars between a government's 'armed forces and dissident armed forces or other organized armed groups'.

In particular, Protocol 2 bans mistreatment of 'all persons who do not take a direct part or who have ceased to take part in hostilities'. Specifically banned is 'murder as well as cruel treatment such as torture, mutilation or any form of corporal punishment'; 'collective punishments'; 'acts of terrorism'; and 'outrages upon personal dignity, in particular humiliating and degrading treatment, rape, enforced prostitution and any form of indecent assault'.

In addition, Protocol 2 allows 'relief actions for the civilian population which are of an exclusively humanitarian and impartial nature 'but only 'if the civilian population is suffering undue hardship owing to a lack of the supplies essential for its survival, such as food-stuffs and medical supplies'.

These humanitarian principles have worked well. Warring parties do trust at least the best known of the agencies to be genuinely independent and neutral. They know they will not be spied on, and they know that their opponents will not get preferential treatment, so they are prepared to allow agencies to work on both sides in the war. In more complex civil wars, naturally suspicious guerrilla leaders have accepted the neutrality and independence of agencies and granted them access to areas they control – often out of self-interest, when food and medical attention were scarce. In areas where control is disputed or patchy, for example if a road has a series of check-points set up by different groups, then neutrality is the only defence an agency will have.

At first glance, humanitarianism seems so obvious as to be unquestionable. It seems a basic human urge to want to ease the suffering of our fellow creatures, but for more than 150 years some have been asking if the urge to 'do something' can make matters worse. Indeed, there are forceful arguments that humanitarian actions, done with good will, can nevertheless increase suffering – by increasing the likelihood of war, by allowing a war to continue, or by allowing other human rights violations to continue. In the next section, we look at the possibility that humanitarian assistance can increase suffering. For some agencies, most notably the ICRC, these humanitarian principles are now seen as 'fundamental', and immediate relief of suffering the only goal. But more recently the fundamentalness of these principles has come under much heavier challenge. In the rest of this chapter, we look at the shifting perceptions of what constitutes humanitarian actions in civil wars, and at how it might be possible to take a more nuanced view of humanitarian principles.

1.4 Nightingale's risk

Florence Nightingale worked in British military hospitals in the Crimean war of 1855–56, was responsible for improved treatment of wounded soldiers and contributed to the development of the nursing profession in Britain. Yet she was strongly opposed to the founding of the Red Cross on the grounds that it would simply 'render war more easy'. The Red Cross would make it easier for militaristic powers to go to war because they knew someone else would take responsibility for the wounded. In effect, the Red Cross would become an ally of the armies. Hugo Slim (2001) calls this 'Nightingale's risk' – the risk that humanitarian action is co-opted and actually assists a warring party or promotes war.

THE HEROINE OF FIFTY YEARS AGO. MISS FLORENCE NIGHTINGALE IN THE HOSPITAL AT SCUTARI.
DRAWN BY W. HATHERELL, R.I.

Florence Nightingale treating wounded soldiers in a British military hospital.

Perhaps the starkest example of this is how humanitarian agencies relate to blockaded populations. Siege and blockade are traditional parts of war, going back at least to Roman times, as the attackers try to starve a city or country into submission. Civilians are always a target because the besieging forces hope to destroy morale in the city; they want civilians to withdraw support from the soldiers and eventually force capitulation. Since the whole point of a siege is to put pressure on civilians to put pressure on the military, providing food behind the lines in a siege is explicitly taking sides against the force laying siege.

As we noted above, both Save the Children and Oxfam were first founded to campaign against blockades in Europe. Oxfam dramatically intervened in an attempt to break a siege in Nigeria in 1968. The state of Biafra had declared independence and was resisting the Nigerian military when the government imposed a siege on Biafra. UNICEF and ICRC were sending food in an impartial operation approved by the Nigerian Government, which then withdrew permission as it tightened the siege. By June 1968 there were harrowing stories on European television and claims that 3000 people a day were dying. Oxfam and some Catholic agencies began shipping food; in August ICRC restarted its airlift without Nigerian government permission; and by October other agencies were involved. By the end of the war, the two airlifts had flown 7800 relief flights into Biafra. It was an extraordinary, heroic achievement. Since then, however, many see this as 'an act of unfortunate and profound folly' (Smillie, 1995, p. 104) and believe that it prolonged the war for 18 months and contributed towards the deaths of 180,000 people.

Bernard Kouchner, a young French doctor who worked as an ICRC volunteer in Nigeria, was shocked by what he saw and by ICRC's initial withdrawal. In 1971 he went on to found a new kind of NGO, Médecins

Biafra, 1968.

Sans Frontières (MSF – Doctors Without Borders), which created rapid response teams that ignored all conventional notions of national sovereignty (although by the 1990s MSF had become a more conventional agency, working on contracts with governments). Oxfam had broken new ground by setting aside issues of sovereignty, using the media to appeal directly to donors, and eventually influencing governments. MSF and established organisations such as ICRC continued in this tradition.

The debate about Biafra rumbled on, and Tim Allen (1998) comments:

> By the time that the Berlin Wall was demolished in 1989, there was ample evidence that the Quixotic altruism of international aid workers in internal wars was less a real solution to the suffering of traumatized populations, and more a response to demands for action among electorates in rich countries who had been disturbed by media coverage.

Oxfam and MSF came to accept that even if the techniques were valid, actions in Biafra were a mistake and actually caused more suffering. Kouchner, however, continues to argue that the intervention in Biafra was correct; 'the victims are always asking for help' (quoted in Allen, 1999). Here is Nightingale's risk played out very clearly – did aid to starving Biafrans actually extend the war and do more harm than good?

The split over Nightingale's risk was shown again in 1994 in Goma in the eastern Congo, in refugee camps for those who had fled from Rwanda after the genocide. We see this dilemma taking place even within individual organisations such as MSF which set up much-needed medical centres in Goma. It soon became clear that the camps were dominated by the militias which had carried out the genocide and who wanted to rebuild their power base; they were stopping more moderate Rwandans from returning home. MSF's French section decided that it had become an accomplice to the granting of impunity to those who carried out the genocide, and withdrew; MSF's Dutch section decided to stay.

1.4.1 Do no harm

But it took two writers in the late 1990s, Peter Uvin and Mary Anderson, to shock the aid community into finally accepting that in some cases they did more harm than good.

Peter Uvin's 1998 book about the Rwanda genocide was titled, explicitly, *Aiding Violence*.

> Rwanda was usually seen as a model of development in Africa, with good performance on most of the indicators of development, including the usual indicators, such as growth in gross national product (GNP), manufacturing, or services; the more social indicators, such as food availability or vaccination rates; and the new bottom-up indicators, such as number of nongovernmental organizations (NGOs) and cooperatives in the country.

Uvin argues that the aid community was fooled by its own indicators and did not see what was happening on the ground. Thus:

> [T]he process of development and the international aid given to promote it interacted with the forces of exclusion, inequality, pauperization, racism, and oppression that laid the groundwork for the 1994 genocide. ... Aid financed much of the machinery of exclusion, inequality, and humiliation [and] provided it with legitimacy and support.

A closer study of aid projects showed that most of the benefits went to the elite, not the poor, through salaries, houses, land, contracts, etc. (Uvin, 1998, pp. 1–8, 114, 231). In what should have been a warning, USAID in its 1992 annual report notes that 'people have attacked local authorities for launching development projects that brought little or no benefit to the community, for being personally corrupt, and for being inaccessible to and scornful of citizens in general' (quoted in Uvin, 1998, p. 126).

Uvin notes that in the four years before the genocide, there was 'widespread violence and massive human rights abuses'. This included the killing and harassment of aid agency and partner NGO staff. Yet there was no protest from the agencies. Indeed, aid increased sharply in this period, in part to support a structural adjustment programme.

> As Rwanda's farmers were facing crises without precedent, as inequality and corruption reached endemic proportions, as hope for the future was extinguished, and as violence, hatred, and human rights abuses became government policy, the international community was congratulating Rwanda ...

Significant amounts of the increased aid was used to import weapons and increase military spending. He notes that:

> Being responsible for as much as 80 per cent of the total investment budget of the government as well as a significant fraction of its current (operating) budget, the donor community's influence was large.

And he concludes that, far from using that power to prevent genocide, 'aid was an active and willing partner' in creating the conditions for the genocide (Uvin, 1998, pp. 85–89, 226, 231, 237).

Finally, Uvin asks the question:

> When societies disintegrate into violence, racism, and hatred, what does development mean? Under what conditions should the repairing of roads and vaccinating people – important things in their own right – take a backseat to more social, psychological, educational, or more outright political work?

(Uvin, 1998, p. 101)

Recognising that 'aid can reinforce, exacerbate and prolong the conflict,' Mary Anderson of the Local Capacities for Peace Project developed the concept of 'do no harm'. The phrase comes from the longstanding guidance to doctors. Hippocrates, originator of the doctor's oath, wrote in *Epidemics* (Bk. I, Sect. XI) that doctors should 'help, or at least do no harm.' The Roman physician Galen is said to have written that doctors should 'first, do no harm'.

Anderson's impact was dramatic and unexpected. Despite all that had been written by the mid 1990s, bilateral agencies and NGOs were shocked by the suggestion that they might be doing harm, and then were even more disturbed by the proposal that analysis of possible harm should be part of their planning process. But field experience of harm done by aid was just too strong, and agencies did change. However, it made many agencies overly cautious, refusing to work where they might do harm. This forced Anderson to warn that 'It is a moral and logical fallacy to conclude that because aid can do harm, a decision not to give aid would do no harm' (Anderson, 1999, p. 2).

In her book *Do No Harm* Anderson sets out how 'aid too often also feeds into, reinforces, and prolongs conflicts'. She argues that:

> Experience shows that aid's economic and political resources affect conflict in five predictable ways:
>
> 1   Aid resources are often stolen by warriors and used to support armies and buy weapons.
> 2   Aid affects markets by reinforcing either the war economy or the peace economy.
> 3   The distributional impacts of aid affect intergroup relationships, either feeding tensions or reinforcing connections.
> 4   Aid substitutes for local resources required to meet civilian needs, freeing them to support conflict.
> 5   Aid legitimizes people and their actions or agendas, supporting the pursuit of either war or peace.
>
> (Anderson, 1999, pp. 37, 39)

Aid can distort local markets, and if aid organisations are not careful, when they are hiring staff, buying goods and distributing assistance they can be benefiting some groups in preference to others, which may actually increase tension. Some form of aid can also give increased credibility to those in power – sometimes the government but other times the local armed group. Uvin's book shows all of this happened in Rwanda. Anderson also shows, as Florence Nightingale saw 150 years ago, that if aid agencies take responsibility for civilians, this reduces the burden on the fighters, and can 'render war more easy'.

Anderson (1999, pp. 55–59) also raises a particularly sensitive issue from the aid community – what implicit ethical messages are they sending out? Hard-working aid staff need breaks and recreation, yet when they use agency cars and petrol for a weekend excursion, when they use their higher salaries for parties with beer and good food at a time when local people have no resources, 'the message is that if one has control over resources, one can use them for personal purposes and pleasure. Accountability is unnecessary.' And when different salaries, different transport rules, and different evacuation rules apply to local and foreign staff, it reinforces the message that inequality is normal and that there should be elites who deserve safety, comfort and convenience.

Perhaps the most difficult dilemmas relate to the choices an agency must make to ensure its own continued presence. Security of its own staff must be a priority, but in its desire to stay and help, can an agency be sending out messages that may actually promote war? Mary Anderson (1999, pp. 55–59) warns that when humanitarian agencies hire armed guards, for example, they say arms are acceptable:

> Aid agencies protest, 'Our aims are worthy; when we employ guards, the weapons support good ends.' Every warlord will make that claim.

A similar problem arises in denouncing abuses. An agency may fear that if it makes public statements about corruption or human rights violations, it will be expelled and be unable to carry out its humanitarian or development mission. But by failing to make the statement, is it colluding with the authorities – government or rebel – in the area in which it is working, and sending out an implicit message that these actions are acceptable?

Bernard Wood (2003) in a study for the UN Development Programme points to the problems caused by agencies needing to act quickly, both because they are anxious to help those in need, and because of the agencies' own need for 'quick and highly visible results'. This often contradicts the need to build local capacities and the need for 'patience and promoting local ownership'. He concludes: 'Helping countries to develop and strengthen their own capabilities to handle their problems, rather than trying to do things for them, offers the only hope for durable results.'

1.4.2 Humanitarian principles no longer protect

'Do no harm' and 'Nightingale's risk' are leading some to believe that a narrow humanitarian approach may do more harm than good. Increasingly, participants in civil wars are also looking anew at the humanitarian principles. As this discussion has become more intense, there has been an explosion of writing and research; for example, the Humanitarian Policy Group (HPG) was set up at London's Overseas Development Institute.

For the agencies, one of the most serious problems is that humanitarian principles no longer provide protection. In an important study for the HPG, a former Oxfam worker Nicholas Leader (2000) points out that the humanitarian principles really were imposed on humanitarian agencies by military elites, granting access in exchange for a promise to raise no questions about the war itself. As Leader says, 'humanitarian principles are a deal between soldiers, not between policemen and criminals.' In particular, this assumed wars between nation-states which would obey the rules they had imposed. In civil wars the belligerents often do not acknowledge the limits of war and may see civilians as a legitimate target; indeed, as we have noted, civil wars are often more brutal precisely because they are between civilians in the same population. Thus the humanitarian agencies find themselves in a paradox – having adopted as 'principles' the rules imposed on them by militaries, they now find themselves trying to impose these 'principles' on civil war militaries. And they do not always succeed.

At the same time, the 1990s concept of 'effects-based operations' (described in Section 1.2.2) is seen by military planners as a return to the concept that military force exists to serve political or strategic ends. Effects-based operations are even seen as 'information campaigns' which persuade the enemy population to act in ways the military wants. Part of this is the desire to build up local allies, and the view that there is no longer a clear military distinction between war and peace. The goal is to use political, military and economic methods – a mix of dissuasion and persuasion to coerce and convince local people to act in certain ways. Aid becomes a part of that package. In Afghanistan in mid 2004, for example, US soldiers were digging wells, building schools and running health posts in villages in an explicit attempt to encourage local people to provide evidence about Taliban insurgents in the area (*Guardian*, 23 September 2004). In Iraq in 2003, the British military used humanitarian aid distributions to draw civilians out of areas it wanted to attack. And the British Navy's 2004 recruitment advertising campaign focused on its humanitarian work.

In wars in Chechnya, Iraq and Afghanistan, humanitarian aid workers became targets in the early twenty-first century, as insurgent forces considered that aid workers were, in effect, supporting the government they were fighting against. The bitter separatist wars in Dagastan and Chechnya saw the kidnapping of aid workers; MSF and the United Nations, among others, were forced to suspend operations in 2002. In Iraq the headquarters of both the United Nations and the International Committee of the Red Cross were bombed in 2003 in unprecedented attacks; attacks on foreigners, including aid workers, increased in 2004, leading many humanitarian agencies to withdraw. MSF had worked in Afghanistan for 24 years under changing wars and governments, but had to withdraw in 2004 when a clearly marked MSF vehicle was ambushed and five aid workers were killed. It brought to 30 the number of aid workers killed in 18 months. MSF blamed the US-led military

> coalition's attempts to co-opt humanitarian aid and use it to 'win hearts and minds'. By doing so, providing aid is no longer seen as an impartial and neutral act ...

> (MSF statement, 28 July 2004)

Commodore Tim Laurence (1999) in his study *Humanitarian Assistance and Peacekeeping* comments:

> The concepts of absolute neutrality and impartiality in war are illusions, and humanitarian personnel providing assistance in time of war will usually be perceived as a threat (and therefore a target) to one or other side.

If the principles no longer buy protection, should they be maintained? Indeed, are they even possible? Consider the three principles:

- Neutrality. How can you be neutral in the face of genocide? Did a false sense of neutrality mean some agencies failed to act in Rwanda? There is a growing view that humanitarians must sometimes take sides; humanitarianism may be better served by publicly denouncing gross human rights violations. Similarly, if an attack is directed at civilians, such as the Biafra sanctions, then an intervention cannot be neutral, because any alleviation of human suffering goes against the military purpose of the action.

- Independence. Many agencies are now dependent on government funding and government contracts, and governments want to use aid for foreign policy and development goals.

- Impartiality. Because they are now dependent on government funding, some agencies can no longer go where the need is greatest, but are forced to become involved in those wars – and those aspects of individual wars – which have the highest political importance for the contracting governments or which meet some other donor need.

1.5   Ethics and choices

Yet another challenge to humanitarian principles is the proliferation of thousands of different agencies. No longer is there only the Red Cross. And each agency has its own goals and its own interpretations of the principles and ethics.

There are two approaches to ethics. 'Deontological ethics' are based on duty, the moral need to act under certain circumstances, and the belief that some actions are good of themselves. This is also sometimes called 'absolute morality'. The ICRC follows this approach – that it has a duty to, for example, care for wounded soldiers. This is contrasted with 'teleological ethics' or 'utilitarian ethics' which are goal-based and are more concerned with wider consequences of actions (Slim, 1997a). This distinction is raised by the intervention in Biafra, where the two approaches to ethics lead to different responses.

Perhaps the most extreme version of absolute morality, in the context of this book, was a statement by the Steering Committee for Humanitarian Response, composed of the Red Cross and a group of humanitarian NGOs, which said baldly: 'The raison d'être of humanitarian action is not the achievement of peace.' Similarly, the Overseas Development Institute

Humanitarian Policy Group says 'Neutrality means not taking sides in hostilities' and 'Humanitarian action is also neutral with respect to the causes of conflict' (Macrae, 2002; Macrae et al., 2004). This means that humanitarian agencies should not take a political position with respect to the justness or otherwise of any particular cause. At this extreme, then, humanitarian agencies with a policy of absolute morality should not denounce injustice.

Increasingly, however, agencies take a view that ethical humanitarian behaviour means they must assess the broader impact of their actions. The automatic response to suffering has been moderated by consideration of the perceived risks of negative impact and of possible alternative actions which might have greater positive impact. This increasingly leads to more 'political' strategies that involve constructive social change. Sometimes this may involve taking sides in the war; at other times, it may mean a more explicit social justice agenda (Leader, 2000) (Box 1.6).

Box 1.6   Peacebuilding and being 'political'

In nearly half of all countries in which a civil war ends, the war begins again within a decade. Despite the initial failure of the concept of a relief-development continuum, it has become clear that interveners must address peacebuilding – efforts to ensure that war does not start again. Instead of being simply a technocratic and managerial issue, however, it is now realised that this is explicitly political. Dame Margaret Anstee, who was Special Representative of the UN Secretary-General in Angola in 1992 when the international community failed to prevent a return to war, wrote in a later report to the UN (quoted in Macrae, 2001, p. 44):

> In the case of peace-building, political considerations take centre stage. In such situations, developmental and humanitarian programmes must contribute to the overall political purpose of consolidating peace and preventing renewed conflict as well as their normal function of improving conditions of life and relieving hardship. Thus, the political objectives should always prevail.

Mary Anderson says that relief and development agencies must work to alleviate human suffering and at the same time promote a durable and just peace. Anderson argues (1999, p. 7):

> By failing to support people engaged in a battle for justice, we support the status quo of injustice. NGOs must be clearly on the side of those who are poor and marginalised, those against whom societies discriminate, and their aid must support systemic change toward justice rather than simply keep people alive to continue to live in situations of injustice.

Our changing approach to ethics and to humanitarian principles relates to what we think is possible. The implicit assumption of humanitarianism from the time of Henry Dunant is that the causes of the war are beyond our control and that the best we can do to reduce suffering is to help everyone equally and neutrally. The implicit assumption of peacebuilding/ development assistance/utilitarian ethics is that we do have influence over the causes of the violence and might be able to reduce suffering by tackling those causes. This difference increasingly affects the way we see and present the question.

In an interview for this book, Jane Barry, a writer on humanitarian aid who remains closer to the absolute morality side, summarised the debate this way. Suppose there is a gangland shooting in a neighbourhood and the victims are brought into the local hospital. The absolute morality view is to treat the victims equally and unquestionably. But suppose the doctors want to take a broader view and try to reduce gang violence. Should the doctors make a judgement as to which of the wounded are gang members and only treat the innocent bystanders, she asks? Or barter treatment to gang members as a condition that they promise not to fight again? Neither is acceptable to her.

By contrast, those who take a more utilitarian approach would accept the challenge, and phrase the problem differently. It is not an issue for the doctor in the operating theatre, but rather a question of: should resources be allocated to improve treatment of gunshot wounds in order to save more lives, or should they go to attempts to prevent gang warfare?

1.6 Chapter summary

In the second half of the twentieth century, there were more than **200 wars** with millions of deaths, and the number increased steadily until the end of the Cold War in 1989. Most were civil wars. There are serious disagreements over the definitions of all key words, leading to the **Humpty Dumpty problem** of words being defined in arbitrary and contradictory ways. There is not even an agreement as to whether the number of wars increased or decreased in the 1990s, because of disagreement over what constitutes a 'war'. We defined war to simply mean 'collective killing for some collective purpose' and **civil war** to be a war 'mainly within one country and where the fighting is primarily between people of that country.' We then defined two other terms. We said **conflict** is any struggle between groups or individuals over resources or power, and we argued that conflict is an inevitable part of change and development. Most conflicts can be resolved, but if they cannot, they can escalate to armed conflict or war. **Peacebuilding** was defined as 'promoting a just and stable peace by helping to end the war and by helping to create the conditions that reduce the likelihood of the war starting again.'

Humanitarian intervention in wars and postwar periods has been going on since the 1860s and the founding of the Red Cross, which also led to the **Geneva Conventions** intended to reduce the harm to non-combatants.

Increasing numbers of agencies have become involved in **humanitarian assistance**, which is traditionally seen to be impartial, neutral and independent. Two issues have been raised, however. One issue is that although neutrality served as a protection for nearly 150 years, in the wars of the early twenty-first century, humanitarian aid workers were **coming under attack** and being killed and kidnapped because they were no longer seen as neutral. The other issue is **Nightingale's risk**, the danger that aid can do more harm than good, and might actually promote or prolong war. This, in turn, led to the concept of **do no harm** and the realisation that the first consideration must be that aid does not make matters worse. It also leads to a discussion of **two kinds of ethics**. One is absolute morality or duty, where an individual feels duty-bound to provide help to the suffering. The other is utilitarian ethics which considers the final outcome and wider consequences, and recognises that immediate reduction of suffering may cause more suffering in the longer term, for example by allowing the war to continue longer than it might have.

References

Anderson, M. B. (1999) *Do No Harm: How Aid Can Support Peace – or War*, Boulder, CO, Lynne Rienner.

Allen, T. (1998) 'Internal wars and humanitarian intervention', essay written for TU872 *Institutional development: conflicts, values and meanings*, Milton Keynes, The Open University.

Allen, T. (1999) 'Whose right to intervene?', audiotape, Milton Keynes, The Open University and BBC.

Collier, P., Elliot, L., Hegre, H., Hoeffler, A., Reynal-Querol, M. and Sambanis, N. (2003) *Breaking the Conflict Trap*, Washington DC, World Bank and Oxford, Oxford University Press.

Eriksson, M., Wallensteen, P. and Sollenberg, M. (2003) 'Armed conflict, 1989–2002', *Journal of Peace Research*, vol. 40, no. 5, pp. 593–607.

Eriksson, M. and Wallensteen, P. (2004) 'Armed conflict, 1989–2003', *Journal of Peace Research*, vol. 44, no. 5, pp. 625–36.

Hegre, H (2005) The PRIO/Uppsala Armed Conflict Dataset, http://www.prio.no/cwp/armedconflict (accessed March 2005)

Iraq Body Count (2005) www.iraqbodycount.org (accessed March 2005).

Keegan, J. (1999) *War and Our World: The Reith Lectures 1998*, London, Pimlico.

Kornbluh, P. (1997) 'The storm over "Dark Alliance"', *Columbia Journalism Review*, New York, Jan–Feb.

Laurence, T. (1999) *Humanitarian Assistance and Peacekeeping: An Uneasy Alliance?* London, Royal United Services Institute for Defence Studies.

Leader, N. (2000) *The Politics of Principle: The Principles of Humanitarian Assistance in Practice*, Humanitarian Policy Group Report 2, London, Overseas Development Institute.

Macrae, J. (2001) *Aiding Recovery*, London, Zed.

Macrae, J. (2002) 'International Humanitarian Action: A Review of Policy Trends', *ODI Briefing Paper*, London, Overseas Development Institute.

Macrae, J. et al. (2004) 'Redefining the official humanitarian aid agenda', *ODI Opinions*, London, Overseas Development Institute.

Pictet, J. (1979) 'The Fundamental Principles of the Red Cross: Commentary', International Committee of the Red Cross, www.icrc.org/Web/eng/siteeng0.nsf/htmlall/5MJE9N (accessed January 2005).

Roberts, L. et al. (2004) 'Mortality before and after the 2003 invasion of Iraq: cluster sample survey', *The Lancet*, vol. 364, no. 9446.

Slim, H. (1997a) 'Doing the right thing: relief agencies, moral dilemmas and moral responsibility in political emergencies and war', *Disasters*, vol. 21, no. 3, pp. 244–57.

Slim, H. (2001) 'Violence and humanitarianism: moral paradox and the protection of civilians', *Security Dialogue*, vol. 32, no. 3, pp. 325–39.

Smillie, I. (1995) *The Alms Bazaar: Altruism Under Fire – Non Profit Organizations and International Development*, London, Intermediate Technology Publications.

Tucker, C. (1996) 'CIA plot or not, drug war preys on minority poor', *The Atlanta Journal Constitution*, Atlanta, GA, 22 September, p. C7.

Uvin, P. (1998) *Aiding Violence*, West Hartford, CT, Kumarian Press.

White, M. (2004) Death tolls for the major wars and atrocities of the twentieth century, http://users.erols.com/mwhite28/warstat2.htm (accessed January 2005).

Wood, B. (2003) 'Development Dimensions of Conflict Prevention and Peacebuilding', New York, UNDP Bureau for Crisis Prevention and Recovery.

2   Intervention

Joseph Hanlon

2.1   Introduction

In this chapter, we will look at the variety of interventions around civil wars and at the rapidly changing attitudes and debates. The 'traditional' view has been that outsiders intervened in someone else's country by invitation and agreement – to provide 'humanitarian' help after a natural disaster or war, to offer 'development' assistance, and through United Nations peacekeeping missions which took place after a ceasefire or settlement and by agreement with the parties. Outside interveners could not violate a country's sovereignty. But sovereignty is increasingly being challenged and forcible intervention is promoted.

Sovereignty means that a state and its government has supreme authority within a territory – a combination of *territory* and *authority* over that territory. The world's land surface is largely divided up into the territories of sovereign states. Traditionally one sovereign state cannot breach the borders of another sovereign state without formally declaring war. Civil wars are usually about authority over the whole territory or a claim that some part of the territory should be separate. Authority also means that other states should not intervene in the 'domestic' affairs of a sovereign state, and this has been interpreted very broadly, for example to mean that one could not cross a border in order to stop human rights violations or stop the activities of even the most heinous dictator.

International organisations like the European Union and the United Nations are associations of sovereign states. The independence of many colonies in Asia and Africa was based on the unquestioned assumption that as independent states they were sovereign and would become UN members.

The UN Charter put great stress on sovereignty and non-interference in what are considered internal affairs. Article 2 of the UN Charter includes:

- 'The Organization is based on the principle of the sovereign equality of all its Members.'
- 'All Members shall refrain in their international relations from the threat or use of force against the territorial integrity or political independence of any state.'

- 'Nothing contained in the present Charter shall authorize the United Nations to intervene in matters which are essentially within the domestic jurisdiction of any state.'

The UN grew out of the Second World War and was seen initially as a body which would try to prevent wars *between* states, especially between the nuclear powers. Sovereignty was seen as a way of preventing states from invading other states.

The 1947–89 'Cold War' dominated the second half of the twentieth century. The Cold War was a conflict between the 'western' capitalist bloc led by the United States and the 'eastern' socialist bloc led by the Union of Soviet Socialist Republics (USSR), itself dominated by Russia. After four decades of spiralling military expenditure, the East cracked first and the USSR split up into its member countries. In a world increasingly divided into 'East' and 'West', the UN and the concept of sovereignty prevented the Cold War from becoming a hot war. Of course, the concept of 'sovereignty' was viewed flexibly. The USSR was allowed to intervene in its neighbouring states, such as Hungary and Czechoslovakia, while the US could intervene in Latin America and the Caribbean, for example in Grenada. There were hot wars between 'East' and 'West' in Korea and Vietnam. And there was a series of proxy 'civil' wars, for example in Angola and Nicaragua. But there was no nuclear war and no world war between East and West.

Three factors have led the concept of sovereignty to be increasingly challenged, at least for weak countries. First was the growth of civil wars, which led to the question of whether 'civil' wars were to be seen as purely 'domestic' issues, and the intervention in Biafra in 1968 marked a permanent change in the rules. Through agencies such as MSF, a belief developed in a humanitarian right to intervene in weak states, independent of sovereignty. Second was the end of the Cold War. Many developing countries made use of the sovereignty principle by playing off East against West to try to gain aid; sovereignty meant that East and West would prevent the other side from intervening without an invitation, leading to a tendency to support dictators and autocratic governments who would invite them in. The Cold War meant that many poor and weak countries had a big brother who would protect their sovereignty, at least in a limited way. The end of the Cold War removed even that limited protection. Third was the debt crisis combined with a fall in aid after the Cold War. Aid during the Cold War had often been in the form of loans, and in the 1980s Western lenders presented the bill; the debt crisis gave lenders a new form of leverage, just when the end of the Cold War meant developing countries had relatively less power. Over a decade and through the use of the International Monetary Fund and the World Bank, the US and the victorious 'West' began intervening heavily in the internal economic and political affairs of poor countries. The fiction was maintained that poor countries were members of the IMF and World Bank and voluntarily accepted their policies, but essential aid and debt relief became conditional on accepting these policy impositions. Tim Allen and David Styan (2000) comment:

> [T]he most remarkable shift that occurred in development practice during the last decades of the twentieth century was the tendency to deliberately and openly set aside sovereignty. The shift has had several aspects, including the structural adjustment programmes of the 1980s and the emphasis on 'good governance' following the ending of cold war alliances.

In this chapter, we look at the changing role of the intervener in the context of the changing nature of sovereignty and the increasing importance of civil wars. We have already noted that humanitarian agencies sometimes intervene in ongoing wars, and in the 1980s this expanded to include development agencies under the term 'complex political emergencies'. This, however, was also by agreement. More recently a view has been growing that there are circumstances in which intervention should be possible without agreement. We conclude the chapter by looking at the responsibilities of such an intervener.

2.2   Postwar peacekeeping by agreement

Some wars end with a victory by one side, in which power is handed over, as in Zimbabwe, or the insurgents are defeated, as in Peru. Often there is an internationally brokered or assisted settlement, as in South Africa or Britain (over Northern Ireland), which leads to some form of power sharing. Sometimes, where a truce or peace settlement has been agreed, the parties agree to the presence of a peacekeeping force. Commodore Tim Laurence (1999, p. 5), assistant commandant at the British Joint Services Command and Staff College, Bracknell, in a study *Humanitarian Assistance and Peacekeeping*, points out that the first modern peacekeeping operation was in the Saar, a disputed zone between France and Germany which was administered under the League of Nations between 1920 and 1935. In 1935 there was a plebiscite under substantial tension, so the League organised a peacekeeping force of 3300 soldiers from Britain, Italy, Sweden and the Netherlands; with a visible presence of international soldiers on the street, the vote passed peacefully, with 90 per cent opting to join Germany, which took place on 1 March 1935.

The United Nations was formed after the Second World War to try to ensure that such a war did not occur again, and Article 1 of the UN Charter commits governments to 'maintain international peace and security'. Perhaps because the founders of the UN did not foresee the kinds of wars that occurred later – despite the experience of the Saar – the UN was not given a formal peacekeeping role in its Charter. But its importance as a trusted and neutral force quickly became obvious. By 2003, the UN had had 56 peacekeeping operations involved in 40 wars, with 14 still in operation. The UN military observer group on the India–Pakistan border has been in operation since 1949 and UN observers in the Golan Heights have been monitoring the disengagement between Syria and Israel since 1974 – an indication that the UN can stand between the two sides but cannot necessarily broker a final settlement.

The UN Charter gives the Security Council the 'primary responsibility for the maintenance of international peace and security'. Chapter 6 of the Charter encourages peaceful settlements of disputes and offers Security Council help. In contrast, under Chapter 7, if the Security Council determines 'the existence of any threat to the peace, breach of the peace, or act of aggression' it can impose economic or military sanctions and take military action 'as may be necessary'. Former UN Secretary-General Dag Hammarskjöld famously described peacekeeping as being 'Chapter 6½' of the Charter, lying somewhere between peaceful Chapter 6 techniques and more robust Chapter 7 methods. Chapter 8 is important because it says:

> [T]he Security Council shall, where appropriate, utilize such regional arrangements or agencies for enforcement action under its authority. But no enforcement action shall be taken under regional arrangements or by regional agencies without the authorization of the Security Council.

Since UN peacekeeping operations must be approved by the Security Council, that means they need agreement of the five permanent members (United States, Russia, China, Britain and France). During the Cold War this was difficult to obtain and tended to be in areas which were not subject to East–West confrontation. Indeed, only 13 peacekeeping missions were approved before 1988, whereas 43 were agreed in the subsequent 15 years. Thus the role of the UN in peacekeeping is largely a post-Cold War phenomenon, has largely involved civil wars, and evolved rapidly in the 1990s. Most peacekeeping missions have been under Chapter 6 of the Charter.

In general, peacekeeping missions involve several thousand international troops, police and civilian observers – often linked to support for demobilisation and disarmament and to humanitarian assistance by other UN agencies. At best, as in Mozambique and Timor-Leste (East Timor), the UN is seen as a genuinely impartial guarantor of the agreement reached by the two sides, allowing the rebuilding of infrastructure and political institutions. Fighters are more willing to disarm if they believe that UN soldiers, in their traditional blue helmets, are there to protect them and to keep the peace. But UN peacekeeping has also had some dismal failures, in Rwanda and Angola, for example.

UN peacekeeping has proved to be effective only when there is the right mix of international and local conditions. Peacekeeping requires approval of the UN Security Council, is funded by voluntary contributions by UN members, and troops are sent voluntarily by UN members. In practice that means those wars of most interest to the big powers are the ones which receive the most attention, such as Afghanistan and the former Yugoslavia. The problem is compounded because the Security Council normally only approves a peacekeeping mission for 30 to 90 days, so approval must be constantly renewed, which makes long-term planning very difficult. Changes in media have also played a role; 24-hour rolling news television brings some wars directly into living rooms throughout the world. When people see suffering on television, they demand that their politicians 'do something'. This has become known as the 'CNN-factor' – a war or disaster given prominence on television gains huge international support from aid agencies and politicians. But the majority of wars are not on television, and they tend to be starved of resources. Many of the UN peacekeeping missions have been severely under-resourced because they were not given TV coverage or were not priority countries for the big powers.

Locally, there must be a peace to keep. Initially, UN forces were lightly armed and served mainly as observers, dependent on the willingness of the parties to the agreement to keep their side of the bargain. Where this did not occur, as in Rwanda and Bosnia in the early 1990s, horrific massacres occurred when the settlement broke down and UN 'peacekeepers' were unwilling or too few in number and too poorly equipped to provide protection.

After the failures in Rwanda and Bosnia, UN Secretary-General Kofi Annan commissioned a report on peace operations by a team headed by the former Algerian Foreign Minister Lakhdar Brahimi. He reported in August 2000, and his report set in train a major change in the UN's approach to peacekeeping. Most importantly, Brahimi argued that:

> impartiality for United Nations operations must therefore mean adherence to the principles of the Charter; where one party to a peace agreement clearly and incontrovertibly is violating its terms, continued equal treatment of all parties by the United Nations can in the best case result in ineffectiveness and in the worst may amount to complicity with evil. No failure did more to damage the standing and credibility of United Nations peacekeeping in the 1990s than its reluctance to distinguish victim from aggressor.

Brahimi (2000) also declared that:

> United Nations peacekeepers – troops or police – who witness violence against civilians should be presumed to be authorised to stop it.

Sierra Leone became the first test, and was an important turning point. After an agreement was signed, the UN entered, as it does traditionally, by invitation of the signatories of the agreement. But in Sierra Leone the agreement broke down and in July 2000 500 UN peacekeepers were captured. Brahimi reported just a month later, and in particular called for more 'robust' rules of engagement. This was taken up in Sierra Leone where UN troops successfully engaged in military action against the forces which withdrew from the original peace accord.

Pakistani soldiers, part of the UNAMSIL peacekeeping force, on patrol in Sierra Leone.

2.2.1 Choosing sides and military intervention

Until now, we have implicitly assumed that outsiders are in a country after a war has stopped, with the agreement of the protagonists. Sometimes there will be peacekeeping forces from the United Nations or regional organisations such as the African Union keeping the sides apart. And it seems clear that, although the UN does not always succeed, UN peacekeepers do reduce the length of wars and stop the killing sooner (Enterline and Kang, 2003). But until now, we have assumed that any outside military forces are there by agreement.

In Sierra Leone, UN, West African and British peacekeepers did intervene on the side of the government and helped to bring the war to an end. But failed interventions in Somalia, questionable interventions in the former Yugoslavia (Box 2.1), and failed peacekeeping missions such as Angola in 1992 where the UN did not take sides when the peace accord broke down, all raise questions. Various studies agree on two points:

- Where competing outside groups back the two sides in a civil war, as often happened in the Cold War, the civil war goes on indefinitely.

- Military or economic support for the government in a civil war makes the war last longer.

Why should backing governments be counterproductive? One guess is that support for a government makes it less willing to negotiate with the rebels, and thus extends the war. Whatever the reasons, the academic consensus is that intervention on the side of the government almost always extends the war. Sierra Leone really was an important exception; there, the international community backed an elected government with popular support faced with a rebel movement which had lost support, and surely brought the war to a speedier end.

On the other side, there is a dispute about what outsiders can do in relation to a rebel movement. We might, perhaps, be able to shorten a war by backing an opposition militarily (strengthening it) or squeezing it financially (weakening it), but there is no agreement on this. Three studies paint a mixed picture:

- Andrew Enterline and Dylan Balch-Lindsay (2002) looked at civil wars going back to 1816 and concluded that where there is no special support for the government, military and economic support for the opposition does increase the chances that the opposition will win, and does, on balance, shorten the war.

- Paul Collier, Anke Hoeffler and Måns Söderbom (2004) of the Centre for the Study of African Economies at Oxford confirm that 'military intervention on the side of the government is ineffective', but find that 'external military support for rebels shortens conflicts'. They find that the impact of economic intervention to *support* either side is 'insignificant'. They also find that a squeeze on rebel finances (for example by reducing their earnings from commodities) shortens the war.

- By contrast, Patrick Regan (2002) of Binghamton University, argues that all third-party military or economic intervention tends to lengthen rather than shorten wars – 'overwhelmingly *any* intervention tends to increase the expected duration of the conflict'.

Researchers have raised two questions about whether the data are skewed. The first is to ask if outsiders tend to intervene in nastier, bloodier, more intractable wars – thus the ones in which there is an intervention are exactly the ones we would expect to last longer. A World Bank study showed that, indeed, 'external intervention is more likely in bloodier wars or when the government fighting the civil war is more democratic'. Nevertheless, the study finds it does not make any difference – intervention tends to lengthen the war (Elbadawi and Sambanis, 2000). The second question about the research is that many of the studies require quite large amounts of data which are often not available, so many conclusions are drawn from only a handful of better studied wars which may not be typical (Suhrke et al., 2004).

Finally, there is a very real political question going back to Mary Anderson's concept of *Do No Harm*. Speeding the end of the war may not always be the best outcome. If a war ends more quickly with the victory of a brutal dictator, it may save lives in the short term but cost more lives in the longer term. Similarly, a longer war to defend a popular elected government might be preferable to a shorter war ending in victory by a military overthrowing that government. The issue of choosing sides in a war has important political, social and humanitarian consequences which may not always be best served by a rapid end to the war.

Box 2.1   Many interveners in the former Yugoslavia

In the late 1980s the Yugoslav federation faced a major economic crisis, and in 1991 broke up. Four states seceded and were soon recognised internationally – Slovenia, Croatia, Bosnia-Herzegovina and Macedonia. Only Serbia and Montenegro remain within Yugoslavia.

The wars that followed showed the whole range of international interventions. The mainly Serb Yugoslav Government forces tried to prevent the breakup and by late 1991 occupied extensive areas of Croatia and Bosnia. In the following decade there was brutal fighting and massacres that later led to war crimes trials. During that period there were eight United Nations peacekeeping missions, four operations by NATO and several missions by the Organisations for Security and Cooperation in Europe (OSCE, made up of all European countries including Russia, plus the United States) and the European Union (EU).

The first UN action was to impose an arms embargo on Yugoslavia in September 1991 and economic sanctions in May 1992. In Croatia the EU eventually negotiated a ceasefire and in December 1991 the UN agreed to send peacekeepers at the request of both Croatia and Yugoslavia. UNPROFOR, the UN Protection Force, was set up initially in Croatia in 1992 to create demilitarised 'UN Protected Areas'. UNPROFOR was later expanded to Macedonia and to Bosnia and Herzegovina and its mandate was enlarged to protect convoys of the UN High Commissioner for Refugees and to monitor a ban on military flights. It was authorised to use force to defend the city of Sarajevo, and to use NATO military power. The concept of 'protected areas' was new and proved difficult to maintain; Dutch troops were unable to protect the town of Srebrenica when it was attacked in June 1995 by Bosnian Serbs and at least 7000 Muslim civilians taking refuge there were massacred. By mid 1995, fighting had escalated and UNPROFOR had grown so large that it was restructured and split into several different peacekeeping missions.

In Croatia, UNCRO, the UN Confidence Restoration Operation, was set up to replace UNPROFOR and monitor a ceasefire and an economic agreement signed in 1994, as well as to facilitate the delivery of humanitarian aid to Bosnia and Herzegovina. In 1996 UNCRO was replaced by two UN missions. Croatia had expelled Serbian forces from Eastern Slavonia and a peaceful handover of Western Slavonia was agreed, but ethnic Serbs in Croatia insisted on international protection and UNTAES, the UN Transitional Administration in Eastern Slavonia, Baranja and Western Sirmium, functioned from 1996 to 1998. There was particular concern about policing, and UNPSG, the UN Police Support Group, monitored the performance of the Croatian police in 1998. Police monitoring was then handed over to OSCE, which continued until 2000.

Also in Croatia there was UNMOP, the UN Mission of Observers in Prevlaka. This was a group of just 28 people which successfully monitored the demilitarisation of the Prevlaka peninsula, a strategic area disputed by Croatia and Serbia, from 1996 until 2002. UN Secretary-General Kofi Annan commented that it showed that even a small UN presence can make a difference.

In Macedonia, UNPROFOR was replaced with UNPREDEP, the UN Preventive Deployment Force, which mainly monitored the border with Kosovo and Albania. UNPREDEP maintained close links with the OSCE Spillover Monitor Mission, the European Commission Monitoring Mission, and the NATO Kosovo Verification Coordination Centre. The UN mission ended in 1999 when China, a permanent member of the Security Council, vetoed its continuation, despite the view of the UN Secretary-General and other Council members that it was useful and should be continued. Indeed, UNPREDEP was one of the most successful UN peacekeeping forces – it kept the war from spreading to Macedonia. In 2001 tension increased between ethnic Albanians and the government but a peace agreement was reached which included a NATO peace force; in 2003 NATO handed over peacekeeping duties to the European Union.

In Bosnia and Herzegovina NATO bombed Serb positions in September 1995, leading to more negotiations and a ceasefire. UN sanctions against Yugoslavia (Serbia) were ended and UNPROFOR was replaced by three teams: IFOR, the NATO-led Implementation Force; an OSCE mission to support democratisation; and UNMIBH, the UN Mission in Bosnia and Herzegovina. UNMIBH was responsible for law enforcement activities and police reform and coordinated UN activities relating to humanitarian aid, refugees, demining, human rights, elections and economic reconstruction. UNMIBH continued until 2002; IFOR was replaced by SFOR, the Stabilization Force, which still had a presence of 7000 troops in Bosnia and Herzegovina in 2004, although NATO intended eventually to transfer the operation to the European Union as it had in Macedonia.

In 1998, the Kosovo Liberation Army began an attempt to break away from Serbia. Serbian security forces responded. Later that year, the UN again imposed an arms embargo on Serbia and in September the Security Council passed a resolution demanding the immediate cessation of hostilities in Kosovo, the withdrawal of Serbian forces, and unrestricted access for humanitarian aid. Because of Russian opposition, the Security Council would not agree military action against Serbia. The OSCE, which includes Russia as a member, sent an observer mission to Kosovo. NATO set up KFOR, its Kosovo Force. Fighting increased and Serbia deployed up to 30,000 troops into Kosovo. With Russia still blocking UN action, a US-led NATO force began aerial bombardment of Serbia. Serbia responded by expelling 600,000 ethnic Albanians from Kosovo. In June an agreement was reached and NATO stopped its air strikes. A joint NATO–Russian occupation force was agreed and a UN Interim Administration Mission in Kosovo (UNMIK) was established, including a 3100 member international police force. Many ethnic Albanians returned, but thousands of ethnic Serbs fled and the UN and NATO were criticised for failing to protect Serbians.

The role of outsiders in the violent break-up of Yugoslavia will be debated for a long time. UN peacekeepers had some real successes, especially where there was a peace to keep – creating a sense of security for minority Serbs in Croatia, keeping the peace in Prevlaka, and stopping the spread of the war to Macedonia. Regional organisations, as set out in Chapter 8 of the UN Charter, also played a key role when they worked with UN agreement. But the NATO bombing of Serbia without UN agreement was widely seen as a violation of international law, as well as being counterproductive and creating more refugees.

2.3   Aid agencies and war

Official aid policy had 'an understanding of development as limited to transferring funds and expertise from the haves to the have-nots', in the words of UN Secretary-General Boutros Boutros-Ghali (1994, p. 235). This also fitted in with the Cold War, because resources could be transferred to allies to buy support. Relief and humanitarian aid were seen as a small part of this, until the sharp increases in aid of the 1980s. Emergency assistance had been shaped by models derived from natural disasters, providing urgent food, shelter and medical help. By the 1980s, most emergency aid was going to war zones, and there was a realisation that in some cases such aid was not short term, but would be required for some years. There was a growing sense that relief and development aid had to be linked in some way, and that it might be possible to use aid to prevent and help to end wars.

Mozambique's 1982–92 war led to the development of the terms 'complex political emergency' and, variously, 'chronic', 'continuing' and 'protracted' emergency – all different euphemisms intended to mean that the emergency was caused by war, but we don't want to say so (Hanlon, 1991, p. 79; Macrae, 2001). All sides realised that Mozambique had become a Cold War battlefield, with the Soviet Union providing some support for the government and the West encouraging apartheid South Africa to create and back an anti-communist insurgent movement. Some European governments and United Nations agencies wanted to help Mozambique, but the mice were unwilling to intervene in a fight between the elephants. So the war continued, with a wide range of donors patching the wounds and clearing up the damage, eventually developing a programme which mixed humanitarian and development aid, and which continued during the last five years of the war.

This was followed by a growing view that relief needed to do more than just feed people and development was more than simple economic growth – they had to reduce vulnerability to war and natural disaster. In 1996 the European Commission issued a paper entitled 'Linking relief, rehabilitation and development'. It defined a new concept of 'structural stability' which was seen as 'the capacity to manage change without the resort to violent conflict'. It was seen as a dynamic concept linked to change, and meant that 'working towards economic development alone is insufficient for an effective policy of peace-building.' It required tackling the root causes of violence, which 'ultimately means touching upon the issues of the distribution of resources and power within the state.' European aid needed to tackle not simply narrow economic growth but democracy, human rights, and viable political structures (European Commission, 1997). Aid should somehow be able to prevent and resolve wars, and even emergency aid should have a developmental content.

The concept of a relief–development continuum triggered a backlash from the humanitarian side. Partly they did not want to be diverted from emergency aid into development and peacebuilding, but also it was seen as a 'technicist fallacy' or 'managerial fix' that was bound to fail (Macrae, 2001, p. 45). But in her book *Aiding Recovery?* (2001, p. 161) Joanna Macrae admits:

> Currently lacking is a critical analysis of how aid practices influence state–society relations, and how aid agencies assess the legitimacy or otherwise of their partners, whether they be governmental or in civil society. Such a debate is clearly a key precondition for any ethical formulation of developmental relief.

2.3.1 Blaming the poor

Meanwhile, the end of the Cold War meant that the West felt less need to buy loyalty, which led to two other changes which had a major impact on the whole attitude towards aid. First, aid levels stopped rising and began to decrease, which led to an attitudinal change in which the blame for poverty was placed more on the poor countries themselves, which were supposed to improve their 'governance' in order to reduce poverty. Second, aid policy, via World Bank neoliberal structural adjustment policies, was increasingly designed to integrate developing countries into a global market dominated by big corporations. This meant smaller government and increasing roles for the private sector as the motor of development. As part of the small state and privatisation model, less aid was going through Southern governments and both development and emergency aid was increasingly being privatised and channelled through NGOs, which had an income of $6 billion by the end of the 1990s (Macrae, 2001 p. 18); this also reflected the growing challenge to the sovereignty of Southern governments.

Taken together with the new neoliberal small government model, wars were increasingly blamed on poor countries themselves – although aid agencies were also blamed for 'doing harm'. The result was an increasingly technocratic and managerial agenda. Aid agencies needed to manage and direct their aid better, targeting it in ways to reduce conflict and war. And recipient governments needed to reform to allow political liberalism and private-sector-led development. There was also a huge growth in 'conflict management' – the view that if competing groups talked more to each other, they could resolve their differences, and reduce the chance of war. Again, the cause of war was placed within the poor countries themselves. But all of these changes took place against a background of falling aid, worsening terms of trade, and generally increasing poverty in poor countries.

There was, however, a growing concern about the narrowness of these international prescriptions, particularly those from the World Bank and IMF. They put major emphasis on economic growth, while the European Commission in its concept of structural stability explicitly says 'experience shows lack of development is not the only major source of violent conflict' (European Commission, 1997).

Indeed, a 2003 World Bank study, *Breaking the Conflict Trap* (Collier et al., 2003), admitted that many World Bank and IMF policies were actually harmful in postwar countries. The study found that 'poor' economic policy, as defined by the World Bank, did not increase the risk of war, but that trying to 'improve' economic policy immediately after a peace settlement did increase the risk of a return to war. 'The results suggest that social policy is relatively more important and macroeconomic policy is relatively less important in post-conflict situations than in normal situations'. Indeed, 'if opportunities exist for modest trade-offs that improve social policies at the expense of a small deterioration in macroeconomic balances, growth is, on average, significantly augmented.' In particular, the report recognises the importance of inequalities as roots of civil war and calls for 'an explicit long-term strategy for intergroup redistribution' and for directing resources to formerly rebel-controlled areas because 'market forces will ... probably agglomerate activity in a way that is disadvantageous to the rebels.' And they call for more stress on rehabilitation of key infrastructure destroyed by war, because of the high rate of return, even though this goes against IMF policy on curbing expenditure (Collier et al., 2003).

2.4 Forcible humanitarian intervention and the end of sovereignty

The growth of often very brutal civil wars has led to an increasing feeling that 'something has to be done'. Meanwhile the concept of sovereignty that was part of the structure that kept the balance between East and West has been challenged. This led in the early 1990s to a call for 'humanitarian interventions' and even 'humanitarian wars' to prevent gross human rights violations and many deaths. The new line is set out by Nicholas J. Wheeler in his 2000 book *Saving Strangers*, where he argues that 'states which massively violate human rights should forfeit the right to be treated as legitimate sovereigns, thereby morally entitling other states to use force to stop the oppression' (Wheeler, 2000, p. 12). This view is still strongly debated.

In the 1970s, there had been three significant interventions by neighbouring states in civil wars. In 1971 India intervened in East Pakistan to support the creation of Bangladesh, in 1978 Vietnam intervened in Cambodia to help overthrow the regime of Pol Pot, and in 1979 Tanzania intervened in Uganda to help overthrow Idi Amin. The three wars did not have significant East–West content and intervention was not seen as a threat by either side in the Cold War. All three saved tens of thousands of lives but at the time were

A young boy watches a convoy of UN vehicles from MONUC, the UN Mission in Congo.

roundly condemned by the international community for violating sovereignty, and for being in the self-interest of the intervening country. But they are increasingly seen, retrospectively, as being acceptable under the new doctrine of humanitarian intervention.

In the 15 years after the end of the Cold War, there has been a series of forcible international interventions which were said to have humanitarian motives. The first time that the Security Council took enforcement action under Chapter 7 to deal with the aggression by one member state against another was when it imposed stringent economic sanctions on Iraq in 1990, and then proceeded to authorise military action by member states. In 1992 Security Council Resolutions 770 and 794 authorised the use of 'all necessary means' to deliver humanitarian aid to civilians in Somalia and Bosnia. There was also military intervention without UN approval in the former Yugoslavia in 1998 (see Box 2.1) and Iraq in 2003. Some of the African states which intervened in Zaire (later renamed Democratic Republic of the Congo) in the late 1990s also claimed humanitarian motives.

Somalia was seen as a particular failure of forcible humanitarian intervention. A civil war in 1991 led to a total collapse of the state, and various ceasefires failed to hold. In November 1992 the Security Council accepted a United States offer of a US-led mission, which was authorised to use 'all necessary means', including enforcement measures, to establish a secure environment for humanitarian assistance. But fighting continued and there was strong opposition to the US-led force; in late 1993, 18 members of an elite US military force were killed in an unsuccessful attempt to capture General Mohamed Aideed, an important clan leader. The US quickly withdrew and the mission collapsed, without having enforced a ceasefire or created adequate conditions for humanitarian aid.

A US soldier breaks down the door of a house in Afghanistan.

One of the strongest proponents of intervention is Chester Crocker, from 1981 to 1989 US Assistant Secretary of State for African Affairs, and later chairman of the board of the United States Institute for Peace. Crocker (2001) argues that the pendulum has swung too far in looking at civil wars as internal, and that there is a 'return of geopolitics'. Crocker stresses the concept of 'bad neighbourhoods', such as southern Africa or West Africa – regions of what he sees as endemic interstate and intrastate rivalry and hostility which leads civil war and violence to spread from one country to another. He and his team go on to argue:

> [S]ecurity-surplus or security exporting regions – sadly too few in number – stand in marked contrast to security-deficit regions where supplies of tinder and matches far outweigh the stock of extinguishers. ... [P]eace initiatives that have borne fruit in Northern Ireland and South Africa would not likely gain the same traction in societies such as Sierra Leone and Afghanistan, where the vital infrastructure of civil society remains far less developed and institutionalised.

> (Crocker et al., 2001b)

He argues that what he calls 'security-exporting regions' such as the US and Europe have a responsibility to intervene and even to undertake 'coercive peacemaking to strong-arm' combatants into agreement, as the US did in Bosnia. With his stress on big bad men within countries at war, there is a bias toward simply going in and simply knocking heads together. 'Evidence suggests that most conflicts in the modern, post-1945, era do not resolve themselves. To bring them under control, some type of external, third-party intervention is required' Crocker (2001) concludes. This can be diplomatic or military, and can involve the UN, regional groups, or individual countries. Pre-emptive action is important to prevent wars.

There are three kinds of arguments against intervention by force. Two argue against any humanitarian intervention by force. The first is the view that the very expression 'humanitarian war' is an oxymoron – the phrase itself is self-contradictory. In general, humanitarian interventions do more harm than good. It is estimated that in 1993 US intervening forces killed more than 6000 Somalis while trying to save them; similarly the bombing of Serbia in 1999 was widely seen to have increased the suffering (see Box 2.1).

The second objection is that states will misuse humanitarianism as a justification to intervene for other reasons, and that humanitarian aims are always a cloak for ulterior motives. In a letter in 1938 to the British Prime Minister Neville Chamberlain, Adolf Hitler justified his intervention in Czechoslovakia on the grounds that 'ethnic Germans and "various nationalities" ... have been maltreated in the unworthiest manner, tortured, economically destroyed and, above all, prevented from realizing for themselves also the right of nations to self-determination' (cited in Wheeler, 2000, p. 30). US and British intervention in Iraq without UN approval in 2003 was similarly justified partly on humanitarian grounds. Both the first and second arguments against forcible intervention agree that, overall, harm outweighs the good. Even if a particular intervention saves lives, it justifies other interventions which do harm and cost even more lives. Proponents of these arguments say a better policy is never to intervene, as was the guideline of the Cold War period.

The third, and more complex, argument against intervention by force is that interventions are arbitrary, saving some people and letting others die. Intervention is mainly determined by the self-interest of the intervening state, will always be arbitrary, and will always be made against weak countries. No matter how gross are the human rights violations of Russia in Chechnya or a US-backed Israel in Palestine, no one would even consider a humanitarian intervention into a permanent member of the UN Security Council or a close ally. The arbitrariness is shown clearly in Iraq. In 1988 the government forces attacked Kurds in the north of Iraq, killing an estimated 100,000 people; the use of chemical weapons against the city of Halabja drew considerable publicity and was seen as particularly reprehensible since it violated international treaties. But the Iraqi dictator, Saddam Hussein, was at that time an ally of the West, so there was no humanitarian intervention. Then Iraq invaded Kuwait and there was a US-led and UN-backed war against Iraq. In 1991 the UN Security Council passed Resolution 688, demanded that Iraq immediately end 'repression' in Kurdish areas of the north and, in a precedent-setting phrase, 'insists that Iraq allow immediate access by international humanitarian organizations to all those in need of assistance in all parts of Iraq', which included opposition forces and refugees in both the north and south of Iraq. Under the cover of this resolution, the military allies imposed a military exclusion zone on Iraqi ground and air military operations in Kurdish areas of the north. But little military protection was given to opposition forces in the south, who were then attacked and massacred by Iraqi forces. Wheeler (2000, pp. 152, 161) argues that the difference was twofold – most importantly that the plight of the Kurds had received extensive television coverage which created political pressure in the US and Europe, whereas there were few TV pictures from the south, but also that there was an interest in establishing allied military control of the north but not of the south. Whatever the reasons, Iraq shows just how arbitrary humanitarian intervention can be: don't help the Kurds in 1988 but help them in 1991, help the Kurds in the north but not equally oppressed Iraqis in the south.

The other element of arbitrariness has been the failure to intervene when it was most needed, most egregiously in 1994 when the UN, and the international community as a whole, did not intervene to prevent a genocide which killed 700,000 people. Indeed, the UN had had a small peace-monitoring force in Rwanda, which it withdrew instead of strengthening. There was more than adequate warning and extensive television coverage of the massacres themselves, but in what was widely seen as perhaps the most shameful failure in UN history, the international community did nothing.

The issue here is far more complex. Proponents of forcible humanitarian intervention accept that it will always be arbitrary and will always require some nation to see it in their self-interest because of the need to spend money and risk the lives of the soldiers. Wheeler argues that humanitarian intervention is morally and legally permitted, but is not required. There is no moral requirement that a bystander jump into the water to save a drowning child. Thus we should be pleased when a country is willing to make a humanitarian intervention, rather than complain about interventions not made – while at the same time working to change the international moral climate so that countries do see it as in their interest to, for example, prevent genocide in Rwanda.

Is it that humanity cares more, or is the new-found enthusiasm for humanitarian intervention simply a way of legitimating the projection of US power, now that the counterpower of the Soviet Union is gone, as Noam Chomsky (1999) argues? He sees 'the resort to force cloaked in moralistic righteousness' as simply 'opening a new era where might is right'. He notes that the US bombed Serbia because of alleged 'ethnic cleansing' of Albanians in Kosovo, yet it backs the Turkish Government which has carried out equally heinous acts against the Kurds. The reason, he argued, is that 'Serbia is one of those disorderly miscreants that impede the institution of the U.S.-dominated global system, while Turkey is a loyal client state that contributes substantially to this project' (Chomsky, 1999, p. 13):

At the end of the decade, UN Secretary-General Kofi Annan summed up the complexities of the new interventionist mood:

> This developing international norm in favour of intervention to protect civilians from wholesale slaughter will no doubt continue to pose profound challenges to the international community.
>
> Any such evolution in our understanding of state sovereignty and individual sovereignty will, in some quarters, be met with distrust, scepticism, even hostility. But it is an evolution that we should welcome.

Why? Because, despite its limitations and imperfections, it is testimony to a humanity that cares more, not less, for the suffering in its midst, and a humanity that will do more, and not less, to end it.

It is a hopeful sign at the end of the twentieth century.

(1999 General Assembly statement, quoted in Wheeler, 2000, p. 285)

Nicholas Wheeler calls for a new agreement on intervention in which the industrialised countries take some responsibility not just for preventing future events like the Rwanda genocide, but also for dealing with the millions in the South who die from a lack of basic necessities, and with the abuses of human rights in the North. He concludes:

developing a new West–South consensus on the legitimacy of humanitarian intervention in the society of states will depend upon a new dialogue between rich and poor. What is needed is a commitment by the West to a redistribution of wealth, and an acceptance by Southern governments that cases will arise where the slaughter of civilians by their governments is so appalling as to legitimate the use of force to uphold minimum standards of humanity.

(Wheeler, 2000, p. 307)

Such a consensus seems a long way away.

2.5 The responsibility to protect

The debate about intervention led the Canadian Government to convene the International Commission on Intervention and State Sovereignty, which reported in 2001. It was co-chaired by Gareth Evans, a former Australian foreign minister, and Mohamed Sahnoun, a senior Algerian diplomat who had been deputy director general of both the OAU and the Arab League. The ten members included a former chair of the military committee of NATO, a former president of ICRC, and human rights and peace activists. One of their starting points was four failures: Rwanda in 1994 which 'laid bare the full horror of inaction', Bosnia in 1995 where the UN failed to protect civilians sheltering in UN-declared safe areas, Somalia in 1992 when an intervention was botched 'by flawed planning, poor execution, and an excessive dependence on military force', and 1999 in Kosovo where an intervention took place, but there were questions as to whether it should have.

The Commission concluded that 'sovereignty does still matter' (p. 7, viii):

In a dangerous world marked by overwhelming inequalities of power and resources, sovereignty is for many states their best – and sometimes seemingly their only – line of defence. But sovereignty is more than just a functional principle of international relations. For many states and peoples, it is also a recognition of their equal worth and dignity.

But the Commission also concluded that:

> sovereign states have a responsibility to protect their own citizens from avoidable catastrophe – from mass murder and rape, from starvation – but that when they are unwilling or unable to do so, that responsibility must be borne by the broader community of states.

Perhaps the most important decision of the Commission was to not talk about a 'right to intervene' but rather to create a new 'responsibility to protect'. It argues that a right to intervene is 'unhelpful' because it focuses on the rights and claims of the intervening state rather than the potential beneficiaries of the action, it focuses narrowly on the act of intervention, it is 'intrinsically more confrontational' and 'at the outset of the debate it loads the dice in favour of intervention'.

By contrast, the 'responsibility to protect' examines the issues from the viewpoint of those needing support (see Box 2.2). It becomes a shared responsibility of a state for its own citizens and of outside interveners. And, most importantly, the Commission said it also entailed a 'responsibility to prevent' and a 'responsibility to rebuild'. The 'responsibility to prevent' means reversing the decline in international aid, tackling the debt crisis, reversing unfair trade policies and taking other actions to help countries 'meet the social and economic development needs of their people.' It also means addressing political needs including support, and pressure if required, for building democratic institutions, power sharing, improved legal protection, and other social and political changes needed to reduce some possible causes of war.

'Too often in the past the responsibility to rebuild has been insufficiently recognised,' warns the Commission. Interveners pull out, leaving the country 'still wrestling with the underlying problems that produced the original intervention action.' Thus 'there should be a genuine commitment to helping to build a durable peace, and promoting good governance and sustainable development.'

On the fraught issue of intervention, the Commission stresses the need to try measures short of military action, particularly sanctions. And it sets six criteria for military interventions: right authority, just cause, right intention, last resort, proportional means, and reasonable prospects. On just cause, it draws a very narrow window, allowing military intervention only to prevent 'large scale loss of life' or 'large scale ethnic cleansing'. In particular, military intervention would not be permitted simply to reverse the overthrow of a democratically elected government – where sanctions are called for instead.

Box 2.2   The responsibility to protect

Proposed by the International Commission on Intervention and State Sovereignty, 2001.

Core principles

(1) *Basic principles*

    A   State sovereignty implies responsibility, and the primary responsibility for the protection of its people lies with the state itself.

    B   Where a population is suffering serious harm, as a result of internal war, insurgency, repression or state failure, and the state in question is unwilling or unable to halt or avert it, the principle of non-intervention yields to the international responsibility to protect.

(2) *Foundations*

The foundations of the responsibility to protect, as a guiding principle for the international community of states, lie in:

    A   obligations inherent in the concept of sovereignty;

    B   the responsibility of the Security Council, under Article 24 of the UN Charter, for the maintenance of international peace and security;

    C   specific legal obligations under human rights and human protection declarations, covenants and treaties, international humanitarian law and national law;

    D   the developing practice of states, regional organisations and the Security Council itself.

(3) *Elements*

The responsibility to protect embraces three specific responsibilities:

    A   *The responsibility to prevent*: to address both the root causes and direct causes of internal conflict and other man-made crises putting populations at risk.

    B   *The responsibility to react*: to respond to situations of compelling human need with appropriate measures, which may include coercive measures like sanctions and international prosecution, and in extreme cases military intervention.

    C   *The responsibility to rebuild*: to provide, particularly after a military intervention, full assistance with recovery, reconstruction and reconciliation, addressing the causes of the harm the intervention was designed to halt or avert.

(4) *Priorities*

    A   Prevention is the single most important dimension of the responsibility to protect: prevention options should always be exhausted before intervention is contemplated, and more commitment and resources must be devoted to it.

B   The exercise of the responsibility to both prevent and react should always involve less intrusive and coercive measures being considered before more coercive and intrusive ones are applied.

Principles for military intervention

(1) *The Just Cause Threshold*

Military intervention for human protection purposes is an exceptional and extraordinary measure. To be warranted, there must be serious and irreparable harm occurring to human beings, or imminently likely to occur, of the following kind:

A   *large scale loss of life*, actual or apprehended, with genocidal intent or not, which is the product either of deliberate state action, or state neglect or inability to act, or a failed state situation; or

B   *large scale 'ethnic cleansing'*, actual or apprehended, whether carried out by killing, forced expulsion, acts of terror or rape.

(2) *The Precautionary Principles*

A   *Right intention*: The primary purpose of the intervention, whatever other motives intervening states may have, must be to halt or avert human suffering. Right intention is better assured with multilateral operations, clearly supported by regional opinion and the victims concerned.

B   *Last resort*: Military intervention can only be justified when every non-military option for the prevention or peaceful resolution of the crisis has been explored, with reasonable grounds for believing lesser measures would not have succeeded.

C   *Proportional means*: The scale, duration and intensity of the planned military intervention should be the minimum necessary to secure the defined human protection objective.

D   *Reasonable prospects*: There must be a reasonable chance of success in halting or averting the suffering which has justified the intervention, with the consequences of action not likely to be worse than the consequences of inaction.

(3) *Right authority*

A   There is no better or more appropriate body than the United Nations Security Council to authorise military intervention for human protection purposes. The task is not to find alternatives to the Security Council as a source of authority, but to make the Security Council work better than it has.

B   Security Council authorisation should in all cases be sought prior to any military intervention action being carried out. Those calling for an intervention should formally request such authorisation, or have the Council raise the matter on its own initiative, or have the Secretary-General raise it under Article 99 of the UN Charter.

C The Security Council should deal promptly with any request for authority to intervene where there are allegations of large scale loss of human life or ethnic cleansing. It should in this context seek adequate verification of facts or conditions on the ground that might support a military intervention.

D The Permanent Five members of the Security Council should agree not to apply their veto power, in matters where their vital state interests are not involved, to obstruct the passage of resolutions authorising military intervention for human protection purposes for which there is otherwise majority support.

E If the Security Council rejects a proposal or fails to deal with it in a reasonable time, alternative options are:

(i) consideration of the matter by the General Assembly in Emergency Special Session under the 'Uniting for Peace' procedure; and

(ii) action within area of jurisdiction by regional or sub-regional organisations under Chapter VIII of the Charter, subject to their seeking subsequent authorisation from the Security Council.

F The Security Council should take into account in all its deliberations that, if it fails to discharge its responsibility to protect in conscience-shocking situations crying out for action, concerned states may not rule out other means to meet the gravity and urgency of that situation – and that the stature and credibility of the United Nations may suffer thereby.

(4) *Operational principles*

A Clear objectives; clear and unambiguous mandate at all times; and resources to match.

B Common military approach among involved partners; unity of command; clear and unequivocal communications and chain of command.

C Acceptance of limitations, incrementalism and gradualism in the application of force, the objective being protection of a population, not defeat of a state.

D Rules of engagement which fit the operational concept; are precise; reflect the principle of proportionality; and involve total adherence to international humanitarian law.

E Acceptance that force protection cannot become the principal objective.

F Maximum possible coordination with humanitarian organisations.

2.6   Chapter summary

This chapter looks at **intervention** and stresses that most intervention is postwar peace support by agreement of the warring parties and local people. In part, this is a recognition of national **sovereignty**, under which a state and its government have supreme authority over their territory. The end of the **Cold War** and the end of states being clients of one of the two big powers brought two changes. First, the **United Nations** was given a much larger role in peacekeeping and peace support. Second, the concept of **sovereignty was increasingly challenged** since there was no longer a concern about the one side breaching the sovereignty of the other side's clients. UN peacekeeping operations had a mixed result, leading to the 2000 **Brahimi Report** calling for the UN to do more to distinguish victim from aggressor and to protect civilians. This, in turn, led the UN to choose sides more actively.

Sovereignty was also increasingly breached, first by **humanitarian agencies** who want to help war victims even if they are not invited, second by military interventions in support of humanitarian goals, and third by the **international financial institutions** which, after the debt crisis and fall in aid of the 1980s, gained the power to impose conditions on previously sovereign governments. Questions are raised about the appropriateness of these conditions in postwar countries.

Forcible humanitarian intervention was increasingly proposed as being necessary to save lives. This was opposed because it was often arbitrary, politically motivated, and harmful. This, in turn, led to the proposal that instead of a right to intervene, there should be a **responsibility to protect**.

References

Allen, T. and Styan, D. (2000) 'A right to interfere? Bernard Kouchner and the new humanitarianism', *Journal of International Development*, vol. 12, pp. 825–42.

Boutros-Ghali, B. (1994) 'An agenda for development', Report of the Secretary-General of the United Nations A/48/935, 6 May 1994; *An Agenda for Development* by Boutros Boutros-Ghali was published in 1995 by the UN Department of Public Information, New York.

Brahimi, L. (2000) *Report of the Panel on United Nations Peace Operations*, New York, UN General Assembly and Security Council, A/55/305-S/2000/809. (Lakhdar Brahimi was the chairman of the Panel and the report is known as the Brahimi Report.)

Chomsky, N. (1999) *The New Military Humanism: Lessons from Kosovo*, London, Pluto.

Collier, P., Elliot, L., Hegre, H., Hoeffler, A., Reynal-Querol, M. and Sambanis, N. (2003) *Breaking the Conflict Trap: Civil War and Development Policy*, Washington, World Bank and Oxford, Oxford University Press.

Collier, P., Hoeffler, A. and Söderbom, M. (2004) 'On the duration of civil war', *Journal of Peace Research*, vol. 41 (3), pp. 253–74.

Crocker, C. (2001) 'Intervention', Chapter 14 in Crocker, Hampson and Aall (eds) (2001a).

Crocker, C., Hampson, F. O. and Aall, P. (eds) (2001a) *Turbulent Peace*, Washington DC, US Institute of Peace.

Crocker, C., Hampson, F. O. and Aall, P. (2001b) 'Introduction' in Crocker, Hampson and Aall (eds) (2001a).

Elbadawi, I. and Sambanis, N. (2000) 'External interventions and the duration of civil wars', World Bank, www.worldbank.org (accessed January 2005).

Enterline, A. and Balch-Lindsay, D. (2002) 'By sword or by signature? A competing risks approach to third party intervention and civil war outcomes, 1816–1997', unpublished, www.psci.unt.edu/enterline/ workingpapers.html (accessed January 2005).

Enterline, A. and Kang, S. (2003) 'Stopping the killing sooner? Assessing the success of United Nations Peacekeeping in Civil Wars', revised version of a paper presented at the annual meeting of the Peace Science Society, Tucson AZ, USA, 1–3 Nov 2002.

European Commission (1996) *Linking Relief, Rehabilitation and Development*, Communication from the Commission of 30 April 1996.

European Commission (1997) *Conflicts in Africa: Communication for the Commission*, Development Collection, Vol. 2.

Hanlon, J. (1991) *Mozambique: Who calls the Shots?* London, James Currey.

International Commission on Intervention and State Sovereignty (2001) *The responsibility to protect: report of the International Commission on Intervention and State Sovereignty*, Ottawa, International Development Research Centre.

Laurence, T. (1999) *Humanitarian Assistance and Peacekeeping: an Uneasy Alliance*, London, Royal United Services Institute for Defence Studies.

Macrae, J. (2001) *Aiding Recovery? The Crisis of Aid in Chronic Political Emergencies*, London, Zed.

Regan, P. (2002) 'Third-party interventions and the duration of intrastate conflicts', *Journal of Conflict Resolution*, vol. 46, no. 1, pp. 55–73.

Suhrke, A., Villaner, E. and Woodward, S. (2004) 'Economic Aid to Post-conflict Countries: Correcting the Empirical and Theoretical Foundations of Policy', paper presented at the conference Making Peace Work, Helsinki, June 2004.

Wheeler, N. J. (2000) *Saving Strangers: Humanitarian Intervention in International Society*, Oxford, Oxford University Press.

3 Roots of civil war: tick 'all of the above'

Joseph Hanlon

3.1   Introduction

Most analysts accept that civil wars have multiple causes, yet there is no agreement on any specific roots – every claim to have identified a cause is disputed. The arguments in the academic literature are acrimonious, arcane and tend to be ignored by policymakers. 'Policymakers have neither the time nor the expertise to choose between competing explanations,' comments Andrew Mack (2002).

There is a host of reasons for this. Mack cites the divisions in both the research and policy communities. Within the academic world, political, sociological and economic researchers develop separate theories, and fight each other and among themselves. In part, this reflects the fact that 'civil war' was never a recognised area for either researchers or policymakers, who look at 'civil war' through their traditional lenses. At government level there are bureaucratic divisions between those concerned with security, foreign policy and aid. International agencies all have their divisions and niches, and prefer explanations which fit their mandates.

Academics coming from very different disciplines lead inevitably to what we have called the Humpty Dumpty problem, with researchers twisting the definitions of words to what they choose them to mean, relating to how they are used in their original fields, and to correspond to what is measurable and gives reasonable results. For example, for the Uppsala group (see Figure 1.1), Rwanda was only an 'intermediate armed conflict' with less than 1000 deaths in 1994, because it only counts those killed in fighting between the government and the Rwandan Patriotic Front; while the more than 500,000 killed in the genocide that year were not 'battle-related deaths' (Gleditsch et al., 2002). The definition of 'ethnicity' can be stretched to all sorts of identifications, including language and religion. It is hardly surprising, then, that academic researchers find contradictory results, and policymakers either ignore them or pick the results which are politically acceptable.

Another root of competing academic explanations was that in the 1990s researchers who had concentrated on the Cold War turned their attention to civil wars such as those in the former Yugoslavia and to the genocide in Rwanda. Anthropologists considered ethnic roots of civil war, environmentalists looked at ecological pressure, and economists applied sophisticated computer modelling. They brought with them fresh approaches, but they also knew little about the history of internal wars. In particular, in the mid 1990s they promoted an argument that that these were 'new wars', somehow ignoring Biafra, Pol Pot in Cambodia, and a history of prior brutal civil violence.

3.1.1 International relations and the role of bad leaders

International relations analysts, who had invested so much in the study of the Cold War, turned their expertise to civil wars. One of the biggest proponents of this approach is Chester Crocker, from 1981 to 1989 US Assistant Secretary of State for African Affairs, and later chairman of the board of the United States Institute for Peace. Crocker argues that with the end of the Cold War, 'the very nature of conflict changed. Conflicts became internal, setting neighbour against neighbour, ethnic group against ethnic group, religion against religion. Breaking all accepted rules of wars, these conflicts targeted civilians and slaughtered non-combatants – men, women and children – just because they belonged to the wrong group' (Crocker et al., 2001b). Other writers, too, picked up on this. Mary Kaldor (1999) coined the phrase 'new wars' and argued that these involve political mobilisation on the basis of identity, that war is often waged by trying to displace people of a different identity (ethnic cleansing), and that the distinction between the political and the economic is becoming muddied. Mark Duffield (1998) coined the phase 'post-modern conflict' for political projects 'which no longer seek or even need to establish territorial, bureaucratic or consent-based political authority in the traditional sense.'

War has been studied for more than 20 centuries and international relations have been an important area of study for many more. Inevitably, interstate war was a central subject of international relations investigations. Over the past 50 years, the study of international relations has been dominated by the 'realist' or 'neo-realist' approach in which the key actors are sovereign states that act rationally to advance their own security, power and wealth. It puts the emphasis on the struggle for territory and resources. It assumes the international system is anarchic and that power determines outcome. And it assumes security is a 'zero-sum game', in which a gain for one state is a loss for another. With the end of the Cold War and the decline of interstate war, these researchers turned their hand to civil war, but their assumptions prove somewhat difficult to apply to a civil war. Most states are not anarchic and most civil war researchers see the possibility of a positive sum game – that there are solutions in which the gains are greater than the losses, for example through changing the share of access to power and resources. And, as we have seen, these are hardly 'new' wars; rather that the international relations scholars had not focused on them in the past.

'Inter'-national relations, by definition, offers a rather narrow way of looking at civil war. In a key article, Chester Crocker and others give a dozen 'sources of conflict' in both interstate and intrastate relations. These include 'bad leaders', 'warlord economies', 'state collapse', 'ethnopolitical/religious extremism', and so on. The emphasis is entirely on the combatants and their leaders, and there is no mention of justified grievances (Crocker et al.,

2001b). All of these ideas of new wars tend to identify big bad men, often called 'warlords', who lead the war for a mix of personal and political gain. Indeed, Michael Brown (1996) sometimes argues that 'bad leaders' are the most important immediate cause of civil war. But it is only certain big bad men, because Crocker makes no mention of the role of the Cold War powers in fomenting civil war.

For these reasons, international relations theories of civil war have been less useful than those of interstate wars. US international relations studies have, however, given three very specific approaches which have clear implications for intervention – 'security exporting regions', discussed in Chapter 2; civil wars as 'political' in Box 3.1; and the 'ethnic security dilemma' discussed in Chapter 4.

3.1.2 Economists and the greed versus grievance debate

The defeat of socialism and the rise to prominence of the international financial institutions such as the World Bank led economists to direct their focus on civil war, and they came to dominate the debate in the late 1990s. The economists brought two important approaches with them – computer modelling and a belief in greed as a driving economic force. This sort of econometric research requires large, computer processable datasets. At least a dozen armed conflict datasets have been created as well as various ways of coding ethnicity, democracy, economic development, etc. But using different datasets gives totally different results, leading to quite dramatic disagreements. This reflects three very basic problems with computer modelling. The first is that the initial data can be surprisingly subjective. Measures of 'democracy' tend to be done by US institutions which have their roots in the Cold War. Economic development tends to be measured by what are called 'proxy variables', such as energy consumption, which are supposed to accurately represent things which cannot be measured, but which in practice are often contentious. Second, countries and wars are often not included if there are no data; one of the most important and widely cited pieces of research on the role of aid in postwar periods turns out to be based on only eight wars, which are all atypical, because they are the only ones for which there is enough data (Suhrke et al., 2004; Collier and Hoeffler, 2004 Table 7). Thirdly, 'It is worth noting that none of the emotions – rage, humiliation or despair, as well as felt grievances – that may affect the propensity of people to resort to violence are directly measured in the econometric literature' Mack (2002) comments.

Perhaps the sharpest contradiction between the economists is the 'greed versus grievance' debate – are civil wars driven mostly by the greed of leaders or by the grievances of ordinary members of the population? This has led to bitter arguments at the highest level. Paul Collier (2000, pp. 10–13), then director of the Development Research Group at the World Bank, wrote that his research showed that 'inequality does not seem to affect the risk of conflict. Rebellion does not seem to be the rage of the poor'. To which WIDER (World Institute for Development Economics Research at the UN University) replied that their research shows 'that objective grievances of poverty and inequality contribute to war and humanitarian emergencies' (Nafziger and Auvinen, 2002). It would be hard to find a more fundamental and more eminent disagreement.

The shift in the 1990s reflects a more fundamental shift in the dominant thinking of international elites. In the 1960s the discourse was driven by the view that the 'third world' had been actively underdeveloped by the European colonial powers and by the United States. Revolutions and anti-colonial wars were seen as fully justified civil wars. Development aid was seen as part of a 'new international economic order'. In part, this was also driven by a fear in the capitalist countries that the socialist alternatives might succeed in the 'third world', which also saw the US actively intervening to overthrow leftist governments, as in Chile. By the 1980s, with the socialist bloc collapsing, underdevelopment was no longer seen as the fault of the rich, but of the poor themselves. Harsh structural adjustment programmes were imposed by the international financial institutions to cut the power of their governments and open markets. In a similar way, civil wars were no longer revolutions justified by the misconduct of the big powers, but instead became mistakes which were the fault of the poor themselves, or at least of their misguided leaders, warlords and corrupt presidents.

Much of the academic research on civil wars has reflected the hegemonic ideas of the era – justified grievance in the 1960s and 1970s, and the fault of the poor in the 1980s and 1990s. But the end of the twentieth century brought an anti-globalisation backlash which had, at its core, a reaction against blaming the victims for their own plight. The Jubilee 2000 campaign to cancel poor country debt argued that the fault lay more with unwise lending and sharp increases in interest rates by Northern lenders, and less with corruption and incompetence of Southern governments. Indeed, Southern campaigners reminded the North of the extent to which they had supported corrupt dictators in the South against the wishes of the people of those countries.

At the time of writing, in the early years of the twenty-first century, the gap between the views of WIDER and those of the World Bank have not been bridged. There are few agreements as to the roots of civil war. In general, Northern policymakers frequently still blame the victims, and Southern leaders frequently tend to blame the North. This inevitably leads to sharp disagreements on the need for and nature of intervention and what actions should be prioritised during a war and in a postwar environment. The dozens (or hundreds) of agencies involved in a peace-support operation will have very different understandings of the roots of the war and thus of the essential postwar actions. The British Government tries to sidestep some of these debates by arguing that war in Africa 'is caused by inequality, economic decline, state collapse and the legacies of European colonialism and the Cold War' (DfID, FCO and MoD, 2001, p. 5).

There is some merit in nearly all of these arguments. Colonialism, the Cold War and misguided policies of the international financial institutions have all helped to create the conditions for civil war; history is important, and the

North has played a central role. Civil wars are, by definition, between forces within a country, but the role of historic and outside factors cannot be underestimated. Nevertheless, internal and contemporary factors such as identity politics, corruption and misguided policies in the South play an equally important role.

Civil wars are complex and caused by multiple factors, thus every war is different. Lip service is paid to multiple causes of civil war, but researchers and agencies are divided by academic discipline, bureaucratic department, agency mission and funding source, and want to stress the single cause that their group prioritises. This leads to real confusion and competition on the ground.

Some of the civil wars research in the 1990s tried to develop models for the start of civil wars. These were often quite mechanistic, using a whole range of conceptual terms such as triggers, proximate causes, root causes, permissive conditions, mobilising causes, and so on. Those fine distinctions are too narrow and contradictory. Here, we do make a relatively vague distinction between (a) those conditions which seem to make civil war more likely, (b) the causes or roots of the actual civil war, and (c) the factors which allow the war to continue without a resolution. The boundaries between these are not clear, however, nor is assignment to categories; for example, different researchers would put ethnicity in the condition, cause and continuation categories. When the 'experts' are themselves in such sharp disagreement, we feel there is a virtue in imprecision.

Finally, we set three contrasts in the explanations given for civil wars. They are caricatures and simplifications, but they do provide a useful shorthand for situating the emphasis of the explanations for war, and give a set of three lenses with which to look at any explanation. They are:

1 *People under pressure versus big bad men*
   Does the explanation put the emphasis on the war being a response to pressure that is not under control of the participants in the war – typically a grievance which cannot be resolved or economic or environmental pressure – or does the explanation put the stress on leaders – warlords, corrupt presidents, World Bank heads (who are almost invariably men) – who are acting contrary to the interests of the people who become involved in the war?

2 *Internal versus external*
   Does the explanation put the emphasis inside the civil war country or outside? For example, diamonds may be seen to be fuelling the war, but is the stress on warlords selling diamonds or on transnational companies buying them? Is the stress on corrupt dictators themselves, or the Cold War powers which supported them?

3 *Historic versus recent*
   Does the explanation put the stress on things which happened some time ago, such as colonial preference for a particular group in society, or does it look at more recent events, such as jobless youth? Ethnicity, for example, can be seen in both contexts – as 'historic antagonisms' or as a newly mobilised resource to support the war.

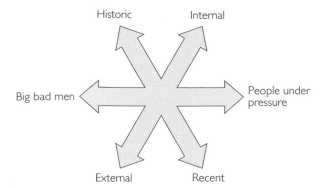

Figure 3.1   Three contrasts in explanations of civil war

Box 3.1 shows just how complex and overlapping the explanations for civil war can be.

Box 3.1   Civil wars are 'political'

The big bad men want state power and this makes civil wars 'political' in the same way as international wars. This perspective from international relations was used to argue that 'in the wars in Liberia and Somalia, the characterisation of the wars as political processes seems to be more illuminating than describing them either as ethnic or resources conflicts.' Isabelle Duyvesteyn (2000) of the King's College London Department of War Studies stresses that the main issue in both wars was 'who should rule?', which is a political issue. 'The factions created a political opposition to the ruling regimes, they moved to the capital to remove the president by force and thereafter the wars gained a new character in the fight over who should replace the president.' Indeed, 'the political power was made tangible by the role of the presidential mansion. Whoever could occupy the building would be seen to be in power. This explains why these mansions were so highly fought over, even after the removal of the presidents.' She goes on to argue that 'these wars were not new in the political arena, the existing form of rule was not questioned, the basis of personal rule remained the same.' She then looks at other similarities between the wars in Liberia and Somalia:

- In both countries a dictator had been kept in place by a Cold War superpower and political opposition suppressed.

- Both 'were violent power transitions which were the only way to change the regimes in which no opposition was possible.'

- Both 'were resource conflicts to the extent that economic advantages of the war economy were used to keep the war machines going... . Economic opportunities were used and the profits made were invested in new weaponry by the faction leaders.'

- Both 'were ethnic or clan wars to the extent that they were made so by the factions. Ethnic and clan identity were highly flexible and fluid, and the invaders consciously choosing an area where an appeal to ethnic identity might find fertile ground were proven wrong. ... The fact that in both cases a mass uprising of the ethnic and clan groups failed to appear significantly undermines the primordialist and constructivist arguments.'

In this chapter (and the following four), we look at the following areas to try to explain the origins of civil wars:

- weak states and state building
- democracy
- recruitment of fighters and the ability to continue the war
- ethnicity and identity
- colonial heritage and Cold War proxy wars
- the impact of globalisation and adjustment
- trade issues
- social contract and horizontal inequality
- economic approaches and greed versus grievance.

We then return to show how these interact with weak states and state building

Here, we look at underlying conditions which make civil war more likely, particularly the view that civil war states are mainly new and weak. This chapter sets out the context under which war is more likely to take place, while later chapters will look at various explanations for the actual causes of war.

3.2 Weak states and issues around state building

We start with a series of explanations for civil war which are not causes, per se, but rather conditions which make war more likely. We have argued that conflict is natural, normal and even constructive, and is linked to the process of change. Conflicts become violent and grow into war when society and government are unable to resolve those conflicts. Here we look at the problem of states and governments which are too weak to resolve conflicts and prevent them from escalating to war.

Most of the civil wars of the past 50 years have been fought in the 'Third World', usually in young countries which were former colonies that gained independence after the Second World War or countries which became independent after the breakup of the Soviet Union. Indeed, it should be noted that civil war countries in eastern Europe, the Balkans and central Asia had been part of the Hapsburg, Ottoman and Tsarist empires in the early twentieth century. Most civil war countries are relatively new countries, and relatively weak. Charles Kupchan of Georgetown University argues:

> [T]he imperial age has left behind deep and lasting scars. The Middle East is still coping with political tensions left over from British and French

colonialism. The violent breakup of Yugoslavia during the 1990s and the ongoing tension between Greece and Turkey have clear links to the remnants of the Ottoman empire. African Americans and American Indians still suffer from the long-term consequences of America's colonial era. And in large swaths of the developing world, the experience of imperial rule and decolonization continue to spawn ethnic conflict, income inequalities and territorial disputes.

(Kupchan, 2001)

In the mid 1970s, Charles Tilly compared developing country state formation with that in Europe and argued that in many ways 'Third World' states look like European states when they are young, and that civil wars are, in many ways, a normal part of state formation. The 1980s and 1990s brought other ideas about the origins of war, some of which are set out in later chapters. But more recently scholars, notably Mohammed Ayoob, have returned to this issue, in part due to the problems of the new countries that had been part of the Soviet Union.

In the previous chapter we noted that sovereignty means that a state and its government has supreme authority within a territory. That means that a state must monopolise and concentrate the means of coercion within its territory and be able to maintain order there; it also must have political authority and it must be able to extract taxes and other revenues needed to run the state and provide services.

In 1975, Tilly wrote:

> The building of states in western Europe cost tremendously in death, suffering, loss of rights and unwilling surrender of land, goods or labor. ... The fundamental reason for the high cost of European state building was its beginning in the midst of a decentralised, largely peasant social structure. Being differentiated, autonomous, centralized organizations with effective control of territories entailed eliminating or subordinating thousands of semiautonomous authorities. ... Most of the European population resisted each phase of the creation of strong states.'

(Tilly, 1975, p. 71)

Tilly and particularly Ayoob point to just how long this process took and just how violent and messy it was. 'One needs to be reminded that the violence generated during the process of state making is the result of actions undertaken both by the state and by recalcitrant elements within the population that forcefully resist the state's attempt to impose order', notes Ayoob (2001). He comments that 'there was no dearth of "Somalias" and "Liberias" in seventeenth and eighteenth century Europe' (Ayoob, 2001). And the first century of the United States involved a genocide of the native population and a particularly bloody civil war.

Nor is the process in Europe complete. The Second World War was the bloodiest in history, and it was 1975 before all of Western Europe was democratic. Ayoob points to the European states which developed last and under the most heavy competition from existing neighbours – Germany and Italy, which emerged as unified national states only at the end of the nineteenth century – and asks if the emergence of Italian fascism and German Nazism was in part a response to the difficulties of state formation in the emerging era of mass politics (Ayoob, 1996).

3.2.1 Faster and more humane

From the Tilly and Ayoob perspective, many of the civil wars of the past half century are an inevitable part of state building, as the state tries to impose order and groups resist. New states are, by definition, weak and the process of state building is, in part, building a stronger state that can satisfy the demands of its citizens – and making inhabitants see themselves as citizens who can make demands on the state. States and their elites are different and there is no single road to state building. Some states remain very weak, and the process even leads to state collapse – as in Lebanon in the 1970s or Somalia in the 1990s – when there is no recognisable government at all. Henk Houweling (1996) points out that this, too, was part of the European process. 'European states have repeatedly been struck by revolutions and periods of total state collapse', notably in the period 1750–1850.

The ruling elites in the new states of the twentieth century face all the problems of the rulers of the new states of Europe and America a century or two earlier, but with a whole series of new constraints. They are under pressure to form modern, democratic, socially cohesive and politically responsive states in just a few years – and to do it in a humane, civilised and consensual fashion. State makers face four constraints today not faced by their predecessors two centuries ago:

- a difficult heritage of colonialism still persists
- human rights must be respected and there is early pressure for democracy
- there is a contradiction between sovereignty and self-determination
- there is a need to move more quickly; they do not have three centuries.

Most of the new states of the twentieth century did not evolve gradually over time but were designed and created by outsiders. The boundaries between states in Africa, South Asia, the Balkans and the Middle East were all drawn in Europe, at conferences or in ministries. The new boundaries creating Iraq out of three former Ottoman provinces were drawn by Gertrude Bell, an archaeologist and official in the British administration, in 1921 in her office in Baghdad (Buchan, 2003). European states and the US had boundaries which evolved over time, through war and treaty, and especially consolidation of smaller states into larger ones. In the Europe of times past, weak or collapsed states were often simply occupied or taken over by neighbouring or more powerful states. Tilly (1975, p. 24) points out that the number of 'more or less independent political units' in Europe fell from about 500 in 1500 AD to 'twenty-odd' in 1900 AD.

Political scientists distinguish between the 'state', which is a geographic and governmental entity, and a 'nation', which is a group of people who share a cultural identity, often but not always a religious, ethnic or linguistic identity. We discuss this in more detail in Section 3.3. below. Europe in the eighteenth and nineteenth centuries prioritised the state, which tended to subsume and if necessary suppress the nations within it. Elite groups were part of that process and thus identified with the emerging state and the building of a new 'nation' within that state. But pressure for increased autonomy by national groups in Britain and Spain, for example, show that that process, too, was not completed.

Colonialism left a particularly difficult heritage for many new states. The colonial powers never intended these to be independent countries, so they did not build appropriate institutions. Economies were geared to raw materials and exports to the mother country; a World Bank study showed that colonies intended mostly for exploitation rather than settlement still have significantly lower growth rates (Collier et al., 2003, p. 66). Kofi Annan (1997), Secretary-General of the United Nations, notes that in Africa 'The challenge was compounded by the fact that the framework of colonial laws and institutions which some new states inherited had been designed to exploit local divisions, not overcome them.' Britain, Belgium and other powers tended to identify and even create an 'ethnic' group to become the more dominant, educated, administrative caste, such as the Yoruba in Nigeria and Tutsi in Rwanda. This has left major ethnic, class and language divisions and tensions which continue into the present. K. J. Holsti (1997) cites 'a tradition of "politics from the top", with colonial authorities commanding and with limited, if any, local participation'. This was frequently adopted by the new governments, who also adopted the colonial position of discouraging civil society and local political action.

In the eighteenth and nineteenth centuries, the growing concept of sovereignty meant that elites were relatively free to carry out the process of state building within their boundaries. To be sure, there were revolutions, consolidations of groups of small states into larger ones, and major interstate wars. But the state was the unit of discussion. State sovereignty was increasingly challenged in the second half of the twentieth century by the increased standing of the individual, through the formal acceptance of a series of rights which were not recognised during earlier centuries in Europe – human rights, democracy, and a new right of group self-determination. For the first time, the individual as well as the state became the legitimate subject of international law. But the rights of states clash with the rights of the individual and this is forcing a new kind of state building.

The adoption of the Universal Declaration of Human Rights in 1948 and the growing recognition of democracy as a check on autocratic leaders meant that states in formation attempting to impose their authority could no longer use force quite so easily. Clearly, dictatorial allies of the big powers in the Cold War and autocratic partners in the twenty-first century war on terror have been less subject to international pressure on human rights and democracy, but there has been a real change in the global climate of opinion which means that elites in new states have less freedom to impose their authority.

The two rights of sovereignty and of self-determination are proving contradictory. The United Nations was created as an association of independent states 'based on the principle of the sovereign equality of all its Members' (UN Charter Article 2.1). This became one of the ground rules of the Cold War – states had sovereignty which could not be violated. The concept of sovereign states, with a legal identity in international law and the capacity to make authoritative decisions with regard to the people and resources of that state, dates from the Treaty of Westphalia of 1648, which confirmed the breakup of the Holy Roman Empire and, among other things, recognised the independence and sovereignty of the Netherlands, Switzerland and the German states (Germany was not unified until more than two centuries later, in 1870). This concept of sovereign states being equal regardless of comparative size or wealth, and the duty of states not to intervene in the internal affairs of other states, has structured international relations since then.

Meanwhile, the concept of 'self-determination' grew out of the Second World War and the debates of the first half of the twentieth century. The principle of 'self-determination of peoples' is established in Article 1 of the United Nations Charter. This has led to many self-defined groups demanding autonomy or even their own country, which conflicts directly with the other new right of a state to maintain its sovereignty and territorial integrity. Not surprisingly, then, many of the civil wars have been about self-determination, separatism and secession.

The colonially imposed boundaries in Africa and Asia took no account of the traditional groups and 'nations' within those boundaries and led initially to a demand for a wholesale redrawing of boundaries. In Africa, that nightmare was rejected with the acceptance of colonial boundaries, however arbitrary or irrational, by the Organization of African Unity in 1964. But many of the post-colonial African states remain weak, having wide ranges of people and languages and little shared national identity. This is often exacerbated by the lack of infrastructure and inherited economies geared to the colonial power rather than to local development. Ayoob (2001) notes that the major powers' endorsement of the breakup of Czechoslovakia and Yugoslavia into ethno-national units 'is bound to augment the challenge to the legitimacy of the principle that postcolonial states in their present form are territorially inviolable. ... [This] too-permissive approach to state breaking ... will add to conflict and anarchy rather than preserve international order.'

The final constraint on state building is that many of the new states are being asked to turn themselves into modern, fully formed states much more rapidly than the states of the eighteenth and nineteenth centuries. This means that several steps which were sequential in the past have to be accomplished simultaneously. In Europe, democracy was the final stage of state building. Today consolidation of power and democratisation must be carried on in parallel. Many new states are facing a rapid change from either a predominantly peasant economy or a socialist economy to a very open contemporary capitalist economy:

> [T]he radical changes of traditional non-capitalist societies lead to far-reaching deformation of the social order and to violent conflicts and wars. Only in exceptional cases can this phase of disorder and social upheaval be managed without authoritarian or violent means, and this applies to the history of Europe as well as to the transitional societies of the 'Third World' and to the current transformation process in the former Eastern bloc. Moreover, this pattern will also be repeated in the inevitable decay of the Chinese empire.
>
> (Jung, Schlichte and Siegelberg, 1996)

We do not take the state-building process and the related problem of weak states as a 'cause' of war. But it is clearly the context in which most wars occur. Established states, especially the more wealthy democracies, have the resources to satisfy grievances and the power to at least keep civil violence in check. Poorer, weaker, newer states often lack the resources and experience to satisfy demands and maintain the peace – violence may seem the only way to force a government to meet group demands, while the government may not have the capacity to respond, leading to civil war.

(**Intervention implication**)

Recognise the need for consolidation of state power and do not overwhelm this with demands for democratisation, human rights, regional autonomy and protection of minority rights. 'Even in today's context, when democratization cannot wait until state building is completed, it cannot thrive in the absence of the political order that only a strongly entrenched state can provide' (Ayoob, 2001).

3.3   Democracy

Richer countries with more established democracies have fewer civil wars. Beyond that, studies suggest that even for relatively poorer countries, strong democracy provides a protection against civil war – probably because individual and group rights are respected and because the relationship between the state and its citizens – the 'social contract' discussed in Chapter 6 – is strong enough to allow grievances to be dealt with. This has led to a frequently cited argument that whereas weak and new states are predisposed to civil wars, democracy is one of the conditions that makes civil war less likely. But further study shows the position to be much less clear. Authoritarian states seem also to have fewer civil wars, perhaps because they can suppress dissent, but in South-east and East Asia it could equally be because they offered rapid growth (See Box 6.1). But 'countries at the middle of the autocracy–democracy spectrum are most at risk of civil

An amputee uses his artificial limbs to cast his vote in the presidential election, Freetown, Sierra Leone. The man was one of many victims of the rebel movement RUF.

war because they are neither autocratic enough to preclude the opportunity of rebellion, nor democratic enough to prevent significant grievance,' comments Sambanis (2001). Alternatively, partial democracies allow some political opposition, but do not give the opponents real influence (Collier et al., 2003, p. 64).

In part this seems to be related to income, in that wealthier states are more stable and have more established democracies. It is also related to state building, as raised earlier in this chapter. Mohammed Ayoob (2001) makes the point that it was 'the European experience that democracy emerged as the final stage of the state-building process and not at the expense of state-building.' If the state itself is still weak, its democracy can be weak and divisive instead of inclusive and protective. Weak and transitional democracies are more prone to civil war, and this does seem to be in some way linked to ethnicity and group and individual rights.

A World Bank study found that for low income countries, autocracies have fewer civil wars. 'At low income levels democracy may be highly desirable for many reasons, but it cannot honestly be promoted as the road to peace,' the study finds. One reason may be that 'even moderate change in political institutions is a risk factor in itself; political institutions must be stable' and institutional stability seems to be more important than democracy (Collier et al., 2003, pp. 64, 65, 123).

3.3.1 Mobilising around identity

A key problem seems to be the ability of leaders to use the democratic process to mobilise around ethnicity or identity. The campaigning process may exacerbate tensions and inflame passions when parties are established and campaigns are run on identity lines. This is especially a problem in a winner-take-all, Westminster or US style of government, where winning 50.1 per cent of the vote gives total power. Marta Reynal-Querol (2002) argues that rights and representation are particularly important and that 'consociational democracies', which she defines as 'proportional representation systems that produce coalition politics', work better than a winner-take-all or presidential systems. Pranab Bardhan (1997) gives the example of Sri Lanka:

> Ethnically based parties in a winner-take-all (or first-past-the-post) electoral system tend to push the parties to extreme ethnic demands. Under such a system in Sri Lanka for the first three decades after independence the two main Sinhalese parties, UNP and SLFP, vied with each other in pandering to Sinhalese ethnic sentiments against Tamils, which pushed the Tamils ultimately to take to arms, a process that the later constitutional changes in the system were unable to avert.

Chester Crocker (2001), explicitly advocates 'deferring elections in societies not yet prepared to hold them and likely to become more polarized and fragile as a result of the election.' He argues: 'Separate elections in the republics of the former Yugoslavia in the earlier 1990s empowered ethnic nationalists and paved the way for the wars of disintegration.'

Intervention implications

'[S]tart with political institutions that provide guarantees against fears of victimhood and subjugation' in a constitution that is difficult to amend to take away guarantees and where 'each party with numerically significant seats should have some veto power, not on day-to-day legislation, but on some predefined set of basic issues' (Bardhan, 1997). 'Wherever possible, the patient building of the institutional preconditions of democracy should precede that unleashing of competitive mass electoral politics' (Mansfield and Snyder, 2001). 'Reducing the risk of civil war is ... a necessary pre-condition for democracy rather than the other way round' (Collier et al., 2003, p. 163). Choose power-sharing systems rather than winner-take-all systems. Do not be afraid to defer elections until other peacebuilding actions have been effective.

3.4   Favourable conditions

Where there is strong pressure to go to war, the decision of the participants will be made at least in part on the likelihood of success. And independent of the justifications, there are some conditions that make it easier to go to war – especially conditions which favour an insurgency. Three of these are:

● poverty, which makes it easier to recruit rebels fighters

- the availability of secure areas
- finance for the war.

These do not cause war; rather, they make violence a more plausible option.

'Poverty increases the likelihood of civil war', according to the World Bank. (Collier et al,. 2003, p. 53). It makes war an easier and more plausible option, because, as James Fearon and David Laitin (2003) comment, 'recruiting young men to the life of a guerrilla is easier when the economic alternatives are worse.'

Most civil wars at least start as insurgencies, characterised by small, lightly armed bands practising guerrilla warfare. Such bands need safe base areas. Mountainous terrain increases the likelihood of civil war (Fearon and Laitin, 2003). Underoccupied rural and forested areas are also significant, as in Sierra Leone. Support from neighbouring states or groups in those states, at least to the extent of having rear bases, has been an important factor in many wars. Dense urban slums can provide this sort of cover; guerrillas can gain protection from identity groups which support the war, or from criminal gangs.

Finally, a successful war is expensive, requiring the purchase of guns, vehicles, food and other supplies. Funding often proves more important in keeping a war going than in the actual start of the violence. In the days of the Cold War, it was relatively easy to gain finance from one of the superpowers. With the end of the Cold War, other sources of finance were needed.

Two other ways to fund wars emerged, and both have extensive international links. First is diasporas – people from the country or group who are now living in the industrialised world and are prepared to provide the money. This has proved a particular factor in financing separatist wars such as those in Northern Ireland, Sri Lanka, and Kurdish areas of the Middle East.

The second source of funding is lootable resources, especially ones which can be sold on international markets. Diamonds in Sierra Leone, timber in Liberia, coltan in the Congo, and drugs in Afghanistan and Colombia have all been utilised to pay for civil wars. Often participants in the war get rich, which leads to the belief that wars are fuelled by greed rather than grievance. But Nicholas Sambanis (2002) makes the point that 'we often cannot distinguish between "war loot" that serves as a means to sustain the war effort and "loot" that is the ultimate aim of the war. Furthermore, even if the financial constraint of mounting an effective rebellion is the most important determinant of the likelihood of rebellion, this need not imply that all underlying motivations for rebellion are subsumed by greed.'

An additional point here is that resources are lootable only if someone will buy them, which usually means international traders of diamonds, timber, drugs or other commodities. This means international funding of wars must be, at least, tolerated by part of the international community. Thus the United States turned a blind eye to opium growing in Laos and Afghanistan and cocaine trading in Nicaragua because it was funding insurgent groups backed by the US. Phil Williams (2001) writing for the US Institute for Peace admits that:

> During the 1980s the cultivation of opium and the sale of heroin were indispensable to the continuation of the mujahideen's campaign to eject Soviet forces from Afghanistan – but were ignored by US supporters intent only on inflicting losses on the Soviet Union.

An international campaign tried to prevent the sale of 'conflict' diamonds, and a registration process was eventually agreed, although its effect remains unclear; similarly the environmental movement has tried to regulate the sale of tropical timber.

Intervention implication

The need for rebel movements to fund their actions leads economists to look outside the civil war country itself, to the buyers of the loot in the industrialised world. A World Bank study (Collier et al., 2003, pp. 129–30, 143–45, 180) looks at key commodities, and suggests changes in developed world policy:

- Virtually all drug production is in war or postwar countries, and current OECD policy to try to force developing countries to discourage production is counterproductive. 'The problem with this production-focused approach is that it makes territory outside the control of a recognised government enormously valuable, and so inadvertently helps to sustain rebellion.' The alternative is to reduce illegal consumption through partial legalisation. The World Bank gives as an example the former British policy of giving legal heroin to registered addicts, because 'this radically reduced the commercial incentive to push heroin'.

- It should be made harder to buy illegally exported diamonds, timber and Columbite-tantalite (coltan). Diamonds paid for the civil wars in Sierra Leone and Angola, where they made UNITA leader Jonas Savimbi rich. Diamonds are easy to transport and smuggle, but marketing is largely controlled by a single company. Following an extensive campaign by international NGOs, the Kimberley agreement was due to take effect in 2003 under which rough diamonds would be certified as having been produced legally in participating countries. Timber, which paid for wars in Cambodia and Liberia, is at the opposite end of the spectrum – it is physically large and easier to monitor, but the trade is in the hands of many small companies. Thailand's ban on Cambodian timber, imposed in 1997, helped to defeat the Khmer Rouge and end the war in Cambodia. The World Bank notes that 'realistically, the effect of better regulation of commodity markets is not literally to shut rebel organisations out of markets, but to make their activities so difficult that they can only sell their illegal booty at a deep price discount.'

Diamond mining, Sierra Leone.

3.5 Environment and migration

In brief, our research showed that environmental scarcities are already contributing to violent conflicts in many parts of the developing world. These conflicts are probably the early signs of an upsurge of violence in the coming decades that will be induced or aggravated by scarcity. The violence will usually be sub-national, persistent, and diffuse. Poor societies will be particularly affected since they are less able to buffer themselves from environmental scarcities and the social crises they cause. These societies are, in fact, already suffering from acute hardship from shortages of water, forests, and especially fertile land.

(Homer-Dixon, 1994)

This Malthusian vision of civil war driven by population growth and the resulting environmental scarcity was written in 1994 by Thomas Homer-Dixon for the University of Toronto Project on Environmental Scarcities, State Capacity, and Civil Violence. Around the same time, a number of writers predicted wars over the growing shortages of fresh water. Later research showed that 'there does not appear to be a convincing case that environmental factors cause major violent conflicts which in turn lead to massive flows of forced migrants,' according to Stephen Castles (2001), director of the Oxford Refugee Studies Centre.

Again, here we have a definitional problem. As environmental scarcity declined in importance as an issue, many of its proponents began to include 'lootable resources' as an environmental factor. International relations writers sometimes use 'environmental factors' to mean a 'hostile and uncertain' social, cultural and political environment. In this section, we do not use these extensions, and stick to the limited concept of 'environmental scarcity' meaning a shortage of resources as a possible cause of war. We do, however, take a broader account here of a related issue – migration. Environmental scarcity might trigger migration, which may be a cause of war, and we consider that here as well.

Debate continues on the impact of environmental factors on the civil wars in Sudan.

Environmental factors do play a role in conflict and war, but they seem far less important than originally feared. For example, land scarcity and degradation is an issue in Sudan, the Congo, Nepal and elsewhere. But a study by the Institute of Strategic Studies in South Africa points out that an important cause of conflict and war is 'grievance related to the unjust and inequitable distribution of land and natural resources in many regions of Africa.' Land issues are more often political than environmental (Black, 1998; Lind and Sturman, 2002).

The Toronto Project on Environmental Scarcities, State Capacity, and Civil Violence (1993–97; www.library.utoronto.ca/pcs/state.htm) also came to accept that the apocalyptic vision of environmental scarcity was not justified, and looked increasingly at the way resource scarcities put stresses on the state. Reduction in resources can cut government income from resource exports, while environmental degradation can expand marginal groups with grievances who are making demands on the state. Political elites may begin to fight over scarce resources. Eventually, groups begin to challenge state authority.

Nils Petter Gleditsch (2001) of the International Peace Research Institute (PRIO) in Oslo summarises:

> In many cases, environmental degradation may be more appropriately seen as an intervening variable between poverty and poor governance on the one hand and armed conflict on the other. In that sense, environmental degradation may be seen more as a symptom that something has gone wrong than as a cause of the world's ills.

Mixed political and environmental factors can trigger landlessness which forces migration. Box 3.2 shows how this happened in the Philippines. Big dam projects similarly create landless people who have to move. These people move into other areas, where they sometimes come into conflict with the people who are already there. By definition, the incomers are a group with an identity (if only defined as coming from outside) and the local people have an identity (if only defined by already living there). Any differences in language, customs or religion help to differentiate the two groups.

Box 3.2   Land struggles in the Philippines and Peru

Colonial policies pushing people off good land onto marginal land is an indirect cause of civil wars in the Philippines and Peru, and can be seen, now, as environmental pressure, according to Thomas Homer-Dixon (1994). Spanish and US colonial policies in the Philippines left behind a grossly unfair distribution of good cropland in the lowland coastal plane, and this imbalance was perpetuated by a powerful landowning elite. People were pushed off the land and into less productive upland areas. Millions of landless poor migrated to the cities. Others continued to farm steep hillsides, often using lowland methods that damaged the fragile ecosystems, eventually causing forest destruction, erosion and landslides, which in turn exacerbated the upland economic crisis. Finally in the 1970s this led landless people to join communist insurgencies to try to displace landlords, and this eventually became a major civil war.

The rise of Sendero Luminoso in Peru can similarly be attributed to people being pushed onto marginal land and the subsequent ecological crisis. During the colonial period, Spanish settlers seized richer valley lands and forced Indian peoples onto steep hillsides with poor soils, where the land became eroded and degraded and people became ever poorer. By the 1980s there was a subsistence crisis, and these areas became the strongholds of Sendero Luminoso.

Irrigation schemes on the Ganges River in India brought dramatic increases in food production in India in the 1960s, but had unplanned effects downstream in Bangladesh. Not enough water passed into Bangladesh in the January to May dry season, disrupting fishing and navigation, changing river flows in ways that caused river bank erosion, and leading to salt water penetration from the Bay of Bengal. Many people lost their land and at least two million Muslim Bangladeshis migrated to mainly Hindu areas of India. In Assam there has been violence between local people and Bangladeshi migrants since the 1980s. Some migrants crossed India to Mumbai (Bombay), and one slogan of communal riots in 1993 was 'kick the Bangladeshis out' (Swain, 1996).

During the 1970s and 1980s more than one million families were moved from the densely populated island of Java to lesser populated islands as part of Indonesia's World-Bank-funded transmigration scheme. The movement was partly political, to settle more 'modern' Javanese people on the outer islands. A substantial number were sent to Timor-Leste (East Timor), which Indonesia had occupied in 1975 and where local people fought a long, and eventually successful, liberation war. In 1998 there was an outbreak of violence on Kalimantan between the transmigrants and the local Dayak, and hundreds were killed (Castles, 2001).

3.6   Chapter summary

All **civil wars have multiple causes**. Academics often propose a single predominant cause of civil war, such as bad leaders or ethnic hatred, which has led to multiple and contradictory explanations. Instead, we say there are always a **range of factors** behind a civil war. There has also been a change in attitudes, with the rich North largely blamed for war and underdevelopment in the 1960s and 1970s, while the poor were blamed for their own underdevelopment and civil wars in the 1980s and 1990s. The contest between these approaches remained in the first years of the twenty-first century.

We categorise differences in explanations of civil war on three axes: **people under pressure versus big bad men, internal versus external, and historic versus recent** (Figure 3.1). For example, the colonial heritage remains important, which would make it an external, historic explanation.

The chapter stresses that most civil wars take place in new states, formed in the past century from the breakup of the nineteenth- and twentieth-century empires. In Europe it took centuries for stable states to become established, and during that period there were many wars and failed states and substantial repression. By contrast, new **twentieth-century states must move quickly through the process of state consolidation, while becoming democratic and respecting human rights and self-determination**, and while overcoming the negative heritage of colonialism. Such demands were never made on older states, and many civil wars come about in part because of problems of rapid state building.

Democracy is a contested issue, with suggestions that the transition to democracy is destabilising. There are several **favourable conditions** which make war more likely: poverty, the availability of secure areas for guerrilla bases, and finance for the war. **Environmental stress** is often cited, but does not yet seem to be causing wars.

References

Annan, K. (1997) *Report of the Secretary-General on the Causes of Conflict and the Promotion of Durable Peace and Sustainable Development in Africa*, New York, Office of the Secretary-General of the United Nations.

Ayoob, M. (1996) 'State-making, state-breaking and state failure' in van de Goor, Rupesinghe and Sciarone (eds) (1996).

Ayoob, M. (2001) 'State-making, state-breaking and state failure', Chapter 9 in Crocker, Hampson and Aall (eds) (2001a).

Bardhan, P. (1997) 'Method in the madness? A political-economy analysis of the ethnic conflicts in less developed countries', *World Development*, vol. 25, no. 9, pp. 1381–98.

Black, R. (1998) *Refugees, Environment and Development*, London, Longman.

Brown, M. E. (ed.) (1996) *The International Dimensions of Internal Conflict*, Cambridge MA, MIT Press.

Buchan, J. (2003) 'Miss Bell's lines in the sand', *The Guardian*, London, 12 March 2003.

Castles, S. (2001) 'Environmental change and forced migration', lecture at Green College, Oxford, 6 December 2001, www.preparingforpeace.org (accessed 2004).

Collier, P. (2000) *Economic Causes of Civil Conflict and their Implications for Policy*, Washington DC, World Bank.

Collier, P. and Hoeffler, A. (2004) 'Aid, policy and growth in post-conflict societies', *European Economic Review*, vol. 48, no. 5, pp.1125–45.

Collier, P., Elliot, L., Hegre, H., Hoeffler, A., Reynal-Querol, M. and Sambanis, N. (2003), *Breaking the Conflict Trap*, Washington DC, World Bank and Oxford, Oxford University Press.

Crocker, C. (2001) 'Intervention', Chapter 14 in Crocker, Hampson and Aall (eds) (2001a).

Crocker, C., Hampson, F. O. and Aall, P. (eds) (2001a), *Turbulent Peace*, US Institute of Peace, Washington DC.

Crocker, C., Hampson, F. O. and Aall, P. (2001b) 'Introduction' in Crocker, Hampson and Aall (eds) (2001a).

Department for International Development (DfID), Foreign and Commonwealth Office (FCO) and Ministry of Defence (MoD) of the UK Government (2001) 'The causes of conflict in Sub-Saharan Africa', London, DfID Information Department.

Duffield, M. (1998) 'Post-modern conflict', *Civil Wars*, vol. 1, no. 1, pp. 66–102.

Duyvesteyn, I. (2000) 'Contemporary war: ethnic conflict, resource conflict or something else?' *Civil Wars*, vol. 3, no. 1, pp. 92–116.

Fearon, J. and Laitin, D. (2003) 'Ethnicity, insurgency and civil war', *American Political Science Review*, vol. 97, no. 1, pp. 75–9.

Gleditsch, N. P. (2001) 'Environmental change, security and conflict', Chapter 4 in Crocker, Hampson and Aall (eds) (2001a).

Gleditsch, N. P. et al. (2002) 'Armed conflict 1946–2001: a new dataset', *Journal of Peace Research*, vol. 39, no. 5, pp. 615–37. The list of conflicts and updates are on a website: http://www.prio.no/cwp/armedconflict (accessed March 2005).

van de Goor, L., Rupesinghe, K., and Sciarone, P., (eds) (1996) *Between Development and Destruction: an Enquiry into the Causes of Conflict in Post-colonial States*, Basingstoke, Macmillan.

Holsti, K. J. (1997) 'Political source of humanitarian emergencies', *Research for Action 36*, Helsinki, WIDER.

Homer-Dixon, T. (1994) 'Environmental scarcities and violent conflict', *International Security*, vol. 19, no. 1, pp. 5–40.

Horowitz, D. L. (1985) *Ethnic Groups in Conflict*, Berkeley, University of California Press.

Houweling, H. W. (1996) 'Destabilising Consequences of Sequential Development', Chapter 9 in in van de Goor, Rupesinghe and Sciarone (eds) (1996).

Jung, D., Schlichte, K. and Siegelberg, J. (1996) 'Ongoing wars and their explanation', Chapter 2 in in van de Goor, Rupesinghe and Sciarone (eds) (1996).

Kaldor, M. (1999) *New and Old Wars*, London, Polity.

Kupchan, C. (2001) 'Empires and geopolitical competition', Chapter 3 in Crocker, Hampson and Aall (eds) (2001a).

Lind, J. and Sturman, K. (eds) (2002) *Scarcity and Surfeit: The Ecology of Africa's Conflicts*, Institute of Strategic Studies, South Africa.

Mack, A. (2002) 'Civil war: academic research and the policy community', *Journal of Peace Research*, vol. 39, pp. 515–25.

Mansfield, E. D. and Snyder, J. (2001) 'Democratic transitions and war', Chapter 8 in Crocker, Hampson and Aall (eds) (2001a).

Nafziger, E. W. and Auvinen, J. (2002) 'Economic development, inequality, war and state violence', *World Development*, vol. 30, pp. 53–163.

Reynal-Querol, M. (2002) 'Ethnicity, political systems, and civil wars' *Journal of Conflict Resolution*, vol. 46, no. 1, pp. 29–54.

Sambanis, N. (2001) 'Do ethnic and non-ethnic civil wars have the same causes?', *Journal of Conflict Resolution*, vol. 45, no. 3, pp. 259–82.

Sambanis, N. (2002) 'A review of recent advances and future directions in the quantitative literature on civil war', *Defence and Peace Economics*, vol. 13, no. 3, pp. 215–43.

Suhrke, A., Villanger, E. and Woodward, S. L. (2004) 'Economic Aid to Post-Conflict Countries: Correcting the Empirical and Theoretical Foundations of Policy', paper given at the UNU-WIDER conference 'Making Peace Work', Helsinki, 4–5 June 2004.

Swain, A. (1996) 'Displacing the conflict: environmental destruction in Bangladesh and ethnic conflict in India', *Journal of Peace Research*, vol. 33, no. 2, pp. 189–204.

Tilly, C. (1975) 'Reflections on the history of European state making' in Tilly (ed.) *The Formation of National States in Western Europe*, Princeton, Princeton University Press.

Williams, P. (2001) 'Transnational criminal enterprises, conflict and instability', Chapter 7 in Crocker, Hampson and Aall (eds) (2001a).

 **Ethnicity and identity**

Joseph Hanlon

4.1   Introduction

Civil wars take place inside a single state, and the most common explanations for the roots of those wars identify the actors themselves. As we will see below, ethnicity and identity are particularly contested areas, and can be seen as pre-existing conditions which dispose a country to civil war, as a more direct cause of the war itself, or as a way of keeping the war going.

US President George Bush (the elder) blamed the war in Yugoslavia on 'age-old animosities' (Snyder, 1993, p. 79). His successor, President Bill Clinton, is said to have decided there was no point in intervening in Bosnia after reading a book which argued that people in the Balkans had been killing each other in tribal and religious wars for centuries (Sadowski, 1998). 'A specter is haunting much of the world today, that of ethnic and sectarian conflict,' wrote Pranab Bardhan (1997). 'The ethnic caldron seems to be boiling over.'

In the few years since those stark views were aired, opinions have moderated somewhat. And yet there is long-running violence in Britain and India between people who claim to be fighting over religion, genocide in Rwanda which is ascribed to 'tribal' differences, and multiple wars in the Balkans which seem to be over both religion and tribe – which all point to a sense that 'identity' has some role in civil wars. But how important is 'identity' as a root of civil war?

We return to the problem of definitions. D. L. Horowitz (1985) says 'ethnic groups are defined by ascriptive difference, whether the indicum is color, appearance, language, religion or some other indicator of common origin.' Ethnic is usually defined very broadly to include 'all racial, tribal, religious or linguistic groupings' (Bardhan, 1997), 'caste' (Horowitz, 1985) and 'nations' and 'communal minorities' (Sambanis, 2002). Ted Gurr (2001) says that 'the "ethnic criteria" used by these groups to define themselves usually include common descent, shared historical experiences and valued cultural traits.' He adds that 'what is important is that ethnopolitical groups organize around their shared identity and seek gains for members of their group.'

We also underline the issue of the definition of 'civil war'. Thus the communal rioting between Hindus and Muslims in India in the 1990s was horrific and deadly, but it was not a 'war' because it was not an ongoing fight between two organised groups which is sustained over time – as, for example, happened in the Balkans.

Gurr runs the Minorities at Risk project at the University of Maryland, which identifies 17 per cent of the world's population, slightly over one billion people, as part of '275 politically significant national and minority peoples in the world's 161 largest countries. ... All but 33 of the 275 groups in the Minorities at Risk survey were subject to one or several kinds of discrimination in the mid-1990s' (Gurr, 2001). By contrast, others estimate that there are between 3000 and 9000 ethnic communities in the world, and note that few of them are involved in violent conflict (Brown, 2001). The Human Genome Diversity Project says that 'using language as a criterion, there are over 5000 distinct human populations in the world' (Bodmer, 1993). UNESCO has catalogued 6000 living languages (Wurm, 2001).

For Gurr, ethnicity takes prominence, so he argues 'it is misleading to interpret the Zapatistas [in Mexico] as just a militant peasants' movement' and instead they must be seen as Mayans. Similarly, although he accepts that in Angola 'during the Cold War the United States and South Africa gave UNITA ample material and political assistance in a proxy war against the Cuban-supported government in Luanda', he still insists that UNITA be seen as a movement 'based mainly on the Ovimbundu people of southern Angola'(Gurr, 2001). So for Gurr, ethnicity is everywhere. He and others see an ethnic basis even for groups like UNITA and the Zapatistas, which reject the label. Similarly, Gurr sees the Sierra Leone war as ethnic, while its participants would describe it as, at most, a regional, North–South dispute. A rebellion in the north of Mali and Niger is described in Box 4.1.

Box 4.1   The Tuareg movement in Mali

The Tuareg rebellion in the north of Mali and Niger is often presented as an ethnic war but it can equally be seen as the protest of marginalised youth. Indeed, the movement was led by 'ishumar', a local word which seems derived from the French word *chômeur*, unemployed. Young Tuareg men who had been soldiers in the Libyan army returned to their homes to find no jobs and few opportunities because they were poorly educated and there had been little investment in their area. General Moussa Traoré of Mali had purchased the support of the Tuareg traditional chieftaincy, but little had filtered down to the rest of the people. The rebellion was as much against these feudal leaders as against the states of Mali and Niger (Azam, 2001).

Similarly, Gurr and others see the Israel–Palestine war as being an 'ethnopolitical conflict', while in fact using a descriptor which actually names a country and a would-be country, Israel and Palestine, and describes a war in which many of its participants would not see the 'ethnic' component as paramount.

Meeting of regional Tuareg, Songhai and other leaders to discuss peace and disarmament after the Tuareg rebellion in Mali.

So the ethnic researchers pose a question for us: is there an advantage in looking at wars through an ethnic lens, even when the description is rejected by the participants in the war?

4.2   Ethnicity: innate or malleable?

In the remainder of this chapter, we look at three issues. First, ethnic researchers divide themselves into 'primordialists' who argue that ethnic identity is innate and largely fixed, and 'constructivists' who argue that it is malleable and changing. These give very different prescriptions for intervention. Then we ask what data are available to show that this approach is useful, and finally we look at the broader question of identity politics to see what that shows.

'Primordialists' view ethnicity as an exceptionally strong affiliation which is often linked to ancient conflicts, age-old hatreds and past atrocities. These identities change little over time. It leads to the view that there are irreconcilable differences between ethnic groups, and that violent clashes are inevitable. The influential Harvard University professor Samuel P. Huntington (1993) identified:

> ...seven or eight major civilizations. These include Western, Confucian, Japanese, Islamic, Hindu, Slavic-Orthodox, Latin American and possibly African civilization. The most important conflicts of the future will occur along the cultural fault lines separating these civilisations from one another. ... These differences are the product of centuries. ... Conflict along the fault line between Western and Islamic civilizations has been going on for 1300 years. ... In Eurasia the great historic fault lines between civilizations are once more aflame.

Countries on the fault lines are prone to civil war, Huntington says; civil wars in Algeria, Chad and Sudan are on the fault line between Islam and Africa, and Yugoslavia was a meeting of three cultures: Islam, Slavic-Orthodox, and Western-Christian. He argues that nineteenth-century wars were between states, twentieth-century wars were between ideologies ('communism, fascism-Nazism and liberal democracy') and the twenty-first century will see the 'clash of civilisations'.

People 'cannot be both black and white or both Hindu and Muslim', argues Ted Gurr, and 'shared physical attributes ("race")' and religion are the main markers of group identity. These are 'strong and durable collective identities'. Language can also be important, but many people in heterogeneous societies ordinarily speak several languages.

Intervention implication

 Primordialists would want guarantees of minority rights, especially through democratic systems, including: the granting of regional and cultural autonomy and improving the distribution of development funds; preferential civil service hiring policies and job creation for disadvantaged groups; active engagement of the major powers, including 'coercive intervention' and 'pre-emptive action' by the UN and big powers in response to 'gross violations of human rights and ethnic wars' (Gurr, 2001).

'Constructivists' or 'instrumentalists' argue for a social construction of identity, moulded by social systems, leaders and circumstances. Identity is malleable, changes rapidly over time, is often recently formed, and is not inherently conflictual. Because of this, constructivists focus on elites and the way they manipulate ethnic, religious or class identity. Perhaps the strongest view is taken by Alexander, McGregor and Ranger (2000), that 'ethnicity is widely understood to be unnatural, to be historically "invented", "constructed" or "imagined" and used "instrumentally" by politicians.' The University of Maryland Minorities at Risk (2000) programme (started by Ted Gurr) notes that in Rwanda, the division between Hutu and Tutsi was originally a class division, not an ethnic division.

> Hutus who accumulated sufficient wealth, for example a large herd of cattle, could become Tutsis, while Tutsis who fell on hard economic times could fall into the ranks of Hutus. ... In 1926 the Belgians decided that the population should be classified as either Tutsi or Hutu (to qualify as a Tutsi, a person had to own at least ten cattle), with no movement between the two groups. Imposing a Belgian practice, all citizens were issued national identification cards which included an entry for tribe.

Often, members of a group define themselves in opposition to another group, and if the two groups become involved in a violent conflict it is very difficult for group members not to take sides and participate in the war

(Sambanis, 2002). Indeed, as Box 4.2 on the Naga shows, a recently constructed identity can still be a strong force for civil war.

Michael Brown (2001), director of the Center for Peace and Security Studies at Georgetown University, notes that:

> It is undeniably true that Serbs, Croats and Muslims have many historical grievances against one another, and that these have played a role in the Balkan conflicts that raged in the 1990s. But it is also true that other groups – Czechs and Slovaks, Ukrainians and Russians, French-speaking and English-speaking Canadians – have historical grievances that have not led to violent conflict in the post-Cold War era.

Constructivist writers put considerable emphasis on 'bad leaders'. Brown (2001) argues that:

> Many ethnic and internal conflicts are triggered by self-obsessed leaders who will do anything to get and keep power. They often incite ethnic violence of the most horrific kind for their own political ends. ... Conflicts triggered by power struggles between opportunistic and desperate politicians are common.

The constructivist view of 'bad leaders' is explicitly rejected by primordialists like Ted Gurr (2001), who writes:

> Given the existence of identity and interest, ethnic entrepreneurs can build militant political movements, but only within limits of group members' expectations about what objectives and actions are acceptable.

A possible middle view is argued by Milton Esman (1994, p. 14):

> Ethnicity cannot be politicized unless an underlying core of memories, experience, or meaning moves people to collective action. ... [But] historical myths can be shaped from imagined pasts to legitimate current goals ...

Many 'ancient hatreds' are actually recent constructions. Nafzifger and Auvinen (2002) cite the way Slobodan 'Milosevic redeemed Serb nationalism by evoking the painful memory of the Kosovo Polje battle of 1389', and in South Africa the apartheid government deliberately created tribal identities to deflect anger away from white rulers.

If identities are constructed, why do followers follow? Many writers cite growing economic problems such as unemployment and inflation, which reduce opportunities, especially for youth. State weakness and collapse increases the pressure and reduces opportunities, increasing the justification to try to exclude the 'other' group so that your group can keep more of what is left.

Note that the intervention implications of constructivist and primordialist interpretations are contradictory. Constructivists try to keep the groups together and resolve underlying problems, while primordialists want to keep the groups apart. Thus differences in academic approach can lead to real and significant differences in choice of intervention on the ground.

Box 4.2   The Naga war in India

After 40 years of intermittent warfare, which began with India's independence in 1947, the Naga and the government of India reached a ceasefire in 1997, although the war started again in 2004. Sanjib Baruah (2003) gives this example of how an artificially created ethnicity can become an extremely powerful collective identity.

A British ethnographic account published in 1922 said that the term Naga 'is useful as an arbitrary term to describe the tribes living in certain parts of the Assam hills'. Nagas speak at least 30 different languages and the pan-Naga organisation Naga Hoho lists 16 different Naga 'tribes'. But the British turned the Naga into a militant group with a strong collective identity. When the British East India Company moved into Manipur in the early nineteenth century, it found the land in the valleys and foothills suitable for large-scale tea production, and it tried to push the local people off the land. Local people resisted and the British responded with relentless brutality. Fighting continued up to 1880. By then the local people had retreated to fortified villages in the Naga mountains. Through their resistance they had developed a sense of Naga solidarity.

During the First World War a labour corps of 4000 Nagas were sent to France, where they saw the 'civilized nations' fighting for their interests. Twenty Naga came together to form the Naga Club; in 1929 they issued a memorandum demanding to be excluded from British plans for India on the grounds that the British 'never conquered us, nor were we ever subject to their rule.' In 1951 the Naga National Council organised its own plebiscite which it said showed that 99.9 per cent of Nagas wanted independence, and it argued with the new Indian Government that the Naga had had a special dispensation from British colonial rule. After an uprising in the late 1950s, India created a separate state of Nagaland in 1963. But an independence movement continued.

Proselytising by the American Baptist Mission, which converted about 90 per cent of the Naga, made Christianity a central part of the Naga identity. In part, the destabilisation of traditional Naga institutions during colonial rule set the stage for this transformation. But it was also about defining themselves as different from India – about half the conversions took place after Indian independence and mark the Nagas as being apart from the Hindu and Muslim population of the Indian heartland.

Nagas may have developed a strong sense of collective identity, but there remain fierce disputes as to just who belongs to this artificially created 'ethnic' group. Naga leaders claim a population of around 4 million, spreading into Burma and three other Indian states, leading to conflicts with other groups and leaders who also claim some of these people.

4.3 International relations and the 'ethnic security dilemma'

In the previous chapter we noted that with the decline in interstate wars, international relations scholars have turned their attention to civil wars. The 'realist' approach to international relations assumes that key actors are sovereign states that act rationally to advance their own security, power and wealth. One of the core assumptions of realist theory, according to Sir Michael Howard (2001), life president of the International Institute of Strategic Studies, is that 'the causes of war remain rooted, as much as they were in the pre-industrial age, in perceptions by statesmen of the growth of hostile power and the fears for the restriction, if not the extinction, of their own.' This fear leads to escalation and what is known as the 'security dilemma', where each country builds up its own defences, which in turn makes the other country (or bloc, during the Cold War) feel less secure and more threatened, so it builds up its defences, in an ongoing spiral. Barbara Walter (1999, p. 305) points 'to the potentially devastating consequences of mistakenly trusting an opponent.' The danger is that one country, acting out of fear, attacks the other, often out of a misperception of the risk.

Jack Levy (2001) says that 'a realist explanation for ethnonational conflict' is what he calls the 'ethnic security dilemma'. Barbara Walter argues there has been too much stress 'on the stated goals of the belligerents' and too little on more general factors that cause civil war to 'erupt inadvertently'. She argues that within countries the security dilemma becomes even more severe because misplaced trust of neighbours could prove fatal and groups may 'find it prudent to act as if neighbouring groups are ruthless predators'. She points out that 'groups have little to fear from each other when the central government can effectively enforce rules and arbitrate disputes', but when governments break down, as in the former Yugoslavia, the security dilemma emerges. She notes:

> Serbs, Croats, and Muslims clearly picked up guns and shot at each other in the early 1990s. In part, this can be explained by their desire for greater territorial control. But it can also be explained by fear and vulnerability they felt as the Yugoslav federation began to disintegrate ...

> Hutus might pick up machetes and kill neighbouring Tutsi because they hate each other. But they might also kill because they fear their own life would be at risk if they fail to act.

(Walter, 1999, pp. 1–10)

The concept of an ethnic security dilemma assumes ethnicity is an issue, and often assumes a primordial interpretation – issues discussed in Section 4.1 above. Barbara Walter, for example, assumes that 'individuals tend to mobilize along ethnic lines rather than along class-based, regional, or ideological lines.' It also assumes that fears are likely to be unjustified and based on lack of information or inaccurate information. 'Domestic groups are often forced to make hurried appraisals of what a neighbour intended to do, since the opportunity for aggression is often short and predators can be expected to act quickly. This short window of opportunity leaves groups little time to collect accurate information and forces them to rely on information that is sometimes inaccurate, misleading, and incendiary,' notes Barbara Walter. With other writers, she goes on to argue that 'the majority of citizens obtain this information from elites who use and manipulate information for their own self-advancement. ... Unscrupulous or predatory leaders ... often have incentives to portray rivals as more malicious than they actually are.' Although there is a primordial assumption here and thus a view of people under pressure, the stress in this explanation often shifts to big bad men who are manipulating the people.

The key problem with this interpretation is caught up in a single sentence by Rui de Figueiredo and Barry Weingast (1999): 'Although most ethnic groups face a security dilemma, the spiral dynamic occurs only occasionally.' As we saw in Section 4.1, there is no reason to assume that 'most ethnic groups', however defined, face a security dilemma. And, having made the assumption, it does not seem predictive – as many writers note, what is striking is how few pairs of ethnic groups act as if they are under threat. Nicholas Sambanis (2001), then of the World Bank, comments that 'neo-realism so far seems not as relevant as some scholars have thought because we have found no evidence of a security dilemma.' These views are not problematic to Chester Crocker, who declares that 'the security dilemma is particularly acute' (Crocker, 2001).

Intervention implication

Among those who accept the existence of the ethnic security dilemma there are conflicting approaches. One group says ethnicity (broadly defined) is the key to peacebuilding. Instead of dealing with grievances, priority should be given to dealing with groups' perhaps irrational fears of each other by dealing with their felt insecurity. Where possible, groups should be geographically separated behind defensible boundaries (responding to the concept of 'people under pressure').

By contrast, Chester Crocker (2001) argues that 'we should be looking beyond the notion of ethnicity' and argues for 'resisting calls for secession and territorial fragmentation'. Allowing the breakup of Yugoslavia is now seen by many writers as having been unwise. (It is important to note that the two views are not totally contradictory. Ted Gurr (2001) notes that 'there are very few contemporary instances in which negotiated autonomy led to independence'. But the line between autonomy and secession can be very fuzzy, as shown in the debate about increasing Basque autonomy in Spain.)

It also puts an emphasis on isolating and marginalising the big bad men who have manipulated their groups through fear and misinformation. But again there is a division of views. Some argue for marginalising by ensuring them an acceptable exit – a 'golden parachute' and guarantee of impunity to ensure they will step aside – while others argue that a war crimes trial is essential.

4.4   Does the ethnic lens help our understanding?

How useful to our understanding of civil war is the concept of ethnicity? One of the primordialists, Ted Gurr (2001), concludes: 'Today, class, ethnicity, and faith are the three main alternative sources of mass movements, and class-based and religious movements may well drain away some of the popular support that now energises ethnic political movements.' Many writers class 'religious' movements as 'ethnic'; Gurr himself accepts that 'some conflicts are hybrids: ethnic wars seen through one set of analytic lenses and revolutionary wars when seen through another'.

Constructivist Michael Brown (2001) makes a similar distinction. He calls an 'ethnic conflict' any conflict that involves an ethnic group in a dispute over political, territorial, economic or social issues. But then he goes on to say that not all conflicts are 'ethnic in character' because the main issues are not ethnic. And there are those which sit somewhere in between:

> The leaders of the Sendero Luminoso and Tupac Amaru movements in Peru were initially motivated by ideological agendas they sought to achieve, but they later placed more and more emphasis on the plight of indigenous peoples. This conflict, therefore, evolved from an ideological struggle into a hybrid.

And, despite going out of his way to stress the primacy of ethnicity and to reject the big-bad-men approach of the constructivists, Gurr (2001) goes a long way toward recognising other views when he says:

> During the last several decades, the entrepreneurs behind ethnic political movements tapped into a reservoir of resentment about material inequality, political exclusion and government predation, and channelled it to their purposes. They drew on the same grievances that fuelled revolutionary movements.

A much debated question is about the utility of the ethnic lens. Does it give us a better understanding of a war and how to respond to it than viewing it through the lens that sees the material and political grievances? The genocide in Rwanda was in part against an ethnic group, but as Box 4.3 shows, ethnic explanations are not adequate. A string of writers have argued against the more popular, media-driven versions of the ethnic approach, which says that primordial hatreds lead to particularly brutal and savage wars. Yahya Sadowski (1998) has pointed out that most of the worst mass killings since the Second World War were not ethnic, including Pol Pot killing up to three million people in Cambodia in the 1970s and Suharto killing one million 'communists' in Indonesia in the 1960s.

Box 4.3   Various explanations for Rwanda's genocide

In the 13 weeks after 6 April 1994, at least 600,000 people were killed in Rwanda. These included 500,000 Tutsi, perhaps three quarters of the Tutsi population, in a genocide organised by the government of President Juvenal Habyarimana. Tens of thousands of Hutu were slain because they opposed the killing and the forces directing it. At least 50,000 people were killed as the Rwandan Patriotic Front (RPF) fought its way across the country, eventually overthrowing the government and ending the genocide (Human Rights Watch, 1999). Subsequent studies have shown there were ample warnings, and that the international community failed to act to prevent or stop the genocide.

The majority Hutu and minority Tutsi look similar and speak the same language and there is much argument as to whether this is a class or ethnic division. As noted in Section 4.1, in 1926 the colonial power, Belgium, decided that a Tutsi was defined as owning at least ten cattle; subsequently, Belgium decreed that only Tutsi could be government officials and receive higher education. This set the domination of the Tutsis, which continued until the end of the colonial period. In the typology of Figure 3.1, this root of conflict sits with the colonial administrators, and is historic, external and caused by big bad men.

With independence in 1962, the Hutu majority took power and extracted their revenge. In a civil war over the next five years, 20,000 Tutsi were killed and 300,000 fled the country, many living in camps in Uganda for the next 30 years. Habyarimana took control in a coup in 1973, and power was increasingly concentrated in the 'akazu' (little house), a small group of people from his northern clan and region.

For more than 20 years, the international community did nothing to help the refugees return home. Rwandan Tutsi fighters from the camps had helped Yoweri Museveni win control of Uganda in 1986. They then formed the RPF and with support from the Ugandan Government in 1991 decided to go home by force. There was a ceasefire and agreement by Habyarimana for a political opening, but he went back on the agreement in 1993. On the way to peace negotiations the next year, Habyarimana's plane was shot down, and the genocide began. Failure to deal with the refugee camps and Ugandan support for the invasion are both external roots of the subsequent war and genocide.

From 1991 the Habyarimana government began a propaganda campaign against the Tutsi minority. The Interahamwe militia was created. In 1993 Hutu hardliners created a radio station, Radio Télévision Libre des Mille Collines. It said the Tutsi were planning a genocide against the Hutu, so it was necessary to kill the Tutsi first – building on the ethnic security dilemma discussed in Section 4.2. Tutsi were seen as 'vermin' that had to be liquidated. A small elite around Habyarimana did use racism and violence to fend off threats to its survival and privileges. This seems like the constructivist interpretation of ethnicity, involving big bad men manipulating the population to build and maintain political power.

Subsequent studies, however, have put much more emphasis on economic factors and the role of external agencies. David Woodward (1997) in a study for Oxfam said that 'economic conditions were important in creating the environment in which the genocide could occur.' In the mid 1980s, coffee and tea accounted for 80 per cent of Rwanda's exports and most of the cash income of rural households. In 1989, the United States ended the 27-year-old International Coffee Agreement, which had kept the price paid to peasant growers artificially high, because US President George Bush (the elder) wanted lower prices for US consumers. Coffee export receipts fell from $144 million in 1985 to $30 million in 1993. To gain aid to fill the gap, Rwanda was forced to accept an IMF/World Bank structural adjustment programme which required civil service wage cuts, higher fees for health and education, and an end to protection of local peasant food producers.

Shortly after the genocide, the Danish Ministry of Foreign Affairs organised an unprecedented joint donor study under the supervision of 37 countries and international agencies. It concluded that 'conditionality on economic restructuring':

- 'exacerbated social tensions and undermined efforts to improve human rights through political conditionality'
- 'fanned resentment'
- 'added to the already heavy burden of Rwanda's poor'.

(Eriksson 1996, p. 15, 43; Sellström and Wohlgemuth, 1996, p. 20; Adelman and Suhrke, 1996, p. 79).

Woodward (1997) called the conditions a 'reckless disregard for social and political sensitivities'.

Peter Uvin (1998, p. 1) notes that 'Rwanda was usually seen as a model of development, with good performance on most of the indicators of development'. Because it was seen as a development success, aid increased substantially at exactly the same time that human rights violations and attacks on Tutsis were accelerating; the joint donor study concludes that donors had significant leverage in Rwanda which they did not use (Sellström and Wohlgemuth, 1996, p. 39). Indeed, 'by not standing firm on human rights conditionality, donors collectively sent the message that their priorities lay elsewhere' (Eriksson, 1996, p. 18). Donors prioritised structural adjustment over preventing genocide. Uvin (1998, p. 229) argues that 'the fact that the development business continued as usual while government-sponsored human rights violations were on the rise sent a clear signal that the international community chose to ignore the racially motivated and publicly organized slaughter of citizens.' Indeed, at a time of increasing aid, the government sharply increased arms imports; France, Egypt and South Africa were happy to send weapons to a government increasingly accused of human rights violations and donors did not object to the diversion of funds. Belgium did end military support to the government in 1990, but France stepped in to fill the gap, even sending troops to support the government (Sellström and Wohlgemuth, 1996, p. 67).

Inequality increased greatly in the 1980s, with only a minority – particularly those with some link to aid through jobs, projects or corruption, or from the President's region in the north – doing well. Environmental stress in what was seen as a tiny overcrowded country (see Section 3.4) is sometimes cited as a root of the war, but in fact Bangladesh, Belgium, Costa Rica, Egypt, South Korea, Tanzania and many other countries have less arable land per capita than Rwanda. In his study of the Rwandan genocide, Peter Uvin (1998, pp. 112,180ff.) admits 'this was a surprise to me' – that there was no link between resource scarcity and the genocide, and he noted that until the mid 1980s Rwanda could feed itself. But he did find a sharp increase in landlessness, as small farmers squeezed by the economic crisis had to sell their land to people earning money from trade, aid, or government.

Uvin (1998, pp. 3, 104, 231) argues that donors obsessed with projects and statistics refused to see that aid was actually benefiting only a small group. Calling his book *Aiding Violence*, he says donors were 'active and willing partners' supporting the 'extreme pauperization and reduction of "life chances" for a majority of the poor' which was creating 'significant frustration and discontent'. Aid supported 'institutionalized inequalities of statuses, rights and power' which worsened during this period. This is 'structural violence' (discussed in more detail in Box 5.3) and is directly linked to a culture of impunity for a corrupt, racist and oppressive but aid-supported elite. According to Uvin (1998, p. 110):

> A population that is cynical, angry, and frustrated is predisposed to scapegoating and projection, vulnerable to manipulation, deeply afraid of the future, and desperate for change. It is this population that bought into the racist prejudice in the 1990s and was willing to kill out of fear, anger, resentment, and greed.

There was a genocide in Rwanda and, most importantly, there was mass participation in the killing. What led ordinary people to feel that they could, and should, exterminate innocent people who had been their neighbours? Seven factors undoubtedly played a role:

- Ethnicity was the key organising factor, although the disagreement between primordialist and constructivist explanations remains.
- Colonial divisions continued after independence.
- Refugees were left in camps in Uganda for two decades with no resolution of their status, followed by Ugandan support for a refugee invasion of Rwanda.
- The economic crisis and the pauperisation of peasants – what is called structural violence – was an essential factor.

- External actions, notably the end of the International Coffee Agreement and the imposition of structural adjustment, exacerbated the crisis.
- The country was ruled by a small and increasingly corrupt and oppressive elite.
- The international community backed that elite and ignored its depredations.

No single one of these factors caused the genocide; probably all were necessary.

Skulls displayed in a church in Nyamata, Rwanda. The remains of genocide victims have been left undisturbed as a monument of remembrance and commemoration.

Perhaps the main point raised by most writers and academics is that ethnic diversity and division does not normally lead to civil war. It is a common-sense point, in that we can all identify historic divisions such as between French and English speakers in Canada that have not led to war. And one of the few things that the builders of computer-based and econometric models agree on is that ethnic or religious diversity or division does not seem to increase the risk of civil violence or war, and cannot be used to predict the likelihood of civil war (Sambanis, 2002; Fearon and Laitin, 2003). Sambanis (2001, 2002) goes as far as to say that it is 'generally accepted' that 'ethnic diversity need not increase the risk of civil violence and may actually decrease it'.

Jean-Paul Azam (2001) makes the point that:

> The ethnic group is the natural component of a rebellion against the state, as the many links that exist among its members provide an efficient way of overcoming the free-rider problems involved in mobilizing a rebellion or insurgency. This is probably why many observers blame African civil wars on ethnic division, while the failure of the state to maintain peace is the root cause of the problem.

Two other factors do seem to significantly increase the risk of civil war – dominance of one group over another and poverty. Both of these can take on an ethnic aspect, as in the 'hybrid wars' discussed above. The dominant group can be ethnically or religiously defined, or can take on that cloak, although the 'horizontal inequality' method is probably a more general way to see this. K. J. Holsti (1997) in a study for WIDER found that spontaneous outbreaks of ethnically based violence are rare, and that in many cases 'it was the state itself which launched the massacres and genocides'. This leads him to argue 'that insecure and weakly legitimate governments rather than primordial hatreds or spontaneous communal strife are the main source of humanitarian emergencies.' This is similar to the points made in the previous chapter.

As we have noted, poverty seems to make war an easier and more plausible option. Pranab Bardhan (1997), then of the OECD Development Centre, says: 'Of course, the foot soldiers in ethnic movements are usually provided by the young, drawn from the ranks of the demoralised unemployed, looking for faith, hope and arms-toting bravado.' Even here, caution is required. Some of the longest running supposedly 'ethnic' conflicts in the twentieth century were in rich countries: the UK (Northern Ireland), the Basque region of Spain, and Cyprus.

Intervention implication

Expressed ethnic divisions need to be taken into account and security concerns addressed, but interveners need to move quickly to look to the political and economic grievances behind what is being expressed as an ethnic dispute. Where the state was an important actor in 'ethnic' violence, emphasis needs to be placed on restructuring the government itself so that it is broadly representative.

4.4.1 Looking at the broader question of identity

Much of the discussion of ethnicity relates to how people identify themselves and how group identity becomes important in civil wars. It may be more useful to look at broader questions of group solidarity and identity. Identity groups often become central to development and to basic social security in weak states. When people cannot gain resources and support from the formal system, be it banks or government, they have to turn to groups of which they are a member – family, clan, village (or, in the city, people with relatives in a particular village), church, caste, ethnic group, etc. A village may work collectively to send their brightest and best off to school in the hope that the boy or girl will go on to gain a formal sector or even civil service job in the city, and be able to send money back to the village and provide a place for others from the village to live in the city and go to school, and then gain further formal sector jobs. In many countries hiring rules for the civil service and state-owned companies are bent to ensure that a fair representation of sons and daughters of different interest groups have jobs. Of course, this system can also be easily corrupted, and can become discriminatory instead of working against discrimination.

A whole series of development and economic changes can disadvantage people – from structural adjustment and squeezes on the poor to modernisation and growth causing structural changes which may disadvantage some groups. To the extent that people feel discriminated against, they will turn to members of their group for support and solidarity. This is likely when there is a political change, for example when a previously privileged group, like the whites in South Africa, loses power, or when there are economic changes, such as when poorer people or people farther from the capital are squeezed by structural adjustment. Where there is an explicit political grievance, people may organise more formal identity groups and protest. Where such protests do not work, violence may be the next step.

Finally, identity is an issue in keeping a war going once it has started. First, there is the issue of money. Group solidarity means it is cheaper to wage war. Sambanis (2001) points to the 'lower within-group costs of coordinating a rebellion as compared to the same costs in highly diverse societies.' And it is easier to raise money by taxing the group, or by drawing on a diaspora (which need not be ethnically defined, although Kurdish, Tamil, Irish and other diasporas have been important).

Second is a cycle of increasing anger, hatred, fear and other emotions toward the enemy which justify intensifying the violence, which we mentioned in Chapter 1. This happens once there has been significant violence and a group has come under attack, property has been damaged, and members have been killed. The response is often to dehumanise the enemy and brand it as evil, which means increasingly vicious conduct is justified. Group identity and cohesion is built in opposition to the other.

Intervention implication

Look for identity groups that cut across the identities that were taken up in the war – for example, youth, women, farmers, the unemployed, trade union members, etc. – and support those new identity groups.

4.5 Chapter summary

Ethnicity and identity are two of the most intensely disputed issues around civil war. Researchers split into **primordialists** who argue ethnic identity is innate and fixed and that there are long-standing disputes between ethnic groups which lead to war. The **constructivists** argue that identity is malleable and changing and often manipulated by leaders. The primordialists would see the roots of war as being historic and a function of people under pressure, while the constructivists would see this as recent and caused by big bad men. Both groups would see this as an internal root of war.

Some international relations theories introduce the **ethnic security dilemma** which argues that one group cannot afford to trust another group and may make a pre-emptive strike, leading accidentally to war.

Despite all the attempts to identify wars as ethnic, **ethnic diversity and division** do not normally lead to war. Also, where one group rebels against being dominated by another, is it a fight between ethnic groups or between an oppressor and the oppressed group – which identification is most important? It may be that people turn to **groups** of which they are members – family, clan, village, etc. – for help in times of crisis, and this same group may be a recruiting pool for fighters and finance for the war, but that does not make group membership a cause of the war. It can, however, be a cause of **perpetuation of the war**; as members of the group are killed or humiliated by the other group, this can lead to group solidarity and a demand for retaliation against the other group.

References

Adelman, H. and Suhrke, A. (1996) *The International Response to Conflict and Genocide: Lessons from the Rwanda Experience, Study 2: Early Warning and Conflict Management*, Copenhagen, Steering Committee of the Joint Evaluation of Emergency Assistance to Rwanda.

Alexander, J., McGregor, J. A. and Ranger, T. (2000) 'Ethnicity and the politics of conflict: the case of Matabeleland', Chapter 9 in Nafziger, E. W., Stewart, F. and Väyrynen, R., *War, Hunger, and Displacement: The Origins of Humanitarian Emergencies*, Vol. 1: *Analysis*, Oxford, Oxford University Press.

Azam, J.-P. (2001) 'The redistributive state and conflicts in Africa', *Journal of Peace Research*, vol. 38, no. 4, pp. 429–44.

Bardhan, P. (1997) 'Method in the madness? A political-economy analysis of the ethnic conflicts in less developed countries', *World Development*, vol. 25, no. 9, pp. 1381–98.

Baruah, S. (2003) 'Confronting constructionism: ending India's Naga War', *Journal of Peace Research*, vol. 40, no. 3, pp. 321–38.

Black, R, (1998) *Refugees, Environment and Development*, 1998, London, Longman.

Bodmer, J. et al. (1993) *Human Genome Diversity* (HGD) Committee Summary Document, Report of the International Planning Workshop held in Porto Conte, Sardinia (Italy) 9–12 September 1993.

Brown, M. E. (ed.) (1996) *The International Dimensions of Internal Conflict*, Cambridge MA, MIT Press.

Brown, M. E. (2001) 'Ethnic and internal conflicts: cause and implications', Chapter 13 in Crocker, Hampson and Aall (eds) (2001a).

Crocker, C. (2001) 'Intervention', Chapter 14 in Crocker, Hampson and Aall (eds) (2001a).

Crocker, C., Hampson, F.O. and Aall, P. (eds) (2001a), *Turbulent Peace*, US Institute of Peace, Washington DC.

Eriksson, J. (1996) *The International Response to Conflict and Genocide: Lessons from the Rwanda Experience – Synthesis Report*, Copenhagen, Steering Committee of the Joint Evaluation of Emergency Assistance to Rwanda.

Esman, M. J. (1994) *Ethnic Politics*, Ithaca, Cornell University Press.

Fearon, J. and Laitin, D. (2003) 'Ethnicity, insurgency and civil war', *American Political Science Review*, vol. 97, no. 1, pp. 75–9.

Figueiredo, R. de and Weingast, B. (1999) 'The rationality of fear', Chapter 8 in Walter, B. and Snyder, J., *Civil Wars, Insecurity and Intervention*, New York, Columbia University Press.

Gurr, T. (2001) 'Minorities and nationalities', Chapter 11 in Crocker, Hampson and Aall (eds) (2001a).

Holsti, K. J. (1997) 'Political source of humanitarian emergencies', *Research for Action* 36, Helsinki, WIDER.

Horowitz, D. L. (1985) *Ethnic Groups in Conflict*, Berkeley, University of California Press.

Howard, M. (2001) 'The causes of war', Chapter 2 in Crocker, Hampson and Aall (eds) (2001a).

Human Rights Watch (1999) *Leave None to Tell the Story: Genocide in Rwanda*, New York, Human Rights Watch, http://www.hrw.org/reports/1999/rwanda/ (accessed 2004).

Huntington, S. P. (1993) 'The clash of civilizations?' *Foreign Affairs*, vol. 72, no. 3, pp. 22–49.

Levy, J. S. (2001) 'Theories of interstate and intrastate war: a levels-of-analysis approach', Chapter 1 in Crocker, Hampson and Aall (eds) (2001a).

Minorities at Risk Programme (2000) 'Data: assessment for Hutus in Rwanda', College Park, Maryland, University of Maryland Minorities at Risk programme, http://www.cidcm.umd.edu/inscr/mar/assessment.asp?groupId=51702 (accessed November 2004).

Nafziger, E. W. and Auvinen, J. (2002), 'Economic development, inequality, war and state violence', *World Development* vol. 30, pp. 153–63.

Project on Environmental Scarcities, State Capacity, and Civil Violence (undated) 'Key findings', www.library.utoronto.ca/pcs/state/keyfind.htm (accessed November 2004).

Sadowski, Y. (1998) 'Ethnic conflict', *Foreign Policy*, issue 111, summer 1998, pp. 13–23.

Sambanis, N. (2001) 'Do ethnic and non-ethnic civil wars have the same causes?', *Journal of Conflict Resolution*, vol. 45, no. 3, pp. 259–82.

Sambanis, N. (2002) 'A review of recent advances and future directions in the quantitative literature on civil war', *Defence and Peace Economics*, vol. 13, no. 3, pp. 215–43.

Sellström, T. and Wohlgemuth, L. (1996) *The International Response to Conflict and Genocide: Lessons from the Rwanda Experience, Study 1 – Historical Perspective: Some Explanatory Factors*, Copenhagen, Steering Committee of the Joint Evaluation of Emergency Assistance to Rwanda.

Snyder, J. (1993) 'Nationalism and the crisis of the post-Soviet state', pp. 79–101 in Brown, M. B. (ed.) *Ethnic Conflict and International Security*, Princeton, Princeton University Press.

Uvin, P. (1998) *Aiding Violence: The Development Enterprise in Rwanda*, West Hartford CT, Kumarian Press.

Walter, B. (1999) 'Conclusion' in Walter, B. and Snyder, J. (eds) *Civil Wars, Insecurity and Intervention*, New York, Columbia University Press.

Woodward, D. (1997) *The IMF, the World Bank and Economic Policy in Rwanda: Economic, Social and Political Implications*, Oxford, Oxfam.

Wurm, S. A. (2001) *Atlas of the World's Languages in Danger of Disappearing*, Paris, UNESCO.

5 External roots of internal war

Joseph Hanlon

5.1 Introduction

Civil wars take place within one country but they do not take place in isolation. We have already looked at external intervention in the wars themselves, but a more detailed look at the roots of the war shows that most explanations have external links. The most extreme were those cases where another country actually fomented civil war; this has been done both by the big powers in the Cold War and by neighbouring countries for their own ends. More common, however, is that causal factors have both internal and external components. Because of globalisation and the importance of trade, any economic factor will have both these components. Aid and the international community play a big role in poor countries, sometimes supporting one group in preference to another and exacerbating tensions, and sometimes promoting a more equitable development that reduces the chances of civil war. In this chapter, we look at five key external aspects: direct foreign intervention, the effects of globalisation, arms and oil, and structural adjustment.

Global Africa.

After a detailed study of civil wars, Errol Handerson and J. David Singer (2000) wrote:

> Although we believe that the root of insurgency is found in the post-colonial states themselves, nevertheless, one is reminded that the fragility of these states is in large measure one of the lingering byproducts of their former colonial domination. Moreover, as was so often the case, the superpowers and their major and minor power allies, who were motivated by imperial reminiscences and/or Cold War exigencies, often threw gasoline on the smoldering conflicts in the post-colonial states.

Intervention implications

Remember that colonialism distorted most things and these distortions continue and can be important roots of the civil war. Ethnic groups and 'traditional' leaders prioritised by the colonial power will inevitably try to maintain that power, and interveners may have to work with marginalised groups to change power relations. Economic distortions by the colonial authorities, which tended to favour particular parts of the country, will need to be redressed; simply allowing the 'free market' to work will continue to favour the better-off areas and normally unacceptable interventions in the market may be required.

We start this chapter with Box 5.1, which suggests that foreign intervention may also prevent civil wars.

Box 5.1   Why were former French colonies in Africa more peaceful?

Up to 1990, civil war rates for former French colonies were much lower than those for other sub-Saharan African countries (Fearon and Laitin, 2003). Of the 16 former French colonies, only two had civil wars – Togo, which had minor wars in 1986 and 1991, and Chad, which has been involved in various serious civil wars since 1965, many of them Cold War related.

This changed suddenly with three civil wars in 1990 – in Niger (which continued up to 1997), Senegal (a Casamance separatist movement), and Mali (minor wars in 1990 and 1994). Congo-Brazzaville has been involved in civil war since 1993. Two civil wars started in 2002, in the Central Africa Republic and Côte d'Ivoire (which involved French troops).

What kept the peace until the 1990s and what changed? Three reasons are put forward. First is French military support for governments, including dictators. France put down a very clear marker by sending troops to help the government of Gabon suppress a coup attempt in 1964. By the late 1980s, there was a shift toward democracy, which is arguably linked in many countries to an increase in violence. James Fearon and David Laitin (2003) comment :

> In the late 1980s, Mitterand's government departed from long-standing French foreign policy by supporting, to a limited extent, democratization in some of its former sub-Saharan colonies. This involved encouraging 'national conferences,' elections, and some political opposition, which all suggested that the prior policy of immediate military support for French-speaking dictators might have changed.

Jean-Paul Azam (2001) puts great stress on the role of the French-backed common currency in many of the former colonies, the CFA franc, and the policy of much higher public sector wages in the CFA zone compared with other African countries. He argues:

> [H]igh public sector wages, purchased at the cost of a smaller number of public agents relative to the population, are strongly associated with a more peaceful society. In other words, private redistribution of state money down through the ethnic channel seems more important than the anonymous provision of public goods by the state for maintaining the political risk at a low level.

He also notes:

> [T]he CFA zone member countries are regarded in most ratings as less corrupt than other African countries, and this may be another channel by which high public sector wages reduce the risk of political violence. When the high incomes of elite members are levied anonymously, through the tax system, this creates less inter-ethnic resentment than petty corruption, which entails extortion by identifiable persons.

Azam further argues that the devaluation of the CFA franc in January 1994, which 'reduced the relative incomes of civil servants and formal sector employees', weakened the states and triggered the coup in Niger and the war in Congo-Brazzaville.

5.2 International actors – colonial wars, proxy wars and neighbours

By definition, civil wars occur inside one state, but sometimes their origin is external. Two sets of internal wars clearly have an international base – colonial independence wars and Cold-War proxy wars. In Africa and Asia many of the wars of the 1950s, 1960s and 1970s were for independence from colonial masters. This phase really only ended in 1990 with the independence of Namibia.

Colonial history still has a strong impact, and some wars still have a colonial component. For example, the 1998 civil war in Guinea-Bissau was partly a result of ongoing Portuguese–French rivalry. Tiny Guinea-Bissau was a

Portuguese colony and neighbouring Senegal was a French colony; Guinea-Bissau joined the French-dominated CFA franc zone (see Box 5.1) and the government tried to build closer links with Senegal, while a faction linked to the military, with covert Portuguese support, backed the Casamance separatist movement in Senegal. After an attempted military coup, neighbouring Senegal and Guinea-Conakry both sent in troops to support the government. The 1998–99 war left several thousand dead and large areas of the capital city of Bissau in ruins.

The Cold War was a period of choosing sides, with Moscow and Washington acquiring allies and backing them in exchange for unquestioning support in international fora such as the United Nations. The US, in particular, backed a series of dictators such as Suharto in Indonesia, Mobutu in Zaire (now Democratic Republic of the Congo) and Marcos in the Philippines. The effect was to stop and often put into reverse the process of state building. Patronage systems developed in which particular groups gained by supporting the dictator and others were discriminated against. Dictators blocked the development of civil society and state institutions which could mediate the demands and grievances of groups in society who found non-violent avenues cut off. As opposition figures, and often anyone who questioned, were suppressed, murdered or forced into exile, systems of transition and peaceful government change were destroyed and change could only come about through violence. Cosseted dictators and their allied elites became increasingly corrupt as they were allowed to divert domestic resources and aid for personal use and foreign bank accounts. Ministries, local government, and services such as health and education atrophied and collapsed; instead of state building there was state demolition. To be sure, some Western-backed autocracies such as South Korea prospered and avoided war. But at the other end of the spectrum were former colonial states such as Sierra Leone and Liberia; there, the West had backed dictators because they opposed Muammar Khaddafi in Libya, and young opponents who wanted to oppose corruption and plunder saw no alternative but violence. It is often claimed that the end of the Cold War brought a set of new wars because of the fall of these dictators, but as Figure 1.1 showed, the number of wars had been increasing steadily as these dictators began to lose control even before the formal end of the Cold War.

During the Cold War the Soviet Union backed some of the liberation movements, notably in Mozambique and Angola, and some opposition movements. The US backed military dictators in many countries, supported military coups in Brazil, Chile and elsewhere, and tended through NATO to back the colonial powers. One of the 'rules' that developed in the Cold War was that national sovereignty could not be violated. Since a country with a government backed by the other side could not be invaded directly, this led to a series of wars in which one side in the Cold War would create or back an insurgent movement which would try to overthrow the government of a country which was backed by the other side. These became known as 'proxy wars'. A proxy is a substitute or something in place of something else; in this case, since the US and Soviet Union did not want a third world war, they fought a series of small proxy wars in developing countries. The wars may have been small and far away, but millions of people died. Box 5.2 looks at southern Africa, one of the worst areas of East–West proxy wars. But they took place elsewhere, too. In Nicaragua, the Sandinistas overthrew a dictator backed by the US and turned to the Soviet Union for aid; the US responded by creating, arming and funding an opposition movement called the Contras between 1981 and 1990; the number dead is estimated at between 10,000 and 50,000.

Zaire, now Democratic Republic of the Congo, is perhaps the most extreme example of the toxic mix of colonial heritage and Cold War intervention. The century of Belgian colonialism had been one of the most brutal in Africa and the country which came to independence in 1960 was impoverished and lacking infrastructure and institutions. But it was rich in minerals. A left-leaning Prime Minister, Patrice Lumumba, was assassinated and replaced in 1965 by the US-backed General Joseph Mobutu. Over the next 25 years, Mobutu backed the West, gave it access to strategic minerals, and allowed Zaire to be used as a rear base for US support for the UNITA opposition in neighbouring Angola (see Box 5.2). In exchange, Mobutu was allowed to become one of the world's most corrupt dictators. In 1978 the IMF appointed Irwin Blumenthal to a key post in the central bank of Zaire. He resigned in less than a year, writing a memo which said that 'the corruptive system in Zaire with all its wicked manifestations' is so serious that there is 'no (repeat no) prospect for Zaire's creditors to get their money back'. When Blumenthal wrote his report, Zaire's debt was $4.6 billion. Despite knowing the money would not be repaid, the IMF, World Bank and Western governments poured in another $8 billion in loans (Hanlon, 2005). Mobutu suppressed or bribed any opposition and shipped money abroad while the state itself was hollowed out. Civil war broke out in 1992 and continued for more than a decade; Mobutu was overthrown and died in 1998. At least three million people died and all of the neighbouring states were drawn into the fighting.

Intervention implications

In states such as Democratic Republic of the Congo (Zaire), Somalia or Malawi where long-term Cold War support of dictators allowed them to destroy the local political class, interveners need to accept that it will take years and even a decade or more to build new institutions. Civil society is normally weak, fractured and often led by exiles with no local base. Almost inevitably, the only political 'leaders' will be people who were ministers or officials who served the old dictator (even if they fell out with him later) and thus have no experience of democratic or inclusive politics. Thus interveners will need to nurture nascent civil and political society, with a particular stress on groups which were marginalised during the Cold War period. There should be constant stress on more openness and inclusiveness. Support for expanded media, such as local radio stations, can also be important.

Box 5.2 Colonial and proxy wars in southern Africa

Southern Africa became a Cold War battlefield with five different wars and various levels of proxy war. With some support from then socialist countries, Angola and Mozambique won independence wars against NATO-member Portugal in 1974. A struggle was building in South Africa against the minority white apartheid government, and there were ongoing independence wars in South-African-controlled Namibia and white-minority-ruled Zimbabwe. Mozambique and Angola announced they were following socialist policies, and looking for aid from the Soviet Union and Cuba. The US saw all five liberation movements as 'communist' and backed white South Africa as a bastion against communism. With US support South Africa intervened first in Angola where they backed the UNITA opposition. The white minority government in Zimbabwe (then Rhodesia) created an entirely new opposition movement for Mozambique, eventually named Renamo, and when the liberation movements won in Zimbabwe, South Africa took over the support and operation of Renamo. The wars in Angola, Mozambique, Namibia and South Africa continued until the end of the Cold War, when there were quickly organised peace agreements in all four countries. In all four, movements or parties which had been opposed by the US won the election. In three there was peace, but in the fourth, Angola, the war started again (see Box 1.2). In Chapter 1 we noted that more than one million people died in the war in Mozambique; a similar number died in Angola.

In Mozambique, Zimbabwe, South Africa, Angola and Namibia, it was local people doing the fighting in what we are describing as a 'civil war'. But external roots can be seen as dominant, at least in Mozambique and Angola, where in each the first war was anti-colonial and the second was a proxy war, with the socialist bloc supporting the government and the US, directly and indirectly, supporting the opposition. South African occupation of Namibia was external and colonial, but South Africa was licensed to hold on to Namibia as part of the Cold War.

The first Zimbabwe war was effectively anti-colonial, as the majority fought against British settlers who had retained control. A second struggle in Zimbabwe, not called a war in some lists, can be interpreted as having been between the two liberation movements (ZANU and ZAPU), or between two ethnic groups (Shona and Ndebele), or as northern Zimbabwe versus south-western Zimbabwe. An important aspect of the fighting was the way in which neighbouring white South Africa provoked the violence in order to destabilise the new and still weak government in Zimbabwe (Hanlon, 1986). South Africa itself had mainly an internal war against minority rule, but external factors were important, again with the socialist bloc supporting the liberation movements and Britain and the US giving at least political support to the white minority government.

> The discussion becomes more confused in Angola, which moved on to a third war when UNITA refused to accept its defeat in the 1992 election and resumed fighting. Although some roots of this third war go back to the anti-colonial and proxy wars, the motivation for the new war was more internal.

Not all foreign involvement was linked to the Cold War; many examples involve neighbours and nearby states. In the Sierra Leone war, neighbouring Liberia played a key role in provoking the war, neighbouring Guinea helped to end it, and five other states in the region were involved in different ways. All of the neighbouring states have been involved in the 'civil' war in the Democratic Republic of the Congo. India has played a role in wars in Nepal and Sri Lanka.

Support for identity groups is also important. A study of 179 minority groups showed that 106, more than half, had received political, material and military support from foreign states in the 1990–98 period. The USA accounted for 18 per cent of all interventions, but many others involved neighbours (Khosla, 1999). In the former Yugoslavia, up to 4000 Muslims from over two dozen Islamic countries were reported to be fighting in Bosnia in 1993 (Huntington, 1993). This has had a direct link to the Cold War, because Islamic fighters trained by the United States to fight the proxy war in Afghanistan then moved on to fight in civil wars in several countries, including Algeria, Bosnia, Chechnya and Indonesia.

Intervention implications

Consider actors outside the country who have an ongoing influence in the war, and what needs to be done to neutralise negative influences and push them to support peacebuilding. Look at the way the actions of some actors may have been influenced by outside support in the past, to help explain their motivations.

5.3   Globalisation

The 'Humpty-Dumpty' prize probably goes to the term 'globalisation', which has as many definitions as authors who write about it. Here, globalisation is used in the most general way to be the increasing volume and speed of international flows of capital, goods, people and information in the latter half of the twentieth century which has led to an increasingly integrated global economy. This has had an inevitable impact on civil wars because individual countries and their wars are less cut off from the rest of the world. Guerrilla movements, even in remote areas, have websites and use satellite telephones to communicate with international radio stations, even if communication on the ground is still by individual messenger. Opposition movements also have better access to arms and money, and are better able to make their case internationally. Global culture also has an impact, from religious fundamentalism to Hollywood movies to radio and the internet; people are less isolated and understand that there are alternatives to the way they live and to what they are being told. One example is young fighters in Sierra Leone, who were shown videos of the Rambo film *First Blood* in the bush as part of their indoctrination (Richards, 1998). Arguably, this aspect of globalisation probably makes it easier to start and sustain a rebellion.

Another aspect of globalisation has been the increase in intervention, both in support of one side in a civil war, and by the international community trying to end the war and build peace. The very large number of international interveners, from small NGOs to United Nations agencies, is itself a mark of globalisation.

Since most civil wars take place in new and poor countries, a central question must be how they have been affected by globalisation. Although some people and countries have gained substantially, perhaps the most important impact has been the sharply increasing wealth gaps, both between countries and within countries. Growth in the latter part of the twentieth century seems to have been greater for the most wealthy. Timmer and Timmer (2004) argue that 'the historical record suggests that – perhaps with the exception of the United States in recent decades – even reasonably wide-spread rapid growth will generate political crises if the very wealthy are allowed to visibly increase their lead too much.' In the face of growing conspicuous consumption, by other countries or elites within countries, the poor sometimes become even more discontented; it is a discontent on which leaders can build.

During the 1980s and 1990s poor countries were faced with two squeezes – falling commodity prices and the debt crisis. In the 1980s, average non-energy commodity prices fell by 5.5 per cent per year; in the 1990s the decline was 2.4 per cent a year. In 1979 there was an international debt crisis; new lending stopped and interest rates jumped dramatically. Between 1984 and 1989 the poor South gave the rich North more than $100 billion – and this is net flow, taking into account aid and new loans (Hanlon, 2002). As Figure 1.1 showed, the 1980s period of worst economic squeeze was exactly the period of the greatest increase in civil wars.

The economic squeeze seems to have a series of effects. Most directly, it reduces the earnings of commodity producers and forces cuts in government spending on services such as health and education, both of which have a direct impact on poorer people. At the same time, elite groups attempt to insulate themselves from the impact of the squeeze, so the poor and disadvantaged groups suffer most. During the Cold War in the mid 1980s, elites frequently had international protection and could suppress growing discontent. Civil war was often the result.

International politics of the second half of the twentieth century has often exacerbated the problem of weak states and state building. The Cold War and then the economic adjustment and liberalisation policies of the international financial institutions both served to weaken states and retard state building.

5.3.1 Elites, the 20:30:50 world and policing the excluded

More than 30 years ago, Johan Galtung (1971) argued that 'the world consists of centre and periphery nations; and each nation, in turn, has its centre and periphery.' Further, relations between the centre and peripheral countries are characterised by an alliance between elites or centres within the two countries, carried out at the expense of the periphery within the peripheral country. This leads directly to the concept of a 'comprador elite', a term which derives from a Portuguese term for those Chinese who served foreign companies in the nineteenth century (Sampson, 2002). It is now used to refer to the Galtung view of centres in poor countries – politicians and a national business class whose position depends on their connection to foreign corporations and aid agencies of developed nations, and who are said to encourage local development that benefits other nations rather than their own.

Since Galtung's paper, this phenomenon has become much clearer, as poorer country elites become increasingly dependent on, and responsive to the demands of, industrialised country elites, and thus respond less and less to their own people. In the Cold War, aid and military support came from East or West and was entirely dependent on the global position that the country's government took. In the post-Cold-War era, aid and debt relief are dependent on having IMF and World Bank structural adjustment programmes which are not subject to local democratic controls. In both cases, widespread corruption and domestic opposition was ignored, so long as elites did what officials in Washington or Moscow demanded. For example, there was often an implicit deal that if elites agreed to privatisation of state assets, a key adjustment demand, then the international financial institutions would look away while those same elites bought the companies at give-away prices and benefited from the privatisation. Thus elites found that state building could be put aside; they were free to turn their attention to personal wealth building.

Ankie Hoogvelt (2001, 2005) has refined the argument, and describes the global architecture as three circles which cut across national and regional boundaries. In the core are the elites of all countries, about 20 per cent of the world population who she calls 'bankable', meaning they have relatively stable incomes and are fully integrated in the world economy. The next 30 per cent are workers and their families who labour in insecure forms of employment and are most affected by global competition and pressure to reduce costs. The remaining 50 per cent of the population are already excluded from the global system, and have no role as either producers or consumers. In the rich or 'core' countries, the percentages are perhaps 40 per cent bankable and 30 per cent in each of the other two groups, while in poor or 'peripheral' countries there is a 10 per cent elite, 20 per cent insecure workers, and 70 per cent excluded. The 10 per cent elite in 'peripheral countries' is the centre-in-the-periphery identified by Galtung, or the comprador elite in the poor countries.

Hoogvelt argues that in the final part of the twentieth century, globalisation has actually changed the nature of capitalism. It has always been assumed, by Marxists and pro-globalisation neoliberals alike, that capitalism would continue expanding to take in more and more people as consumers and producers. Hoogvelt argues that this expansion has stopped, and instead capitalism is now deepening, providing more (particularly information-based) products for the rich minority. For example, the percentage of foreign investment that goes to non-oil peripheral countries is falling as the transnational corporations write off the periphery. This means that the excluded 50 per cent appears set to remain excluded. The income gains from globalisation in all countries have gone to the bankable centre group; as Galtung predicted, income inequalities are increasing.

There is an active response from at least some of the 70 per cent excluded majority in the poor states, Hoogvelt notes. Some attempt to migrate to richer countries. Others become violent, fight other groups or their own elites, or simply loot; this has become a major source of civil wars and international terrorism. The result, she argues, is that the rich countries have realised the need to reinforce the state system and uphold the concept of sovereignty – so that governments in peripheral countries become responsible for controlling their own excluded, curbing violence and migration. In the post-Cold-War world, however, powerful states now assert the right to intervene when comprador elites fail to carry out their tasks. This is particularly important for countries with resources the core needs, notably oil.

The whole process, Hoogvelt concludes, is simply 'the management of exclusion'. In order to maintain this system, the core countries are propping up the elites of peripheral countries, politically and militarily, to police their own countries. Aid is used to keep the support of those elites, but extensive conditions on that aid keeps the elites in line. But, notes Hoogvelt, some of these conditions have had perverse outcomes. Privatisation has fuelled conflicts between elites and increased the potential for criminal activities, while cutting the size of the state sector has undercut the patronage power base of many elites and decreased the opportunities to keep all groups within the system, as we saw in Box 5.1, which actually increases violent conflict. This, in turn, will lead to increasingly military responses and repression, and a return to the Cold-War-style support of dictators, which we have already seen fuels civil wars.

5.3.2 Adjustment

There was a widespread agreement that some shift was needed away from the very heavy presence of the state in the economy that characterised the development model of the 1960s and 1970s. In 1978, the Marxist president of Mozambique, Samora Machel, commented that 'Our state cannot waste its energies selling needles and razor blades', and the government began to privatise small state-owned businesses (Hanlon, 1984, p. 77). In the early 1980s a new era of conservative economics known as neoliberalism came to dominate international thinking. It went much farther than the earlier consensus view, involving much more bias toward the private sector and a sharp reduction in the role of the state as developer, promoter and regulator,

International Monetary Fund Headquarters, Washington, DC.

and was to prove highly controversial and contested. With the end of the Cold War and the end of the most recent socialist experiment, neoliberalism was triumphant, at least as far as the World Bank and International Monetary Fund (IMF) could impose it on developing countries. One of the key difficulties for the new countries was that the older industrialised countries had already had their state-led development and it was at least possible to argue that the state apparatus had become too large and too interventionist. Most developing countries, however, had still not passed through this era, and they were being told by Washington-based officials that they had to cut back on states which had not yet been built. Cuts in state services such as health and education undermined the legitimacy of the new state; IMF-imposed wage cuts forced civil servants to be corrupt to survive, which further undermined the legitimacy of the state.

Adjustment policies do not cause wars, but as we saw in Box 4.3 they can be an important factor. Researchers have pointed to a number of examples. Nafziger, Stewart and Väyrynen (2000, p. 18) say that IMF 'austerity budgets were a major element in the disintegration of the former Yugoslavia.' K. J. Holsti (1997) notes, 'the correlation between the successes of the Sendero Luminoso in Peru and the imposition of severe economic retrenchment policies in that Andean country.' Thomas Homer-Dixon (1994) states that under pressure from international financial agencies, Philippines dictator Ferdinand Marcos was forced 'to adopt draconian stabilization and structural adjustment policies. These caused an economic crisis in the first half of the 1980s, which boosted agricultural unemployment' and reduced alternative employment opportunities. This forced a migration into the uplands which was already under heavy environmental pressure, and encouraged people to join the growing communist revolution in the hills.

For Samuel Huntington (1993), IMF adjustment policies feed directly into the 'clash of civilizations' because, 'through the IMF and other international economic institutions, the West promotes its economic interests and imposes on other nations the economic policies it thinks appropriate.'

The image of the efficiency of the market and the leaner, meaner, smaller, less interventionist state could have some resonance in the industrialised countries (although it has proved less acceptable there too). But it cuts to the core of state building, which is not lean, mean or efficient, but rather, when done well, about promoting opportunity, trust and access. The international financial institutions are charged with creating international openness and efficiency, not equality and domestic accessibility. But economic conditions and even budget outlines imposed by these institutions mean that elected parliaments have no say about the most important aspects of government and development policy, which undermines the credibility of the entire democratic process, further undermining modern consent-led state building. Adjustment may create a state which is more willing to leave space for the market, but it also creates a state which is less able to respond to challenges which could lead to civil war.

So the twentieth century ended with many weak states further weakened by the Cold War and adjustment, and with leaderships and elites more concerned with personal advancement than state building. This corresponded to the growth in civil wars, as weak states and distanced elites could not respond to demands coming up within their countries. Pressure increased on people in some countries in what is sometimes called 'structural violence', as described in Box 5.3, and the result was violence and war.

Box 5.3   Ignoring global structural violence

The concept of 'structural violence' was developed by Johan Galtung (1969). He starts by arguing that 'if people are starving when this is objectively avoidable, then violence is committed, regardless of whether there is a clear subject-action-object relation.' There is no difference between people starving because they are under siege or people starving because of an unjust economic system; in both cases, they are the victims of violence. He distinguishes between 'personal' or 'direct' violence, in which there is an actor that commits the violence, and 'structural' or 'indirect' violence where there are no specific actors, but 'the violence is built into the structure and shows up as unequal power and consequently as unequal life chances.' And he notes that structural violence can lead to personal violence, for example in a rebellion against an oppressive government, if the actors decide that the cost of the personal violence would be less than the cost of structural violence. In particular, Galtung concludes, peace cannot simply be seen as the absence of direct violence; people who are the victims of structural violence are being violently killed, just as if they were shot, and may see a turn to personal violence as a way of reducing the total violence against them.

Civil wars involve personal violence. But the increase in the numbers of wars in the 1980s could be seen as a response to increased structural violence caused by Cold War and economic adjustment policies. Richard Cornwell (2002, p. 59), at the Institute for Security Studies (ISS), South Africa, writes that the issue is:

> ... structural violence at the international level, which consists in the deliberate maintenance of a global system based on fundamental and self-reinforcing inequity. We know that structural violence within countries and communities, even families, may lead eventually to actual, physical, violence, yet too many people persist in the belief that structural violence on a global scale will have no such consequences. In a 'globalising world' this is all the more unsafe an assumption, and we see a number of conflicts that, while ostensibly local, also have global linkages to essential 'external' actors. Systemic structural violence may not be a sufficient explanation for the incidence of conflict, but it seems, in its manifestation of the increasing polarization of the haves and have-nots and the marginalisation of ever larger portions of mankind to be a necessary component of any comprehensive explanation of most conflicts, including those in Africa.

> Those who seek to narrow the security debate to areas of traditional concern not only condemn their analysis to an ineffective shallowness, they also, sometimes unintentionally, provide an alibi for the wealthier, more influential countries, allowing them to ignore their role in perpetuating this systemic imbalance. This is a welcome escape for politicians unwilling to take the long view or to persuade their electorates that their present pain is a precondition for global peace, and that equity, and self-interest, will demand that the citizens of the wealthy countries limit their claim to the bulk of the world's resources.

5.4   Arms and oil

International trade can have significant and unexpected effects which make civil war more likely and then make it easier for the war to continue. In many ways the arms trade is the most obvious. Arms-producing countries refuse to impose any serious controls. During the Cold War both sides provided weapons to their clients, and the end of the Soviet Union threw huge arms stocks onto the market. Thus criminal gangs and opposition movements have no difficulty obtaining handguns, lightweight AK-47 machine guns, mines and even sophisticated weapons such as shoulder-launched Stinger missiles. The easy availability of weapons must have some impact on the decision making of a group which goes to war in response to structural violence. And easy access to arms and ammunition helps to keep the war going once it has started.

Ordinary commodities play a role as well, often in surprising ways. We have already pointed to the fall in commodity prices. A sharp fall in cocoa prices indirectly led to the civil war in Côte d'Ivoire (see Box 6.3). In 1989 the United States ended the 27-year-old International Coffee Agreement, which had kept prices paid to producer countries and farmers stable and artificially high. The US wanted lower coffee prices for consumers, but this triggered two civil wars. One of these was in Rwanda. Before the decision was taken, Colombian president Virgilio Barco warned then US President George Bush (the elder) that a failure to extend the agreement would reduce producer prices so much that it would push peasant farmers to switch from coffee to coca (*Independent*, London, 15 September 1989). Bush did not listen but the forecast proved correct; when peasants switched to coca, the response was an escalation of military action against the peasants and escalating civil war. A key point here is that the impact was indirect and unexpected; President Bush wanted lower coffee prices, not two civil wars.

Mineral-exporting countries seem to be especially at risk of war. A high dependence on primary commodity exports substantially increases the risk of civil war according to Collier and Hoeffler (2002), and when they descend into conflict, mineral-resource-abundant countries also tend to have longer conflicts than those without resource abundance (Fearon, 2001). With the exceptions of Botswana, Indonesia and Malaysia, most mineral-exporting countries had a poor growth record in the 1970–2000 period. A key issue seems to be that mineral-rich countries often have weaker institutions. In part, this may be because governing elites have treated mineral earnings as personal wealth which could also be used through patronage networks to reward loyal followers. Thus those elites felt no need for development, strong institutions or other methods of gaining popular support to stay in power. However, Tony Addison and Syed Mansoob Murshed (in the next chapter) argue that at independence the mineral-rich countries had weaker institutions – both political and economic – within which to contain conflict and prevent it turning violent. Colonies where the climate and resource endowment suited settler agriculture and related manufacturing and services had better institutions at independence than those territories whose climate and conditions deterred settlement, and which were colonised primarily for their minerals and port facilities – both enclave activities (Acemoglu, Johnson and Robinson, 2001). Mines and related transport infrastructure need few public goods: Kenya and Zimbabwe were diversified settler economies whereas Sierra Leone provided diamond revenues and a naval base, but not much else.

There are four different reasons for minerals to be linked quite directly to civil war:

- Dictators have used the revenues from mineral exports to keep themselves in power and to build up their military. During the Cold War period, support for dictators was partly to ensure access to minerals and this has continued, particularly for oil.

- Minerals have been a source of grievance, as the poorest people or people in particular areas want a larger share of the earnings.

- Easily lootable or transportable minerals such as diamonds have been an important income for rebel movements, allowing them to buy arms and other goods needed by their fighters – and in some cases prolonging the war as some leaders began to profit.

- Easily obstructable mineral transport systems, such as oil pipelines, are hard to protect and can be cut by rebel groups.

The end of the Cold War cut off one supply of revenue, and many ruling elites had neither the legitimacy created by a popular mandate nor the political support generated by rising living standards as enjoyed by authoritarian leaderships in much of South-east and East Asia. Angola provides a classic example. After the end of the Cold War, oil and diamonds paid for the war to continue. Oil funded the government war machine, diamonds paid for the opposition UNITA's fighting ability, and both sides siphoned off a substantial percentage as corrupt income.

Oil is a particular issue. More than one third of the wars on the 2002 Uppsala University list are in oil-producing or oil-pipeline countries. Demands for a higher share of oil revenues have fuelled separatist movements, for example in Aceh in Indonesia, Cabinda in Angola, and Biafra in Nigeria. Concern about controlling oil supplies in the early twenty-first century seemed to suggest a return to Cold War style struggles and support for dictators. In Sudan, for example, China was backing the government while the United States had thrown its political weight behind rebel movements in oil-producing areas. Uzbekistan had a very poor human rights record and economic growth and living standards were among the lowest in the former Soviet Union, yet it continued to have US political support, probably because it was an important oil producer and willing to support the US in its 'war on terrorism'. Concern was growing that as oil supplies begin to decline and demand continues to rise, major powers may intervene militarily to secure their oil supplies. At the very least they may be more willing to back the comprador elites discussed earlier in this chapter.

Oil pipeline construction, Azerbaijan.

Several international NGOs argued that transnational corporations were actually fuelling the Angola war and others by buying the diamonds and oil without asking questions. This led the main diamond buyers, de Beers, to agree eventually to a diamond certification system, known as the Kimberley process, which would make it harder for rebel groups such as those in Sierra Leone, Angola and the Democratic Republic of the Congo to sell what were called 'conflict diamonds'.

Meanwhile, pressure is growing on international oil companies to make public the amounts of money being paid to poor countries for oil, so that patronage payments and money put into foreign banks can no longer be hidden so easily. Peter Eigen (2004), Chairman of Transparency International, sees externally fuelled corruption as a particularly severe problem in oil-rich countries:

> As the Transparency International Corruption Perceptions Index shows, oil-rich Angola, Azerbaijan, Chad, Ecuador, Indonesia, Iran, Iraq, Kazakhstan, Libya, Nigeria, Russia, Sudan, Venezuela and Yemen all have extremely low scores [indicating rampant corruption]. In these countries, the oil sector is plagued by revenues vanishing into the pockets of western

oil executives, middlemen and local officials. ... Looking at the oil industry worldwide, Transparency International has been urging western governments to oblige their oil companies to publish what they pay in fees, royalties and other payments to host governments and state oil companies. Access to this vital information will minimise opportunities for hiding the payment of kickbacks to secure oil tenders, a practice that has blighted the oil industry in transition and postwar economies.

> **Intervention implications**
>
> Tighter control of arms sales by arms-producing countries
>
> Fairer trade and systems to prevent sudden falls in commodity prices
>
> Transnational corporations extracting resources such as oil should be required to publish payments to governments and other bodies. The main purpose of transparency is to reduce corruption and to allow citizens to see the flows of revenue from natural resources to see if they are well used. This could also reduce the risk of secessionist movement in oil-rich areas by making clear the actual revenues and their distribution, which would prevent exaggeration of possible gain by separatist leaders.

5.5   The greed versus grievance debate

As we have seen, studies of civil war had been mainly carried out by political scientists, anthropologists, international relations analysts, and environmentalists. In the mid 1990s, economists, particularly those linked to the World Bank, came to dominate the debate, using large databases and sophisticated analytical techniques to try to discover the underlying patterns of civil war. The result was their view that war, like other aspects of society, was driven mainly by greed and lust for wealth and power. This line fitted well with the views of many of the international relations realists and some of the ethnic primordialists. But to many other economists and development studies professionals it seemed totally opposite to what they were seeing.

Although it has been widely accepted that diamonds and drugs can fuel war, that people often grew rich from war, and that some leaders prolonged wars for personal gain, the question is whether this 'greed' was the driving force for civil wars or whether these 'lootable' resources were mainly being used to pay the costs of wars fuelled by grievance. This debate between economists is one of the most important ongoing debates on the roots of civil wars, which is discussed in more detail in Chapter 7. In this section, we look at the implications of this debate for international factors in civil wars.

On the greed side of the debate, Morris Miller (2000) states:

> Poverty is associated with societal stress and with sporadic and endemic societal violence, but stress does not lead to war or play a major role in

enabling the rise to power of war prone leaders and their associated elites unless other factors are at play. The causal factors conducive to war making are varied but all are characterised by tribal, religious, and ethnic rivalries that political leaders exploit to mobilise support for war, and/or the lust for money or hegemonic power of the political leadership.

The World Bank view is expressed by Paul Collier and Ankie Hoeffler (2002), who claim their research shows that land and income inequality have no effect on the risk of war. To them, the key is ease of recruitment. A World Bank team headed by Collier found that 'low and declining incomes, badly distributed, create a pool of impoverished and disaffected young men who can be cheaply recruited by "entrepreneurs of violence"' (Collier et al., 2003, p. 4).

The response comes from E. Wayne Nafziger and Juha Auvinen (2002) at WIDER, who ask: 'Can we really argue that the East Timorans, the Kashmir *mujahidin*, Chechnyans, Palestinians, the Hutu, Nuba and southern Sudanese, to name just a few, are motivated only by greed rather than grievance?' And a report from the Institute of Development Studies at Sussex said simply, 'poverty and inequality remain among the major sources of conflict' (Luckham et al., 2001). Critics go further and accuse the World Bank economists of being highly selective in the choice of countries and databases, and believe that many of their answers are actually built into their models as assumptions. Nafziger and Auvinen use a different database from the World Bank groups and conclude exactly the opposite of Collier and Hoeffler – that high-income inequality clearly does increase the risk of war.

The reaction was so forceful that the World Bank economists eventually partially retreated their position. In 1999 Paul Collier wrote:

> Discussion of civil conflict is dominated by the narrative of grievance. ... The evidence on the causes of conflict really does not support this interpretation. ... Greed seems more important than grievance.

> (Collier, 1999, p. 14)

In a 2003 report *Breaking the Conflict Trap*, Paul Collier and his team said:

> *So is the Root the Loot?* We have already argued against a greed-based interpretation of rebellion. Most entrepreneurs of violence have essentially political objectives, and presumably undertake criminal activities only as a grim necessity to raise finance. However, over time the daily tasks of running a criminal business may tend inadvertently to develop a momentum of their own. ... At this point, any political agenda has withered away.

> (Collier et al., 2003, p. 79)

This, in turn, gives rise to what he calls 'the conflict trap', where a rebellion has a momentum of its own.

This change in view may be smaller than it seems. Low income countries are more likely to have wars, and 'extremely unequally distributed income' makes wars last longer (Collier et al., 2003, p. 81). But to the economists, it is still greedy and corrupt leaders drawing in young men without a future who keep the war going, rather than the underlying grievances.

In the greed and grievance debate, greed is often ascribed to the insurgent side. But government corruption is another form of greed which seems to play a role in creating grievances: as resources are siphoned off by corrupt groups they are not available for other groups or for development or social services in general. This becomes more of an issue if resources dry up, for example because of declining aid or falling commodity prices. We have noted elsewhere that corruption was often supported when the superpowers backed dictators during the Cold War; the withdrawal of that support had already begun in the late 1980s and meant a fiercer competition for resources at the same time that the dictator had reduced military and police power to repress dissenting groups. This happened in the Democratic Republic of the Congo (then Zaire) and Indonesia, for example, where the international financial institutions had been pushed by the United States to support hugely corrupt governments in the 1970s and 1980s.

Another way of looking at the issue is that war might be caused by a government diverting attention from poor economic policies. S. Brock Blomberg and Gregory D. Hess (2002) noted that the probability of war 'for the United States tends to double when the economy has recently been in recession and the president is running for re-election.' They wondered if something similar might happen more generally, and they looked at 152 countries from 1950 to 1992, and discovered that 'the occurrence of a recession causes an increase in the probability of internal conflict starting in a given year to almost double.'

Intervention implications

Look North. What is striking about the greed and grievance proponents is that they agree on the need to target the industrialised countries as well as the civil war countries. Those stressing loot want changed drug policies including partial legislation, tighter banking regulations and corporate transparency. Those stressing grievance want changed economic policies with more aid and more open Northern markets to promote more trade.

5.6   Implications for weak states and state building

Each of these approaches to the causes of civil war interacts with the problems of weak states and state building. We have already noted that ethnic wars were not particularly common and that ethnic division could not be used to predict war. But combining increasing poverty, grievance, and group identity does seem to provide some explanation.

Susan Woodward (1999) attributes high levels of anxiety between Bosnian Serbs, Croats and Muslims at least partially to the 'budgetary austerities of macroeconomic stabilization, debt repayment and economic reform in the 1980s.' In particular, the middle classes whose standards of living had risen from 30 years under communism were squeezed and they became more suspicious of their neighbours and more susceptible to nationalist rhetoric.

'Economic malaise also implies that there are fewer avenues open for economic advancement and this encourages in some people particularistic attempts to seek ways of climbing up that are more tightly dependent on ethnic connections', comments Bardhan (1997). And some groups are differentially squeezed.

> [T]he budgetary axe often falls more heavily on social and economic programs for the poor, which include some of the already disadvantaged minorities (in Latin America, for example, the indigenous people are among the poorest of the poor)... .
>
> [T]he adjustment package may lead to a contraction of the non-traded sector which includes the informal services sector where many of the lower income groups earn their livelihood. ...
>
> [T]he reduced role of the government diminishes its ability to insure the losing groups against these hardships and external shocks and to assuage conflicts through redistributive transfers.

As the state is squeezed, corruption and rent-seeking increases and becomes more competitive. Political authority and access to resources may increasingly be monopolised by a single identity group to the exclusion of others. State collapse and cuts in state spending both reduce the ability of the state to provide jobs and social welfare. This forces people to provide for their own needs and to look for group solidarity, which increases the importance of the family, clan or ethnic group as a means of social security.

Adjustment and economic reform can also work against some of the interventions suggested in earlier sections. For example, in the primordial ethnic section the proposed intervention was 'granting regional and cultural autonomy and improving the distribution of development funds.' But faced with administrative and fiscal constraints, central governments are increasingly cutting regional development funds and trying to devolve fundraising and fiscal responsibility to local units. Pressure on central government for fiscal reform could sharply reduce the value of regional autonomy.

Similarly, we noted the importance of civil service jobs to provide salaries and urban posts for representatives from groups such as clans or villages and this has often been a way of keeping peace between groups. It may not be the most efficient way to run the state and parastatal companies, but done with some skill this sharing of the spoils of office can reduce group envy without compromising operating efficiency too much. Privatisation and civil service reform as pushed by the international financial institutions may lead to more efficiency, but it also means fewer jobs in general and fewer jobs in particular for already disadvantaged groups, which could fuel group tension.

Finally, Bardhan (1997) argues that adjustment and economic squeezes lead to poor migrants from rural areas moving into urban slums where they remain poor and marginalised and are easily mobilised by sectarian and criminal leaders. '[T]oo often some disadvantaged groups find that agitational politics and street violence are the only way they can make the government respond to their concerns about the unfairness of the pain that is inflicted on them.' When rival leaders belong to different communities, fights can take the form of communal riots.

Environmental issues also come into play with weak states and state building. Stephen Castles (2001) points to the important role of the state:

> [A] strong, efficient state can deal with environmental problems better than a weak and possibly corrupt state. The key problem then is perhaps not environmental change itself but the ability of different communities and countries to cope with it. This, in turn, is closely linked to problems of underdevelopment and North-South relationships. ... [I]f we really want to deal with the root causes of forced migration, the first step is to stop Northern practices that make things worse for poor countries of the South.

And the University of Toronto Project on Environmental Scarcities, State Capacity, and Civil Violence, which set out to find environmental causes of war, in fact found that the main effect of environmental scarcity is to weaken the state, through reduced revenue and more intense elite competition, and to increase the number of marginalised groups with grievances.

> A widening gap between rising demands and state performance, in turn, erodes state legitimacy, further aggravates conflicts among elites, and sharpens disputes between the elites and the masses. As the state weakens, the social balance can shift in favor of groups challenging state authority.

Finally, there are real questions about imposing the normal World Bank/IMF structural adjustment programmes on countries coming out of civil war. Chris Cramer (2004) points out that European reconstruction and Marshall Plan aid after the Second World War followed a very different pattern. He notes there was a diversity of policies rather than the one-size fits all of adjustment. But he also points out that the things all European countries did as part of their successful reconstruction are exactly the things which are opposed in present structural adjustment programmes for postwar countries: extensive economic involvement by governments, with high levels of government spending and a commitment to full employment. 'Private sector investment boomed too. However, there is good evidence suggesting that this private sector expansionism would not have happened without the stimulus of public spending.'

The World Bank remains very divided on policy for postwar countries. Its study, perhaps surprisingly, argues against imposing rapid changes on weak postwar states, and argues that in terms of democratisation, fiscal adjustment and stress on the market, past donor policy was wrong. The report explicitly challenges the World Bank's own Low Income Countries Under Stress (LICUS) approach (Collier et al., 2003).

Intervention implications

Three areas are highlighted in the World Bank report (Collier et al., 2003, pp. 87, 123, 154–56, 166, 177):

- Conventional adjustment is inappropriate for countries just coming out of war. 'The conventional sequence is that the top priority is to correct macroeconomic imbalances', but this is wrong. Instead, the stress should be on 'social policies – specifically policies for social inclusion', particularly widening access to education and health – even 'at the expense of a small deterioration in macroeconomic balances.' Similarly, the returns on early rehabilitation of destroyed infrastructure can be very high which means such spending can be higher than has been assumed in the past. Furthermore, a strategy of rehabilitation and social inclusion is a signal of intent to respect a peace agreement and move forward in an inclusive way. This promise of peace encourages investment and draws in rebels far more than macro-economic stability, the World Bank study argues.

- The market is not the only answer. 'Some policies may raise growth but enhance either grievances or opportunities for rebellion'. In particular the private sector is likely to move very slowly into formerly rebel-controlled areas, which means that public expenditure needs to be distributed more to those areas. Public expenditure needs to be seen as fair rather than having the highest return.

- Do not push institutional reform and democratisation. 'Even moderate change in political institutions is a risk factor in itself; political institutions must be stable', the report notes. 'Historically, to the extent that bilateral donors have included political institutions in their conditions, the focus has been on encouraging political change. Understandable as this is, it may be quite dangerous as well as being highly intrusive. An alternative approach is to attempt to reinforce existing democratic institutions, where they exist.'

5.7   Chapter summary

On the internal–external axis, previous explanations of war have been largely internal. But **colonialism** and the **Cold War** were two key external factors in setting off civil wars. Colonialism distorted both economic and social relations between groups of people, regions, etc., and these distortions remain and can become a root of war. Some civil wars were **independence wars**. In the Cold War, the socialist bloc led by the Soviet Union and the capitalist bloc led by the United States did not want a new world war, but they did fight a series of **proxy wars** in which one side backed the government of a developing country and the other side backed or created an opposition movement. Many of the civil wars of the 1980s were in fact Cold War proxy wars. Also in the Cold War both sides **backed dictators** who were allowed massive corruption and oppression, which had the effect of destroying the possibility of peaceful change and peaceful resolution of conflict, thus promoting civil war. Some of the civil wars of the 1990s were extensions of independence and proxy wars. In the contrasts of Figure 3.1, these can be seen as external and people under pressure, although big bad men can be seen to play a role, both as colonial dictators (notably in Portugal) and as increasingly misguided local opposition leaders. These events fit at various places on the historic–recent scale, ranging from colonial wars going back 30 years or more to recent involvement of dictators and rebel leaders.

Globalisation with its increasing flow of goods, money and information has also had an impact. In the 1980s and 1990s developing countries were squeezed by **falling commodity prices** and the **debt crisis**, which had a destabilising effect on many countries, increasing the chances for war. Some writers are now arguing that up to 50 per cent of the world's people are **excluded** from the new globalised world while small elites in the poor countries make their links with elites in rich countries rather than their own poor. We introduce the concept of **structural violence** – it is argued that where people are killed by hunger or economic crises, it is as much 'violence' as if they were shot. This creates conditions for violent reactions and becomes a root of war, while elites in poor countries are expected to **manage exclusion**. The poor and marginalised see the **structural adjustment** policies of the International Monetary Fund and World Bank as promoting the economic interests of the rich North. Here the big bad men can be seen as either in the international financial institutions, or as being leaders of local elites who do not promote the interests of their own people. On the historic–recent scale, these are recent events.

Another external component is **trade** which is essential to keep a war going. Sales of **arms** by industrialised countries are important in fuelling the war. **Oil** exports are a key source of government revenue, and Northern governments will back dictators to ensure an oil supply, possibly leading to situations similar to the Cold War. Exports of **diamonds and timber** have earned money for rebel movements. This is both external and internal, because it is international trade of the civil war country. All of these external factors compound the problems of weak states.

References

Acemoglu, D., Johnson, S. and Robinson, J. A. (2001) 'The colonial origins of comparative development: an empirical investigation', *American Economic Review*, vol. 91, pp. 1369–401.

Azam, J.-P. (2001), 'The redistributive state and conflicts in Africa', *Journal of Peace Research*, vol. 38, no. 4, pp. 429–44.

Bardhan, P. (1997) 'Method in the madness? a political-economy analysis of the ethnic conflicts in less developed countries' *World Development*, vol. 25, no. 9, pp. 1381–98.

Blomberg, S. B. and Hess, G. D. (2002) 'The temporal links between conflict and economic activity', *Journal of Conflict Resolution*, vol. 46, no. 1 pp. 74–90.

Castles, S. (2001) 'Environmental change and forced migration', lecture at Green College, Oxford, 6 December 2001, www.preparingforpeace.org (accessed 2004).

Collier, P. (1999) 'Doing well out of war', World Bank 10 April 1999, www.worldbank.org/research/conflict/papers/econagenda.htm (accessed 2004).

Collier, P. and Hoeffler, A. (2002) 'Greed and grievance in civil war', Working Paper 2002–01, Oxford, Centre for the Study of African Economies, www.csae.ox.ac.uk/workingpapers/wps-list.html (accessed November 2004).

Collier, P., Elliot, L., Hegre, H., Hoeffler, A., Reynal-Querol, M. and Sambanis, N., (2003), *Breaking the Conflict Trap*, Washington DC, World Bank and Oxford, Oxford University Press.

Cornwell, R. (2002) 'Conclusion – where to from here?' in Lind, J. and Struman, K. (eds) *Scarcity and Surfeit: The Ecology of Africa's Conflicts*, Pretoria, South Africa, Institute for Security Studies.

Cramer, C. (2004) 'The great post-conflict makeover fantasy', paper given at the UNU–WIDER conference 'Making peace work', Helsinki, 4–5 June 2004.

Eigen, P. (2004) 'Corruption robs countries of their potential, especially oil-rich countries', statement at the Foreign Press Association, London on 20 October 2004, www.transparency.org/cpi/2004/cpi2004.pe_statement_en.html (accessed November 2004).

Fearon, J. (2001). 'Why do some civil wars last so much longer than others?', http://hypatia.ss.uci.edu/gpacs/newpages/agenda.htm (accessed November 2004).

Fearon , J. and Laitin, D. (2003) 'Ethnicity, insurgency and civil war', *American Political Science Review*, vol. 97, no. 1, pp. 75–9.

Galtung, J. (1969) 'Violence, peace, and peace research', *Journal of Peace Research*, vol. 6, no. 3, pp. 167–91.

Galtung, J. (1971) 'A structural theory of imperialism', *Journal of Peace Research*, vol. 8, no. 2, pp. 81–117.

Handerson, E. and Singer, J. D. (2000) 'Civil war in the post-colonial world', *Journal of Peace Research*, vol. 37, no. 3, pp. 275–99.

Hanlon, J. (1984), *Mozambique: the Revolution Under Fire*, London, Zed.

Hanlon, J. (1986), *Beggar Your Neighbours: Apartheid Power in Southern Africa*, London, James Currey and Bloomington, Indiana University Press.

Hanlon, J, (2002) 'Defining "illegitimate debt" and asking when creditors should be liable for improper loans', Development Policy and Practice Working Paper 46, Milton Keynes, The Open University, Development Policy and Practice Department.

Hanlon, J. (2005) 'Defining "illegitimate debt": when should creditors be liable for improper loans?' in Jochnick, C. and Preston, F. (eds) *Sovereign Debt at the Crossroads*, Oxford, Oxford University Press.

Holsti, K. J. (1997) 'Political source of humanitarian emergencies', *Research for Action* 36, Helsinki, WIDER.

Homer-Dixon, T. (1994) 'Environmental scarcities and violent conflict', *International Security*, vol. 19, no. 1, pp. 5–40.

Hoogvelt, A. (2001) *Globalization and the Postcolonial World* (second edn), Basingstoke, Palgrave.

Hoogvelt, A. (2005) 'Globalisation and imperialism; wars and humanitarian intervention', in TU875 *War, intervention and development*, Readings, Milton Keynes, The Open University.

Huntington, S. P. (1993) 'The clash of civilizations?' *Foreign Affairs*, vol. 72, no. 3, pp. 22–49.

Khosla, D. (1999) 'Third World states as intervenors in ethnic conflict', *Third World Quarterly*, vol. 20, no. 6, pp. 1143–56.

Luckham, R. et al. (2001) 'Conflict and poverty in Sub-Saharan Africa', IDS Working Paper 128, Brighton, Institute of Development Studies.

Miller, M. (2000) 'Poverty as a cause of wars?', *Interdisciplinary Science Reviews*, vol. 25, no. 4, pp. 273–97.

Nafziger, E. W. and Auvinen, J. (2002), 'Economic development, inequality, war and state violence', *World Development* vol. 30, pp. 153–63.

Nafziger, E. W., Stewart, F. and Väyrynen, R. (2000) 'Case studies of complex humanitarian emergencies: an introduction', Chapter 1 in War, Hunger and Displacement: The Origins of Humanitarian Emergencies, vol. 2, Nafziger, Stewart and Väyrynen (eds) (2000).

Project on Environmental Scarcities, State Capacity, and Civil Violence (undated), 'Key findings', www.library.utoronto.ca/pcs/state/keyfind.htm (accessed November 2004).

Richards, P. (1998) *Fighting for the Rain Forest: War, Youth and Resources in Sierra Leone*, Oxford, James Currey.

Sampson, S. (2002) 'Beyond transition: rethinking elite configurations in the Balkans', pp. 297–316 in Hann, C. (ed.) *Postsocialism*, London, Routledge.

Timmer, C. P. and Timmer, A. S. (2004) 'Reflections on launching three books about poverty, inequality, and economic growth', *Wider Angle* 1/2004, Helsinki, WIDER.

Woodward, S. (1999) 'Bosnia and Herzegovina: how not to end civil war', Chapter 3 in Walter, B and Snyder, J. (eds) (1999) *Civil Wars, Insecurity & Intervention*, New York, Columbia University Press.

6 The social contract and violent conflict

Tony Addison and S. Mansoob Murshed

6.1 Introduction

In this chapter we shift the focus somewhat and look at what it is that holds societies together so that peace, rather than civil war, prevails. To answer this question Section 6.2 of this chapter sets out the concept of the social contract: that is, the set of rules, formal and informal, that guide the behaviour of citizens, entrepreneurs and governments and allow conflict to be expressed and resolved peacefully rather than violently. In this context, we underline the point previously made that civil wars – the breakdown of social contracts – are not purely internal affairs, but can have strong international dimensions, both in cause and effect. We then go on to discuss development failure as a cause of war, focusing on sub-Saharan Africa, where lack of economic progress seems to have undermined the construction of a working social contract. Section 6.4 addresses the issue of whether war can be explained by the erosion of the social contract as a result of high inequality across a society, in particular large differences in living standards between groups. Section 6.5 concludes by restating the importance of national action to build institutions that work to restore the social contract, and by emphasising that those institutions may show considerable variation across countries. In other words, there is no single template that can be imposed to obtain peace, certainly not by outsiders.

6.2 A framework for understanding violent conflict

6.2.1 The social contract

Violent conflict is a complex social phenomenon with many dimensions – ethical, humanitarian, economic and political – all of which are highly controversial and much debated. To introduce you to this debate, we need to provide a framework through which to interpret the particular experiences of different countries, specifically why it is that war occurs in some countries, while others manage to avoid it. Our framework acts as a guide and we hope will encourage you to explore the issues further and to deepen your own views.

Conflict is a fact of everyday life for families, workplaces, communities and nations. This may seem a rather obvious point, but it is an important one, and worth emphasising. Every day, people express, negotiate and settle their differences in a peaceful way, without threatening or resorting to violence.

No society has a complete consensus on family issues, religion, the economy or the right way to be governed – and indeed many societies are marked by radically different views, often stridently expressed. Yet in most societies, the majority of people do not feel compelled to use violence, either to make their point or to try and achieve change. They express their differences vocally, but peaceably, and work towards settling them in a peaceful manner, creating and using *institutions* which constitute the 'rules of the game'. The use of the terms 'institutions' and 'rules of the game' reflects a debate among economists over the past 20 years as part of 'the new institutional economics'. Some people may still reject the rules of the game and resort to violence but this is, thankfully, a minority (Murshed, 2002b).

When a society operates according to widely accepted rules of the game, we say that it has a viable *social contract*. The term 'social contract' is a very old one in political philosophy; it was famously expounded by the philosopher Jean-Jacques Rousseau in his book *The Social Contract*, published in 1762, but like all such concepts it has taken on different meanings over time. It is a 'contract' in the sense that citizens concede complete freedom of action for the benefits of living in a system governed by rules. In other words, they concede the right to be governed. Before that the philosopher John Locke also expounded on a contract between the ruler and his or her subjects, which the latter could rightfully repudiate in the event of mis-governance by the sovereign. The notion of a contract between the ruler and the ruled is not confined only to the European tradition; Khaled Abou El Fadl (2004, p. 11) notes that in Sunni Islam the rule of the Caliph, or leader, is based on a contract between the Caliph and the people, who give their allegiance and consent to the Caliph in exchange for him carrying out his responsibilities.

When the social contract is well-established, the rules of the game create expectations of how people will behave towards each other, thereby reducing the costs and increasing the benefits of their interaction. This interaction has three possible dimensions:

1   It may be *political*, such that the debate and resolution of issues of governance takes place within accepted parameters of behaviour – ranging from assemblies of elders in an African village to the parliament of a European nation.

2   It may be in the area of personal conduct guided by *moral values* which often stem from religious faith and cultural tradition, for instance interactions between men and women and between adults and children.

3   It may be in the *economic* sphere, in the exchange of goods and services in markets, and in the organisation of the production process, as well as in the rights, both property rights and rights of use, to productive assets, particularly natural capital (i.e. arable and grazing land, forests, water, and fisheries, etc.). Natural capital is one of the most important productive assets in low-income societies where most livelihoods are typically agrarian. Human capital is also important, and a developing society invests in human capital by education and better nutrition and adds to the productivity of human and natural capital by investment in physical capital.

This is not to imply that such a society has reached some kind of nirvana or that there are no grievances. A society that has a viable social contract may be marked by deep disputes, with people sometimes flouting laws and conventions to make their point, or even resorting to violence. Societies must therefore work hard to keep disagreements in peaceful channels, repairing and at times radically overhauling the rules of the game. And some people may be driven by greed for wealth and political power to try and overturn the rules or to manipulate them to their own ends. Societies with a viable social contract must therefore impose sanctions against those who step outside the rules of the game – either formal sanctions under the rule of law and/or informal sanctions such as ostracising rule breakers.

However, when the rules of the game are particularly well-established, complete strangers are reasonably certain that their agreement will be honoured. In other words, high levels of trust characterise societies with strong social contracts. When this is not the case, people become reluctant to interact in ways that expose them to *opportunistic behaviour* by the other party, where opportunistic behaviour is defined as taking advantage of others by unfair means. Opportunistic behaviour also reflects an inability to commit or honour commitments. If opportunistic behaviour is anticipated, it is difficult to trust one another and enter into implicit or explicit contracts.

Traditional societies are often characterised by disputes over natural capital and livestock since these are the foundation of livelihoods and group status. However, violence between groups is often conducted according to strict rules. This is summed up by a Somali historian writing of camel raiding in pre-colonial Somalia: 'although war was a constant feature ... acts of excessive brutality were seldom committed. Since no group liked to be on the end of such excessive violence, they took great care not to be the first to perpetuate it. They had every reason to believe that the example they set in victory would be the one followed by their opponents in the event of their own defeat' (quoted in Peterson, 2000, p.9). The same rules governed food raids (*gazu*) in pre-Islamic peninsular Arabia.

Relatedly, the social contract has a strong *temporal* dimension: the willingness of people to work today to maintain the social contract is strongly influenced by how they view the future. If the future starts to become very uncertain – and indeed so uncertain that we doubt the safety of our own lives – then we may see little worth in cooperating with others to keep the social contract in repair. This might be lending money to someone else for an investment that yields only a future return, or agreeing to abide by a rule that limits our present freedom of action in return for individual and social gain in the future. The value today of these future benefits falls as the future becomes more uncertain. People in countries that are sliding into violent conflict, or are passing through it, face high levels of uncertainty which can eventually destroy any working social contract – and which can make its 'postwar' resurrection extremely difficult.

In this chapter we will focus chiefly on the political and economic elements of the social contract, with examples of the moral element being discussed to a lesser extent. The moral element is of course important, but it is less relevant to the issues being discussed here.

6.2.2 The social contract in different societies

Our discussion so far has used the term 'society' in a very general way. In fact, the concept of the social contract can be applied to discuss anything from a *nation state* to a much smaller community or ethnic group. It is quite possible for a clan or other group to create a viable social contract among its members at local level, but to live in a nation state which has a weakly developed social contract, or indeed to live in a territory which is not a nation state in the modern sense. Although conflict between such groups may occur – for instance over natural capital – we are concerned here with violence on a large scale, and therefore with the breakdown of modern nation states, and any social contract that has underpinned their *legitimacy*: the state's right, in the eyes of the citizenry, to rule.

At this point it might be asked: is the social contract written down? If so, where? Does it exist in the form of a country's constitutional document? Is it the written body of law and precedent? Certainly, societies that have achieved a *modus operandi* in each of the three areas of the social contract will have taken steps to codify or 'formalise' it in these ways. But a country may have all the panoply of constitutions and laws but not yet have a viable social contract. This was true of many African countries at independence in the 1960s, and is true of many of today's 'postwar' countries. And a moment's reflection will yield to the reader many examples from their own society of rules of behaviour that are not in any way formalised, but which nevertheless constitute a strong element of how society organises itself. In summary, the social contract of a peaceful society may have elements that have never been formalised in any way.

Our use of the term 'contract' may also be questioned, since when we think of contracts in ordinary life, we think of people entering them willingly. In fact, however, it is the case that every society uses a degree of coercion, including the use of state violence, or the threat of it, to enforce the rules. The degree of coercion will depend on the politics of any particular country, but generally speaking there are three 'classes' of government.

First, there are mature democracies in the sense that they have passed through many elections, resulting in peaceful changes in government. Political parties are strong, there are strong formal checks and balances on the use of power, and a free and independent media as well as an active civil society acts to expose wrong-doing. Although mature democracies are generally high-income countries, Botswana, Costa Rica and India are three examples of long-standing democracies in the developing world. Normally, peace characterises social life but coercion is used when people break the rules, and force may periodically be used to contain outbreaks of violence. As noted in Box 1.2, at the beginning of the twenty-first century there were between three and five civil wars in India; the United Kingdom, Spain and other European democracies have also had recent civil wars. However, in well-functioning democracies the use of force derives its legitimacy from democratic control. The end of the Cold War has seen a sharp rise in nominal multi-party electoral democracies in the developing world. Civil society pressure contributed to this wave of democratisation and so did pressure from donors who made multi-party elections a condition of their aid, often in the context of collapsing states with disintegrating social contracts. We can label these processes 'exogenous democratisation'. Furthermore, it is in the first few years of democratisation that embryonic democracies are most vulnerable to collapse (Gates and Strand, 2004). By contrast, the demand for democracy can be internal or home-grown (endogenous), and if these demands follow economic development the process of democratisation may indeed be stable and long lasting (see Box 6.1). There have also been instances in history where a ruling elite has gradually extended the franchise to pre-empt a social revolution thereby largely preserving its wealth and a measure of influence (the history of nineteenth-century Britain, for example) and instances where the elite has acted too late, thereby losing both power and wealth (Russia in 1917 and Iran in 1979 are examples).

Box 6.1 South-east and East Asia: authoritarianism and economic development

From the 1960s to the late 1980s leaderships in Indonesia, Malaysia, Singapore, South Korea and Taiwan offered their populations the prospect of rising living standards in exchange for acquiescence to limited political freedom. These regimes ranged from South Korea's tight controls to the looser 'semi-authoritarianism' of Singapore (Ottaway, 2003, p. 4).

Irrespective of their personal motives, rulers justified their actions by citing the need to sacrifice political liberties to achieve, as early as possible, a higher living standard. This strategy is summed up by Park Geun-hye, daughter of the late Park Chung-hee, who took power in South Korea's 1961 military coup, and whose presidency (1961–79) became synonymous with the country's phenomenal economic growth: 'Industrialisation and democratisation could not be achieved at the same time. When my father became president, this country was in terrible poverty. The first thing he had to do was to save the country through industrialisation and from that followed democratisation' (Ward, 2002, p.16).

There is, in fact, no consensus among economists that democracy is harmful to growth. Studies show both positive and negative effects, and authoritarianism was generally a disaster for growth elsewhere in the world, including much of Latin America and most of Africa. Nor did it work well in all of South-east Asia; Burma and the Philippines went into steep decline under dictatorship. We should not therefore presume that democratisation has to wait for economic development. But certainly Asia's authoritarian and semi-authoritarian states achieved rates of economic growth and structural change unprecedented in global economic history. Whereas it took the United Kingdom – the world's first industrial nation – 54 years to develop from a low-income economy to a middle-income economy, it took Singapore and Taiwan only ten years to achieve middle-income status (Parente and Prescott, 2000).

Economic growth, combined with redistribution, enabled Indonesia, South Korea and Taiwan to mobilise considerable popular support, notwithstanding their use of coercion as well. This also assisted the regimes in a second objective which was to organise their nations against external threats, particularly the case for South Korea and Taiwan and, relatedly, to undermine domestic communist insurgency, uppermost in the minds of Indonesia's military leaders in the 1960s.

After China's 1949 revolution, China's communist party consolidated its rule with a similar agenda, but the failure of collectivised agriculture and central planning led it to reverse direction and initiate economic reform from 1976 onwards. The growth delivered by successful reform secured considerable popular support for the regime, making it difficult for political dissidents to encourage wider opposition. This enabled the Chinese communist party to retain power after the 1989 massacres of the pro-democracy movement which for a time raised the spectre of civil war. China's fast economic growth and poverty reduction over the last ten years has further reinforced this social contract, but widening inequality between poorer and richer regions, together with the social change attending rapid growth, imply that a single-party political system must eventually give way. A radically different social contract, one involving a multi-party democracy, will then be necessary – a major challenge for China's future (Gilley, 2004).

However, a lack of progress in development can undermine popular support for democracy. The second class of countries consists of those authoritarian or semi-authoritarian states in which people acquiesce to constraints on political freedom because they derive other benefits. Such benefits may include protection from external aggression by other states or societies, or economic benefits, whereby people are offered the prospect of rising living standards in return for acquiescing to limited freedom. Citizens may dislike this lack of political freedom, but any desire to rebel is held in check by the prospect of losing the benefits that the authoritarian system delivers, and not just the fear of the violence they may experience if they rebel. In this sense, there is a measure of agreement to the rules of the game, and order is maintained not just by coercion alone. This type of social contract has been characteristic of the South-east and East Asia regions: first Malaysia, Singapore, South Korea, Taiwan and later China. These regions have experienced the world's fastest rates of economic development over the last 50 years (see Box 6.1).

It is worth highlighting a survey (UNDP, 2004) that found that only 43 per cent of Latin Americans fully support democracy, and more than 54 per cent of people polled said they would support an authoritarian government if it improved the economy. Given the gross human rights violations committed by past authoritarian governments in Latin America, this is a rather worrying trend which raises concerns that a similarly extremist government might be allowed to come to power again, with the related implications for the safety and well-being of its citizens.

This brings us to the third class of countries, which consists of nations held together largely by terror: authoritarian states that fail to deliver economic prosperity generally resort to intensifying state violence to discourage large-scale rebellion. North Korea is the major contemporary example. Few people benefit from North Korea's system since the country has failed to achieve sustained economic growth. The country's rulers and their military and security apparatus absorb the limited resources that are available, to the detriment of the populace, which has periodically experienced major famine. This is one example of how the absence of civil war does not necessarily imply that a society currently has a viable social contract, and peace – defined as the absence of large-scale violence – does not mean that a society is working well for the majority of people, nor that some major breakdown isn't going occur in the future. For the purposes of our study here, however, this trajectory obviously holds few lessons compared with the first and second set of countries.

Regarding democracy, autocracy and the possibility of civil war, it has been suggested that the risk of internal war is at its lowest during autocracy and mature democracy (Hegre et al., 2001). This means that war is most likely during a transition from one system to another, because that is precisely the time when the state is at its weakest and the social contract may be collapsing.

6.2.3 Evolution and breakdown of social contracts

At any point in time, we will see societies where a long-standing social contract is strengthening, others where it is undergoing fundamental change for the better, and still others where it is weakening or has broken down.

The social contract evolves over time, and that evolution in part reflects what has gone before. In that sense, the social contract and its three dimensions (political, moral and economic) have the characteristic of *path dependence*: the past influences the present. Changes in each dimension of the social contract affect the other dimensions, sometimes causing profound stresses and tensions. For instance, economic development – in particular industrialisation and urbanisation – alters social values as people become more mobile, exposing them to different values from those of their parents and changing their role in society. For example, history shows that rising female labour-force participation has profound effects on the status and social role of women.

The pace of change may sometimes provoke a counter-reaction. For example, in the 1970s the Shah of Iran's attempt to accelerate industrialisation while maintaining an autocracy culminated in his being overthrown and the establishment of a theocracy. This reflected a reaction not only against the Shah's authoritarianism, but also against the increasing forced secularisation of Iranian society under his rule. The religious establishment in Iran always maintained close contact with the poor, whose cause it championed during the widening gulf between the rich and poor during the Shah's regime. Iran's post-1979 regime proved no more successful in creating a viable social contract, perhaps because of its external threat perception, as in many post-revolutionary societies. By the end of the 1990s the theocracy was under pressure from the country's pro-democratisation and human rights movements which have an entirely different vision of the social contract necessary for Iran's development. The challenge for Iranian society is to move towards a new social contract through peaceful means, rather than through violence.

We have shown that much of the change that we see in society over time originates from global forces that intrude, powerfully, on the internal dynamics of individual societies. One example which we met in Chapter 5 is the Cold War (1947–89), the effects of which are still felt in many developing countries. Box 6.2 examines the impact of the Cold War for social contracts in the specific cases of Cambodia, Afghanistan and Ethiopia. Another factor is global climate change, which may also destabilise societies, and not just in the developing world. A study for the US Department of Defense concludes that global warming, if not halted, will be a significant catalyst for future civil wars and interstate wars (Schwartz and Randall, 2003). A third source of change is globalisation, which is a powerful force reshaping societies – for good and bad – through increased flows of trade, finance, technology and information (Murshed, 2002a; Nayyar, 2002).

Historic income gaps between the richest and poorest nations are an important example of changes across society. UNDP (1999) reproduces figures to show that this gap was only 3:1 during the dawn of the industrial revolution in 1820, rising to 11:1 by the end of the first episode of globalisation in 1913. More recently, it grew to 35:1 in 1950, rising slightly to 44:1 by 1973. After the commencement of the present round of globalisation around 1980, this figure has acquired a staggering magnitude of 72:1. Rising global inequality means that poorer countries are falling ever further behind the affluent world, intensifying pressure on many of their social contracts.

Box 6.2   The legacy of the Cold War

The Cold War was a disaster for a number of long-standing, but fragile, social contracts. Its role in sustaining internal war in the developing world cannot be overemphasised. In Cambodia a pre-1970 social contract, built around a monarchy that had survived French colonial rule, provided a measure of peace if not much economic development. But growing rebellion, arising from lack of economic progress and deep inequality, became larger and deadlier as the war in neighbouring North Vietnam spilled over into Cambodian territory – particularly after the United States attacked Vietnam's Cambodian bases in

1970. The subsequent Khmer Rouge regime killed tens of thousands of its political opponents between 1975 and 1979, and over a million more people died from malnutrition and forced labour. After the overthrow of the Khmer Rouge, a Vietnamese-backed regime was subject to Khmer Rouge attacks, aided by covert assistance from China and the Western powers. Cambodia's subsequent reconstruction has been marked by weak government and political instability, and the country continues to live with problems first created more than 30 years ago (Le Billon and Bakker, 2000).

In Afghanistan, political institutions with a lineage going back to the eighteenth century provided a measure of peace – and successfully resisted incursions by the nineteenth century's great powers – but were overturned in a coup by communist military officers in 1978 and the Soviet Union's invasion in 1979. The Soviet Union, the United States and their respective allies fought a vicious proxy war in Afghanistan through the 1980s, which devastated the country and created millions of refugees (Rubin, 2000; Rashid, 2002). Further turmoil and civil war followed, culminating for a while in the Taliban regime which enforced their own (extremist) interpretation of Islamic values and provided a base for the *Al Qaeda* terrorist network until the Taliban's overthrow by a US-led coalition in 2002. Since then the country's new leadership has been attempting to construct a new social contract – with a new constitution and elections – but is largely unable to wrest control of the country from its powerful warlords, some of whom hold ministerial positions in the government. The representative assemblies that have been convened following the expulsion of the Taliban from the capital Kabul underrepresent the majority Pashtuns and overrepresent the communities from which the Northern Alliance is drawn.

In Ethiopia, the 1975 military coup ended a feudal monarchy that had successfully resisted Italian colonialism in the early twentieth century but which had largely failed in economic development, and the country experienced major famine in the early 1970s. The military regime ('the Derg') engaged in brutal suppression of internal dissent and switched sides from the United States to the Soviet Union. It also stepped up the war on the secessionist province of Eritrea, a war which had begun during the monarchy.

Ethiopia also fought a border war with Somalia which had, in the meantime, switched sides to the United States (Lefebvre, 1991). Somalia's regime received generous US economic and military assistance in the 1980s, with the regime eventually crumbling with the run-down in foreign aid as the Cold War wound down in the late 1980s.

In summary, in each of these countries there was a working, if fragile, social contract until the late 1960s, although it was already under considerable stress from poorly performing economies. Whether their prewar institutions would have transformed themselves in such a way as to restore stability and achieve growth is now a moot point: their institutions were swept away by the more powerful dynamics of the Cold War.

6.3   Development failure as a cause of violent conflict

Just as economic prosperity is an important underpinning to peace, poor nations are at greater risk of civil war; low income and poverty are the most important factors when measuring civil war risk (Collier et al, 2003). Such 'development failure' is often linked to failing states, declining institutions and disintegrating social contracts.

In this section we focus on Africa, which has both the worst economic performance of any region, and the highest incidence of war (SIPRI, 2003, p. 111). These factors, rooted in Africa's colonial past and subsequent Cold War proxy wars, have undermined the construction of a working social contract in many African countries, and the few 'success stories' remain highly vulnerable.

Africa is land and mineral-resource abundant and in colonial Africa economies were based on the extraction of valuable minerals and export-agriculture by large European-owned estates – with Africans supplying the labour (sometimes forced). Colonialism also created a class of African smallholders producing food for the national market and export crops such as cotton for the imperial and global markets. But the needs of African farmers for infrastructure and marketing were given a low priority, and the prices of their crops were sometimes kept artificially low for the profit of the colonial administration and its imperial power, as in the Belgian Congo (Nzongola-Ntalaja, 2002, p. 71). The economies of settler colonies – those that received large inflows of European settlers, such as Angola, Kenya, Mozambique and Zimbabwe – were more diversified, although investment was overwhelmingly geared to the needs of colonialists rather than indigenous populations. In addition, colonialism often exacerbated or created a dangerous imbalance in political and economic power between ethnic groups. As Box 4.3 shows, in Rwanda the racial ideology of Belgian colonialism sharpened the distinction between Hutus and Tutsis – peoples who had lived alongside each other relatively peaceably in pre-colonial times (Chrétien, 2003).

The transition to independence in sub-Saharan Africa (SSA) lasted from the late 1950s, starting with Ghana in 1957, through the independence wars of the 1960 and 1970s, ending with Namibia in 1990. Many of the newly independent nations had been colonies for less than a century and as we have already detailed in the last chapter, some of the conflicts that took place in Africa were as a result of the struggle for colonial independence and Cold War proxy wars. The liberation struggle was long and bloody in Portuguese Africa (Angola, Guinea-Bissau and Mozambique) which then went through a chaotic transition to independence following the 1974 Portuguese revolution and the swift exit of the colonialists. In Rwanda, Hutus massacred 20,000 Tutsis, and 100,000 more fled as refugees in the years immediately prior to independence in 1962. The Belgian Congo went through a badly organised independence in 1960, marked by escalating violence and then, just after independence, an army mutiny and an attempted secession by the country's two mineral-rich provinces, Katanga and Kivu, backed by Western mining interests. A UN peacekeeping operation (its first in Africa) was a major failure. With the Soviet Union and the United States competing for influence over the new state – Congo possessed many strategic minerals, and supplied uranium for the first atomic bombs – the country's first prime minister was murdered and army chief Joseph-Desiré Mobutu seized power and was allowed to become one of the world's most corrupt dictators.

In summary, many countries were already fragile, both politically and economically, at independence. Even those that did not undergo war during or shortly after independence were faced with daunting problems. They had small numbers of African professionals available to meet the requirements of governments and private sectors for skills, they were largely dependent on a few minerals or export crops for foreign exchange, and public revenues were low in relation to the overwhelming needs of the population for basic services and infrastructure. Their aid dependence was consequently very high.

Africa's new leaderships offered their people a social contract not too dissimilar to what was on offer elsewhere in the developing world from the 1950s to the 1970s: the promise of rising living standards in return for support for single-party rule. Leaderships also argued that multi-party politics would be ethnically based, thereby undermining nation building – though in the event it was single-party rule that proved fatal, allowing dictators to come to power in several countries. Aid donors were happy to go along with this; both East and West accumulated client states, while France and the UK gave priority to stability and the protection of commercial interests in former colonies.

SSA undertook considerable institution building in the 1960s and 1970s to make up for colonial deficiencies, and some countries managed to improve schooling, health-care and infrastructure. But social progress was undermined by a lack of sustained economic growth. This was the result of many factors including: the neglect of smallholder agriculture, indeed overtaxing it for the benefit of politically influential urban groups; ill-conceived industrial projects serving tiny domestic markets in contrast to East Asia's successful strategy of competitive manufacturing for the global market; and the oil price shocks of the 1970s and the volatility in world commodity prices which undermined commodity-dependent economies. SSA's aid dependence accordingly rose, and the region began to accumulate external debt to private creditors, and also increasingly to the aid donors themselves, at an alarming rate.

In summary, development strategies mostly failed to deliver higher living standards, with the exceptions of Botswana and Mauritius. By 1980 many SSA countries had a per capita income that was below its level at independence. This continues for some countries, notably the Democratic Republic of the Congo (DRC). Governments began to undertake economic reforms ('structural adjustment') supported by IMF and World Bank loans, involving market liberalisation, privatisation of state-owned enterprises (SOEs), and macro-economic reform to restore the public finances and reduce high inflation. As Chapter 5 has discussed, these reforms were highly controversial, both in design and implementation, and indeed were sometimes distorted to benefit special (and corrupt) interests; most governments had little room for manoeuvre in their donor relations, given the importance of aid to national budgets.

Economic reform went through a stop–start cycle as reforms were tried, stalled, and tried again. When the public finances were brought under control it was often at the cost of deepening recession – and further deterioration in the coverage and quality of basic services and infrastructure – as the economy passed through an adjustment process that involved major fiscal restraint, public expenditure cuts and greater revenue mobilisation. Fiscal reform was certainly very necessary; public spending was not adequately focused on the needs of the poor, and ethnic discrimination in spending was also evident. But effective reform is difficult to achieve under rapid adjustment because expenditure cuts tend to undermine already weak state capacity (Kayizzi-Mugerwa, 2003). A paradox of IMF and World-Bank sponsored reform is that while it is often seen as the retreat of the state – with the dismantling of market controls and the privatisation of SOEs – effective state institutions are still crucial to achieve reform's intended results. Better public expenditure management, better tax and customs systems, better central banks, and institutions to protect the public interest in the now-liberalised markets (and to fill the gap when markets fail in credit, and food marketing for instance) are all needed.

Some success was achieved in restoring growth to the collapsed economies of Ghana, Tanzania, Mozambique and Uganda – the latter two were also recovering from civil war. But even the 'success stories' remain highly vulnerable to global economic shocks, their economies not yet having diversified from commodity dependence, and they – along with the rest of SSA – accumulated large unserviceable debts to the donors. In the case of the worst performers such as Zaire (DRC) the IMF and the World Bank continued to lend beyond the point at which it was economically rational to do so, acting under political pressure from France and the United States which were eager to maintain Mobutu's regime as their client state. This 'odious debt' remains a serious drag on the DRC's prospects for postwar recovery. And there were many unmitigated failures. Adjustment programmes failed to pull Sierra Leone out of a deepening economic slump, and some reforms made matters worse. For example, Sierra Leone's public food-distribution system was dismantled as part of an ill-conceived liberalisation of agricultural markets that was a condition of World Bank lending (Griffiths, 2003). Côte d'Ivoire's post-independence economic performance was among Africa's best until the 1980s, but a steep fall in commodity prices, combined with a badly designed adjustment programme foisted on the government by the IMF, the World Bank and the French Government, led to a deep economic depression in the 1980s which contributed to civil war in the 1990s (Box 6.3). Likewise, as noted in Box 4.3, the patronage practised by the Habyarimana regime in Rwanda was undermined by a commodity price shock – a fall in the international coffee price at the end of the 1980s – and the regime increasingly resorted to repression in the lead-up to the genocide of 1994 (Verwimp, 2003).

Box 6.3 Civil war in Côte d'Ivoire

Côte d'Ivoire accounts for 40 per cent of the world supply of cocoa. The economy boomed during the 1960s and 1970s when world cocoa prices were high. Houphouet-Boigny, the country's first and long-serving president, built a successful post-independence social contract that contained regional tensions. His government redistributed the country's cocoa wealth, via a tax on cocoa exports, to reduce inequality between the rich Christian south – the cocoa-producing area – and the drier, poorer, Muslim north (Azam and Koidou, 2003). Houphouet-Boigny co-opted leaders from the different ethnic groups into the government and civil service, thereby providing them with patronage opportunities to spread the country's wealth (Azam, 1995). Public investment in education across Côte d'Ivoire provided a steady flow of young graduates from all ethnic groups into well-remunerated jobs in an expanding public sector and a vibrant private sector.

Processing cocoa beans, Côte d'Ivoire.

However, overproduction and the collapse of world cocoa prices in the 1980s led to an economic slump, which dragged down pubic revenues via the export tax on cocoa. The price shock was compounded by a badly designed adjustment programme. Instead of devaluing the CFA franc – the currency of Côte d'Ivoire and other members of the CFA franc zone – the government, with the backing of the IMF, the World Bank and France attempted to resolve the crisis by fiscal restraint, leading to deep cuts in public expenditure. This failed to restore growth, and eventually the CFA franc was devalued, thereby encouraging an export recovery in the early 1990s. However, by this time the damage had been done to both the patronage system and to the employment prospects of the young, who became increasingly frustrated. They provided ready recruits for ethnic demagogues, particularly those stoking up hatred against the northerners as well as the millions of migrants from Burkina Faso, Mali and Guinea who had settled in Côte d'Ivoire to work in the booming cocoa economy of the 1970s.

Houphouet-Boigny died in 1993, and succeeding presidents reversed his policy on immigrants and barred them from owning land. People from the north who shared the same ethnicity as emigrants from Burkina Faso and Mali also became targets of discrimination and were denied public jobs. Alassane Ouattara, a leading opposition figure with a power base in the north was barred from the 2000 presidential elections on the grounds that his father was born outside Côte d'Ivoire.

During the election campaign supporters of the then president, Laurent Gbagbo, attacked and killed supporters of Ouattara. Northerners in the army then rebelled in September 2002 and civil war began, drawing in mercenaries from Liberia and other parts of West Africa. The rebels seized the northern half of Côte d'Ivoire. Acting under a UN mandate, French peacekeepers intervened and separated the two sides, creating a buffer zone, and a peace treaty was signed in January 2003 calling for the creation of a temporary power-sharing government and new elections in 2005.

In general, aid donors in the 1980s and early 1990s had little understanding of the likely social effects of the reforms that they were requiring, nor the internal dynamics, and often the extreme fragility of the societies with which they were dealing. This became very apparent in Rwanda, a country that had been lauded as an aid 'success story' right up to the 1994 genocide (Uvin, 2000). A former United Nations Development and Humanitarian Co-ordinator for Rwanda, Stephen Browne, summarises this debacle in the following statement:

> Before the genocide Rwanda was implementing a programme of structural adjustment, supervised by the IMF and the World Bank. The country enjoyed an unusually good image with the donors, the most important of which had resident missions in Kigali. Thus, the aid donors had a major stake in Rwanda in the months prior to the genocide, and indeed many saw the country as an African model of development. What seems extraordinary now is that none of the donors appears to be aware of the Government's careful preparations for one of the worst massacres in human history. Yet information was available from which the cataclysm could have been predicted. Indeed, some observers have argued that aid, in supporting the Government's policies and programmes, may have contributed to the conditions that incubated the genocide. Rwandan society has suffered from high levels of 'structural violence' – inequality, marginalization, and ethnic bias – which were often rooted in, and exacerbated by, state action.

(Browne, 1999, p. 3)

> **Intervention implications**
>
> Look more closely at the social effects of interventions and reforms. Recognise the fragility of the social contract and ensure that interventions do not further weaken it.
>
> Look for inequalities and distortions created or increased by colonialism, the Cold War, and adjustment, and try to redress them in an intervention.

6.4 Inequality and the social contract

Section 6.3 highlighted the role played by economic factors, principally low economic growth and resource endowments, in the breakdown of social contracts and the causation of war. But this does not complete our discussion of war's economic dimension. We now turn to a deeper discussion of *inequality*, which we have mentioned from time to time, without being too precise as to its meaning. In this section we outline several different concepts of inequality and we discuss their possible link to violent conflict.

6.4.1 Definitions of inequality

If a sample of a hundred people were taken at random it would be possible to rank their standard of living in many different ways. A monetary measure, such as annual income or expenditure, might be used; or a non-monetary measure might be employed, such as life expectancy, level of educational attainment measured by literacy, health status explained by number of days of illness this year, or nutritional status as assessed by ratio of body weight to height. Individuals could then be ranked in order from the person with the highest income to the lowest, the person with the best health to the lowest, and so forth. Alternatively, because a lot of income is jointly produced by household members working together and some of it is consumed jointly (for example electricity that lights a house), analysis often uses *households* as the basic unit of comparison.

Other types of information on people can be collected, for instance their gender, where they live, as well as their ethnic, cultural and religious characteristics. It is then possible to make comparisons of monetary and/or non-monetary measures of living standards in terms of groups – i.e. between males and females, urban and rural dwellers, or finer spatial divisions by region and subregion. Such an analysis is said to be looking at *horizontal inequality*, whereas considering the inequality for individuals or households, but ranking them without regard to group characteristics, focuses on *vertical inequality*.

Note that such information might be used to take a look at *poverty* in particular. Poverty can, for example, be defined in terms of income or expenditure. The World Bank defines a poverty line of less than US$1 per day, adjusted for its comparable purchasing power across countries, below which a person is said to be living in poverty. There are also other ways of defining monetary poverty. Alternatively, or better still as a complement to the monetary measure, someone can be defined as poor if their health, literacy, or other elements of non-monetary well-being fall below a defined level.

Self-built housing, Mumbai, India.

A great deal of information has now been gathered on living standards in developed and developing countries through household surveys. Much of it has been used to construct vertical measures of inequality as well as poverty measures. But if group characteristics such as ethnicity or province are available – and this is not always the case – then horizontal measures can be constructed as well. Care must be taken in assessing this data, however, because each individual belongs to several groups. For example, if particular ethnic groups are concentrated in particular regions, it may be difficult to determine whether the data are showing differences between ethnic groups or differences between regions. This can be even more complicated if the regions have different income patterns – say a coastal area with fishing and rice growing and an upland area with cattle and maize. Is the group difference between ethnic groups, between regions, or between fishing people and cattle herders?

Clearly, inequality is an important social phenomenon in its own right, but does it have a causal role in violent conflict? Does the 'rage of the poor' lead to violence against the wealthy, and do the latter respond with violence in return? High inequality may contribute to a society's political instability – frequent changes of government including by military coup – and the instability may lead to some violent deaths, for instance in demonstrations and through the human rights violations associated with military regimes, but not to the large-scale fighting and death associated with civil war.

Central and South America's experience is particularly relevant in this respect. A nation such as Brazil, with perhaps the highest income inequality in the world, has a history of political turmoil, including military regimes that committed gross violations of human rights, but not civil war. El Salvador, Guatemala, Nicaragua and Peru are high inequality societies characterised by civil wars involving rural-based insurrections, often involving much-abused indigenous populations, but the Central American republics were caught up in the Cold War, and their civil wars in the 1970s and 1980s were not purely domestic in cause. Colombia has very high inequality and a long-running civil war, but again there are other factors – notably the criminal violence of the drugs trade.

6.4.2 Horizontal inequality and violent conflict

Conflict can be between rich and poor, in other words emanating from vertical inequality – to produce a classic revolutionary movement of the Russian (1917) type. In Marxism–Leninism an increasingly impoverished working class cooperates to pursue its class interest, setting aside any ethnic and religious differences. But in societies that have not undergone industrialisation and urbanisation, or which are still in the early stages, class interests may be much less important than ethnicity and religion as ways to mobilise and organise people. And even in industrial societies, ethnicity and religion may still retain their power, as is evident in the wars of the former Yugoslavia, the former Soviet Union, and in Northern Ireland. Regional differences played a role in Sierra Leone, Côte d'Ivoire (see Box 6.3) and Sudan. The debate on inequality's role in war has therefore increasingly focused on horizontal inequality. Horizontal inequality is important because any group seeking to organise itself to pursue a common agenda faces a 'collective action' problem, whereby the group may be unable to co-operate due to mutual suspicion (Olson, 1965). Having a common ethnicity may reduce suspicion among group members, and promote cooperation, thereby reducing the collective action problem.

Still, it is one thing to say that ethnic or regional characteristics are a powerful mobilising force for groups, and quite another to say that they lead people to murder each other. There are, after all, plenty of societies, both developed and developing, where people from different ethnic groups and religions live alongside each other, using those characteristics to organise their day-to-day activity. What causes societies to move beyond their 'tipping point' and into violence? The following aspects of horizontal inequality have been emphasised as powerful forces (Addison and Murshed, 2002; Murshed and Gates, 2005):

- *Unequal access to assets*. Assets are crucial to the livelihoods of the self-employed (smallholder farmers, micro-entrepreneurs, etc.). Unequal access to land and other natural capital upon which livelihoods depend, and the dispossession of groups by more powerful groups, can over time breed an increasing sense of desperation, ultimately leading to insurrection. Typically this is seen as war led by indigenous peoples, who were forcibly removed from access to natural capital during colonial times and then converted into wage labourers for European settler populations and their descendants as the latter created increasingly larger estates, i.e. in Central America and Southern Africa. But smallholder communities can also come into conflict in land-scarce territories, and this is an important dimension of interethnic violence in Burundi and Rwanda.

- *Unequal access to wage employment.* Those without productive assets for self-employment, or those whose assets are too meagre to sustain them, must seek wage employment. This is especially important for young males, who otherwise constitute the recruits for competing warlords. Economic growth provides the ultimate source of rising private-sector employment and wages – both in the formal and informal sectors – but if growth is low then the public sector becomes the main source of formal employment. Public jobs therefore become very valuable – particularly their opportunities for patronage – and may be allocated to ethnic groups that dominate the government. As we saw in our earlier discussion of development failure in Africa, this has provided a powerful force in the descent into violence (see Box 6.3 on Côte d'Ivoire).

- *Unequal access to public services and overtaxation.* In addition to discrimination in public employment, some ethnic groups may suffer from discrimination in access to public services, reflecting allocations of public spending for the social sectors and development towards more powerful groups (Addison et al., 2004). At the same time, they may be disproportionately taxed to pay for public spending that provides them with little benefit; the net effect of the fiscal system is therefore negative for them. The fiscal dimension has been important in the wars of Burundi and Rwanda (Ndikumana, 2004), and also elsewhere (Keefer and Khemani, 2003).

- *Unequal burden-sharing during crisis.* Shocks to a society – environmental, economic, and external attack – are a tough test of whether its social contract is working well. If the costs of those shocks are borne disproportionately, resentment can grow. Safety nets such as famine relief and food-for-work programmes, and more advanced social security systems not only reduce the magnitude of shocks, but also give those affected the sense that they are part of a society that will try to protect them. In SSA, commodity-price shocks undermined the patronage systems in Côte d'Ivoire and Rwanda (see Section 6.3 and Box 4.3).

- *Unequal benefits from windfalls.* For many societies a windfall – for instance the discovery of new valuable mineral resource or a boom in commodity-export prices – can be even more destructive than crises, since such windfalls are often mismanaged. This is the 'resource curse'. When the area producing the windfall mineral receives little benefit in return, resentment can build – a long-running problem in Nigeria's oil-producing Delta region – and natural-resource wealth is a powerful incentive to try and secede.

In summary, resentment between groups may build up over differences in living standards *between* the groups, and this may be much more important to people within a group than differences in living standards *within* the group so that rich and poor join together to fight the rich and poor of other groups. This may be one reason why some researchers find that large vertical inequalities do not increase the risk of war (Collier and Hoeffler, 1998). Box 6.4 provides an example of applying horizontal inequality to the war in Nepal.

But there are still difficulties with the horizontal inequality line of argument. First, people need to be inspired and led into violent conflict: genocide is not some disorganised frenzy – murdering large numbers of people needs careful planning, as Rwanda showed. Demagogues can resort to religion and ritual, as is the case with the 'Lords Resistance Army' in northern Uganda, and as was the case in Sierra Leone (see Ellis, 2001), and an appeal to ethnic pride or some misplaced sense of nationalism, as in the former Yugoslavia. Warlords and 'war entrepreneurs' can make a straight appeal to greed – promising loot to acquire followers (Gates, 2001). Leaderships therefore make a difference as to whether groups become organised enough to pursue war, and the loss of leaders can make a big difference to peace: for example, in Angola, UNITA's will to fight collapsed with the death of its long-running leader, Jonas Savimbi, in 2002 (see Box 1.1).

Second, high inequality societies may experience high levels of violent crime, including of the poor having to resort to criminal livelihoods, but may still avoid civil war. South Africa, which has one of the highest levels of income inequality in the world and high horizontal inequality as a result of the former apartheid racial policies, is an important case. Apartheid ended after a long civil war; there were also high levels of violent crime and, as part of the war, an attempt to make the country ungovernable. In 1994, as the country's first post-apartheid elections took place, many observers were convinced that civil war would resume. Yet these dire predictions have not come to pass despite continued high levels of violent crime – except perhaps in Kwa-Zulu Natal, where there was extensive political violence which some researchers classed as a war and others did not. Elsewhere, and even eventually in Kwa-Zulu Natal, a remarkable consensus was forged across ethnic groups, and democratisation has been consolidated. But nearly everyone recognises that the new social contract requires much faster and more equitable growth, together with large improvements in basic services, to meet the high aspirations of South Africa's black poor and to close the gap with the higher-income, mainly white, population.

In summary, when all of the evidence is taken together, inequality starts to look important in the causation of war, and horizontal inequality especially so. There is no direct mechanical relationship between inequality and war, but then there is no direct causal relationship between other variables and war, except perhaps high per-capita income because richer societies have better institutions for conflict resolution, the most to lose from internal war and are more able to redistribute income. Conflict is a complex phenomenon, and we should not expect there to be any one lever that can be pulled to achieve a solution.

> ## Intervention implications
>
> Identify strongly felt horizontal inequalities which have led to violence and war. Aim to redress those inequalities through more equitable growth and development, as well as redistribution, and support the building of a new social contract.

Box 6.4 Horizontal inequality and the social contract in Nepal

by Martha Caddelll

In February 1996, the Communist Party of Nepal (Maoist) launched a 'People's War', denouncing parliamentary democracy and adopting a 'path of armed struggle against the existing state power'. By early 2004 over 10,000 people had been killed as a result of the war. Reported human rights abuses committed by both the Maoists and the state security forces escalated.

What is the arena where this conflict has unfolded? Nepal is characterised by a dramatic degree of geographical diversity. The south of the country, the *terrai*, is predominantly flat, plain land, only a few metres above sea level. In contrast, the northern boundary of the country is marked by the Himalayan mountain range. The country is also divided east–west by five major river networks, which demarcate five development regions. Nepal's diversity is not just geographical. A diverse array of languages, cultures and peoples characterise the population: 103 caste and ethnic groups and 92 languages were officially recognised in the 2001 census report. The Constitution, however, recognises the country as a 'Hindu kingdom' and privileges Nepali as the 'language of the nation'.

Within this diversity, there is significant horizontal inequality, with a considerable disparity in levels of access to employment, services and levels of development within the country, and between social groups. Incomes in mid-western and far-western regions are one quarter, or less, of those of the capital. The UNDP's Human Development Index for those regions is less than half the Kathmandu level, with shorter life expectancy and much lower literacy levels. Gaps between caste and ethnic groups are similarly large. Despite an attempt at land reform, there are still major land inequalities (Murshed and Gates, 2005).

Failure of the social contract and failures of development help to explain why this social inequality tipped over into civil war. A return to multi-party democracy in 1990 raised expectations about popular participation and development, but these remained largely unfulfilled. Despite repeated commitments to decentralisation, power and authority remain concentrated in Kathmandu. Indeed, the domination of civil service posts by Bahun and Chettri elites has escalated since the restoration of multi-party democracy in 1990 (Bhattachan, 2000; Dixit, 2001). Similarly, 50 years of 'development' efforts by the government and international agencies have been largely ineffective.

In such an arena, the Maoists were able to offer alternative forms of participation, even an alternative 'social contract'. Rather than NGO-style participation and 'empowerment', the power of direct action and the gun were on offer. The initial appeal of the Maoists also arose from their ability to speak to the grievances of specific groups, to address directly inequalities that mainstream politicians had talked about, but failed to act on. Concerns of women, ethnic groups, *dalits* ('untouchable' castes) and the landless were addressed in a direct way. Landowners were attacked, bans on alcohol consumption introduced and alternative systems of government and justice mechanisms introduced.

Activities were initially concentrated in the mid-west, where a history of radical leftist politics and the experience of state repression had made the population particularly receptive to the Maoists' approach. In addition, it has been argued that ethnic divisions and local divisions led to the political conflict, taking on particular salience in the districts of Rukum and Rolpa (de Sales, 2003). These districts also had the tactical advantage of being remote from urban centres, had poor communications networks, and had extensive forest to provide refuge for the guerrillas. The war steadily spread over the entire country. A brutal and heavy-handed response by the government, including the army being drawn into the conflict in 2001, pushed more people into the arms of the insurgents. This was combined with the continued failure of mainstream political parties to address effectively issues of inequality and grievance.

Nepali Maoists.

> But the Maoists too face problems in maintaining and extending their support. Populism was increasingly replaced by coercion and forced recruitment. Divisions between the rhetorical claims of the Maoists and their actual practice are evident. Popular concern about the tactics and use of force adopted by both sides— and the impact this will have on the longer term future of the country – is increasingly voiced. A number of ethnic activist and *dalit* groups questioned the prominence of upper caste Hindus among the Maoist leadership. Increasing contradictions in the Maoists' position on women have also been noted (Pettigrew and Schneiderman, 2004).
>
> The Maoists were able to speak to multiple horizontal inequalities and political disillusionment. While these inequalities were widely acknowledged by mainstream political parties, the Maoists offered a more direct means of tackling them and an alternative vision of 'development'.

6.5   Conclusion

A well-functioning social contract is essential to prevent the outbreak of violence and civil war. In the broadest possible sense the social contract is multi-dimensional, taking on a moral, political and economic dimension. It can also be implicit rather than explicit. But as far as the risk of the outbreak of large-scale violence is concerned, the social contract refers to the institutions of dispute settlement. For that to happen, the contract must be seen to be just, credible and well functioning. Alongside these institutional arrangements for dispute settlement are mechanisms for distribution, which refer to the fiscal system. Every well-functioning society has in place devices for redistributing a portion of the economic pie between the rich and poor, between distinct ethnic groups, and between better off and worse off regions of the country. Normally this is done through the fiscal system, involving taxation that is general and social-sector expenditure that is broad based. Recruitment into the civil service, political power sharing and the granting of government contracts also fall into the purview of this argument. Therefore, these redistributive processes address inequality, but particularly horizontal or intergroup inequality.

The ultimate function of redistribution is inclusiveness. The lack of inclusiveness often takes the form of a real or perceived rise in horizontal inequality, and therein lie the seeds of war. Very often this occurs because of the degeneration of an earlier, functioning, social contract that has over time become unworkable because its inclusive, power-sharing, dispute settlement and economic redistributive mechanisms simply lack credibility, perhaps because of a fall in income due to changing commodity prices, or to the discriminatory actions of factional leaders. These are linked, with discriminatory behaviour more likely when economic development is not taking place, and specifically when there is a lack of growth or economic progress. This is because growth enlarges the economic pie, and makes redistribution and sharing all the more feasible. Furthermore, economic growth in the developing world is less likely in countries endowed with a very large share of lootable or obstructable mineral resources, because these profits that can be siphoned off encourage corrupt practices which eventually lead to economic decline via institutional degeneration. Such countries also run the risk of civil war.

Thus, the avoidance of war and the fostering of economic progress both require institutional building and regeneration. Poorly functioning institutions can cause war as well as economic stagnation, and we have demonstrated how economic decline can contribute to war by putting the existing social contract under stress. Despite some circularity or reverse causation in the arguments that link war to the breakdown of the social contract and on to the lack of economic growth, one factor is clear: the primacy of institutions. Institutions define the superstructure within which policy is conducted, and therefore determine the efficacy of mechanisms for conflict resolution and policies that promote economic progress. By institutions we refer to such things as the rule of law, voice and accountability, political stability, the control of corruption, the regulatory framework and the quality of the bureaucracy. In promoting institutional development so as to make the peaceful social contract feasible, there is no one-size-fits-all policy for all nations in war, or in danger of war. Externally imposed policies for democratisation, say in Iraq, are fraught with difficulties. The end of the Cold War saw a spurt of multi-party electoral democracies appearing in the developing world. Many of these countries have slid back into autocratic practices even when periodic elections are held. One reason for this decline could be that these new democracies and the institutional framework and social contract sustaining them are not entirely home grown.

In postwar situations reconstituting the social contract that sustains peace is imperative. This requires broad-based development and growth to tackle the horizontal inequalities that produced the war in the first place. Thus inequality has to be dealt with as well as poverty. Sustained economic growth is essential for ensuring the livelihoods of the poor after war, so that the new social contract can be maintained and horizontal inequalities narrowed.

Intervention implications

Rebuilding the social contract requires redistributive processes to address horizontal inequalities, and to make the country more inclusive.

Institutional development is essential for economic development and reconstructing the social contract. But institutional development must be home-grown, and not imposed from outside.

In postwar situations it is imperative to reconstitute the social contract that sustains peace. This requires broad-based development and growth to tackle the horizontal inequalities that produced the war in the first place. Thus inequality has to be dealt with as well as poverty. Sustained economic growth is essential for ensuring the livelihoods of the poor after war, so that the new social contract can be maintained and horizontal inequalities narrowed.

6.6   Chapter summary

Conflict is a part of everyday life and normally people settle their conflicts peacefully, within a framework of **institutions** or rules of the game. When a society operates according to a widely accepted set of rules of the game, it is said to have a viable **social contract**, which operates at political, moral and economic levels. A strong social contract implies higher levels of **trust**, less **opportunistic behaviour**, and more willingness to think towards the future. The social contract is at least partly informal, and when it involves the agreement of people to be governed, it underpins the **legitimacy of the state**. Social contracts are often **democratic**, but in South-east and East Asia there have been examples of successful authoritarian social contracts based on rapid income growth for most people. The social contract need not be fair, but a viable social contract should provide a framework to resolve grievances by groups who feel they are being treated unfairly.

As with any contract, the **social contract can be broken**, for example when a significant portion of the population withdraws consent from a government seen not to be keeping its side of the bargain. Breakdown in the social contract can lead to violence and civil war. The **Cold War and globalisation** have both put the social contract under heavy pressure in many countries – the Cold War because of the way the big powers backed particular groups breaking the balance of the social contract, and globalisation because of the way it sharply increased income inequalities.

Colonialism left many countries weak at independence, and exacerbated imbalances in power between different groups. In the post-colonial period the aid donors often supported autocratic one-party states and in the Cold War backed dictators in client states. African governments **failed to deliver higher living standards**, and World Bank/IMF adjustment programmes did not help, leading to breakdowns in the social contract. **Aid donors failed to understand the social effects of the reforms** they were requiring, which often weakened states and their social contracts.

To function, the social contract must be seen to be **just, inclusive and credible**. Where there is no economic growth plus discriminatory behaviour, the social contract may degenerate. To prevent a war, or after a war, it will be necessary to create a new social contract.

Inequality between groups is called **horizontal inequality**; comparisons can be made between various kinds of groups, including gender, class, religion, language, and ethnicity. If not redressed, these can lead to discontent and violence. Five aspects of horizontal inequality are important **mobilising forces for groups** and can lead to civil war: unequal access to **assets, jobs** or **services**, as well as unequal **burden sharing** and unequal **benefits from windfalls**. Horizontal inequalities can create a vicious circle: a weak social contract may mean that horizontal inequalities cannot or will not be redressed, which can lead to violence and a further weakening of the social contract. Civil war can be seen as the breakdown of the social contract.

References

Abou El Fadl, K. (2004) *Islam and the Challenge of Democracy*, Princeton, Princeton University Press.

Addison, T. and Murshed, S. M. (2002) 'On the economic causes of contemporary civil wars', pp. 22–38 in Murshed, S. M. (ed.) *Issues in Positive Political Economy*, London, Routledge.

Addison, T., Chowdhury, A. and Murshed, S. M. (2004) 'The fiscal dimensions of conflict and reconstruction', in Addison, T. and Roe, A. (eds) *Fiscal Policy for Development: Poverty, Growth and Reconstruction*, London, Palgrave Macmillan for UNU-WIDER.

Azam, J.-P. (1995) 'How to pay for the peace? A theoretical framework with references to African countries', *Public Choice*, vol. 83, no. 1–2, pp. 173–84.

Azam, J.-P. and Koidou, C. (2003) 'Rising threats: containing political violence in Côte d'Ivoire', *IDEI Working Paper*, January 2003, http://idei.fr/activity.php?a=1578 (accessed November 2004).

Bhattachan, K.B. (2000) 'Possible ethnic revolution or insurgency in a predatory unitary hindu state, Nepal' in Kumar, D. (ed.) *Domestic Conflict and Crisis of Governability in Nepal*, Kathmandu, CNAS, pp. 135–62.

Browne, S. (1999) 'Aid and conflict in Rwanda', *WIDER Angle*, no.1/99: 3 (available at: www.wider.unu.edu).

Chrétien, J.-P. (2003) *The Great Lakes of Africa: Two Thousand Years of History*, New York, Zone Books.

Collier, P. (2003) 'The market for civil war', *Foreign Policy*, vol. 136, pp. 38–45.

Collier, P. and Hoeffler, A. (1998) 'On economic causes of war', *Oxford Economic Papers*, pp. 563–73.

Collier, P. and Hoeffler, A. (2004a) 'Conflicts', pp. 129–56 in B. Lomborg (ed.) *Global Crises, Global Solutions*, Cambridge, Cambridge University Press.

Collier, P. and Hoeffler, A. (2004b) 'The challenge of reducing the global incidence of war', Centre for the Study of African Economies, Oxford University, Paper prepared for the Copenhagen Consensus (March 26), www.copenhagenconsensus.com/Files/Filer/CC/Papers/Conflicts_230404.pdf, (accessed November 2004)

Collier, P., Elliot, L., Hegre, H., Hoeffler, A., Reynal-Querol, M. and Sambanis, N. (2003), *Breaking the Conflict Trap*, Washington DC, World Bank and Oxford, Oxford University Press.

Dixit, K. M. (2001) 'Bahuns and the Nepali state', *Nepali Times* 65, 19 October 2001.

Ellis, S. (2001) *The Mask of Anarchy: The Destruction of Liberia and the Religious Dimension of an African Civil War*, New York, New York University Press.

Gates, S. (2001) 'Recruitment and allegiance: the microfoundations of rebellion', *Journal of Conflict Resolution*, vol. 46, pp. 111–30.

Gates, S. and Strand, H. (2004) 'Military intervention, democratization, and post-conflict political stability', mimeo, Centre for the Study of Civil War, PRIO, www.prio.no (accessed November 2004).

Gilley, B. (2004) *China's Democratic Future: How it Will Happen and Where it Will Lead*, New York, Columbia University Press.

Griffiths, P. (2003) *The Economist's Tale: A Consultant Encounters Hunger and the World Bank*, London, Zed Press.

Hegre, H., Ellingsen, T., Gates, S. and Gleditsch, N. P. (2001) 'Towards a democratic civil peace? Democracy, civil change, and civil war 1816–1992', *American Political Science Review*, vol. 95, pp. 17–33.

Kayizzi-Mugerwa, S. (ed.) (2003) *Reforming Africa's Institutions: Ownership, Incentives, and Capabilities*, Tokyo, United Nations University Press for WIDER.

Keefer, P. and Khemani, S. (2003) 'The political economy of public expenditures', *Working Paper* 26953, Washington DC, World Bank.

Le Billon, P. and Bakker, K. (2000) 'Cambodia: genocide, autocracy, and the overpoliticized state', pp. 53–88 in Nafziger, E. W., Stewart, F. and Väyrynen, R. (eds) *War, Hunger and Displacement: The Origins of Humanitarian Emergencies*, Vol. 2: *Case Studies*, Oxford, Oxford University Press for UNU-WIDER.

Lefebvre, J. A. (1991) *Arms for the Horn: US Security Policy in Ethiopia and Somalia*, 1953–1991, Pittsburgh PA, University of Pittsburgh Press.

Murshed, S. M. (ed.) (2002a) *Globalization, Marginalization and Development*, London, Routledge for UNU-WIDER.

Murshed, S. M. (2002b) 'Conflict, civil war and underdevelopment: an introduction', *Journal of Peace Research*, vol. 39, no. 4, pp. 387–93.

Murshed, S. M. and Gates, S. (2005) 'Spatial-horizontal inequality and the Maoist insurgency in Nepal', *Review of Development Economics*, vol. 9, no. 1, pp. 121–34.

Nayyar, D. (ed.) (2002) *Governing Globalization: Issues and Institutions*, Oxford, Oxford University Press for UNU-WIDER.

Ndikumana, L. (2004) 'Fiscal policy, conflict, and reconstruction in Burundi and Rwanda', in Addison, T. and Roe, A. (eds) *Fiscal Policy for Development: Poverty, Growth and Reconstruction*, London, Palgrave Macmillan for UNU-WIDER.

Nzongola-Ntalaja, G. (2002) *The Congo: From Leopold to Kabila*, London, Zed Books.

Olson, M. (1965) *The Logic of Collective Action*, Cambridge MA, Harvard University Press.

Ottaway, M. (2003) *Democracy Challenged: The Rise of Semi-Authoritarianism*, Washington DC, Carnegie Endowment for International Peace.

Parente, S. L. and Prescott, E. C. (2000) *Barriers to Riches*, Cambridge MA, MIT Press.

Peterson, S. (2000) *Me Against My Brother: At War in Somalia, Sudan, and Rwanda*, New York, Routledge.

Pettigrew, J. and Schneiderman, S. (2004) 'Women and the Maobaadi: ideology and agency in Nepal's Maoist movement', *Himal South Asian*, January 2004, www.himalmag.com/2004/january/essay.htm (accessed November 2004).

Rashid, A. (2002) *Jihad: The Rise of Militant Islam in Central Asia*, New Haven, Yale University Press.

Rubin, B. R. (2000) 'Afghanistan: the last Cold-war conflict, the first post Cold-war conflict', pp. 23–52 in Nafziger, E. W., Stewart, F. and Väyrynen, R. (eds) *War, Hunger and Displacement: The Origins of Humanitarian Emergencies*, Vol. 2: *Case Studies*, Oxford, Oxford University Press for UNU-WIDER.

de Sales, A. (2003) 'The Khan Magar country, Nepal: between ethnic claims and Maoism' in Thapa, D. (ed.) *Understanding the Maoist Movement in Nepal*, Kathmandu, Martin Chautari.

Schwartz, P. and Randall, D. (2003) 'An abrupt climate change scenario and its implications for United States national security', Emeryville CA, Global Business Network, www.gbn.com (accessed November 2004).

SIPRI (2003) *SIPRI Yearbook 2003: Armaments, Disarmanent, and International Security*, Oxford, Oxford University Press for the Stockholm International Peace Research Institute.

UNDP (1999) *Human Development Report 1999*, New York, United Nations Development Programme.

UNDP (2004) *Democracy in Latin America: Towards a Citizen's Democracy*, New York, United Nations Development Programme.

Uvin, P. (2000) 'Rwanda: the social roots of genocide', pp.159–85 in Nafziger, E. W., Stewart, F. and Väyrynen, R. (eds) *War, Hunger and Displacement: The Origins of Humanitarian Emergencies*, Vol. 2: *Case Studies*, Oxford, Oxford University Press for UNU-WIDER.

Verwimp, P. (2003) 'The political economy of coffee, dictatorship, and genocide', *European Journal of Political Economy*, vol. 19, pp. 161–81.

Ward, A. (2002) 'Former first lady exposes divisions in South Korea', *Financial Times*, London, 12 March, p. 16.

7 Greed versus grievance: conjoined twins or discrete drivers of violent conflict?

Christopher Cramer

7.1 An introduction to the neoclassical economic theory of violence and war

As we have seen in the preceding chapters, until quite recently studies of civil war had been carried out mainly by political scientists and anthropologists, joined later by international relations analysts, and occasionally environmentalists. During the 1990s, however, mainstream economists came to dominate the debate, using large databases and sophisticated analytical techniques to try to discover underlying patterns of civil war. This work helped to correct a bias against economic analysis in many earlier studies of war in developing countries, and a clear argument emerged that the main sources of civil war lay in economic factors and, moreover, the key economic driver of civil war was the opportunity to exercise individual 'greed'. This argument fitted well with the fundamental assumptions of orthodox, neoclassical economics. Economists use 'utility' as a piece of jargon encapsulating what an individual wants in terms of individual well-being, income, satisfaction, power, etc. Neoclassical economists assume that people's behaviour is governed by rational choices made so as to maximise individual 'utility'.

To many in the Development Studies field, however, this line of argument seemed to oppose what they were seeing on the ground. It was widely accepted that diamonds and drugs could fuel war, that some people grew rich from war, and that some leaders prolonged wars for personal gain; but it was not generally accepted that such aspects could be the original driving force behind wars. In addition, some other economists – so-called heterodox economists – also opposed the view of mainstream or orthodox economists, arguing that although economic factors were relevant they could not be boiled down to mere 'greed'.

Around the turn of the millennium this debate crystallised around a simple dichotomy: between greed and grievance. The stark terms of this debate helped to popularise this distinction as a way of organising analysis of and policy responses to violent conflicts in developing countries. For example, Collier and Hoeffler (2002) argued that land and income inequality have no effect on the risk of civil war. Yet Nafziger and Auvinen (2002), summarising research from a project at WIDER (part of the UN University), argued that high income inequality was one of the strongest predictors of the incidence of civil war.

This chapter sets out the terms and the evolution of the debate and shows how orthodox economic thinking came to be applied to the study of violent conflict. It also argues that the debate has been distorted by a tendency to make simplistic and misleading analytical distinctions. First, therefore, we will discuss this issue of classification and false distinctions. Section 7.3 then looks at the theoretical roots of the greed hypothesis and shows how the claims made have shifted over time. In Section 7.4 some of the main methodological and empirical critiques of the neoclassical economic perspective on violent conflict are summarised. The final section focuses on the 'collective action problem', which is central to the rational theory of the greed hypothesis and, indeed, is a central issue that requires explanation for any collective violent conflict: in what circumstances do individuals engage in collective action, in this case violent collective action, and how are some of the common obstacles to collective action overcome?

7.2   Analytical boundaries and false distinctions

Oversimplification begins with the very idea that there can be a clear 'either/or' explanation of the causes and motivations for war, whether it is either greed or grievance or any other binary forcing apart of principal causes. As we will see, greed and grievance are less easy to separate than the debate has acknowledged.

It might help to clarify this point, and to show some of the older roots of the debate, by recalling an exchange in the 1930s between Einstein and Freud on the reasons for war. Einstein opened the discussion, trying to draw Freud into an explanation of the persistence of war but in the process succinctly setting out a kind of model of his own. For Einstein, the key at a relatively proximate level of causation was the combination of two factors. First, there was the 'craving for power which characterises the governing class in every nation'. Second, this political power hunger is 'often supported by the activities of another group, whose aspirations are on purely mercenary, economic lines ... that small but determined group ... composed of individuals who, indifferent to social considerations and restraints, regard warfare ... simply as an occasion to advance their personal interests and enlarge their personal authority'. Einstein acknowledged that it was necessary then to explain how this coalition of interests could manipulate large numbers of people to take part in wars. At a superficial level, he argued, the mechanism was the control by the powerful of the organs of organisation and persuasion – schools, the press, the Church, etc. But at a more essential level, this mechanism only works because it is easy to generate a collective psychosis out of the 'lust for hatred and destruction' that people have within them.

Freud's reply elaborates on Einstein's ideas. Freud discusses the persistence of violence as the principle by which conflicts of interest are resolved. He picks up on Einstein's identification of a destructive instinct. Freud first divides all instincts into two main types – those that conserve and unify ('love') and those that are aggressive, acquisitive and destructive ('hate') – and then argues that they *cannot neatly be separated*. 'It seems that an instinct of either category can operate but rarely in isolation: it is always blended ("alloyed", as we say) with a certain dosage of its opposite, which modifies its aim or even, in certain circumstances, is a prime condition of its attainment ... As a rule several motives of similar composition concur to bring about the act ... Thus, when a nation is summoned to engage in war, a whole gamut of human motives may respond to this appeal – high and low motives, some openly avowed, others slurred over' (Freud quoted in Nathan and Norden, 1960).

This is an insight that the supporters of a 'greed versus grievance' distinction appeared to ignore. It is an example of the more general problem of categorisation or classification, a problem that afflicts the study of violent conflict in various ways, as it does most scientific endeavour. Social scientists are driven by a common and necessary human impulse to classify. However, most classification systems impose artificial discontinuities onto a reality that is more of a continuum.

One classification issue that matters greatly to the greed versus grievance debate and more generally to the discussion of the causes of violent conflict is the question of how to define a civil war. Those conducting individual case studies perhaps have less need to commit to a specific and explicit definition of civil war. However, those who carry out comparative studies, especially those involving large samples, have to be more precise in their definitions. The classification challenge is to define criteria for inclusion in, and exclusion from, the set of phenomena to be called civil wars. Briefly, a number of complications arise.

First, the borders around the set of civil wars might be artificial, porous, or fuzzy. On the one hand, civil wars may shade into regional or international wars. A classic example is the Spanish Civil War, which the historian E. H. Carr referred to as 'the first battle of the Second World War' and in which a number of other countries were embroiled, as combatants, as influences, as financiers and arms suppliers. Violent conflict in the Democratic Republic of the Congo (Zaire) in the 1990s and 2000s was at the same time a *civil* or *intrastate war*, a series of *localised conflicts* (e.g. in the eastern Kivu districts, a calamity sustained, and perhaps partly caused, by specific market linkages to the world economy), and a *regional international war* stoked by interventions by Rwanda, Uganda, Angola and Zimbabwe.

On the other hand, civil wars may shade into non-war violence. There is some disagreement over whether or not the conflict in the 1980s in South Africa between the African National Congress (ANC) and Inkatha, fought out in what is now KwaZulu-Natal and around migrant worker hostels in the townships of the Witwatersrand industrial heartland, represented a civil war or a different form of localised conflict. Certainly, this was collective killing and while there were overlapping reasons for much of the killing, these reasons included a collective purpose. However, beyond the fact of its collective organisation, there is the question of the role of the state. Most definitions of civil war turn partly on whether a violent conflict pits one party against the state: in that particular conflict neither party was the state, though of course the violence was folded into the broader political conflict over apartheid and the evidence suggests that the apartheid state carefully nurtured both the underlying political and social conflict and the violence. Elsewhere, in India and Brazil there is widespread urban and rural violence, some of it highly organised and collective and much of it involving state complicity (and complacency) in one way or another. It is common, for example, to read discussions of urban violence in Brazil that apply the 'civil war' label, though this would not be included in quantitative datasets of civil wars.

The second complication regarding the classification of civil wars is the question of whether all those conflicts that qualify as civil wars can really be treated as equivalent. For obviously there is, as Sambanis (2003) puts it, 'unit heterogeneity'. In other words, having applied a formal set of criteria to produce a set of civil wars it is then immediately obvious that this set includes very varied experiences. Were the causes and characteristics of war in Liberia identical to those in Angola, let alone those in Colombia or Afghanistan or Sri Lanka? Can we use exactly the same model to explain the outbreak of conflict in Chechnya in the 1990s and the civil war in El Salvador in the 1980s or Greece in the 1940s? Doubtless, these conflicts have things in common – in the logic of violence and in the meddling of imperial powers; but it is surely stretching the truth to think of them as equivalent conflicts.

Third, there is the 'Rwanda problem'. The most widely used definition (for purposes of quantitative analysis) of civil war relies on a particular 'battle death threshold' of 1000 deaths per year. Aside from the massive problem of data reliability that afflicts all studies of violent conflict and that undermines the stability of any inferential claims from large sample statistical studies, there is a qualitative difficulty; for civil wars often involve vast numbers of deaths by direct violence that does not take place in classic battlefield confrontations. Furthermore, a huge number of the casualties of such conflicts are killed by indirect violence, i.e. by the increase in disease or (for example, as a result of the strategic bombing campaigns conducted by the Derg in Ethiopia in Wollo and Tigray during the mid 1980s) in famine fatalities. Despite the high numbers of people killed, the genocide in Rwanda in 1994 does not qualify as a civil war – though of course, as we saw in Box 4.3, one of the causes of that paroxysm of viciousness was the civil war following the invasion in 1990 from Uganda of Rwandan Patriotic Front (RPF) forces, a group that had emerged among Tutsi refugees in Uganda..

Therefore, it can be seen that the very definition of a civil war is unstable. In addition, even if a relatively precise civil war definition is accepted, quantitative analysis and inference remain highly sensitive to small changes in the definition or in which cases are deemed to fit the definition. The University of Michigan's Correlates of War (COW) Project, first begun in 1963 and still ongoing, is widely accepted 'to have one of the top data collection programs in the field of political science'. Most quantitative studies have employed the COW dataset of civil wars and, therefore, it has been assumed that they are applying identical 'rules' in categorising conflicts for inclusion or exclusion under the title of 'civil war'. However, Sambanis (2002) argued that there are in fact inconsistencies over time within the

COW project and, therefore, between the datasets used in models of civil war. Applying some of the variables most commonly used in such models – including GDP growth rates and per capita levels, inequality, and degree of democracy – to a range of subtly varying versions of the COW dataset, Sambanis found that not only does the degree of significance in correlations vary but also, in some cases, the sign of the correlation relationship varied depending on which dataset was used.

Classification questions are, therefore, at the heart of debates about the causes of violent conflict. Inevitably, any classification will involve imposing artificial discontinuities onto continuous reality. What matters is whether the classification systems used provide explanatory clarification or whether they actually obscure the issues. The greed versus grievance debate itself is based upon a distinction that, it has been argued, is conceptually misleading; below, some of the empirical evidence that also undermines the usefulness of this distinction will be discussed.

7.3   Evolution of the greed versus grievance debate

7.3.1   History of economics and conflict

We have seen that it wasn't until the 1990s that economics was brought to bear in the analysis of civil war. This may owe something to the historical tradition of thinking in economics, which through the nineteenth century came to have a rather positive conception of human behaviour and especially of the effects on society of capitalism. Keynes captured precisely this idea, arguing: 'Dangerous human proclivities can be canalised into comparatively harmless channels by the existence of opportunity for money-making and private wealth, which, if they cannot be satisfied in this way, may find their outlet in cruelty, the reckless pursuit of personal power and authority, and other forms of self-aggrandizement' (Keynes, cited in Hirschman, 1992, p. 134). Meanwhile, the slightly naive gaze of economics was reinforced by the paradox made famous by Adam Smith – that the selfish pursuit by individuals of their own interest produced, by the waving of the wand of the invisible hand, the optimal social outcome.

However, this attitude changed as the movement known by some as 'economics imperialism' gathered momentum during the 1990s. This phrase describes the process by which the principles and methods of orthodox economics were applied to an increasingly wide set of social phenomena; or from another perspective, it describes the colonisation of the social sciences by economic principles and methods.

One of the most important roots of the greed versus grievance debate was Jack Hirshleifer's application of neoclassical economic theory to the study of violent conflict. Hirshleifer (1994) sought to refresh and complete economics by showing that it could be applied also to what he calls 'the dark side of the force'. Hirshleifer makes the point that people are rational, utility-optimising individuals, with choices – typically between cooperation and conflict. Hirshleifer proposes that while there may be a 'way of Coase', after

Shanty town along the railway track at Senen contrasts with newly built apartment blocks on Jakarta's Golden Mile.

Ronald Coase's proposition that individuals never willingly pass up an opportunity for mutually beneficial exchange, there is also a 'way of Macchiavelli', since neither will people pass up an opportunity to exploit, extort, and appropriate by force. Given preferences, individuals will simply work out which activity maximises their utility at least cost. Preferences, for Hirshleifer, include broad categories like 'xenophobia'.

One other determinant of people's choices in analyses by Hirshleifer and others – choices between conflict and cooperation – is the concept of 'opportunity cost'. This captures the idea that if a person buys something, or allocates resources to one action, there is both a direct cost (the resources committed) and an opportunity cost, which is the set of alternative things or actions that are forgone by this choice. If the opportunity cost of violence is low, then it becomes more likely that people will choose violence. The opportunity cost of violence is lowest where there are fewer alternatives for peaceable gain and this is true mostly for the poor. In other words, the poor have a comparative advantage in violence.

Economists who have made empirical studies of civil war in developing countries have drawn directly on Hirshleifer's pioneering work in this field. There is a direct route from Hirshleifer's treatment of preferences to a measure of the cost of coordinating different people and getting them to commit to organised violent action. There is also a direct route from Hirshleifer's idea of the opportunity cost of violence to Collier's suggestion that greed is a motive for violence in the particular case where there is evidence of a large number of unemployed young males in the presence of direct material benefits through instant taxation or looting. Attacking a town and looting it do not, in this case, involve giving up safe jobs and bright prospects.

7.3.2 Changing models

The greed versus grievance debate emerged against this background. Collier (Collier and Hoeffler, 1996) developed a sequence of models that sought to put empirical flesh on what otherwise remained an elegant but entirely abstract, and hence speculative, theory. These models changed: they contained different propositions, they drew on different data, and they made evolving empirical claims over time. The models spanned the range from an early model on the conditions under which the utility of rebellion would be maximised, to the World Bank's 2003 report *Breaking the Conflict Trap*, and an associated output of World Bank research in this field, Sambanis's (2003) study of the 'fit' between the model and detailed case studies.

Before outlining some of the key features of this evolving model, it is worth stressing that the claims that were made shifted rather substantially. *Breaking the Conflict Trap* retreated from the explanatory confidence of the earlier models on which it was built, and acknowledged that the causes of wars are multiple. Because of this, the report proposed that the focus should be not on the clear identification of causes but on statistical 'proneness'. Further, while the core model presented in the report was little changed from earlier models, it was argued that greed is less important than formerly suggested: 'While the prevalence of natural resource secessions suggests that greed cannot be entirely discounted, it does not appear to be the powerful force behind rebellion that economic theorists have assumed' (Collier et al., 2003, p. 64).

Let us, then, look at these models, chiefly by focusing on the evolution of the models of Collier (2000), and Collier and Hoeffler (1996). An early version proposed that the utility of rebellion could be assessed by the interplay of several factors: the probability of victory, the gains to victory, the expected duration of the conflict and the costs of organising a rebellion. However, these things are difficult to measure, certainly in precise quantitative terms. Therefore the authors proposed to capture them indirectly, by using proxy variables. Proxies are used commonly in quantitative analysis where the variable of direct interest cannot be quantified but where, arguably, a close substitute can be quantified and can be trusted to represent the actual object of interest.

The early model therefore proposed:

- that the utility of rebellion was a function of the probability of victory, which itself was a function of potential government defence spending and the resource endowment of the country; and
- that the utility of rebellion would be greater where the conflict was expected to be over quickly, where the windfall gain to victorious rebels was likely to be higher, and where it was relatively easy and costless to organise a rebellion.

Potential government defence spending was 'proxied' by the natural resource endowment – with a hefty endowment of natural resources, a government should be able to adjust the temporal flow of revenue, raising resource extraction and/or taxation in order to pay for increased military spending to rebuff a rebellion. An obvious example was the way that the Angolan Government in the 1990s raised oil-backed commercial loans, partly to finance military expenditure. By contrast, natural resources also provide a windfall to victors, so this proxy has to perform two contrary roles.

In this same model, potential defence spending was also proxied by a quantitative measure for inequality, the Gini coefficient (see Box 7.1). This inequality variable in the model produced an intriguing claim: high inequality appeared to be correlated with a low incidence of civil war. This is at odds with the findings of other models and explanations both by Collier and by others. The explanation given was that high inequality would indicate the existence of a wealthy elite that was so content with the status quo that its members would welcome a temporary tax hike to cover the costs of maintaining this status quo. Therefore, knowledge of a high degree of inequality would be a deterrent to prospective rebels. This captures a very important dimension of Collier's argument: that there may well be reasons to start a rebellion (and inequality may be one of them) but what matters is whether or not there is a sufficient opportunity for successful rebellion. In this case, high inequality, because of its supposed effect on fiscal politics and government defence capacity, represents a lack of opportunity.

Box 7.1   Inequality and the Gini coefficient

The Gini coefficient is the most common measure used by economists to capture the distribution of income. Data are collected from household surveys carried out across a 'representative' sample of the population of a country. On the basis of the data collected, it is possible to calculate what proportion of the total income of the country flows to the richest 10 per cent of the population, the next richest 10 per cent, and so on down to the poorest 10 per cent. This information is converted into an index that produces a 'score' between zero and one. A country with a Gini coefficient closer to one (like Finland) has a much more even distribution of income than a country with a score closer to zero (like Brazil or South Africa). It should be noted that this is only one among a number of ways in which economists measure inequality and that this – like other measures – needs to be treated with great caution. Typically, scores for different countries hide differences in the type of information collected, in the quality of data collection procedures, and in the degree to which the sample was really representative of the total population. These problems mean that quantitative data on inequality are an unreliable guide to changes over time and to comparisons between countries.

The other proxy worth highlighting here is that used to stand for the coordination costs of rebellion. This is where the ethno-linguistic fractionalisation index (ELF) enters the fray. This index measures the probability that any two people encountering one another will come from a different ethnic group. The evidence appeared to show that more ethnically diverse or fragmented societies were *not* more volatile and more likely to be rent by war. The evidence suggested that something in between total homogeneity and ethnic diversity was associated with the statistical risk of conflict, i.e. polarisation. The answer to why this might be was that in a diverse society it would prove too difficult to coordinate a coherent rebellion. The costs would be least in an ethnically polarised society with starkly rival ethnic 'preferences'.

In subsequent years this basic model changed. The mix of variables shifted, the emphasis shifted, the rational explanations varied, and the dataset changed. The simplest variation was in Collier and Hoeffler (1998). Here the model was adjusted to include religious difference as well as ethnic fractionalisation (though this innovation was then dropped in some subsequent models such as the more widely read Collier (2000) greed or grievance model). In spite of these changes however, the 1998 model generated more or less similar findings and some predictive claims. Nonetheless, it is also worth noting that inequality slipped quietly out of the model at this stage, though it reappeared in later versions, to play a different role.

7.3.3 Proxies for motives

The most well known version of the model was Collier (2000). Proposing simply to explore whether conflicts take place more because of grievance or greed, Collier designed proxies for each of these categorically distinct motives. Grievance was proxied by:

- economic stagnation, captured in the rate of growth of GDP in the five years before the outbreak of war
- evidence of repression, measured through indices of political rights
- inequality, quantified in the Gini coefficient
- and possible ethnic tension, applying the scores for the ethno-linguistic fractionalisation index.

The proxies for greed were:

- the share of primary commodity exports in total GDP
- the share of 15–24 year old males in the total population
- and the average years of schooling in the society.

These proxies were designed to capture the possibility that, whatever grievances might exist, a civil war would only happen where there was the mixture of unemployed young men with no economic opportunities and the easy spoils of war, like alluvial diamonds. Perhaps not surprisingly, given the proxies examined, the empirical tests produced stronger correlations between the 'greed' proxies and civil war than between war and 'grievance' proxies.

Can this finding be justified in the real-world context, however? Collier's answer began from the reasonable point that grievances are extremely common but the incidence of civil war is less so. Whatever the objective conditions of society and the scope for grievance, it has often been observed that poor and oppressed people are politically quiescent, even fatalistic. Whether this means they have a high 'tolerance for inequality', or a rational awareness of the high coordination costs of rebellion or the low probability of victory, or whatever, is not very clear. Collier then argued that the answer lay in the collective action problem. The classic collective action problem – i.e. the obstacle to collective action by rational, choice-making individuals – is that it is hard naturally to produce public goods, goods whose enjoyment cannot be exclusive to individuals, through collective action (street lighting or security, in the textbook examples) when some people will be 'free riders': they will benefit from the public good without willingly contributing to its provision. Usually, it will take some form of coercion, like government taxation, to ensure the provision of public goods. In the application of the idea to the problem of rebellion, conditions of grievance will not produce sufficient conflict to overcome injustice because of this free-rider phenomenon. Why would someone risk their life and give up their fishing or farming work to try to win social benefits that other people, who do not lift a rebellious finger, will be able to enjoy? There is another problem too. People will not naturally, so the argument goes, trust in the lofty promises of leaders that after the victory a bright new day will dawn, and the society will be converted into a just and egalitarian society. But if there are immediate rewards that can be enjoyed individually by participants, like diamonds, gold watches, other people's daughters, and so on, then the collective action problem vanishes.

Collier (2000) was followed by the World Bank's 2003 report, *Breaking the Conflict Trap*, of which Collier was one of the main authors. In the light of previous versions, as highlighted above, this was a remarkable document. It appeared in many ways to retreat from any sharp analytical focus, moving away from previous hypotheses and placing more significance on variables that had been downplayed in Collier (2000) and Collier and Hoeffler (1996, 1998). In addition, the report appeared to contain many contradictions. In one place the text distanced itself from the claims of 'economic theorists' that greed is a significant cause of conflict, but at the core of the report, the Collier and Hoeffler model appears to be essentially unchanged. While the report took pains to stress the multiple causes of war and to pay due respect to the specifics of individual cases, in practice such specificity and context were arguably overwhelmed by the emphasis on establishing generalised statistical models. This approach, which treats all civil wars as equivalent, is counter to the idea of 'unit heterogeneity' that we met at the beginning of this chapter (Sambanis, 2003).

The next section will look in more detail at these shifting models and examine the methodology applied in more detail.

7.4   Social science or smoke and mirrors?

There are several possible explanations for the shift over time in these models. Plausible reasons include changes in the dataset, shifting ideological nuances, institutional pressures, the inevitably cumbersome outcome of multiple authorship, and a bid to be seen to accommodate at least some of the criticisms of the neoclassical economic perspective on violent conflict. Beyond purely speculating on what lies behind these changes, it is worth highlighting some of the major features that critiques of these models have identified and considering the empirical efforts to test the propositions made. Some argued that the models discussed above were characterised by a combination of truism and falsehood. Some argued that the models did capture an important dimension of at least some specific conflicts but that there could be no single explanation for all civil wars. Others focused more on the lack of emphasis on international causes and contributing factors to the incidence of civil wars.

A range of criticisms has been levelled at this kind of approach. Sambanis (2003) noted the 'simplistic distinction' between greed and grievance (see also Cramer, 2002 and Richards, 2005) and pointed out that state strength and weakness was not well theorised in the Collier models. Fearon and Laitin (2003) criticise the empirical findings on various counts, claiming that in their own statistical research they find no evidence, for example, for an association between primary commodity dependence and civil war onset. Cramer (2002) challenges the appropriateness of the methods, the quality of the evidence and the logic of the assumptions underlying the models. Lichbach et al. (2003), criticising both Fearon and Laitin's (2003) and Collier's models, stress the ambiguity of the proxies used. Lichbach et al. also criticise the lack of consideration in these models of political dynamics, that is, of the processes of historic political mobilisation and prior conflict. This relates to the discussion of collective action in violent conflict and echoes at the general level the arguments of Wood (2003) and Gutierrez (2003) (see below). Meanwhile, Richards (2005) argues that Collier and Hoeffler completely misunderstand the ways in which non-economist social scientists collect and treat evidence. Collier's approach turns on the assertion that if people are interviewed about their participation in violent conflicts they will inevitably hide their greed and dramatise their grievance, therefore obscuring their true interests and motivations. Econometric analysis of behaviour (through indirect, proxy measures) is supposedly more 'objective'. To this, Richards responds that Collier 'seems to be basically misinformed about how other social scientists approach their research. Anthropologists and others who take what people say seriously are not as naive as he assumes' (2005, p 11).

Authors of quantitative models of civil war drawing on neoclassical economics purport to be objective and to apply good social science. They say there are weaknesses in the way the empirical tests were designed. The predictive claims were unconvincing, even on their own methodological terms and without any grander critique of econometric methods. The data were so unreliable that they could not support any of the empirical claims made. And the rationalisations deployed to 'explain' the findings of tests could appear arbitrary and overly abstract, whereas actual case study evidence of political dynamics often suggested alternative explanations. The rest of this chapter summarises briefly these methodological and empirical problems and then discusses in a little more depth some evidence from a range of conflicts on the collective action problem – why people participate in warfare and how they are recruited.

What was basically abstract speculation and logical thought experiment in Hirshleifer (1994) was tested in a range of models that relied on quantifiable proxy variables to represent purported causal linkages. The main problem with this arises if the proxies are poor approximations of reality. A model proposing that those (young men) with no economic opportunities have a comparative advantage in violence and, therefore, that a society with a large concentration of such young men is likely to experience civil war, depends on average years of schooling as a proxy for unemployment. This is, however, a confused set of propositions. In particular, it is not obvious that available data on average years of schooling accurately represent lack of economic opportunities or unemployment. Nor is it at all clear that it is the unemployed exclusively or mainly who are the solid fuel of collective violence. There are many countries with a high level of supply of educated youth but where this is not matched by demand for educated labour. And lack of education does not always translate directly into unemployment – especially where there are many economic activities that do not necessarily fit standard categories of employment, where much labour market and other economic activity is unrecorded, and where labour demand is often seasonal rather than permanent.

Further, it is somewhat naive to claim that violence is supplied by the unemployed and ill-educated. The same argument was made about suicide bombers, yet the evidence showed that the bulk of suicide bombers in the Lebanon, for example, were educated and relatively middle class (Krueger and Maleckova, 2002). The appalling pogrom in Surat in India in the early 1990s against Muslims was a cataclysm of poorly regulated labour markets characterised by desperate conditions, low pay, seasonal migration and political stoking, not by simple unemployment. Landless agricultural workers in El Salvador – many of whom had made up an unfree labour force, with restrictions on mobility, etc., on large plantations – were a critical component of the voluntary support for and participation in the Farabundo Marti National Liberation (FMLN) insurgency of the 1980s, alongside self-employed family farmers. In Sierra Leone, young unemployed males in the countryside and the towns were an important part of the Revolutionary United Front (RUF), but there are three qualifications to this. First, employed young men were also recruited, i.e. not exclusively those with no prospects at all other than violence. Second, many of the young people (not just boys) who were recruited to fight for and to provide logistic and sexual support to the RUF were forcibly recruited and kept virtually as slaves. Third, even though some people did secure direct material benefits from access to diamond transactions (and so might be thought of as 'greedy') there is plenty of evidence of an age-based grievance motivating voluntary RUF recruits. Lack of education seems more likely to be a proxy for grievance rather than for greed. In rural areas the institutions of gerontocratic chieftaincy had for many years continued to dominate society but with a profoundly compromised legitimacy. Since the state system of taxation had disintegrated, chieftaincies replaced it with arbitrary levies that were sorely resented. Indeed, Fanthorpe (2003, p. 58) argued that: 'Modernised, educated and individuated youth, once jettisoned by contracting patrimonial networks, may have had little opportunity, let alone desire, to return to rural communities governed by chiefs. Readily recruited by belligerent groups on both sides, they were already primed to sow chaos by their double alienation.'

The use of the ethno-linguistic fractionalisation index was another crude and frequently misleading proxy for the coordination costs of rebellion. The validity of using this index in large statistical studies depends on three conditions: there must be an agreed score for each country and there must be a consistent unit of measurement across countries; ethnicity must be the principal source of collective identity and the main basis for collective action and preferences in all the countries in the sample; and ethnicity must have the same social and political significance across time and space within the sample. However, none of these conditions holds. For example, there are problems in 'scoring' Rwanda, given that there is no racial or linguistic or religious basis for the Tutsi/Hutu ethnic distinction. In Afghanistan, meanwhile, different estimates for the number of ethnic groups vary between 50 and 100.

In addition, there is no empirical foundation for the assumption that ethnicity is the main source of collective preference or collective action and coordination. Sure enough, ethnicity or race often overlap with ideology and class as sources of collective action – as they did, for example, in Chiapas in Mexico in the early 1990s and in El Salvador in the 1980s, and as they did in Angola in the 1970s to the early 2000s, and elsewhere. But ethnicity is far from obviously the main source of collective action in conflict. In Sierra Leone, over time during the war there were ethnic phenomena, like the kamajoisia militia, but ethnicity played very little role in the cause of war. Similarly, in Angola it is easy to divide the population into three main ethnic groups, the Bakongo, the Mbundu, and the Ovimbundu, each of which maps roughly onto the constituencies of the FNLA, the MPLA and UNITA, respectively. However, there is little mileage in explaining the war as an ethnic war. The overlap map of liberation movements and ethnic groups is not very exact, and in any case, many people in Angola had very little sense of ethnicity during the colonial period. Ethnicity was not institutionalised in the same way it was both before and during Belgian colonialism in Rwanda, for example. And during the war – despite some efforts by leaders to play the ethnic card – for many people ethnicity faded rather than sharpened as a source of collective identity, as a result of mass migration to cities, the increasingly widespread use of Portuguese, and the fact, for example, that there were Ovimbundu fighting in the government's armed forces as well as for UNITA. Further, there was considerable internal conflict within Ovimbundu areas rather than a homogeneous and instinctive reflex of support for UNITA. To summarise, ethnolinguistic diversity is unstable within countries over time, it is inconsistent as a driver of political allegiance across countries, and it is not even clear how precisely it can be measured. Therefore, it is not likely to work effectively as a proxy for how collective action is taken or avoided.

These examples suggest that the empirical tests are not designed very robustly. Furthermore, they wield data that are extremely untrustworthy. It has already been shown in Section 7.2 of this chapter that the correlations on which inferences are made are highly sensitive to variations in the sample. More generally, data on political violence are often unreliable, especially as a basis for comparison. So too are the data for many of the other variables used in these models – data on unemployment, on economic performance, on degrees of freedom or political repression, and on inequality, are all often highly questionable. Cramer (2003), for example, showed how poor data on inequality internationally undermines the quest for event regularities linking inequality to the incidence of violent conflict.

These empirical problems help to explain why the models have so far not achieved any convincing empirical claims or predictive success. Leaving aside the methodological and philosophical argument about whether or not predictive success can be achieved in the social sciences, the shaky claims made by analyses of these models are compounded by contradictory empirical claims made in other analyses testing similar variables. Collier and Hoeffler (1998) 'predict' 14 and fail to predict 13 of the 27 'civil wars' in their sample of 95 observations. Thus their model appeared to have a roughly 50:50, coin-tossing success rate in predicting where wars actually took place. Sixty-five non-wars are predicted correctly: i.e. in 65 cases where there was not a civil war their model correctly expected this outcome, as against the six cases where there was no war but the model had expected a war. Non-war simply is statistically more common than war. Further, it is not clear how dazzling are the insights of a model claiming to predict civil wars between 1960 and 1992 that tests a sample arguably skewed by the inclusion of 20 OECD countries out of a total of 98.

More significantly, there was little agreement in the literature on the significance of key factors, or variables, used in statistical studies. Nafziger and Auvinen (2002, p. 156) claimed that high income inequality was correlated with the incidence of humanitarian emergencies. In an early version of the Collier and Hoeffler model discussed above (1996), high inequality is said to reduce the risk of civil war (because the elite beneficiaries of the high Gini coefficient can be relied on to fund a war effort to repel the rebellion). In the 1998 version of the model, inequality vanishes from sight. In Collier's greed and grievance model of 2000 inequality appears but, lined up on the grievance side of the divide, is deemed irrelevant to the incidence of civil war. Then, in *Breaking the Conflict Trap* (2003), inequality did appear to be one of the root causes of conflict: 'Thus our central argument can be stated briefly: the key root cause of conflict is the failure of economic development. Countries with low, stagnant, and *unequally distributed per capita incomes* that have remained dependent on primary commodities for their exports face dangerously high risks of prolonged conflict' (Collier et al., 2003, p. 53, emphasis added). Meanwhile, Cramer (2003) found no clear pattern linking Gini coefficient data to the incidence of civil war, but qualifies this by questioning the value of the Gini coefficient as an indicator of the way in which inequality might matter to the causation of conflict. For it might be that inequality does matter to conflict but that its contribution cannot be captured by the Gini coefficient or other quantitative measures. The significance of inequality might lie more in the specific political history of social group relationships in any given country and in the ways in which these institutionalise what Addison and Murshed in Chapter 6 call 'horizontal inequalities', e.g. between Catholics and Protestants, Hutus and Tutsis, immigrants and indigenous inhabitants, black and white, and so on.

There is a similar story for other variables. Fearon and Laitin (2003) argued, for example, that the preponderance of young men in a population does appear to be positively correlated with the incidence of civil war but that, since most wars are in lower or middle income countries where the demographic structure is skewed towards the young, we cannot be sure of causality. Fearon and Laitin also found that there was no evidence to support Collier's claims about the causal significance of primary commodities.

Intervention implications

Look beneath the claimed justifications of the combatants for economic motivations. Economic betterment can be an important cause of war – leaders and combatants may be fighting to redress serious horizontal economic inequalities, but they may also be fighting for personal gain. Often, both are occurring. Interveners need to look to ways of blocking sources of personal gain while simultaneously trying to redress serious economic inequalities between groups.

7.5   Collective action

Neoclassical economic theories and models of violent conflict quite rightly questioned the circumstances in which people will engage in violent collective action. They answered the question, as we saw above, in a particular way: the constraints on collective action are overcome by offering direct and selective material benefits to individuals (who may exclude others from the enjoyment of these benefits) and by reducing the need to defer their enjoyment until some putative victory.

This argument chimes nicely with evidence of conflicts fuelled by loot. At first sight, it appears to tally with UNITA's capacity in Angola to mobilise people after the end of the Cold War through control of diamond fields; with the RUF insurgency in Sierra Leone, again linked to diamonds and other sources of instant taxation; with the militia groups mixing warfare with control of and participation in the coltan commodity chain in the Kivus in the Democratic Republic of the Congo; with participation in violence and the opium economy in Afghanistan and Burma/Myanmar; and with the overlapping guerrilla warfare and drug, and kidnapping, economy in Colombia.

However, this abstract argument is actually a rather poor guide to the ways in which collective action challenges have been met in a variety of wars around the world. For example, from this perspective insurgency in Colombia and El Salvador presents something of a puzzle. Participation in the FARC in Colombia and in the FMLN war in El Salvador was largely voluntary; however, the risks in both cases were high relative to not participating. Further, the rewards were neither material nor exclusive to the volunteers. Life in the FARC was extraordinarily tough (Gutierrez Sanin, 2003). No contact with families was allowed, sex was discouraged, and conditions were often physically gruelling. The risks were high, and higher than for non-participants. FARC members were not paid, looting was prohibited, and material rewards and profits were channelled upwards to the apex of the organisation. Yet volunteer numbers were high. Indeed, the FARC was competitive in recruitment compared with other militias and paramilitary groups, even though these rivals did pay recruits.

In El Salvador during the civil war the FMLN also attracted a lot of voluntary support (Wood, 2003). Again, conditions were difficult and the risks high. There were rewards – in the form of access to occupied plantation land, and local landowners did pay coffee taxes, for example, and peasants supplied tortillas to the guerrillas – but these rewards hardly took the form of 'loot'. The instant taxation that took place scarcely fits the stereotype of marauding and unruly troops preying on the local population. Further, the chief rewards were not exclusive to FLMN volunteers. Other local landless people and smallholder families could benefit from improved land access and new cooperatives even if they were not FMLN members. The evidence suggests that more complex forces than maximisation of individual material utility drove voluntary participation. Rationality was relational and social and ideological norms played a dominant role. Historical experience does matter – for example, the history of land dispossession in El Salvador, the enduring unfree labour relations, a rural society characterised by National Guardsmen being stationed on the larger plantations, continued repression and the historical memory of *La Matanza*, the massacre in 1930 of thousands of Indians in the wake of a labour protest. Economic variables are an important way into the understanding of conflict in El Salvador but the timing of the uprising owes more to two factors other than the previous five years of economic growth: a specific cycle of action and reaction that ratcheted up the scale and intensity of violent conflict; and years of political mobilisation in the countryside, by leftwing leaders and by liberation theologians.

Social norms and political ideas were important in Colombia too, where the other dominant factor was the organisational learning and effectiveness of the FARC leadership. Certainly, as the cocaine sector expanded this had a dramatic effect on the scale potential of the FARC but cocaine production and trade does not explain the origins of the FARC rebellion or the success of its recruitment. The neoclassical economic perspective – with its argument that the poor have a comparative advantage in violence – suggests that, in the old cliché, 'life is cheap': where there is no opportunity life is a throwaway thing. However, the behaviour of volunteers for the FARC, the

FMLN, the Zapatistas in Chiapas, militias in Sierra Leone, and so on suggests that life is not simply being thrown away because of its low value: rather, it suggests that joining violence can be an assertion of the value of life, not its devaluation. It is always right to question the veracity of motives expressed by the actors during the war and rationalisations of causes claimed after the war. However, there is an intriguing comparative consistency in some of the imagery of rebellion across contexts. Repeatedly, in Africa or Latin America for example, interviewed rebels suggest themes like wanting no longer 'to be treated like dogs' or to escape 'being treated like slaves'. Keen's (2002) interviews in Sierra Leone generate a repeated emphasis on a quest for *respect* and an assertion of *humanity* through violence, as well as a precise formula of turning the tables on those – especially the chiefs – who had humiliated young people previously for non-payment of arbitrary taxes. 'Let's see why the war emerged,' said a cooperative leader in El Salvador. 'Perhaps – the majority say so anyway – because the Catholic Church gave a certain orientation. Perhaps the words of the Bible connected with a very deep injustice – they treated us like animals, it was slavery. In the Word of God, there was something that would touch you. In truth, we had been living as though the Word was in the air, when it was something to live within ourselves. I am grateful that there were such people, many of them now dead' (quoted in Wood, 2003, p. 87).

Zapatistas, Chiapas, Mexico.

A further factor in the overcoming of private, individual deterrents to collective violent action is that wars typically emerge from a background of layer upon layer of social and political conflict and previous violence. Layer upon layer of private and local social agendas are folded into the actually manifest 'civil war'. The scope for score settling may decide at the margin whether one individual chooses to join rather than not join a rebellion. And the success of collective violence organisationally depends typically on its fusion between goals and agendas. One of the best analyses of this is Norma Kriger's (1992) research into 'peasant voices' on participation in the liberation war in Zimbabwe, where, for example, local agendas of women's conflict against patriarchy and young men's conflict against rural gerontocracy were often more important mobilising forces than the grander project of nationalism.

Finally, one of the most common sources of collective mobilisation, which violates rational choice precepts, is coercion of one kind or another. This is more important in some conflicts than others. In Angola both the MPLA and UNITA routinely press-ganged, kidnapped, and forced people to join their armed forces as combatants, sexual servants, or logistical workers, cooks, porters, and so on. This was especially so for the recruitment of children. The same has been true of the violence in the Democratic Republic of the Congo. By now, it is also well known that in Mozambique, Cambodia, Sierra Leone and elsewhere a common form of recruitment to atrocity involved forcing individuals to perform extreme acts of violence, usually against family members.

> ### Intervention implications
>
>
>
> Think about the collective action problem and why people have been willing to risk their lives in a civil war. Interveners should respond to those reasons. People who were fighting for what they saw as an important cause can become key actors in peacebuilding, while those who were forced to fight may need special support. For those who fought simply for lack of other opportunities, the priority may be education and jobs.

7.6 Conclusion

The neoclassical economic perspective injected a much-needed dimension to the study of violent conflicts. This perspective focused on the economic and material in a way that many analyses of violence did not. For example, two excellent readers on violence, published in 2002 and 2004, failed to include any economic analysis of note. And the neoclassical economic perspective helped to bring the study of violence closer to the heart of development economics and development studies. That this was necessary is clear from the fact that most development textbooks, until 2000 at least, barely mentioned a subject that is obviously central – through the incidence of war and the prevalence of non-war violence – to the lives of vast numbers of people in the world.

Yet from another perspective the neoclassical economic theories of violent conflict combined inaccurate proxies with unreliable observations, to test an abstract model concocted out of platitudes mixed with an extraordinarily restricted set of precepts about human behaviour and rationality. The theories and models did not produce a good fit with any detailed observation of reality. Finally and to return to the first point made in this chapter, the neoclassical economic framework for the explanation of violent conflict tended to produce and rely upon too many artificial distinctions. The future of this field of study lies in probing the porous borders of these categories and distinctions. Most notably, the distinction between greed and grievance has proven unhelpful, as indeed the World Bank itself acknowledged (Collier et al., 2003). Quantitative studies are important but need to be conducted and advanced with considerable caution: they are often best as ways of raising questions rather than answering them. And there is a need for far more interdisciplinary, detailed and historical case studies. These should definitely make use of political economy and economic analysis; they should learn from the ideas and questions raised by orthodox economists; but they should not become trapped by the abstractions of neoclassical economics.

7.7 Chapter summary

The debate between economists is characterised as **greed versus grievance**. Economists use 'utility' as a word encapsulating what an individual wants. Orthodox neoclassical economists assume that people's behaviour is governed by rational choices made so as to maximise individual 'utility' and thus that the key economic driver of civil war was the opportunity to exercise individual **'greed'**. The so-called heterodox economists responded that economic **grievances** rather than greed were the driving force. The split was clearest over **income inequality** – orthodox economists said high income inequality did not increase the risk of civil war, while heterodox economists said high income inequality was one of the strongest predictors of civil war.

Orthodox economists hoped their methods would be more **objective**, and that by applying modelling techniques to databases on civil wars they could determine roots and even predict wars. But in trying to treat all civil wars in the same way, they faced major difficulties with defining wars, as well as problems obtaining sufficient statistical information about civil war countries. With no precise way of defining and measuring motives, economists were forced to use alternatives that could be measured – so-called **proxies** – to stand in, and there was debate about the validity of these choices. These studies gained international prominence, particularly with the World Bank, but the methods proved unable to predict wars. The problem may be that far from being objective, the choices of models, data sets and especially proxies became **subjective**.

But the entry of economists into the study of civil wars forced serious consideration of economic motivations and also of the **collective action problem** – why do people choose to participate in civil wars, at potential great personal cost, rather than just be **free riders** who take no risks but share the benefits of victory? A variety of answers may apply, even to different people in the same war. For orthodox economists, the issue is maximising personal utility – people feel they have **more to gain than to lose** by fighting. This applies both to pure greed and to lack of alternative opportunities. But, as has already been seen, there are many examples of people fighting for **altruistic and political** motivations or out of **group solidarity** – they join the war because they agree the group will gain through violence, even if they may lose personally.

References

Collier, P. (2000) 'Doing well out of war: an economic perspective' in Berdal, M. and D. M. Malone (eds) *Greed and Grievance: Economic Agendas in Civil Wars*, Boulder CO, IDRC/Lynne Rienner.

Collier, P. and Hoeffler, A. (1996) 'On economic causes of civil war', mimeo, Oxford, Centre for the Study of African Economies.

Collier, P. and Hoeffler, A. (1998) 'On economic causes of civil war', *Oxford Economic Papers*, vol. 50, pp. 563–73.

Collier, P. and Hoeffler, A. (2002) 'Greed and grievance in civil war', Working Paper 2002–01, Oxford, Centre for the Study of African Economies, www.csae.ox.ac.uk/workingpapers/wps-list.html (accessed November 2004).

Cramer, C. (2002) 'Homo economicus goes to war: methodological individualism, rational choice, and the political economy of war', *World Development*, vol. 30, no. 11, pp. 1845–64.

Cramer, C. (2003) 'Does inequality cause conflict?', *Journal of International Development*, vol. 15, pp. 397–412.

Fanthorpe, R. (2003) 'Humanitarian aid in post-war Sierra Leone: the politics of moral economy', Chapter 4 in Collinson, S. (ed.) *Power, Livelihoods and Conflict: Case Studies in Political Economy Analysis for Humanitarian Action*, HPG Report 13, London, Overseas Development Institute.

Fearon, J. and Laitin, L. (2003) 'Ethnicity, insurgency, and civil war', *American Political Science Review*, vol. 97, no. 1, pp. 75–90.

Gutierrez Sanin, F. (2003) 'Criminal rebels? A discussion of war and criminality from the Colombian experience', Crisis States Programme Working Paper 27, DESTIN, London, London School of Economics.

Hirschman, A. O. (1992) *The Passions and the Interests: Political Arguments for Capitalism before its Triumph*, Princeton, Princeton University Press.

Hirshleifer, J. (1987) 'Conflict and settlement' in Eatwell, J., Milgate, M. and Newman, P. (eds) *The New Palgrave Dictionary of Economics*, London, Macmillan Press.

Hirshleifer, J. (1994) 'The dark side of the force', *Economic Inquiry*, vol. 32, pp. 1–10.

Keen, D. (2002) ''Since I am a dog, beware my fangs': beyond a 'rational violence' framework in the Sierra Leonean war', Crisis States Working Paper No. 14, DESTIN, London, London School of Economics.

Kriger, N. (1992) *Peasant Voices: Zimbabwe's Guerrilla War*, Cambridge, Cambridge University Press.

Krueger, A. B. and Maleckova, J. (2002) 'Education, poverty and terrorism: is there a causal connection?', paper prepared for the World Bank's Annual Bank Conference on Developing Economies, April 2002.

Lichbach, M., Davenport, C. and Armstrong, D. (2003) 'Contingency, inherency and the onset of civil war', mimeo, University of Maryland.

Nafziger, E. W. and Auvinen, J. (2002) 'Economic development, inequality, war, and state violence', *World Development*, vol. 30, no. 2, pp. 153–63.

Nathan, O. and Norden, H. (eds) (1960) *Einstein on Peace*, New York, Schoken Books.

Richards, P. (2005) 'New war: an ethnographic approach' in Richards, P. (ed.) *No Peace No War: An Anthropology of Contemporary Armed Conflicts*, Athens, Ohio University Press and Oxford, James Currey.

Sambanis, N. (2002) 'Defining and measuring civil war: conceptual and empirical complexities', mimeo, Department of Political Science, Yale University.

Sambanis, N. (2003) 'Using case studies to expand the theory of civil war', CPR Working Papers No. 5, Conflict Prevention and Reconstruction Unit, Washington, World Bank.

Wood, E. (2003) *Insurgent Collective Action and Civil War in El Salvador*, Cambridge, Cambridge University Press.

World Bank (2003) *Breaking the Conflict Trap: Civil War and Development Policy*, Washington, World Bank.

Reflections on development in a context of war

Alan Thomas

8.1   'Don't just do something – stand there!'

The exhortation: 'Don't just do something, stand there!' (Minear and Weiss, 1993) comes from a handbook for practitioners of 'humanitarian action in times of war'. The point is that even in an emergency – perhaps we should say *particularly* in an emergency – it is worth stopping to think carefully rather than jumping in without analysing the consequences of actions. It is also very important to consider one's 'stance', not least in order to work out *how* actions should be carried out consistently with what one stands for.

One of this book's main themes is how external agents should act, or 'intervene', in violent conflict and post-violence situations. The implication is that war is so dreadful and so destabilising that the suffering of the populations affected and the need to avoid further damage outside the areas already caught up in violence make it imperative to 'do something'.

'Intervention' can mean outside agencies 'interfering' in the internal affairs of states, thus breaching their sovereignty (Allen and Styan, 2000). For example, the idea of 'humanitarian intervention' is used as a justification for NGOs such as Médecins Sans Frontières to cross borders in bringing relief to destitute populations. 'Intervention' can have a stronger meaning, implying 'coming between' warring parties, and there have been several recent examples of 'forcible interventions', using outside force to bring a halt to violent conflict or human rights abuses.

However, using force to end the use of force is a somewhat contradictory idea. Also, as we have seen from previous examples, forcible and other interventions often have unforeseen consequences, and it is notoriously difficult to create positive and sustainable outcomes without allowing those in conflict with each other to play out their differences in some way. Hence there are strong arguments against just 'doing something' because of the awfulness of a situation, but to do a lot of clear thinking before acting.

What is implied by the injunction to 'stand there'? Not rushing into action does not imply ignoring the escalation of violence or acquiescing in gross abuses of human rights. It first implies letting one's presence be known, making it clear that events are observed by outsiders. Second, it means holding to one's position. This implies working out the justification for one's actions, including the basis of legitimacy for any intervention. It also implies being clear about the values underlying one's position. Before embarking on any intervention, it means working out a way to act which is consistent with those values. Third, there is an imperative to adopt a 'reflective practitioner' mode, learning from experience and from what one observes before undertaking any further intervention.

Intervention implications

Even when it is not yet clear what intervention may be correct, make it obvious that events are being observed by outsiders.

In particular, taking time to think allows consideration of the development context. The rest of this chapter is about the concept of development, how it is contested, and how the different ways in which it is used relate to war and intervention. It summarises some ways of thinking about development worked out elsewhere (Thomas, 2000a, b) and applies them to the context of war.

The next section outlines the various ways in which development and war have been related to each other. It is followed by a section introducing the main meanings of development, and then by three sections taking each of the main meanings in turn in the context of war. Finally, we argue for consideration of values and consistency with one's vision of development, and for promoting the conditions for development in all interventions, even in the midst of violent conflict – with the proviso that being clear what you think development *should* mean will not necessarily make it so.

8.2 Development and war

Development and war have generally been considered separately. The simplest definition of development is probably Chambers' (1997) 'good change'. War, by contrast, is clearly bad – although, as has been pointed out in previous chapters, wars can also have some positive outcomes. Even the most brutal wars (as in Sierra Leone) are seen by at least some of the proponents as necessary in order to achieve what they regard as 'good change', by removing those who block that change.

Nevertheless, it is easy to see development as a process of improvement which is only possible in 'normal' times, i.e. in times of peace. War then seems to be an entirely negative interruption to this process. In this way of thinking, in a war or postwar situation, peace must be re-established before considering development again.

However, in practice things are always messier than this. If we waited until humanitarian relief was no longer necessary and peace was embedded, we could wait forever before beginning to think about development. In actuality, development always takes place, or development efforts are made – whether or not they succeed – in a context of conflict. This conflict may be more or less serious, involving violence to a greater or lesser extent. War may be regarded as the most extreme version of conflicts in which

Demonstration calling for children's rights, at Children's Commonwealth Day events, Durban, South Africa.

development is always an issue. Forcible interventions, humanitarian relief, peacekeeping, peacebuilding and development interventions can all be considered as types of intervention which can be happening at the same time. Development cannot be kept apart from war contexts but always needs to be considered at the same time as other forms of intervention.

There are also negative aspects of development. Although in everyday usage 'development' is virtually synonymous with 'progress', there is no agreement on what exactly constitutes progress, whether it is taking place and how it is to be achieved. Nevertheless, over the long term development implies increased living standards, improved health and well-being for all, and the achievement of whatever is regarded as the general good of society at large. However, the wholesale change required to obtain such improvements may be impossible without disrupting established living patterns, and there are almost inevitably losers as well as winners. Some, such as Alvares (1992), go further, equating development with violence and arguing that those who promote and benefit from the particular forms of development which dominate the modern world do so in the full knowledge that such development requires the exploitation, impoverishment and displacement of millions of others.

To say that development is about achieving 'whatever is regarded as the general good of society' masks the fact that what constitutes 'the general good' is regarded very differently by people with different values or interests. These can be basic differences over visions of development, which, as we will see, often underlie conflicts which can become violent. There are also a number of ways in which development processes can accentuate conflict (as detailed by Goodhand in Chapters 11 and 12). Generally speaking, development can bring new sources of wealth which can become the focus of ethnic or other tensions. Development aid can also exacerbate divisions. For example, in the case of Rwanda, Peter Uvin argues in his book *Aiding Violence* (1998) that interventions aimed at development in fact contributed to the situation which resulted in genocide.

By contrast, as noted earlier, although war intrinsically involves extreme brutality and causes huge amounts of suffering and destruction, good change can happen during wars, and wars can help bring about the conditions for development. This is not an argument *for* war, if only because war cannot generally be controlled and the result cannot be known in advance. It is certainly not to propose deliberate killing and destruction in the uncertain hope of some positive outcome. Nevertheless, within one side of a war, social solidarity can be extremely high, with a willingness to support collective endeavours that can continue into high levels of motivation towards development and reconstruction efforts after the war. The liberated zones of revolutionary movements can constitute experimental sites for putting ideals into practice. Civil wars and internal conflicts have brought about good change, obvious examples being the abolition of slavery in the United States and the overthrow of apartheid in South Africa. One can even argue that all the main examples of countries which have succeeded in achieving thoroughgoing socio-economic development in the last 50 years (Japan, South Korea, Taiwan) have done so via reconstruction efforts following major wars.

War and development relate to each other in a number of other ways. 'Development' is surely the ultimate aim of both forcible and other interventions in war situations, beyond the immediate objectives of halting violence and then avoiding a return to war. Many of the agencies involved in conflict situations are also 'development' agencies. The general commitment of international agencies and governments to 'development' provides the context in which much of the work of development agencies takes place in wars or postwar situations. As we shall see, these agencies tend to have a rather restricted view of what development is, and in fact the meaning of development is tending to be equated with what these agencies do. Thus 'development' is now *defined* by the practice of agencies like Oxfam, the UK's Department for International Development, or the World Bank, whether in attempting to reduce poverty in the world's poorest countries or in providing relief in war or postwar situations.

8.3   Meanings of 'development'

The first thing to realise about the concept of 'development' is that there is no agreement on what it means, let alone on how to achieve it. It is a concept which is contested both theoretically and politically, and is inherently both complex and ambiguous.

The international journal *Development* defines its concerns in terms of 'the search for alternative paths of social transformation towards a more sustainable and just world'. However, many of the agencies involved in development, as well as writers on development, do not allow alternatives but use the word to mean what they want it to mean. As Cowen and Shenton put it (1996, p. 4): 'Development comes to be defined in a multiplicity of ways because there are a multiplicity of "developers" who are entrusted with the task of development.'

I'm sure you recognise the Humpty-Dumpty problem introduced in Chapter 1. The different ways of using a term such as development are not equal. It's worth quickly looking at *Through the Looking Glass* again to hear how the conversation continued:

> 'When I use a word,' Humpty Dumpty said, in rather a scornful tone, 'it means just what I choose it to mean – neither more nor less.'
>
> 'The question is,' said Alice, 'whether you CAN make words mean so many different things.'
>
> 'The question is,' said Humpty Dumpty, 'which is to be master – that's all.'

In other words, we have to consider the power relations between the various agencies; power and agency are concepts taken up by El-Bushra in the next chapter. For now, we can see that only some of the multiplicity of 'developers' can be 'master'. Only some have sufficient power for their interpretation of 'development' to be effectively imposed on others.

8.3.1 A complex and ambiguous concept

It's very important, then, to understand some of the complexity and ambiguity of the concept of 'development', to be able to counter the partial and simplistic definitions promoted by those in powerful positions.

We have already seen that even Robert Chambers' definition of development as 'good change', quoted above, is not as simple or straightforward as it sounds. If we look more closely at the two words, we see that 'good' implies a vision of what is desirable in society, something to aim at, a state of being with certain positive attributes which can be measured so that we can talk of 'more' or 'less' development. 'Change', by contrast, is a process. *Vision* and *process* are two of the three senses which will be introduced below as the main ways in which the term 'development' is used. The third is the idea of *deliberate action*, and this may or may not apply to 'good change'. However, we already noted that there are big differences over what is regarded as 'the general good'. 'More' of some kinds of development may not be regarded as 'good' by all. More national infrastructure may not be 'good' for those more interested in safeguarding the environment and preserving local cultures; more material wealth may not be seen as 'good' by those whose idea of 'development' is about promoting religious education. As we have noted, 'change' is disruptive. It is never likely to create benefits all round, but to increase things which some see as 'good' while neglecting or actively harming others.

'Development' as an idea can of course apply to many fields, from child psychology and livestock breeding to religion and politics. In many of these fields there are similar inherent contradictions. For example, development can mean moving from a simpler to a more complex state. There is no implication that more complex is necessarily 'better', although there may be more chance of achieving improvement with more options available. Alternatively, something developing can mean it is becoming what it should be, as in a plant, or child, growing to its full potential. There is a tension between these ideas and the idea of progress, where more complex is usually regarded as better, and development can mean improving even on the best so far.

With development comes increased consumption.

Here our prime concern is with the development of societies, although within that the development of localities and of individuals is also important. Also, particular building projects may be called 'developments', and development as building is an important idea when considering *how* development occurs or may be brought about. Thus, in the context of war or its aftermath, 'development' can often mean physical reconstruction, building roads and other infrastructure, schools and health facilities. For this type of development, the notion of reaching inherent potential, and hence being limited by it, does not really apply. However, the imperative of supplying basic public needs or restoring disrupted services as soon as possible may make it difficult to think in terms of improving on previous arrangements.

'Building' is also much used as a metaphor for developing institutional infrastructure. There is a clear danger in assuming institutions such as courts, civil society organisations or democratic structures can be 'built' or copied from designs brought in from outside. It is important to realise that in the case of building institutions, as with building infrastructure, there are different ways of building, different priorities, and hence choices to be made. Even the building of physical infrastructure is not a question of technical imperatives and therefore politically neutral. Choices over the form of institutions may be even more critical. One should also realise that in both cases it is not the immediate result of the 'building' which is important for development, but the way it interacts with the society around it and its longer-term impact.

At another level, it is useful to think about 'personal' development and its relationship with development at the societal level. What people learn from their experiences may be regarded as their individual 'development', which ideally helps them to reach their potential. One of the most influential attempts at defining what is meant by development is based on the idea of creating the conditions for 'the realisation of the potential of human personality' (Seers, 1969; see below). What people learn from war may damage them rather than help them realise their potential, but it may also open up new possibilities in unpredictable ways. The relationship between development at individual or local levels and at national or societal levels also brings in the idea of equity between various localities or between different social groups or classes. This is another important consideration in relation to conflict and our main focus on development at the societal level.

Let us conclude this general discussion of the idea of development, and how it goes beyond simply 'good change', with some summary points which demonstrate its inherent ambiguity as a concept. First, development does not mean improvement in just one aspect but implies an all-encompassing change. Second, development is not just a once-off upgrading, but implies a process of continuous change which builds on itself, creating more and more complexity, and where new 'improvements' build on previous changes. Third, development means changes occurring at the individual level and at the level of society at one and the same time. Changes in society have implications for the people who live in that society, and conversely, changes in how people think, interact, make their livings and perceive themselves form the basis for changes in society. Finally, we have noted that development is not always seen positively. These points often go together, in that what some see as a general improvement may have losers as well as winners, and if social change is all-encompassing and continuous then the implication is that previous ways of life may be swept away, with the loss of positive as well as negative features.

8.3.2 Three senses of 'development'

We have already introduced the suggestion that 'development' has three main senses. This formulation has been used elsewhere (Thomas, 2000b, p. 29) to distinguish the following ways of using the term 'development':

- as a *vision, description or measure of the state of being of a desirable society*
- as an *historical process of social change* in which societies are transformed over long periods

- as consisting of *deliberate efforts aimed at improvement* on the part of various agencies, including governments, all kinds of organisations and social movements.

Note that, whenever anyone uses the term 'development', their usage embodies particular ideals, but these ideals are not likely actually to be achieved. So we still refer to 'development' when the actuality does not live up to the ideals espoused. Thus, measures of development may be used to analyse partial development or even a complete lack of development. As we have noted, development as an historic process means a continuous transformation which has negative as well as positive aspects. As for development efforts, not only are there disagreements over what they should be aimed at, but they do not necessarily succeed even in their own terms.

The three senses of 'development' relate to each other in various ways. The historic process of development supposedly results in the state of being a desirable society; deliberate efforts at improvement are probably motivated by and aimed at a particular vision of a desirable society. 'Doing development' is not rendered worthless by the idea of development as historic social change. In fact, it is millions of deliberate actions which add up to form historic processes. Conversely, one's view of history and of how social change occurs must help determine what efforts are seen as worthwhile and as likely to succeed in leading to 'improvement'.

The next three sections take each of these senses of 'development' in turn, and explore them a little further in relation to war and intervention.

8.4 Competing visions of development in a war context

In the first sense, development is a vision or description of a desirable society. Different political ideals lead to different visions of what is desirable, and what is one person's utopia could be another person's nightmare.

We can contrast three broad types of vision of development. While some of these can be partly combined in different ways, there are elements which are strongly at variance with each other and could cause conflict, potentially even violent conflict.

8.4.1 Modern industrial society

The first vision of development is a *modern industrial society*. In these terms, a 'developed' society has not only reached certain levels of wealth as measured in material terms (income per capita), but it is also continually 'growing' economically. To achieve development means to modernise, to 'follow in the footsteps of the West', or, in Bernstein's words, to follow Western advice like this: 'If you want what we have (and have achieved), then you must become like us, and do as we did (and continue to do)' (Bernstein, 1983).

Particularly since the demise of the Soviet Union, the vision of modernity and industrialisation is also a vision of a capitalist market economy with a global reach. It is certainly a vision of a more and more complex society both technologically and institutionally. Note too that virtually all 'advanced capitalist economies' are also Western liberal democracies. Although some East Asian countries have joined the ranks of those regarded as 'developed' in this sense, the underlying vision has not really changed. Writers such as Fukuyama (1995) argue that the combination of capitalist industrialisation with liberal democracy is now the only viable model for development.

> Today virtually all advanced countries have adopted, or are trying to adopt, liberal democratic political institutions, and a great number have simultaneously moved in the direction of market-oriented economics and integration into the global capitalist division of labour.
>
> ... As modern technology unfolds, it shapes modern economies in a coherent fashion, interlocking them in a vast global economy. The increasing complexity and information intensity of modern life at the same time renders centralized economic planning extremely difficult. The enormous prosperity created by technology-driven capitalism, in turn, serves as an incubator for a liberal regime of universal and equal rights, in which the struggle for recognition of human dignity culminates. ... [T]he world's advanced countries have no alternative model of political and economic organization other than democratic capitalism to which they can aspire.
>
> (Fukuyama, 1995, pp. 3–4)

8.4.2 Human development and 'alternative development'

Second, there are visions of development in terms of *the realisation of human potential*. This is not such a monolithic idea as the first, allowing space for the notion that different people or groups may prefer to develop themselves in different ways. Sometimes termed 'alternative development', it combines visions of 'people-centred development' based on principles of justice, sustainability and inclusiveness (see e.g. Korten, 1990) with those based on notions of participation, empowerment and freedom (Friedmann, 1992; Sen, 1999).

This approach lends itself to the creation of lists of dimensions of 'human development'. Seers originally proposed three conditions for 'the realisation of the potential of human personality': the capacity to obtain physical necessities; useful and fulfilling employment; and equality, which 'should be considered an objective in its own right' (Seers, 1979, pp. 10–11). The idea of measuring development through a combination of dimensions was taken up by Amartya Sen and others in the United Nations Development Programme (UNDP) and its work on a Human Development Index. This was originally based on material well-being measured via income, health measured by life expectancy and educational levels measured through literacy rates, but has since been refined in various ways.

By now there are very many different lists of dimensions of human development. Seers himself recognised the political dimension and suggested participation, political independence and educational levels as further 'conditions for development' in addition to the three mentioned above (Seers, 1979, p. 12). Since Seers originally wrote his article (in 1969), several further aspects of importance have gained recognition, notably the position of women and the need to safeguard the environment, as well as the issue of human security or freedom from violence. Thus we can extend Seers' six to a list of nine 'conditions for human-centred development', one of which is 'human security' (see Box 8.1). This implies the ideal of the absence of war as a condition for development.

Box 8.1   Nine conditions for human-centred development

1   low levels of material poverty

2   low level of unemployment

3   relative equality

4   democratisation of political life

5   'true' national independence

6   good literacy and educational levels

7   relatively equal status for women and participation by women

8   sustainable ability to meet future needs

9   human security.

Source: Thomas, 2000b, p. 34 based on Seers, 1979, pp. 10–12.

The alternative development vision also lends itself to cultural diversity. People who are empowered to develop themselves will do so in different, culturally distinctive ways. One might then ask whether cultural diversity can be seen as an aspect of a single 'alternative development' vision – or whether there are differing visions of cultural or national development which are specific to particular groups or nations. Religious and cultural identity would play a big part in such visions. There is a balance between the very positive aspects of identities such as these in terms of self-esteem, self-reliance and so on, and the potentially negative aspects of exclusivity which can easily become a cause of conflict and intercommunal violence.

One then has to ask how specific cultural preferences relate to principles such as Korten's justice, sustainability and inclusiveness, which may be argued to have universal validity. While 'alternative development' may not give rise to a unified vision, there are considerable commonalities among its specific forms. Hence 'human development', 'people-centred development' or 'alternative development' all create rivals to the notion that there is only one feasible vision for the development of all human society, that of the modern, industrial, market democracy.

A classroom in Benin

8.4.3 'Ameliorating the disordered faults of progress'

A third type of vision for development is less thoroughgoing in its value basis than the two discussed so far. On the one hand it can be thought of as pragmatic – ambitious perhaps, but within a managerialist framework which does not envisage full-scale social transformation. On the other hand, it is how development is portrayed by a radical critique of the language of 'development', and of what has historically been entailed by development, which has roots in Marxism but finds more modern form in the 'post-development school' (Sachs, 1992; Escobar, 1995).

This critique of development is encapsulated by a quote from Cowen and Shenton (1996): 'Ameliorating the disordered faults of progress.' It is easy to relate this view to agreements by world leaders and powerful international organisations about the imperative to act to improve the human condition and avert global catastrophe. Here development means reducing the incidence of poverty, improving the health of populations, mitigating environmental degradation, and so on. It may be recognised by positive changes in a number of indicators corresponding to the whole range of different dimensions of human existence.

In one way this vision could combine aspects of the other two. Thus modern industrial society could be accepted as a global reality even though it might not be thought of as an ideal since the progress which achieved it also brought enormous problems. The rather minimal 'vision' for development, in this case, would be to make sufficient small improvements to keep these problems manageable and prevent degeneration into chaos. The nine conditions for 'human-centred development' given above could then be one way of providing a checklist of areas in which these small improvements would have to be made.

There are other indicators or targets representing different versions of the dimensions of human or economic development. The best known set is probably the eight internationally agreed Millennium Development Goals (MDGs), which form an excellent example of this type of vision. They are:

- eradicate extreme poverty and hunger
- achieve universal primary education
- promote gender equality and empower women
- reduce child mortality
- improve maternal health
- combat HIV and AIDS, malaria and other diseases
- ensure environmental sustainability
- develop a global partnership for development.

The MDGs do not include human security and freedom from violence and war as a separate item. Arguably, it is useful to separate war from development conceptually in this way. However, one could well include intervention in war situations as part of 'ameliorating the disordered faults of progress' – especially if war is conceived as a by-product of progress. Some wars are easy to conceive in this way. If a particular conflict involves competition for control of resources given value by capitalist globalisation, such as oil or diamonds, then ameliorating its effects could be part of this third vision of development. The rather minimal nature of the vision, however, means that this does not imply intervening in all such conflicts. If a contested resource was sufficiently far away, competition over it was relatively marginal to global capital, the political disruption caused by the conflict was not too great and the human cost mainly localised (as with the war in the Democratic Republic of the Congo), then it would not be worth much effort in this direction. However, in other cases this idea of development may be invoked as the justification for substantial and expensive interventions.

Arguably, there is a consensus among powerful development agencies in which development has taken on a restricted meaning and is often in the name of the third (limited) vision. In other words, the dominant meaning of development is amelioration: small improvements in a range of human development indicators such as those associated with the MDGs, as well as limited interventions to ensure that conflicts do not get out of hand. At the same time, this consensus maintains the assumption that only the first development vision – of a modern, globalised, industrial society – is fully viable in the long term. This consensus holds particularly for humanitarian relief and other interventions in conflict and post-conflict situations. It also holds for many 'developmental' interventions, where the consensus between development agencies does not usually involve the 'search for alternative paths of social transformation towards a more sustainable and just world'.

8.4.4 War and visions of development

We may ask how these visions of development relate to war and intervention. Some wars are clearly about conflicts between visions of development. In other cases, it may be possible to interpret conflicts at least partially in this way, while recognising that the causes of conflict are usually unclear and ambiguous. In particular, those motivated by visions of human or 'alternative' development are likely to be in conflict with those promoting a vision of modern industrial society, although this need not necessarily lead to violence.

One clear example is the Zapatista insurgency in Chiapas, Mexico, which has since 1994 been promoting local 'people's power' in specific opposition to neoliberalism and globalisation. In other cases, culturally specific alternative visions of development may be in conflict with the consensus towards limited development activities or humanitarian interventions in conflict situations. However, where war has ensued, it is almost certain there were other factors in play to exacerbate the differences.

It could also be useful to consider intervention in a different sense: that of 'coming between' the warring parties. Such interventions would be set out specifically to avoid recreating or accentuating the differences which led to violent conflict. They would not, for example, promote market reforms or Western multi-party democracy in a situation where local cultural identities are at odds with the Western notion of 'modern' society as the only basis for development. Various types of intervention in this sense are discussed in Chapters 11 and 12 under the headings of 'peace building' and 'conflict transformation'. Somehow, such interventions would attempt to provide the basis for political (non-violent) contestation of the competing values and visions for development.

8.5 War and development as historic change

In this second sense, 'development' is seen in terms of 'grand narratives' describing how societies change and progress over long periods of time. For much of the second half of the twentieth century, development writing was dominated by theoretical debates between two broad schools of thought: the neoliberal (including modernisation theory) and the structuralist (including various forms of neo-Marxism).

To neoliberals, history is the sum of the actions of individuals and firms, as well as governments and other organisations, all acting in their own material interests. Their 'grand narrative' is about the resulting inexorable rise of global capitalism and hence modernisation. An absolutely crucial aspect of capitalism is that it is intrinsically dynamic. Capitalism tends to build on itself and become more complex, growing or 'developing' from within, with no need for outside intervention. In this 'narrative', the spread of market society throughout the world is also more or less inevitable. Many go further, as in the quote from Fukuyama, to link market orientation, globalisation and liberal democracy in a model to which there is 'no alternative'. War, if considered at all, is an aberration, since it would disrupt commerce and destroy the fruits of capitalist accumulation. Indeed, another part of this 'narrative' is that 'advanced' liberal democracies are said never to go to war with each other.

By contrast, while 'structuralism' denotes several related but distinct strands of thought, their 'grand narratives' are about political and economic struggles between large social groups, particularly classes, as new structures and systems replace old ones across the globe. Both revolutionary violence and war have their place in these 'narratives', as for example with the Marxist idea of war as a necessary corrective to capitalism's recurrent 'crises of overproduction'.

Since the end of the Cold War and the demise of the state socialist model of development, it has been easy for neoliberals not only to assert that their model of liberal capitalism is the only viable model of development (see above), but also that their 'grand narrative' has been proven correct.

However, while structuralists' prescriptions have not led to a practically successful model of development, one should not discount the way structuralists explain historical change. Structuralists tend to criticise global capitalism as a system of exploitation. While applauding its dynamic character, they do not attribute the growth of capitalism simply to that of internal dynamism. Karl Polanyi (1957), for example, writing in the middle of the twentieth century, argued that the 'development' of capitalism is better explained by reference to a struggle between movements representing pro-market and 'protectionist' interests. One can see similar struggles today in the clashes between corporate interests and anti-globalisation protesters over the role of the World Trade Organization.

In terms of the management of development interventions, there are at least two main points to be taken from a consideration of development as historic change. First, it is crucial to understand the developmental and historic context in order to appreciate the constraints and possibilities for intervention. Second, seeing development in terms of long-term historic processes does not make it pointless to try to influence those processes. The way that structuralists such as Polanyi explain historic change is in terms of the balance between forces represented by different interests struggling against each other. A useful intervention could be to support those forces which most closely accord with one's own vision for development, while avoiding intensifying the struggle to such an extent that unnecessary violence is created.

8.6   Deliberate improvement in a war context

The last sense of the term 'development' incorporates deliberate efforts at improvement, in other words, *intentional* development. In this third sense, development means, somewhat tautologically, whatever is done in the name of development. Such deliberate attempts at improvement are often called 'development *interventions*'.

In this sense, it appears that as we enter the twenty-first century development has become less about the transformation of the economic and social basis of societies than in previous periods. For the most powerful 'development agencies', it has taken on a more limited meaning, referring specifically to the practice of attempting to reduce poverty and achieve the other MDGs, or engaging in humanitarian relief to mitigate the effects of internal wars and other disasters. This fits closely with the third vision of development discussed above – 'ameliorating the disordered faults of progress.' It is taken as given that the context is the globalised market and the dominance of liberal democracy.

There are also examples of development interventions undertaken in the name of the second, 'alternative' or people-centred development vision, though these are often localised. They tend to be lost in situations of violent conflict. The point is that, whatever the underlying vision, development in this sense is the practice of intervening deliberately in order to create improvement.

The sense in which 'intervention' is used here does not specifically relate to situations of war. It does not necessarily imply a breach of sovereignty, interference in others' affairs, or a forcible attempt to prevent or end human rights abuses or conflict. A 'development intervention' is an input into a situation from outside which changes the relationships and influences the ongoing processes within that situation. It could be any kind of deliberate outside influence on any socio-economic or livelihood system, where the aim is development rather than simply relief.

8.6.1   The management of development tasks

What is implied is that a development agency engages in activities designed to bring about progressive change. Management of development tasks of this kind has been characterised elsewhere as:

> the management of deliberate efforts at progress on the part of one of a number of agencies, the management of intervention in the process of social change in the context of conflicts of goals, values and interests.

> (Thomas, 1996, p. 106)

In the same paper, it was argued further that 'there is something specific about those tasks which may be called development tasks' (Thomas, 1996, p. 101). This characterisation was broken down into four distinctive features of development tasks (Thomas, 1996, p. 106):

- external social goals rather than internal organisational ones
- influencing or intervening in social processes rather than using resources to meet goals directly
- goals subject to value-based conflicts
- the importance of process.

The implication of the last point is that development involves public action on the part of a number of agencies; it is not a prescription for actions to be undertaken by the state alone (see Wuyts et al., 1992). For that matter, it is not appropriate for any particular development agency to intervene alone.

While the practice of development agencies is a very important aspect of development, the fact that this has become the *dominant* meaning of development means that development has become limited in several ways. The fact that the same agencies are involved both in poverty reduction and humanitarian relief tends to make the latter appear to be a kind of development activity, and thus limit the meaning of development still further.

It is not just that development has come to have a rather tautological meaning, and is now used to mean *practice* more than vision or process. While the dominant notion of development as practice cannot exclude ideas of development as vision and as process completely, it is limited in that it incorporates rather simplistic versions of these. The vision of development tends to be reduced to targets and the process of development to techniques.

The targets may be extremely ambitious, as with the well-known target derived from the first Millennium Development Goal for halving the proportion of the world's population in extreme poverty by 2015. Nevertheless, targets are inherently unidimensional and as such represent a very limited vision of social transformation. One might also question how adopting the first MDG means admitting at the outset that even the most successful programme of development that can be envisaged will leave at least half of the world's absolute poor in the same state.

As for the techniques, they may be relatively sophisticated, based on some broad theory of social change. However, the use of techniques designed to achieve such targets directly tends to oversimplify theory and to depoliticise development. It implies that large-scale social change may be achieved straightforwardly by deliberate actions. It also implies that poverty reduction may be achieved by targeting the poor without the need for broader social change. Both of these provide an extremely limited view of the historic process of development.

War can be seen as interrupting development projects and making it impossible to carry out development activities. However, as we know, other types of interventions are made into war or postwar situations. Earlier in this chapter we listed a number of these. Thus, forcible interventions, aimed at bringing a halt to violent conflict, humanitarian relief, peacekeeping, and peacebuilding, aimed at building institutions in order to transform conflictual relationships and make violence less likely, can all be differentiated from interventions aimed directly at development. However, we should not make the simple assumption that these types of intervention occur in sequence, so that once a war has started there can be no more development until after forcible intervention and humanitarian relief have given way to peacekeeping and peacebuilding. In practice one cannot separate the types of intervention so cleanly. To some extent, several of these types of interventions, particularly peacebuilding, can have developmental aims. In such cases, you might consider to what extent they share the four features of development tasks listed above, and whether the limitations of restricting development to mean the practice of development agencies apply equally to such interventions.

8.6.2 A developmental style of intervention

Two further limitations which are even more acute in conflict situations are the huge uncertainty over the outcomes of interventions and the inevitable questions on the legitimacy of interventions by any agency, particularly those from outside. This puts a premium on the *way* in which an intervention is carried out and how it 'carries' particular developmental values, rather than looking for efficiency in achieving results, by whatever means. This implies a style of managing interventions which promotes developmental values.

- This emphasis on *how* an intervention is carried out applies readily to humanitarian interventions and peacebuilding, as well as to interventions aimed directly at development or poverty reduction. It fits well with our injunction to 'stand there' – and think how to act before acting. In Chapters 11 and 12, Goodhand takes up this discussion in more depth with respect to peacebuilding, or 'conflict transformation' as such initiatives are characterised there.

> **Intervention implications**

Developmental values can be promoted while undertaking interventions in several ways:

- Emphasising *how* tasks are done, not only the achievement of results. For example, undertaking reconstruction activities by employing members of the local population may slow the reconstruction down but could lead to capacity building and a degree of empowerment as well as build local livelihoods.

- Acting consistently with one's own values (and/or those of one's organisation). If one's values include participation, inclusivity, and transparency then it is incumbent on one to put these into practice in dealings with all parties as far as possible.

- Promoting values which define what is to be regarded as development at the same time as trying to meet development needs consistent with these values.

- Ensuring that the same values which underpin one's vision of a well-developed society also underpin one's actions at the lower levels.

Questions remain about the right to intervene (Allen and Styan, 2000), whether considering immediate humanitarian actions, peacebuilding initiatives, or longer-term developmental activities. If development is simply what development agencies do, we must ask what entitles them to undertake development interventions. This leads us to consider the concepts of trusteeship and legitimacy. The former arises, according to Cowen and Shenton (1996), in response to the basic 'problem of development' that those adversely affected are generally powerless to help themselves. Trusteeship means that one agency is 'entrusted' with acting on behalf of another, in this case to try to ensure the 'development' of the other. Legitimacy, by contrast, depends both on having the power and capacity for action, and on being able to represent the interests of those for whom one is acting. However worthy the values by which an agency operates, there is a degree of subjectivity about deciding whether they are legitimate operators in the field.

8.7   Conclusion

The previous section points towards managing interventions in a way which challenges the dominant view of development as simply the practice of development agencies in trying to ameliorate poverty and other 'problem' situations such as those involving violent conflict. It implies actively considering how to promote the conditions for development. It means thinking about values and visions of development and how one's actions embody or contradict these.

Making interventions more developmental implies considering alternative visions and processes. Interventions can be aimed at capacity building and inclusivity and hence be in line with the vision of development as the 'realisation of human potential'. Or they can be aimed at promoting markets and competitive opportunities for individual advancement, in line with a neoliberal vision of development.

It is important to be transparent about the choices involved in promoting one vision over another; the aim is to try to avoid just taking one model for granted. For example, the dominant version of development tends to represent a market-led vision as the only possibility for development. This could mean undertaking 'reconstruction' activities through competitive tendering and using overseas contractors on the basis of their superior efficiency, thus losing the opportunity for local participation, but doing this as though there were no choice involved. Even if it is impracticable to go entirely towards the values of 'people-centred development' in the constraints of a real situation which may be only partially post-conflict, there may be choices about the degree of intervention appropriate in what is certainly not likely to be a 'free' market.

Intervention implications

Be clear and transparent about your vision of development – are choices based on the free market approach, a people-centred vision, or some other process?

Consider alternative visions and processes.

It's also useful always to consider development as a process. This perspective implies not just responding to specific needs but considering how development is about all-encompassing (holistic) change. Future development has to be a process building on what is put in place now. Once again, this implies that it may be more important to embody those principles which one would like to see built into future development, than to get current projects completed with maximum efficiency, even if there is urgent need for the services or infrastructure which they are to provide.

In any case, the uncertainties of a conflict or post-conflict situation mean it is difficult, if not impossible, to make and implement specific long-term plans for development. It may be best not to try. The alternative, once again, is to build developmental principles into peacebuilding and other current actions.

What comes out of this discussion consistently is the conflict between different values and visions of development. But, as we know by now, it is impossible to avoid the contradictions behind the idea of development by laying down a single, simple definition of one's own.

'The question is,' said Humpty Dumpty, 'which is to be master – that's all.'

8.8   Chapter summary

The exhortation 'Don't just do something – stand there!' means not rushing into action, while at the same time not acquiescing to human rights abuses or escalations of violence. Make it clear that outsiders are watching, and be clear of one's own position and how to act within your own values.

Development has been defined as **good change**, but it can often be disruptive. Sometimes war can bring about good change. So one needs a better definition of **development**. It can be seen as a **vision** of a better society, an **historic process** of social change, and as **deliberate efforts** at improvement. Development agencies frequently take only the third definition and use it to describe what they do, but that is much too restrictive.

Two versions of the historic process are the **neoliberal modernisation** view, which sees the inexorable spread of growth through markets and a dynamic capitalism, and the **structuralist** view which sees change occurring through political and economic struggles between groups.

Three **visions** of development are presented: **modern industrial society**, which is particularly linked to the capitalist market economy and sometimes to democracy; **human-centred** development, which is linked to realisation of human potential and has more social and political content; and **cleaning up** the messes created by modern capitalist development, which includes dealing with poverty and environmental problems. In the early twenty-first century, the deliberate efforts, neoliberal, cleaning up view dominated. This narrow approach is characterised by the Millennium Development Goals.

Civil war can be triggered by a clash between alternative visions of development and alternative versions of the historic process. Development need **not wait for peace,** and developmental interventions can be **peacebuilding** if they meet **social goals** and put a greater stress on **process** and emphasising how tasks are done, rather than on simple efficiency in carrying out projects. Development is not done by the state or an agency alone, but through broader public action.

References

Allen, T. and Styan, D. (2000) 'The right to interfere?: Bernard Kouchner and the New Humanitarianism', *Journal of International Development*, vol. 12, no. 6, pp. 825–42.

Alvares, C. (1992) *Science, Development and Violence: The Revolt against Modernity*, Delhi, Oxford University Press.

Bernstein, H. (1983) 'Development', in Thomas, A. and Bernstein, H. (eds) The Open University course U204 *Third World studies*, Block 1, 'The 'Third World' and 'Development'', The Open University, Milton Keynes.

Chambers, R. (1997) *Whose reality counts? Putting the first last.* London, Intermediate Technology.

Cowen, M. and Shenton, R. (1996) *Doctrines of Development*, London, Routledge.

Escobar, A. (1995) *Encountering Development: The Making and Unmaking of the Third World*, Princeton NJ, Princeton University Press.

Friedmann, J. (1992) *Empowerment: The Politics of Alternative Development*, London, Blackwell.

Fukuyama, F. (1995) *Trust: The Social Virtues and the Creation of Prosperity*, Penguin, Harmondsworth.

Korten, D. (1990) *Getting to the Twenty-first Century Voluntary Action and the Global Agenda*, West Hartford CT, Kumarian Press.

Minear, L. and Weiss, T. (1993) *Humanitarian Action in Times of War: A Handbook for Practitioners*, Boulder CO, Lynne Reinner.

Polanyi, K. (1944, republished 1957) *The Great Transformation*, Boston, Beacon Press.

Sachs, W. (ed.) (1992) *The Development Dictionary: A Guide to Knowledge as Power*, London, Zed Books.

Seers, D. (1969; 1979) 'The meaning of development', in Lehmann, D. (ed.) *Development Theory: Four Critical Studies*, London, Frank Cass.

Sen, A. (1999) *Development as Freedom*, Oxford, Oxford University Press.

Thomas, A. (1996) 'What is development management?' *Journal of International Development*, vol. 8, no. 1, pp. 95–110.

Thomas, A. (2000a) 'Development as practice in a liberal capitalist world', *Journal of International Development*, vol. 12, no. 6, pp. 773–87.

Thomas, A. (2000b) 'Meanings and views of development', in Allen, T. and Thomas, A. (eds) *Poverty and Development into the Twenty-first Century*, Oxford, Oxford University Press.

Uvin, P. (1998) *Aiding Violence: The Development Enterprise in Rwanda*, West Hartford CT, Kumarian Press.

Wuyts, M, Mackintosh, M. and Hewitt, T. (1992) (eds) *Development Policy and Public Action*, Oxford, Oxford University Press.

9 Power, agency and identity: turning vicious circles into virtuous ones

Judy El-Bushra

9.1 Introduction

This chapter turns the spotlight on power and power relations, as an important dimension in explaining war. For many commentators, it is the unjust, unacceptable or oppressive use of power by political leaders which leads to war and to the continuation of war. Studying power helps to understand how wars are started, and, just as important, how they continue, often generation after generation. Studying power leads us to focus on the powerless as well as the powerful – not only the overt, coercive, power of politicians, warlords, and institutions, but also the power that ordinary citizens living in war zones have, to transform their situations and their relationships, turning vicious circles of violence into virtuous ones. The task of reconstructing societies torn apart by war includes redefining how power is to be exercised and shared in that society. Power does not exist in the abstract, but only within social relations; thinking about power relations in the different contexts in which we work helps us identify their specific nature, and ensures that our interventions are as appropriate as possible to that context. Finally, those among the international community who intervene in postwar reconstruction processes must be aware of the power they themselves hold, and the thin line they tread between representing universal values on the one hand, and furthering the interests of globally dominant cultures on the other.

Addison and Murshed have set as our starting point the belief that war represents a breakdown of the social contract. This 'contract' is the unspoken agreement whereby the governed agree to accept the imposition of a political disposition which may fall short of the full realisation of their wishes, in return for at least partial representation and security. At this level, war is the ultimate form of challenge by one power interest to another; peace, in contrast, is not the exchange of one controlling power interest for another, but rather a new consensus on how power is to be constituted and managed. The challenge of peacebuilding, then, is to establish a new set of political relationships in which all interests can be represented and in which a new social contract can be negotiated. However, the literature on power suggests that causes for war need to be sought not only in relationships between different components of a political system, and not only in relationships between the governed and the governing, but more broadly in the quality of relationships in society at large.

In this chapter we will consider how power has been understood in the fields of sociology, philosophy and gender studies. We aim to identify insights from these disciplines which will help us gain a better understanding of war – as it is initiated, perpetuated, supported and brought to an end. In order to understand how power works, we will need to observe how it is manifested in social processes such as decision making, governance and the functioning of institutions. Indeed, a large part of the work we will be drawing on does focus on this big picture. However, these broad processes are acted out by individual people, whose behaviour is influenced by their individual aspirations and motivations, which are in turn derived in part from their social and cultural contexts. Consequently, we will need to consider how power relations work at an interpersonal level as well as on a mass scale. We will see that power is not always overt or violent, but can also be internalised, as people are socialised to accept their place in power hierarchies. Our investigation of this invisible sort of power will lead us to pick up again the discussion of identity begun in Chapter 4. However, here we will focus particularly on gender identity, an area in which differing interpretations have generated contentious views about the involvement in war of women and men, young and old.

9.2 Power, democracy and the Western model of the state

In the classic sociological definition of power, it is described as a relationship between two people or groups, in which there is a conflict of interest between the two and in which one obliges the other, through the existence of sanctions, to submit to the other's wishes.

Power is often exercised in subtle ways, making it hard for both the insider and the outside observer to recognise when and how it is being exercised. Although war is about the exercise of power – and resistance to it – on a mass scale, it may be easier to understand how it works when we examine relatively small-scale and stable situations. For example, seeking to identify what enables a person or group to prevail in a conflict of interest, Bachrach and Baratz studied local government institutions in the United States in the 1960s. They analysed local council meetings to see how the decision-making process served, or failed to serve, the interests of different constituencies within the community. Their key observation was that political factions aiming to acquire or maintain power often relied not on winning arguments in council, but on being able to set the terms of debates: indeed, some were ingenious in finding ways of *preventing* issues from being discussed when it was not in their interests to air them. Bachrach and Baratz used the term 'nondecisions' to describe the way in which powerful interests managed to control agendas, thereby effectively depriving those who challenged their values or interests of a voice that could be heard, even under the guise of democratic participation. In their view, an effective decision-making structure would be one which welcomed and paid serious attention to new or minority voices (Bachrach and Baratz, 1970).

Non-decisions can be effected by a variety of means. These include *intimidation, co-optation, deflection* (for example, postponing the impact of contentious decisions by shunting them into special commissions) and *blocking* (for example, by changing the rules so as to prevent certain types of issues from being discussed). The idea of a non-decision clearly has implications in political work. Bachrach and Baratz themselves cite 'participatory democracy' as a form of non-decision, since it involves granting to the political opposition 'the illusion of a voice' (Bachrach and Baratz, 1970, p. 45). The question for them is not so much 'who rules' as 'who is disfavoured' by a political system – does the system perpetuate 'unfair shares', and do mechanisms exist to thwart new sources of power, authority and influence? These manipulations of democratic process can be as important as outright abuses of power in generating a sense of 'unfair shares'. Bachrach and Baratz lead us to sound a note of caution in stating our belief that democratic decision-making is a prerequisite for stable peace. They suggest that the *form* of decision-making structures may be less important than their *practical outcomes* in meeting a diverse and perhaps contradictory range of interests. Systems which represent their constituents in form only are unlikely to quell unhappiness at 'unfair shares'. This has important implications for those whose task in postwar reconstruction is to decide on what sort of political structures need to be put in place to guarantee the representation of diverse groups.

Intervention implications

A rapid move to elect a parliament or congress and a president through the creation of a US or British system is often seen by the international community as an essential part of the postwar phase of political reconstruction. The implication of Bachrach and Baratz' view is that this may give only the illusion of democracy, because powerful interests, by manipulating political agendas (and the way the media deal with them), can effectively exclude minority or weak interests.

Alternative structures, often based on consensus decision making between unelected elders, are sometimes seen as more successful at representing all groups, but they often suppress the interests of powerless components (such as women or younger men) within those groups.

Is it possible to design a decision-making framework which fully represents all interests, and which encourages those who are not already politically involved to have the confidence to do so?

9.2.1 Power and the Western state

Power relations take different forms in different political cultures. The Western model is often held up by the international community as an ideal to which states emerging from civil war should aspire. However, it is the product of a particular history, in which forms of power have evolved over centuries and have been challenged in particular ways. It may not necessarily fit other contexts.

The general view is that in the Western model of the state, power 'from below' combines with power 'from above': the institutional superstructures which create formal power depend on, and draw their strength from, the dynamism of exchanges among the grassroots. However, while for some analysts this is a harmonious relationship characterised by consensus, for others it represents oppression and struggle. For Habermas, for example, debate at the grassroots level gradually merges into consensus, and is then translated through the legislative system into the institutions of governance. Consensus born out of communication and deliberation is a form of popular power ('communicative power') and the basis of 'deliberative democracy' (Habermas, 1996). In Habermas' optimistic view of Western political culture, mainstream views are representative of the whole population, popular debate translates seamlessly into popular power, and tensions between governed and governors, or between different sections of the population, exist but are managed constructively. His description of political life airbrushes out knotty problems such as the exclusion of minority interests, or politicians using the tactic of 'nondecisions' to silence unwelcome voices.

For Foucault, power can never be a manifestation of consensus. Violence, whether real or threatened, is 'its primitive form, its permanent secret, and last resort, that which in the final analysis appears as its real nature' (Foucault, 1983). Seen in historical context, Western culture can be characterised by three types of struggle – against domination, against exploitation and against individual subjection, i.e. the reduction of the individual to a 'subject', controlled by and dependent on another. It is this latter struggle which in Foucault's view has predominated in the West since the nineteenth century. The centrality of the individual in Foucault's analysis is both its strength and its limitation: one is obliged to ask whether a concern with individual freedom – a product of a particular combination of historical circumstances – is a luxury that only the West can afford.

9.2.2 Power and knowledge

Foucault described as 'pastoral power' the form of power which was adopted originally by the medieval church and which, by guaranteeing spiritual salvation, enabled it to exercise control over the minds and consciousness of its flocks. Pastoral power spread into the institutions of the state, institutions such as the police, the public health authorities and the school system. All these, while appearing to exist for the benefit of the people, serve as means whereby the state controls their attitudes and values and ensures acceptance of the status quo. For Foucault, European history since the Middle Ages has been in effect the history of struggle against this imposed 'subjectivity', in which leaders have claimed power on the basis of superior knowledge about the right way to live.

Intervention implications

How should public debate be managed in the context of postwar peacebuilding? Should we see the role of the media as being a forum for 'deliberation' leading to consensus, as Habermas would suggest? This plays an important part in reconciliation and rebuilding national institutions, and in minimising the role of those driven by hate and anger who are always present in the postwar period.

Foucault, by contrast, would say that consensus is not democracy: the existence of the media – even open media – is not by itself sufficient to prevent manipulation of political debate by powerful interests. Indeed, the media might become a means for suppressing dissent, or for eliminating challenging or minority views, encouraging the emergence of new sources of grievance. This could lead to the suppression of grievances which might lead to a return to war. To maintain a balance, those in power would need to be active in seeking out the views of those not normally represented in mainstream society and ensure that these views were fully aired and legitimated.

Interveners need to consider balancing Foucault and Habermas. They too must actively seek out the views of those whose voices are not heard to provide a balance to the consensus view. Indeed, interveners need to support voices that are not being heard, to rise above the combination of non-decision, pastoral power, and consensus media – while at the same time exercising some constraint on the voices of hate and anger and those who try to organise in divisive ways.

The relationship between how people see the world and how those in power attempt to influence this perception is a major theme in conceptualisations of power. Lukes, for example, discussing Bachrach and Baratz' use of the term 'nondecisions', suggests that the most effective form of power is that which does not require to be exercised in overt and direct ways, because it shapes people's 'perceptions, cognitions and preferences in such a way that they accept their role in the existing order of things, either because they can see or imagine no alternative to it, or because they see it as natural and unchangeable, or because they value it as divinely ordained and beneficial' (Lukes, 1974, p. 24). In other words, the horizontal inequalities described in Chapter 6 are often seen as natural and normal.

Interpreting power as control of knowledge and self-perception, and not merely as the violent or dictatorial imposition of will, has implications for those who seek effective ways of resisting or neutralising oppressive power and of replacing it with a more constructive set of relationships. Two thinkers who have had considerable influence in the development of methods and approaches for political action are the Brazilian educator Paulo Freire and his collaborator, the theatre director Augusto Boal. Freire described how the fact of being oppressed impacts on the consciousness and self-perception of the oppressed, as well as on that of their oppressors, so that those who wish to act in solidarity with the oppressed must find ways of breaking both these moulds. Freire discussed the role of the outsider in support of other people's struggles, warning against the dangers of paternalism and enjoining them to 'think *with* the people, not *for* them' (Freire, 1996).

Boal's work focuses on using drama to help people analyse the unquestioned perceptions referred to by Lukes. Boal believes that people are led to internalise social norms which limit the range of behaviour they consider possible, a notion to which we return below when looking at gender identity. For him, personal development consists in imagining previously unimaginable possibilities, and he developed techniques of roleplay and drama in which people 'rehearse' ways of resisting and transforming internalised power (Boal, 1995). Boal later used this experience to identify hundreds of legislative changes suggested by the poor with whom he had worked, which he then proposed to the municipal council of Rio de Janeiro, of which he is a member.

Intervention implications

When an external agency intervenes in a postwar reconstruction exercise with the aim of supporting local people's own initiatives, what does it do when it observes them making mistakes? Ignore the problem in order to avoid imposing? Offer training followed by support, which adds up to coercion? Withhold funding until a change of heart comes about?

The question is a critical one for intervention agencies which are mandated to uphold international policy, such as the UN agencies. What happens if the values which inform policy are not shared in the community under discussion – if for example, women's rights in international law are not reflected in local customary law? Does policy represent the unjustified imposition of one culture over another? Those who uphold policy point out that international conventions have been adopted as a result of a global consensus, so that the challenge is not to debate the values inherent in them but to ensure their implementation.

Freire's answer would be to engage in critical dialogue, recognising that both outsiders and insiders have valid views. Critical dialogue consists of joint identification of a problem followed by joint investigation, leading to a decision about strategies which both are committed to upholding. Even if policies are 'right', they cannot be imposed but must be interpreted on a case- by-case basis by those most directly affected by them.

In the real world, interventions aiming at post-conflict reconstruction are dominated by international laws, conventions and procedures designed to strengthen and democratise institutions of the state, and following a particular interpretation of what 'democracy' and 'the state' mean. Indeed, adherence to these models is increasingly a condition for the benefits of participating in the international arena, for example accessing loans from international financial institutions. While thinkers such as Habermas rightly underline the critical importance of open discussion as a basis for democratisation, others point to the messiness of politics, and the difficulties of building a political arena in which constituencies with highly varying histories and self-perceptions feel confident enough to participate. And, as Foucault and Freire emphasise, the question is not just who counts in political debate, but rather whose knowledge counts, and what forms of expression can be found to bring alternative ways of thinking and acting into the political framework.

9.3   Power, patriarchy and gender identity

As we have seen, power is manifested in complex ways, ranging from overt physical aggression at one end of the spectrum to subtle forms of mind control at the other. Opinion is divided on whether consensus and debate can lead potential opponents to share power or whether consensus is an illusion. For some, power can be a benevolent force, while for others its exercise is inherently unhealthy, however well intentioned. In other words, the Western model of democratic governance is both defended by some as a model of consensus politics and popular power-sharing, and resisted by others as a form of oppressive – and largely hidden – social control.

9.3.1   Patriarchy and hegemonic masculinities

A major stream of thinking exploring these questions in more depth is around identity, and in particular the issue of gender identity and the construction of patriarchy as a dominant form of power. We have seen the different ways in which ethnic identity has been considered to contribute towards civil war, especially when it serves to mobilise groups in support of common action to defend or promote common interests. Gender identity (see Box 9.1) and ethnic or group identity go hand in hand; indeed, the two are often said to define each other and can hardly be dissociated. However, the reason why gender identity is an important dimension of power relations is not just because it provides a further layer of description, but also because it throws particular light on how forms of 'insidious power' influence people's behaviour. It may be, then, that the issue of gender identity can provide pointers explaining why cycles of violence are initiated and perpetuated in some cases, and in others not.

'Patriarchy' describes power systems which favour the interests of dominant men, and which, in doing so, suppress the interests of women and of men who do not fall into dominant categories. These 'subaltern' or lower-status categories of men might include younger, poorer men, men of lower-status ethnicity or occupational category, of poorer education, of minority religions, or men whose lifestyles or sexual behaviour are not accepted by mainstream society. A particular concern here is with younger men, since many civil wars appear to be related to struggles between generations of men. A similar distinction needs to be made between women of dominant categories and subaltern women; however, the assumption behind the concept of patriarchy is that within a particular class, men are most likely to dominate over women. Patriarchy is an important concept in understanding war, because it helps to identify who is advantaged and who is disadvantaged by systems of power, in what ways, and triggering what response. It suggests that women and younger men experience war (the ultimate struggle for power) in different ways from older men, and that their contribution to war may also take different forms from that of male elders. As we shall see in the next chapter, they may also contribute to peacebuilding in different ways.

Kate Millett introduced the notion of 'patriarchy' as a system of power relations in which the power of male elders universally subordinates women and younger men (Millett, 1977). However, Millett's work – and that of feminist scholars who followed her – focused mainly on social relationships between men and women. It was left to others to spell out in more detail how patriarchy divides men, and we return to this below. For Millett, men's power over women is exercised in all areas of life, and is so complete that it appears natural – it is 'perhaps the most pervasive ideology of our culture and provides its most fundamental concept of power' (Millett, 1977, p. 25). Millett suggests that this 'pervasive ideology' is constructed through the process of socialisation within the family, reinforced by other cultural institutions such as education, religion and literature, and further maintained by economic exploitation and the threat of force.

Box 9.1 Gender identities: two views

Opinions differ as to how far gender identities have a fundamental or fixed nature. There are two broad interpretations. The first considers the distinction between men and women as being the most fundamental division within humanity. In this view, women are essentially nurturing and creative, a feature which is derived from their capacity to give birth, while men are essentially aggressive and territorial as befits their origins as hunters and protectors. These characteristics are thought to be part and parcel of being a man or a woman: the fact that not all men and women follow these patterns of behaviour all the time is a testament to the power of social control.

The second view is that gender differences are 'performed', i.e. not an intrinsic part of human nature. Far from being natural and immutable, they are socially constructed and can therefore be changed. However, here too there are different interpretations. For some, gender identities are constructed through social relations and social institutions, but constructed in the same way everywhere, i.e. society everywhere oppresses women. For others, this is not necessarily the case: those who adopt the 'social relations' approach (Kabeer, 1994; Jackson and Pearson, 1998) consider that gender differences are embedded within other factors of difference such as age, ethnicity or class, and so need to be understood in context. For those who hold this view it follows that differences *within* genders may be as important as differences *between* them. Rather than seeing all women and all men as forming homogeneous categories, this view suggests that a range of 'masculinities' or 'femininities' (different masculine and feminine identities) may be produced through the intersection of different social and historic factors. In other words, it is impossible to generalise about what 'women' or 'men' are like, even within one society.

'Masculinities' and 'femininities' represent a shared perception of right or appropriate behaviour. These help determine the claims that individuals can make on the support of family and friends. Men and women who offend against the commonly accepted norms for their gender and class run the risk of losing support: for example, in a culture where men are expected to serve in the national army, men who desert, or lodge conscientious objection, can suffer various forms of abuse ranging from humiliation to imprisonment or death. In this sense, gender is not so much about differences between men and women, but about divergence between *ideals* (identities) and the *realities* lived by individual men and women.

In the essentialist view, war is a masculine trait, and peace a feminine one. Agencies intervening during and after war should therefore invest resources in ensuring women's protection from men. However, if we take the alternative view, the precise forms of disadvantage faced by both men and women have to be studied in context, and cannot be read off from a hypothetical universal condition.

The notion of patriarchy has become a standard tool of analysis and strategy among feminists and others since the 1970s, albeit with different interpretations. Criticisms have centred on two main points: one, the representativity of Western models, and the other the place of men in a feminist analysis of power. Millett's view of patriarchy has been said to ignore the different lives and different perspectives of women in different parts of the world, encouraging white, middle-class Western feminists to assume that their own concerns are representative of all women everywhere. The question this raises in relation to development and humanitarian intervention is: to the extent that the tenets of Western feminism have found their way into international policy, does this mean that policy is an instrument of cultural imperialism? In the following chapter we examine the implications of this question for women's rights in and after periods of war in more detail. For the moment, however, we should note that, as we will see below, feminist understandings of power and patriarchy are not uncontested, even among feminists.

Second, there has been much debate about the nature of men's power and how individual men access it. For Millett, it was clear that men as a group and women as a group have different interests, and that men's power, rather than some amorphous 'system', is what oppresses women. This has been taken by some radical feminists as a charter for separatism. Others have pointed out, in contrast, that many men are not in positions of power over women, and indeed may be subordinated to women, and that men may be disadvantaged by patriarchy as much as women.

R. W. Connell (1995) developed the concept of 'hegemonic masculinities' to explore the idea of men being disadvantaged by patriarchy. Connell sought to explain how those who hold power, i.e. set the terms of decision making in institutions, are everywhere mostly men. This led him to trace the historical evolution of a 'Western' model of masculinity from its roots in sixteenth-century European capitalism. Connell described how hierarchies of masculinities came into being, in which particular groups of men came to dominate over others. Under the influence of political and economic trends, these hierarchies changed their nature and were transformed into new hierarchies in which different qualities gained the ascendancy. The end result of this process in the West is that white, heterosexual, educated, adult men came to dominate not only over women but also over other groups of men (particularly black, gay or young men).

In focusing on the 'Western' model, Connell's purpose goes beyond using the European case as just one example of how dominant masculinities come into being. An important part of his theory is the idea that the 'European/ American' model has developed into a global hegemony. In this process, the fraught relationship between elite and lower-status or subaltern men in Europe was eventually exported across the world through colonialism and globalisation. There are many different ways of being a man; these differences are not haphazard, however, but structured into a hierarchical arrangement which now, in the post-Cold War period, has a global reach.

Connell suggests that attributes of masculinity and femininity are closely related to class and occupation, and have been influenced by the political and economic movements of the time. So, for example, the introduction of management systems in recent decades has given rise to a version of masculinity which emphasises knowledge and interpersonal skills above physical prowess. In fact, he believes that such changes have served to rationalise and soften hegemonic masculinity in the West in colonial and post-colonial periods, so that men in Western societies have had the luxury of developing 'soft' values under the guise of 'civilisation'. Meanwhile, the violent and oppressive elements which capitalism required were 'exported' to the colonies in the form of forced migrations of workers and the subordination of indigenous labour. In many cases the version of the 'gender order' which came to be exported through the colonial encounter was more rigid, more violent, and less egalitarian than the versions it replaced. The assumption often made that the 'European/American model' is the highest point of progress is therefore open to question.

In short, there are two general views of patriarchy. In the first, patriarchy enshrines the domination of all men over all women. In the second, it is a system of power relations whose component institutions favour forms of power more easily accessible to men; individual men, however, are themselves arranged in a hierarchy, with men who fail to fit the dominant type reaping less of the 'patriarchal dividend' than others.

9.3.2 Gender identities and violence

Gender identity is part of some sociological explanations of violence and war. Firstly, particular cultures may at particular times give stronger value to aggressive behaviour (for example, by encouraging children to enjoy games involving physical contests) than to complementary values such as justice or protectiveness. Some commentators suggest that male violence can sometimes be explained by *distortions* of masculine identities, rather than being a trait inherent in men. Evidence from Sierra Leone, for example, suggests that warlords have indeed deliberately attempted to play on young men's sense of self, combining enforced violence with exposure to violent films and to drugs. Richards further provides evidence that these patterns of enmity and abuse have been perpetuated over generations (Richards, 1996). Boas similarly suggests that explanations for the extreme inhumanity of the conduct of the war in Liberia may be found in the experience of the ex-slave settlers from the United States who reproduced master–slave identities in their own relationship with indigenous groups. Master–slave identities and relationships were perpetuated – and twisted – at each historical turn (Boas, 1997).

Secondly, the notion of 'thwarting' describes a link between the ideal patterns of behaviour represented by gender identities on the one hand and the reality which most people live on the other. Thwarting suggests that people who are unable to live out their gendered identities in a satisfactory way, because of circumstances they cannot control, are more likely to resort to violence because of the frustrations this generates. The process is interpreted in different ways, however. For some writers, it may arise because of conflicting self-images. Wade, for example, describes the lives of men in a working-class Colombian community who are torn between the image of the family protector and provider on the one hand, and the sociable, free-spending buddy figure on the other, between the demands of the family and the demands of the male peer group. These tensions – between two seemingly contradictory 'masculinities' – are often channelled into abusive domestic relationships with wives and children (Wade, 1994).

Dolan, by contrast, understands 'thwarting' as a process in which the conditions of war, state collapse and deprivation restrict the range of 'masculinities' that are available for men to adopt (Dolan, 2002). He suggests that institutions such as the state and the national army have a duty to provide the conditions and the means whereby men and women can effectively perform the roles expected of them: 'it is impossible to dissociate power relations between individual men from the power relationships existing between individual men and the state' (Dolan, 2002, p. 79).

Dolan uses the concept of thwarted gender identity to explain how men resort to violence in some circumstances and not in others, and suggests that the state exercises a profound influence over the interpersonal behaviour of individuals. He uses the example of northern Uganda, where the state has failed to protect the Acholi from rebel attacks and from the consequences of the war and at the same time it has failed to prevent abuses carried out by its own institutions. Dolan describes how men are unable to attain the ideal characteristics of manhood – the capacity to provide and protect, to marry and beget children, to provide responsible leadership and maintain respect – for the reasons indicated in Box 9.2.

Box 9.2   The role of men in northern Uganda

The ideal man should ...	But in reality...
Provide for the material needs of women and children	High percentage of population lives in protected villages, cut off from agricultural land Limited job/income-generation opportunities Cattle raided by UPDF, LRA and others World Food Programme rations inadequate, irregular
Marry and beget children, providing them with guidance and leadership	Limited cash/cattle for bridewealth means men cannot marry, continue to be 'youth' Limited access to education and jobs; soldiers are better off No privacy in displaced camps Limited cash to pay children's school fees
Provide physical protection for women and children	Rebels raid villages, kill and abduct adults and children, destroy property UPDF fails to protect or pursue UPDF rapes local women with impunity Men also vulnerable to rape and other forms of physical violence by all combatants Fear that men joining UPDF will be sent to wars in Congo or Sudan
Resolve differences through discussion	Other Ugandans perceive Acholi as backward, primitive, professional warriors Youth are denied opportunities, take up arms to achieve goals Alternative forms of achievement (through education, enterprise, etc.) not available.

The problem is particularly acute for younger men, who are not taken seriously as adults until they marry and beget children, something which is increasingly difficult to achieve in the circumstances of the war. Some young men, finding their aspirations for education and employment blocked, join rebel groups or take to violent crime. However, options are limited for all men. The hopelessness of their situation causes many to resort to various forms of abuse and self-harm (including alcoholism, domestic violence and suicide). The war has seen 'a growing polarisation between those who are able to attain the markers of masculinity and exercise the power which these bring, and those who are unable to fulfil expectations and are thus deeply disempowered' (Dolan, 2002, p. 78). It follows that for the average male citizen, violence, far from being a component of a masculine model, is the 'last resort of those who are unable to achieve "masculinity"'. For the military, violence is part and parcel of a form of masculinity which is legitimated by the state, used both as a tool for control and to create a situation where a violent expression of masculinity is an almost inevitable outcome.

This analysis is important for several reasons. Firstly, it seeks an explanation for male violence in terms of psycho-social, as well as economic and political factors (we turn to the issue of female violence below) – indeed it underlines the importance of bringing psycho-social factors into the economic and political analysis. Secondly, it describes how the way that people live on the ground and the broader course of war at a macro level are intimately linked. We have described the tensions between 'big bad men' and 'local people under pressure' as explanations for war. Dolan's evidence suggests that both explanations work, and indeed that there is an iterative relationship between them. Although everyday behaviour by ordinary citizens is influenced by events on the bigger canvas, it also *contributes* to those events, so that

Chechen rebel fighter.

understanding the way ordinary citizens view their roles and their situations is an important element in understanding the war. In particular, one begins to discern a vicious circle of oppression, violence, deprivation and impoverishment, frustration and more violence – a vicious circle in which the thwarting of gender identity plays a role in perpetuating conditions of intractable conflict.

Intervention implications

Violence against women often reaches extraordinarily high levels during war and after it, and the need to protect women from this violence is gaining more attention in international humanitarian interventions. Dolan's argument is that male violence can be explained as the outcome of hegemonic masculinity pushed to an extreme of oppressive control, in which choice of lifestyle is restricted and only one, dispossessed and dehumanised, version is possible. This suggests that both men and women are equally being victimised. Indeed, Dolan suggests that women might be best protected through projects to help men regain the role of protector and provider into which they have been socialised.

Some feminists and women's organisations on the other hand believe that gender equality is a vital element in the democratisation of postwar societies, and that encouraging a return to patriarchal values would compromise this equality. While helping men might have short-term advantages in terms of reducing levels of violence, it might at the same time be putting the clock back for women who have gained economic independence and who may wish to keep hold of it. Women's organisations are willing to concede that men need help too, as long as the pendulum does not swing back too far.

The majority of combatants in most wars are men, but this does not mean that women play no part in war. There are two contending approaches to the issue of women and war. In one view, war is in effect war on women, in which men are the perpetrators and in which women suffer, both directly in the form of physical attack and rape, and indirectly because it is largely they who cope with the consequences of war. War and violence against women in its many forms are seen as being manifestations of one principle, that of male violence. Women, as the principal victims of war, are also the ones who resist it most strongly and are hence the driving force within peace movements (Kelly, 2000). The second view holds that even though patriarchal interests (position, territory, political power) may be the main motivation for war, it is important to distinguish between patriarchy as a principle and men as a sex. Both men and women have gendered roles and identities which have been elaborated historically within a patriarchal framework, and as a consequence of these each is differently violated by war.

It is impossible to deny the huge catalogue of horrors that women have experienced in war (Rehn and Sirleaf, 2002). At the same time it is also impossible to deny their role in carrying out and perpetuating violence (see Box 9.3). Women influence the attitudes of their children and grandchildren through the knowledge and values they pass on, and in this way are often key vehicles for perpetuating intercommunal mistrust across generations. They are often the first to demand that men defend their and their group's interests aggressively. They contribute to nationalist or liberation movements both as fighters and in support capacities, and indeed have often been seen as more vicious fighters than men (Bennett et al., 1996). Where they achieve political power at a global level they may be as ardent as men in promoting the global hegemonies that underpin wars.

Box 9.3   Women supporting and participating in conflict

'Warfare between clans (among the Acholi in northern Uganda) was further regulated by the necessity to carry out certain cleansing rituals before making an attack. ...The chief's wife or mother pronounced a blessing as part of the ritual. In this way the war initiative was established as a legitimate – and indeed unavoidable – duty, supported by the clan as a whole.' (Lumoro, 2002)

'Women joined the guerrillas (in El Salvador) because their lives and outlooks had been changed by other experiences, and because they believed they would be listened to in these organisations ... Above all they were carers, whether they took care of logistics or houses and sites. They participated in marches and mobilisations. They supported the militancy of their men by nurturing committed families. And they led the defence of human rights when repression spread throughout the country. They were crucial to the survival of the guerrilla camps, whether as combatants or cooks; they were in charge of communications and the supply of food, clothing, medicine and munitions. And it was also they who, in the villages, gave shelter to the guerrilla women who were about to give birth; it was they who took care of the new-born children.' (Ibanez, 2001, pp. 120–1)

Women involved in Maoist activities (in Nepal) are engaged mainly in four areas: people's militia, the party, the party's sister organisation for women, and as common supporters, feeding and hiding the fighters in the villages and gathering information for them. In some districts, 40 per cent of the militia are women. Women party workers promote social justice and reform, and raise the awareness of women who are still bound by the patriarchal system of the society. Their work in fighting alcoholism, polygamy and other social anomalies attracts more and more women to the Maoists. (Adapted from Gautam, 2001)

Women in right-wing Hindu nationalist movements in India have been in the forefront of attempts to marginalise and make illegitimate the claims of minority Muslim communities. They have done this by encouraging a highly aggressive Hindu masculinity among the men, by extending the reach of extremist parties through their women's wings, and by sanctioning (and encouraging) specific acts of anti-Muslim violence such as the demolition of the Ayodhya mosque. (Mukhta, 2000)

'I was captured in 1996 at Tombodu (Sierra Leone) by a woman captain. She took me to be part of her squad... I was trained to use an AK 47 gun and a pistol. We attacked Tongo, Koidu, Kongoteh, and a Guinea border town called Fokonia, where we burnt houses and foodstuffs and chopped off people's hands. When we were forced to move out of Koidu, we went near to the Liberian border and then started attacking right up to Freetown. I used to infiltrate into enemy territories to spy. We smoked marijuana, took capsules, had cocaine injections.' (Finda, a girl aged 16, quoted in Jusu-Sheriff, 2000, p. 48)

Does an understanding of gender relations help us to understand violence better? We have seen how male violence can be the outcome of thwarted aspirations towards ideals of manhood, ideals which are intimately bound up with ethnic or other group identities. We have also seen how women participate in or support such violence in circumstances where they believe that doing so will advance the interests of their group. We can perhaps envisage war as the struggle of some men to maintain their dominant position in hierarchies, and of others to escape from the constraints which these hierarchical relations impose on them and which restrict their potential to achieve their aspirations. In this struggle, relationships are of primary importance – relationships between women and men, between men and other men, between individuals and the state, between individuals and their society, between different clans and ethnicities within the context of the state. So if we want to remove the underlying causes of violence, we need to reconstruct not only the structures and procedures of public life, but also the nature of these social relationships, and in particular, how they change in response to different trends or events.

9.4 Power and social relations – a case study

To illustrate how these questions of changing power relations have been explored in more detail, we will describe a research project investigating the connections between gender identity and war in several African war-affected situations, carried out by the development agency ACORD. The project was based theoretically in the 'social relations' approach to gender (see Box 9.1 on different views of gender relations) and in the social exclusion analysis framework (SEA), which helps analyse the power relations existing in a given situation. SEA evolved in ACORD's Namibia programme, where it formed the basis for a community-level analysis of the social consequences of Namibia's experience of apartheid (Kandirikirira, 2003). These consequences included violent, aggressive behaviour on the part of adolescent boys and widespread passivity by girls in the face of sexually exploitative relationships. Much of the community research was carried out using the drama techniques developed by Boal (see above), and the resulting programme design was developed through this collaboration between the agency and the communities concerned.

SEA aims to build up a picture, in any given context, of the social, economic, cultural and political factors which permit powerful groups to exclude others. These factors provide individuals and groups with the 'power to act' – derived from wealth, influence or decision-making authority – in ways that deprive others of economic or other resources and opportunities, or which deny them self-respect. Discrimination can be active or passive, and includes inflicting injustice by turning a blind eye to the oppressive behaviour of others; indeed, inaction may be as devastatingly discriminatory as overt actions. A pattern of discrimination becomes an 'ideology of superiority' when it is embedded in society so deeply that people 'can see or imagine no alternative to it, or ... see it as natural and unchangeable, or ... value it as divinely ordained and beneficial' in Lukes' words. This embedding takes place through a long process in which relationships between different groups evolve in adaptation to economic and political factors, in much the way that Connell describes for the evolution of 'hegemonic masculinities'. The power relationships involved are built up over a long period of time and are usually based on unequal, but to some extent symbiotic, economic relationships. Both the exploited and the exploiters come to accept the situation, and indeed the relationship is often structured in such a way that both appear to gain some advantage from it, or at least that the exploited would lose stability and security if they overthrew it. The dismantling of these embedded unequal relationships cannot be accomplished quickly or painlessly, and attempts to change those horizontal inequalities can cause war if managed poorly. This suggests that strategies for democratisation in a postwar context need to take a long view.

The ACORD research project drew on SEA as a basis for detailed research design and in analysing the results. SEA emphasised the idea of war as a struggle between patriarchal interests, a struggle which leaves the ordinary citizen suffering and which cannot be fully neutralised unless a different and more inclusive form of power is able to flourish. The research focused on gender as an axis of power relations which cuts across distinctions of class and ethnicity. It was carried out in five programme areas (in Sudan, Mali, Angola, Uganda and Somalia), and explored the experiences of war of people living in those areas (El-Bushra, 2003). Based largely on testimonies from 135 respondents (more or less evenly divided between men and women), it assessed the relevance of gender difference both in terms of the impact of war, and in terms of its underlying causal factors. The research focused on two main questions. First, it examined the frequently made assumption that gender relations change as a result of war, offering a 'window of opportunity' for transforming gender regimes and for enhancing women's status. Second, it investigated the proposition that gender identities might themselves be a factor in perpetuating war.

In relation to the first question, that of the impact of war on gender relations, the findings initially appeared paradoxical and confusing. On the one hand, that change had come about was clear from all the study areas. In particular, women acquired new responsibilities for providing for their families economically, while men had essentially lost their roles. For example, a man in a peri-urban squatter area near the Angolan capital, Luanda, in despair at depending on his wife even for personal purchases such as cigarettes, said 'My wife is responsible for what is mine – she comes and goes, and I don't have a cent ... is that a life?', while a man in the Somalian coastal town of Brava said 'Now we obey our women ... they are taking us through this difficult time'. Many of the men interviewed described role reversals within the household with mixed feelings: they were grateful to their womenfolk and recognised the need for attitudes to women's participation in decision making to change in future, yet felt devastated by the erosion of their power and status.

Women also had mixed feelings: they welcomed the opportunities war had provided to acquire new skills and to demonstrate their capacities under pressure. A Malian woman returning from refuge in Mauritania, commenting on the impact of living abroad, said 'The most notable impact for me was that I learned to read and to cook well. That wasn't possible before. We understood there is a better life than ours ... and we came back because we were promised (i.e. by our men) consideration and respect.' A southern Sudanese woman displaced to Khartoum summed up the change by saying 'This is the benefit of war, if wars have benefits ... We cannot maintain the division of labour because there is no room for that.' However, women took on greater work burdens as a result of this change. Moreover, for some, economic independence came with a loss of personal relationships and social support.

On the other hand, though evidence of change was clear within households, it did not appear to extend far into the wider community. Community decision-making structures, such as elders' committees or the chiefship, continued to place power in the hands of men. In Somalia for example, male members of a clan are expected to provide financial contributions to cover the costs of war, including compensation payments to other clans – this is a primary basis for men's role as decision makers within the clan, a role from which women are essentially excluded. Nowadays, some men depend on their wives to provide the money required, since they themselves have no source of income – the ultimate role reversal. In such cases the men's position within the community is deeply undermined, to the extent that they may be excluded from clan meetings. However, women continue to be excluded from such meetings too. The Somalia researchers expressed doubts that women's new powers would last once a new government was established.

In similar vein, researchers from Uganda noted a widespread backlash against women's and children's rights. While it was mostly older men who expressed these views, some older women also expressed disapproval of 'modern' women's behaviour, in particular of their sexual assertiveness. Generally the case studies demonstrated that the gains women had acquired seemed tenuous at best outside the immediate household; they had gained increased responsibility, but not increased power.

The ACORD research team found it difficult to agree on how to interpret these apparent contradictions. What appeared to one researcher as a massive change, to another seemed merely a reworking of previous attitudes. 'Gender relations' proved too broad a term to describe the different types of change that were happening, and so it was necessary to assess how change was happening in four separate elements of the gender order:

1   Gender *roles*, i.e. the everyday tasks of men and women, had changed most. In every community taking part in the study, women had generally taken on bigger workloads and bigger responsibilities for providing for their families. Conversely, many men, finding that war had destroyed or moved them away from the resources which they previously controlled (such as agricultural land for example) had retreated into enforced idleness and frustration.

2   Gender *identities* (see above) had changed in that neither men nor women were able to live up to the behaviour expected of them because of their reduced circumstances, although the expectations themselves had not changed.

3   Power relations within *institutions* had changed slightly, and inconsistently from one case to another. Women's increased family responsibilities had to some extent resulted in greater de facto decision-making power for them within the household: since they now earned a greater proportion, if not all, of the family income, they were more likely to decide how to spend it. However, decision making was often retained by men. Not much had changed at community or national level, where decision-making bodies continued to be dominated by men: women had acquired greater responsibility but without a concomitant increase in power.

4   Gender *ideologies* had not changed at all and in some cases had become more firmly patriarchal. Gender ideologies can be described as the values, attitudes and beliefs which underpin the roles, identities and institutions that make up the gender order.

This analysis suggests that even though the everyday lives of individual women and men may change significantly as a result of war, change in terms of broader institutional practice or at the fundamental level of ideology is extremely slow. Projects designed to capitalise on the potential for change in postwar periods cannot realistically be expected to find more than superficial success, especially if they operate within the time frame normally applying to postwar rehabilitation projects, and may not work in women's favour at all if they are based on policy formulas alone rather than on deep analysis of context. However, other studies provide evidence that positive *change* can come about through a combination of popular organisation and political will, neither of which existed in the ACORD study areas. For example there is evidence that in Rwanda attitudes and values are beginning to change, largely because a broad coalition of women's organisations has levered high-level political will to reform policy (UNIFEM, 2003).

Intervention implications

On of UNHCR's 'five promises to refugee women' is 'to ensure that 50 per cent of refugee representatives on management committees are women'. The aim is to give the validation of the international community to the notion that women can and should be seen as active participants in decision-making at the community level. There are positive and negative consequences to such a strategy. On the one hand, many women refugees have affirmed the positive changes that have come about in camp facilities and management as a result of this initiative. On the other, the ACORD research suggests that any changes might be superficial, disguising hidden resistance within the community institutions, and possibly leading to a backlash against women if the strategy is seen as an imposed one. In fact, evidence for such an outcome has been document in the Burundian refugee camps in Tanzania (Turner, 2000), where this policy was introduced without discussion.

The second question which the research project addressed was: can gender identity be considered as a causal factor in war? Although this was a more difficult question to answer from the empirical data available, the testimonies did provide indications that it can. In all five of the case study areas, patriarchal struggles for power and control of resources are implicated in the war, at both the macro political levels and in terms of local and domestic violence. Sudan respondents, for example, despaired at what they saw as the causes of the war: intolerance, greed and intransigence over religion, traits which they observed on both sides. One respondent described it explicitly as 'gender-based violence – man against man fighting for position. The Somalia study brought out clearly the way in which national-level struggles for armed supremacy between the 'big' clans impacted on relations between clans at the local level. The Angola team talked about the 'two-way relationship between patriarchy and violence' in describing the way political groups had manipulated issues of women's sexuality, while the Sudan team brought to the fore the connection between the increased availability of small arms and violent robbery, rape and forced marriage. As the Ugandan research team put it, 'aggressivity and militarization represent both a vision and a strategy to restore the possibilities of ethnic and gender identity' (Lumoro, 2002).

Figure 9.1 depicts how violence leads to, and is in turn generated by, poverty, humiliation, frustration, loss of livelihood, failures of governance, political manipulation and breakdown of intercommunal relations. The situation becomes a breeding ground for a wide variety of manifestations of violence, including domestic and sexual abuse, alcoholism and drug abuse, depression, suicide, armed criminality and adherence to militias. These in turn, by reinforcing poverty and humiliation, lead to a continuation of the conditions which perpetuate war.

Gender identities, which influence the way people perceive themselves in relation to their social environment, are closely bound up in this vicious circle. The question, then, is: can gender identities be turned round, to

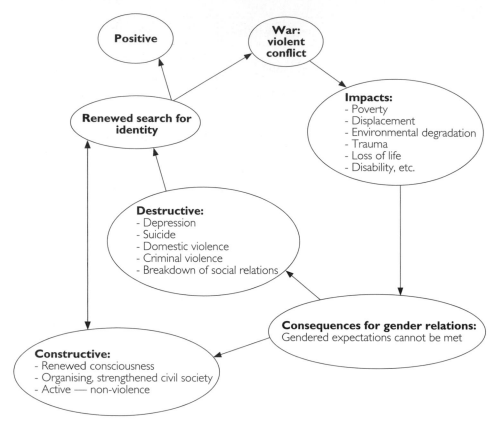

Figure 9.1   Gender impact flowchart: 'how gender identity can contribute to cycles of violence'

provide a new and more constructive set of relationships? Figure 9.1 suggests that there are points in the vicious circle where public debate, a renewed consciousness and commitment to active non-violence can turn the situation around, by emphasising socially constructive identities and values rather than destructive ones.

9.5   The challenge of social transformation

How might this transformation be achieved? We examine this in more practical detail in Chapter 10, but for the moment in this final section we consider what further pointers we might find in the literature on power which might help conceptualise the task of overcoming and reversing the vicious cycles of violence.

9.5.1   Resistance, solidarity and agency

We referred at the beginning of this chapter to the suggestion that the oppressive exercise of power – and resistance to it – is at the root of war. How do people respond when power is imposed on them? We have seen above that the dehumanisation that results from violence and poverty brings about a chain-reaction of self-harm and harm to others, often linked to the pursuit of goals which relate to the reclamation of identity. This suggests that for those whom Freire describes as the 'oppressed', emancipation begins only when they become conscientised, i.e. when they develop the consciousness which will enable them to free themselves. For the outsider, merely wanting to help is not enough, since the 'false generosity of paternalism ... makes the oppressed the objects of its humanitarianism' and perpetuates this dehumanisation (Freire, 1996).

Ideas about 'conscientization' (and 'subjectivity', Foucault's term for the freely determined self-image to which he believes all human beings have a right) seem very abstract, but are worth thinking about since they have shaped international resistance movements of different sorts which, as in the feminist movement for example, address some very concrete manifestations of oppressive power relations. What can children kept in bonded labour, or women who suffer domestic violence, for example, do to escape their situation, in the absence of supportive projects, refuges or alternative means of surviving?

Intervention implications

 Humanitarian relief interventions in and after war may be much needed as short-term measures, but most of us recognise the need also to address the underlying abuses of power that generate and perpetuate many emergency situations. Without addressing these abuses of power, humanitarian support will provide only sticking-plaster solutions. But as outsiders, are there limitations on our moral right to undertake this on our own initiative? And what should we do if those who are abused feel unable to challenge their abusers? For example, there can be no doubt that providing assistance to women in rape epidemics, such as have been documented in Somali refugee camps in Kenya for example (Kagwanja, 2000; Musse, 2004), is a critical necessity. However, raped women may want some forms of support more than others. Kagwanja's point is that neither UNHCR nor the Kenyan Government took their protection responsibilities seriously, while Musse describes how Somali elders resisted taking responsibility for pursuing rapists unless they were themselves likely to gain from compensation payments. In these circumstances, would it have been right for outsiders to encourage women to follow cases through the courts? Many women preferred to take no action, since they had no confidence that the system would provide them with the support they needed; on the contrary, they simply expected that they would be ostracised by their families and communities.

Individuals attempt to create a viable and satisfying life for themselves, in spite of the limitations their social context imposes on them. Lack of formal power does not deprive people of resilience or of capacity to resist what they consider to be unwanted pressures. Whether they engage in deliberate analysis of their situation or not, people living in areas affected by war are responding on a daily basis to crises and dilemmas about which they make choices – where to live, which market to frequent, or what stories to tell their children. 'Agency' refers to the capacity of individuals to act, in furtherance of what they perceive to be their own interests. The importance of the concept of agency in understanding war is that all individuals exercise agency, whether or not they have power. Keeping in mind that individuals have the potential to change their lives and their situations, and are not simply swept along by tides of history, 'agency' reminds us that power can be found in places and in forms that we may not expect. Rather than focusing attention on the larger-than-life figures of history – the warlords, politicians and bankers for example – 'agency' encourages us to recognise how 'ordinary' men and women influence the course of war.

The concept of agency is particularly relevant when considering the issue of gender and violence raised above. The notion that women are victims of violence, and men the perpetrators of it, pervades much discussion of humanitarian intervention. However, we cannot simply conclude that people are victims of their circumstances, tossed around by history and exercising no personal choice to influence the world around them. 'Agency' suggests that women and men respond to their experiences in active ways, that they have the capacity to assert their own interests as they see fit, and to be resilient in the face of the constraints imposed on them.

9.5.2 Empowerment

Is all power necessarily oppressive? Rowlands, discussing the way development agencies adopted strategies of 'empowerment' (Rowlands, 1997), identifies different sorts of power, namely:

- power as domination, or *'power over'*
- leadership which helps people achieve their goals, or *'power to'*
- *'power with'*, achieved by collective action to tackle problems
- *'power from within'*, which equates with spiritual strength.

In Rowlands' formulation, 'power over' is thought of as being in finite supply and a 'zero-sum game', i.e. it always needs both winners and losers. If women, for example, are to gain power, men will necessarily lose it. When power is conceived in this way, those whose power is under threat are bound to respond by resisting attempts to erode it. However, seeing power as a creative and productive process, and one in which everyone can share, may result in different outcomes. Thus those who are marginalised through 'power over' can find a different sort of strength to make changes to their situation, by drawing on their own resources and on resources which derive from solidarity with others.

Rowlands' main interest is in examining how the concept of 'empowerment' has been employed by development projects aiming to advance the situation of women in Honduras. Her conclusion is that the concept of empowerment tends to be defined too loosely and too variously, and often fails to reflect the aspirations of the women whose empowerment is intended. In this respect, her work recalls that of Freire, insisting that only the oppressed can decide how to alter their situation. Promoting self-confidence, self-worth and a sense of agency enables the excluded to challenge the internalised oppression highlighted by Lukes and others, and to maximise their inner potential or 'power to' and 'power from within'.

A women's group in Sierra Leone discuss income generation and new business development projects, in a scheme supported by UNICEF.

9.6   Conclusion

In this chapter we have drawn from the literature of power to gain insights into how wars begin and how they are perpetuated. Looking at the way power is manifested in decision-making institutions and in society at large, we see that it often operates in subtle and insidious ways: powerful interests control not only people's behaviour but also their knowledge, values and self-perception. Systems of democratic participation in decision making can channel power into constructive directions, but can also be abused and manipulated. Power systems developed in the West may not be the best models for other cultures to follow: indeed, the export of the Western 'hegemonic masculinity' model of patriarchal power across the globe may have generated new forms of tension and oppression.

Looking at gender relations as an aspect of power, we have seen how the construction of gender identities both reflects and underpins power relations generally: gender identities are built up – through socialisation practices in the home and in other institutions – to encourage acceptance of unequal relations as being normal and morally right. A concern with gender is important, not just to ensure justice and equality in relations between men and women, but also because it gets to the heart of the nature of power, cutting across other forms of discrimination and colouring the relationship between different clans, classes and age groups. Gender identities – and the ideologies and structures which underpin them – can be critically important in shaping the responses of men and women affected by war, and in determining whether they react in destructive and violent ways or by redefining their values and relationships positively.

It could be said that the challenge of postwar transition is to develop a new consensus on how different kinds of power in society are to be valued and managed. In this chapter we have considered some approaches to the task of transforming oppressive, exclusionary power. The main lesson to be drawn is that such relationships *can* be changed; if identity is in large part socially constructed, altering the conditions of its construction will engender different patterns of behaviour. This implies that the task is not so much to replace oppressive power-bearers with less oppressive ones, but rather to rethink the values we attach to the quality of relationships. In this, we need to look at *all* relationships, not just the formal structures of political decision making. We also need to accept that change takes place at different speeds at different levels, and that institutional and ideological changes are likely to be extremely slow. This suggests that our interventions may be less effective in generating lasting change than we think they are.

9.7 Chapter summary

Civil war is a struggle for power, and reconstructing postwar societies requires redefining how **power** is exercised and shared, which requires a better understanding of how power works. Power can be seen as a **relationship** between two people or groups in which one obliges the other to submit to its wishes. For Habermas, in the Western democratic state power is exercised by **consensus,** while for Foucault, power is always the subject of **struggle** with the threat of violence. Power can be exercised in **hidden and subtle** ways, including preventing issues from being discussed. Power can also come through control of **knowledge** and promotion of social **norms** which keep groups oppressed; the social contract sometimes accepts major inequalities of power.

Patriarchy describes a power system in which **dominant men** suppress the interests of women and lower status, or subaltern, men. In patriarchal systems, subaltern men often have power over lower status women. Civil wars can sometimes be seen as struggles for power and resources between groups of dominant men, but with the fighting being done by subaltern men (and some women). Attributes of **masculinity** vary over time and place, and violence can be promoted by building on particular aspects of male self-image. Dolan argues that in war or collapsed states, men cannot fulfil the social role they expect of themselves, and that **thwarted** aspirations of masculinity can also lead to violence. Young men may not be treated as adults until they have a wife and children who they support; war may stop them from becoming 'men' in this sense and they may choose an alternative masculinity involving violence. Women are often the victims of that violence.

Ending violence means reconstructing power relationships between men and between men and women, as well as changing the social view of what it means to be a man or woman. That means changing four kinds of **gender** relations: **roles, identities, power within institutions, and ideologies**. War tends to change roles and institutions, but not identities and ideologies.

Civil wars can also be seen as coming from the oppressive exercise of power and the resistance to it, which may, in turn, require new understandings of power relations. **Agency** is the capacity of individuals to act, independent of whether or not they have formal power, and can be used to change power relations. Rowlands defines four kinds of power: it is normally defined as domination or **power over**, but there is also **power to** achieve goals, **power with** others for collective action, and **power within** or spiritual strength. These other forms of power need to be tapped to change power relations, and to create a new social contract. This means changing relationships between different groups – men and women, young and old, citizens and the state – and changing the way people think about power, including understanding that individuals have the capacity to decide and act in their own right, even under restrictive circumstances.

References

Bachrach, P. and Baratz, M. (1970) *Power and Poverty: Theory and Practice*, Oxford, Oxford University Press.

Bennett, O. et al. (eds) (1996) *Arms to Fight, Arms to Protect: Women Speak Out About Conflict*, London, Panos Institute.

Boal, A. (1995) *The Rainbow of Desire: the Boal Method of Theatre and Therapy*, London, Routledge.

Boas, M. (1997) 'Liberia – the hell-bound heart? Regime breakdown and the deconstruction of society', *Alternatives*, vol. 22.

Connell, R. W. (1995) *Masculinities*. Cambridge, Polity Press

Dolan, C. (2002) 'Collapsing masculinities and weak states – a case study of Northern Uganda' in Cleaver, F. (ed.) *Masculinities Matter! Men, Gender and Development*, London, Zed Books.

El-Bushra, J. (2003) 'Fused in combat: gender relations and armed conflict', *Development in Practice*, vol. 13, nos. 1 & 2.

Foucault, M. (1983) 'The subject and power' in Dreyfus, H. and Rabinow, P. (eds) *Michel Foucault: Beyond Structuralism and Hermeneutics*, Chicago, University of Chicago Press.

Freire, P. (1996) *Pedagogy of the Oppressed*, Harmondsworth, Penguin.

Gautam, S. (2001) *Women and Children in the Periphery of the People's War*, Kathmandu, Nepal, Institute of Human Rights Communication.

Habermas, J. (1996) *Between Facts and Norms: Contributions to a Discourse Theory of Law and Democracy*, Cambridge MA, MIT Press.

Ibanez, A. (2001) 'El Salvador: war and untold stories – women guerrillas' in Moser, C. and Clark, F. (eds) *Victims, Perpetrators or Actors? Gender, Armed Conflict and Political Violence*, London, Zed Books.

Jackson, C. and. Pearson, R. (eds) (1998) *Feminist Visions of Development: Gender Analysis and Policy*, London, Routledge.

Jusu-Sheriff, J. (2000) 'Sierra Leonean women and the peace process' in Lord, D. (ed.) *Paying the Price: the Sierra Leone Peace Process*, London, Conciliation Resources.

Kabeer, N. (1994) *Reversed Realities: Gender Hierarchies in Development Thought*, London, Verso.

Kagwanja, P. (2000) 'Ethnicity, gender and violence in Kenya', *Forced Migration Review*, vol. 9, pp. 22–25.

Kandirikirira, N. (2003) 'Deconstructing domination: gender disempowerment and the legacy of colonialism and apartheid in Omaheke, Namibia' in Cleaver, F. (ed.) *Masculinities Matter: Men, Gender And Development*, London, Zed Press.

Kelly, L. (2000) 'Wars against women: sexual violence, sexual politics and the militarised state' in Jacobs, S., Jacobson, R. and Marchbanks, S. (eds) *States of Conflict: Gender, Violence and Resistance*, London, Zed Books.

Lukes, S. (1974) *Power: a Radical View.* Basingstoke, Palgrave.

Lumoro, I. (2002) *Uganda Case Study, Gender-sensitive Design and Planning in Conflict-affected Situations*, London, Agency for Co-operation and Research in Development (ACORD).

Millett, K. (1977) *Sexual Politics*, London, Virago Press.

Mukhta, P. (2000) 'Gender, community, nation: the myth of innocence' in Jacobs, S., Jacobson, R. and Marchbanks, S. (eds) *States of Conflict: Gender, Violence and Resistance*, London, Zed Books.

Musse, F. (2004) 'War crimes against women and girls' in Gardner, J. and El-Bushra, J. (eds) *Somalia, the Untold Story: the War Through the Eyes of Women*, London, Pluto Press.

Rehn, E. and Sirleaf, E. J. (2002) *Women, War And Peace: The Independent Experts' Assessment on the Impact of Armed Conflict on Women and Women's Role in Peace-Building*, New York, UNIFEM.

Richards, P. (1996) *Fighting for the Rain Forest: War, Youth and Resources in Sierra Leone*, London, Heinemann.

Rowlands, J. (1997) *Questioning Empowerment: Working with Women in Honduras*, Oxford, Oxfam.

Turner, S. (2000) 'Vindicating masculinity: the fate of promoting gender equality', *Forced Migration Review*, vol. 9, pp. 8–9.

UNIFEM (2003) *Report of the Learning Oriented Assessment of Gender Mainstreaming and Women's Empowerment Strategies in Rwanda, 2–12 September 2002*, UNIFEM.

Wade, P. (1994) 'Man the hunter: gender and violence in music and drinking contexts in Colombia' in Harvey, P. and Gow, P. (eds) *Sex and Violence: Issues in Representation and Experience*, London, Routledge.

Transforming power relations: peacebuilding and institutions

Judy El-Bushra

10.1 Introduction

Our discussion of power indicates that it is a basic component of social relationships, such that no strategy for change can succeed unless it takes power dynamics into account. Just as the breakdown of power relations can lead to war, so reconstituting them can lead to peace. Understanding how power relations perpetuate war can help to identify points in the vicious circle where the downwards spiral can be reversed. In Chapter 9 we saw that this task is wider than changing the formal structures of political decision making; it also means changing the nature of relationships between different groups, between men and women, young and old, between citizens and the state, and that this means changing the expectations that each has of the other, both in terms of daily practice and in terms of attitudes and values. We also saw that changing the way people think about power – whether they give value to collective and individual power as well as the power of some to control and dominate others – is as important as changing the structures of power. To do this it is important to conceptualise the individual as possessing the capacity to decide and act in his or her own right, even under restrictive circumstances.

In this chapter, we examine some of the broad intervention strategies which might be suggested by this approach to understanding power relations. We do this with an eye to the concrete intervention situations – where prioritising one's goals is a difficult, though crucially necessary, task. We start by discussing the overall framework of 'conflict transformation', i.e. the process of transforming conflicts of interest from being violent, destructive forces to being positive channels for communication and dialogue. We then look at what conflict transformation might mean, from two perspectives: firstly, from the point of view of gender and intergenerational relationships, and secondly at the level of institutions, focusing particularly on the state, civil society and the international community. We hope to show that the power relations which operate within institutions, and those in the wider society, are in fact closely linked. Our overall argument is that social reconstruction after war requires interveners not only to deal with the obvious power holders – the governments, military factions, warlords and business interests – but also to create institutional frameworks in which those without a voice can find an acknowledged and respected place in the political landscape.

In this chapter we assume the reconstitution of social and political relationships at all levels – locally, nationally, and internationally – to be a key part of postwar reconstruction. The accent is on creating a culture in which different elements in society regain confidence that their voices will be heard and their interests acted on – in short, on the redefinition of the social contract. Following Galtung, we accept that 'positive peace' is not just the absence of war but a situation where major conflicts of interest have been resolved, where violence is at a minimum, and where exclusion, inequality and injustice cannot be practised with impunity (Galtung, 1995). Putting such a society in place means transforming conflictual relationships into cooperative ones: ensuring political representation for all groups, establishing a constitutional framework which protects the rights of all citizens, opening up public debate, and dismantling structures and practices built on prejudice and exclusion.

10.2 Conflict transformation

Conflict transformation is an approach to conflict management which recognises that divisions and tensions exist in every society. These divisions and tensions are natural and potentially positive features of society since they represent basic human aspirations to self-realisation. War happens when these tensions are allowed to become destructive; peace involves transforming them into strengths. This might be achieved by looking for the 'connectors' (Anderson, 1999) and supporting these, or by setting up platforms of open debate where the rights and aspirations of all parties can be recognised. Conflict transformation as a strategy has been informed by the notion of transforming 'power over' into 'power to' and 'power with', i.e. emphasising the gains that can be made by everybody when all parties' interests can be satisfied, at least to an acceptable degree.

The professional field of conflict transformation has very old and very broad roots, being based on the notion of non-violent resistance, of which elements can be found in most major religions. In terms of practice in the early twenty-first century, however, it is a relatively new field of work, and its theory and practical tools are still being developed. 'Conflict transformation' as a term grew out of, and became distinct from, 'conflict resolution' around the mid 1990s. The focus of 'conflict resolution' is on mediation, i.e. on effecting a negotiated settlement between two parties in conflict. Conflict resolution often tends to be carried out at relatively high levels of politics and to involve elite players in national and international conflicts, resulting in formal or legally binding agreements between these official players. The actual processes of conflict resolution revolve round the skills of specialised negotiators who themselves become part of the same elite groups in the process.

Much criticism (and self-criticism) was directed at the exclusiveness of the process of conflict resolution work (Rupesinghe, 1995). It was pointed out, for example, that the conflicts inherent in war operate at a number of different levels, and that peace will not be sealed unless local disputes are solved within the larger ones. Conflict resolution in the sense of high-level mediation often fails to address underlying grievances and inequalities. The lack of involvement of 'ordinary citizens', themselves potential catalysts for peace, places limitations on the commitment of broad populations to abide by formal peace settlements. (The accuracy of this criticism can be seen in the repeated pattern by which negotiated settlements bring only temporary reprieve, with violence breaking out again if complex roots are not acknowledged.) Conflict in and of itself is seen as a natural expression of social difference and of humanity's perpetual struggle for justice and self-determination. The challenge is not to abolish conflict, but rather to put a stop to the cyclical nature of violent conflict by acknowledging and channelling this struggle into constructive directions, and by addressing the structural issues that perpetuate armed conflict (Lederach, 1995).

'Conflict transformation', which has come to be used in preference to 'conflict resolution', describes a broad range of activities which are aimed at bringing out the potential of conflict to be a positive force for change. These activities might include:

- providing social services to ensure that survival and basic needs of all, especially the more disadvantaged amongst the different populations, are met
- peacemaking (dialogue, mediation, contributing to and monitoring peace accords)
- advocacy to promote awareness of peace, disarmament, justice and human rights issues
- leadership and involvement in political processes; encouraging popular participation and confidence in political processes
- contributing to and strengthening civil society
- community-level development and social reconstruction work.

The stress is not so much on what is done, as on how it is done – running a soup kitchen, for example, might fall under the heading of conflict transformation if it is managed in a way that emphasises the principle of equal rights and shared responsibilities, whereas running it as a service for one group from which others were excluded would exacerbate conflict. In this sense the approach of 'Do no harm' lies firmly within the conflict transformation ethos, since both emphasise how any specific action, whatever label is put on it, can contribute either to the reduction of tension or to enhancing it. The challenge is to see opportunities for acknowledging difference and providing channels for it to be expressed and legitimised. Conflict transformation is about creating new institutions and new practices of social relations, in which divergent interests are regulated constructively and equally.

10.2.1 Conflict transformation and power

The conflict transformation profession, however, tends to have an uneasy relationship with the notion of power, and does not always acknowledge the centrality of power relations as both a cause of conflict and a potential instrument of transformation. Within power relations we must include, crucially, not only those that operate within the society where war has been conducted, but also those that shape the relationship of that society with wider national, regional and global forces. And the latter clearly includes institutions and networks which purport to provide assistance, including the institutions of conflict transformation itself. Some of this critique has come from within the profession itself.

John Paul Lederach is a foremost exponent of the peacebuilding practice pursued by the Mennonite Church (a church based mainly in the USA and dedicated to peacebuilding; see Sampson and Lederach, 2000). Lederach describes how the experience of 25 years as a conflict resolution trainer led him to move on from the approaches in which he had originally been trained in North America, which he described as 'too narrow, often out of context, and presumptious' (i.e. based on a presumption of superiority on the part of the trained specialists) and displaying a 'rhetoric of cultural sensitivity' (Lederach, 2000). Lederach's own experience led him beyond this rhetorical sensitivity towards 'an orientation rooted in the centrality of context, culture and empowerment' (Lederach, 2000, p. 47). Whatever external or international forces have generated or supported war, the fact remains that it is the local society that suffers the consequences and that it should therefore be paramount in shaping the solutions. Ready-made, one-size-fits-all solutions developed elsewhere and imported by conflict professionals will be both oppressive and ineffective. Outsiders have a role, but it involves dialogue with, acknowledgement of and support to local initiatives. Lederach's account suggests that the 'centrality of context, culture and empowerment' is all too frequently overlooked.

Intervention implications

Imagine that, in the interests of postwar reconciliation, a local women's group is proposing to organise a 'cultural day'. Performers representing the two previously opposed parties will share a platform and be treated to examples of each other's dances and songs.

For many interveners, this sort of activity has high value because it sends peace messages in a form that is easily understood, locally initiated, and enjoyable to boot. For some doubters, however, there is a danger that the performances might simply serve to exacerbate existing prejudices, if power imbalances between the groups are not recognised and addressed in the planning of the day. A possible alternative approach might be to involve a third party (of professional dancers perhaps) to perform the dances of both sides, emphasising parity between the two groups (El-Bushra and Kerr, 2005, forthcoming).

Applying what we have learned about power relations to conflict transformation suggests that dismantling deeply rooted structures of oppression is not something that can be achieved overnight. If the roots of injustice are embedded in our closest and most intimate relationships, in our history, language and religion, if those who suffer from injustice may have internalised and accepted it, and if our very identities and values are brought into question by the existence of structural violence, then the solutions must be fundamental and far-reaching. Most importantly, external interveners must acknowledge their own role in the power structures which are to be transformed, and the extent to which their social position and background colours their response to the situations they are trying to ameliorate.

A goal of conflict transformation in the context of postwar reconstruction is to restructure relationships which were previously out of balance, and where the imbalance may have contributed to the process of 'normal' conflict becoming violent. These relationships may, in different circumstances, include those between different classes, ethnic groups or occupational categories, ages and sexes. Restructuring relationships has a double importance in so far as a consolidated impact can be obtained: for example, changing negative attitudes of the wealthy towards the poor can also raise awareness of discrimination against groups which are associated with poverty, such as disabled people or disadvantaged ethnic groups. To get a more detailed picture of some of the issues around the reconstruction of power relations, we will explore two types of power relation which are universally present (those based on gender and on age) and then consider an analytical framework which may help bring some of these issues to the fore.

10.3   Reconstructing power relations (1): gender and age as axes of social organisation

Both women and young people are groups that might well be sidelined by the 'nondecision' processes of politicians. Both are likely to have been socialised to think of themselves as subordinate to male elders, a process which effectively suppresses their voices and imposes compliance with a set of expected behaviours which may not be either beneficial or feasible. Their insights and their efforts are needed in rebuilding after war. Women and youth are not the only categories of whom this can be said: others might include particularly disadvantaged ethnic groups such as the Batwa in Rwanda and Burundi, occupational groups such as the potters of southern Somalia, and refugee and displaced populations everywhere. However, we take women and youth as representative examples of groups that need to be brought into any reconstruction strategy if the emerging political culture is going to withstand postwar stresses.

10.3.1 Women as peacebuilders

Since the end of the Cold War there has been a notable expansion in the women's peace movement. This movement has been met with indifference by some sections of the international community, and with uncritical support by others. The adoption by the UN Security Council of Resolution 1325 on Women, Peace and Security is a reflection of the importance, in rhetoric at least, which the world community accords to women's participation in

Garment-factory workers protest against the killing of several workers by police at a demonstration demanding the payment of back pay and holiday bonuses as stipulated by Bangladeshi labour law.

conflict transformation. Resolution 1325 promotes women's involvement in formal negotiations and in peacekeeping, and requires all parties to provide adequate protection for women and for women's rights as part of their obligations under international law (Anderlini, 2001).

The growth in women's peace organisations, and the expansion of international policy and funding support available to them, is an important feature of post-conflict transition periods in the present era (Date-Bah, 1996; Kumar et al., 2000). Although, as Kumar's team suggests, the existence of financial support may have been a powerful incentive to their emergence, it may also be the case that the experience of war acts powerfully on the conscience of those most disadvantaged by it, leading them to recognise the advantages of organising to achieve improvements in their lives and the lives of those close to them.

Box 10.1 Women organising for postwar social transformation

Women in Somalia and Somaliland became involved in the peace movement (supporting political negotiations, running demobilisation and reconstruction projects, joining teams of community-based conflict negotiators, for example) because of their frustration at seeing their families being torn apart. Although they protested against men's persistent refusal to allow women to take part in political negotiations, they also tended to believe that they could go far in influencing peace processes without seeking to revolutionise their status (Gardner and El-Bushra, 2004).

In postwar Bosnia-Herzegovina, women's organisations formed for a variety of reasons, including both for women-specific benefits and for some more general good. These included acquiring economic independence, taking action against violence against women, encouraging women to get involved in politics, and working for reconciliation (Cockburn, 2002).

In Rwanda, women's organisations shouldered a large part of the burden of social care in postwar and post-genocide Rwanda from the height of the crisis onwards – they organised food supplies and cooking for their families, took in orphans, encouraged fleeing soldiers to come back, looked after rape victims, and so on. This laid the foundations for an extensive network of women's organisations, representing women in rural communities, in parliament, in the media as well as women genocide survivors and women's legal rights groups. These are now grouped under an umbrella which acts as an important interlocutor with government and with external assistance providers (UNIFEM, 2003).

The fact that women tend generally not to engage in actual combat does not mean that they do not suffer and witness – and perpetrate – extreme violence, with all the psychological and social consequences that that entails. Moreover, in many societies women are responsible for the provision of food and care both within the household and at a community level, and this responsibility is likely to increase as a result of war. At the same time, social institutions are unlikely to change fast enough for these increased responsibilities to be matched by increased power. Often it is this experience which catalyses women's organisations, as it gives women a stake in peace: women peace activists do not want violence, nor do they want to go back to the way things were before.

Women tend to be few in number in formal peace negotiations, being rarely acknowledged as competent actors in formal processes. However, they have broken through this barrier in some cases (such as the Burundi women invited to the peace table by Nelson Mandela), often gaining acceptance at the peace table *as women* (i.e. with a non-partisan agenda) rather than as members of delegations. In addition to national level negotiations, they are often involved in local peace processes, for example interceding with militias on behalf of vulnerable civilians. Women's peace activism in post-conflict reconstruction periods includes roles advocating for women's rights and for their participation in local and national politics, both locally and at regional and international levels. It also includes a range of service delivery activities such as providing food for returning refugees, supporting women who have been victims of sexual violence, and providing for orphaned children (El-Bushra, 2003).

These various activities contribute to peacebuilding, inasmuch as they challenge existing power relations and attempt to replace them with an inclusive framework. The aim is twofold. On the one hand, a society which has the capacity to negotiate a sustainable peace (a peace which responds to the needs of all sections of society) is necessarily a society in which women and men are fully represented in decision making. Women's peace movements therefore work towards their own rights and equality as a contribution to sustainable peace. On the other hand, many also work towards the broader societal goal of ensuring that all sections of the population have access to political processes and the opportunity to participate in them. This task – involving a transformation of attitudes, practices and structures – is a further potential contribution to peacebuilding (El-Bushra, 2003).

Within the women's peace movement, however, there are a number of dilemmas to be faced, revolving around the question: why women? Such a movement runs the risk of falling into the essentialist trap of seeing women universally as peace-loving victims. This assumption denies women's agency, i.e. the capacity to act in what they see are their interests and make their own decisions about their own lives. Members of women's peace organisations often consider themselves to be developing a common 'women's agenda' as a counterpoint to the failed politics of violence, an agenda which links women across political divides on the basis of their common identity and shared experiences of war. Some see their traditional gender roles (as mothers and carers) as being the basis of their peacebuilding activities, while for others it is precisely the need for women not to be restrained within those roles that motivates their activism. Women have varying views about how far they should participate in 'men's politics' – for some, the aim is to influence governments; for others, confrontation against oppressive authorities is the only possible response. For some, women's organisations are still too young and lacking in confidence to venture far into alliances with other groups, while for others, a style of 'women's politics' is developing – one based on expressing differences without aggression – which can influence mainstream politics and peace activism (El-Bushra, 2003).

These dilemmas are important for the international community to consider. Support – financial and otherwise – has been provided to women's peace groups in postwar situations, but it is not always clear how far this is the result of unthinking application of policy prescriptions and how far it is the outcome of genuine understanding of the potential of such organisations. Women's organisations still tend to be consigned to the 'local' level, with no questions asked about their marginalisation within formal national and international decision-making structures. As with new organisations generally, to be lionised by the international community may not be the most effective form of support, and could indeed deprive them of valuable assets such as conviction, solidarity and the capacity to represent grassroots memberships.

Moreover, there is sometimes a conflict of organisational cultures operating in the relationship between donors and women's organisations, since donors expect women's groups to submit funding applications based on standard criteria and planning methods, while many such organisations choose to operate on the basis of intuition, inspiration, and solidarity rather than in logical planning frameworks (El-Bushra, 2005 forthcoming). At the same time, women's organisations recognise their own organisational weaknesses, and in particular the need to become more strategic in their planning, not only in order to access funds but also to increase their effectiveness and their capacity to enter into alliances across civil society. Below, we return to the question of how the international community can best support such groups.

Intervention implications

Commentators on women's participation in the Sierra Leone peace process have suggested that the women's peace movement there had strong influence on public opinion during the mid 1990s, but that it later allowed itself to be eclipsed by politicians because the women themselves had failed to develop a strong political analysis, and hence political leadership, of their own.

Given that many women find the male-dominated political arena intimidating, is it best to support women's organisations in making their own 'women's' politics, in which case they run the risk of being ignored? Or should they be supported to take part in mainstream politics, running the risk that they may be obliged to compromise their own analysis?

Women activists at a workshop organised by International Alert in Oxford in 2002 concluded that women's groups should move into the mainstream, but only when they had developed their own political analysis, identified their agenda and strategies, built up strong and skilful organisations, and developed clear consensus between women from different factions. The workshop recommended donors to support capacity building for women's peace groups, and asked donors to help them address 'the often significant barriers that women face between themselves' (El-Bushra, 2003, p. 63).

10.3.2 Intergenerational relations and conflict transformation

Intergenerational relations have figured in conflict transformation initiatives in a somewhat different way: here, rather than forming the basis of a global movement, age has been a factor of polarisation (mostly among men) which has been a powerful driver, both of conflict and of attempts at conflict resolution. 'Youth', in international parlance, tends to refer to the 15–24 age group. The term is often used alongside, and overlapping with, the category of 'children', defined as persons under the age of 18. Though 'youth' covers both males and females, young men are likely to dominate in any organised activities involving youth.

Conflict between generations is a feature of many societies all over the world. As the International Crisis Group maintains for Central Asia, for example:

Responding to the demands of young people means giving them a say in how things are run and understanding that they will challenge the present generation of leaders. But most Central Asian governments regard young people as a group to be controlled rather than included.

International Crisis Group, 2003

And as has been seen in earlier examples of war situations, for example Sierra Leone, wars are often in essence wars between generations of men. In other cases, conflictual interethnic relationships take violent form when the elders of the different groups prevail upon their youth to take up arms to defend the group's interest. For example, demobilisation of child soldiers in the Democratic Republic of the Congo has been overshadowed by the not entirely unjustified worry among assistance providers that returning ex-combatants may be sent back to fight by their elders (Verhey, 2003). Dolan (2002) makes the point that in northern Uganda (as in many other contexts) the category 'youth' is not defined by physical age so much as by social status: a youth is a man who by definition has not yet married. The practical difficulties of marrying in the circumstances of war ensure that many men fail to enter social adulthood – despite having sexual partners and begetting children – and endure a continuing status as youths. His contention is that the frustration and humiliation suffered by these men goes some way towards explaining widespread domestic violence and self-harming behaviour, as well as the decision by some to join armed forces.

In many societies, respect for (usually male) elders was in the past enshrined in institutions that placed older men at the centre of processes of local dispute settlement. Many of these institutions have died out, but are now in the process of being resuscitated as 'traditional mechanisms for conflict resolution'. Calls for their reinstallation have been made on the grounds that

Young female government fighters stand guard, Liberia.

'indigenous' methods of conflict resolution are likely to be more effective than imported ones, since they are better understood and accepted by the perpetrators of violence. 'Traditional' mechanisms may play a critically important role in the cultural reinstatement of groups or ethnicities such as the Acholi of northern Uganda which have been marginalised over decades, and may contribute positively to their sense of inclusion.

However, there are some difficult questions around such institutions. Firstly, there are bound to be practical problems around the reinvention of 'traditions' which have died out (Box 10.2). Secondly, such mechanisms often depend on, and provide support to, the power of male elders, and are associated with codes of behaviour that validate the subordinate position of women and youth. For some women and young people, the reintroduction of traditional structures can only reinforce, rather than transform, unequal relations, and so can never be instruments of transformation. Even where modern adaptations have been made (such as training women to be judges in Rwanda's *gacaca* community genocide courts – see UNIFEM, 2003) people may feel that such changes are cosmetic only.

Box 10.2   Traditional conflict resolution: the case of northern Uganda

In 1999 in northern Uganda, the anointment of clan elders was seen by some as an essential step in enabling Lord's Resistance Army (LRA) rebels to take advantage of the government's amnesty and give themselves up, since the return of the rebels was believed to be contingent on the performance of cleansing rituals which only properly anointed chiefs could perform. However, the institution of clan leadership had undergone numerous changes in the course of British colonial administration, as a result of which there was much uncertainty about how to do this. Some clans had forgotten how to perform the anointment ceremonies, others failed to mobilise the necessary costs or had lost the appropriate insignia, while others were riven by sometimes violent disputes about who should be anointed. Moreover, young people had little confidence in the authority of the elders. Women's opinion was divided, many believing that the reinstitution of the Acholi code of behaviour would be a backward step.

A deeper problem lay in the fact that Acholi healing rituals applied to disputes within the Acholi community, not to relations with other groups. The reinstallation of the chiefs thus supported an interpretation of the violence which saw its cause as lying exclusively within the Acholi community, rather than one which explored the position of the Acholi within the Ugandan state (Dolan, 1999).

Nevertheless, the emotional appeal of the strategy of reinstalling the chiefs was strong enough to overcome these objections, and the anointments went ahead with the support of the central government and of some international NGOs.

The period in which the anointments were conducted coincided with a steep increase in rebel attacks, which was followed by a drive by the army, in collaboration with the Sudanese army, to drive the LRA out of its bases in the Sudan. There was an increase in the number of rebel soldiers escaping, as a result of this military operation.

After the anointments, the issue of the chiefship rapidly became non-controversial. Many of the cleansing rituals were indeed performed, but these were mostly to resolve disputes between existing residents. It is unlikely that the possibility of traditional reconciliation contributed greatly to the return of LRA cadres.

Few formal organisations of young people have come about in response to the problems faced by young people in war. This suggests a major black hole of disempowerment. The international community places considerable emphasis on the vulnerability of youth and children in conflict and has created substantial initiatives to support them; the UN Secretary-General has appointed a Special Representative for Children and Armed Conflict, for example. International alliances working on youth issues in war (such as the Coalition to Stop the Use of Child Soldiers, for example) mostly include organisations 'working with or on behalf of child soldiers'. However, young people organise in many ways, often with the deliberate intention of challenging prevailing realities, and are often suppressed or manipulated as such. An example in the Uganda context is the *lukeme* groups of young male singers and musicians, who resisted calls to take part in a government-sponsored competition to write a song in praise of universal primary education (El-Bushra and Dolan, 2002). Such organisations are often unsupported by the NGO community, a fact which perhaps limits their scope financially, but paradoxically protects them from the need to operate in a world which is potentially politically hostile.

10.3.3 The social relations framework

Organisations – whether government or civil society – are the product of their social environment, and of the power relations which exist both within the organisation and in society at large, including the global society. To understand more about power relations within and between institutions, it is useful to draw from the social relations framework (SRF), an analytical device developed by the Institute of Development Studies, University of Sussex (Kabeer, 1994).

SRF is useful for understanding violent conflict (although not specifically designed with this in mind) because it helps unpack sources of tension and conflicting interests within institutions, and shows how resources, relationships and practices in and between institutions can exacerbate those conflicts. Furthermore, if applied periodically it permits a description of changes that have taken place over time (for example, before and after war). This may suggest possible future scenarios in terms of changing institutional practice. For Kabeer, changing institutional practice is a critical strategy in transforming relations of inequality.

SRF evolved within the field of gender and development, but throws light on processes of inequality generally; indeed, like the social exclusion analysis framework described in Chapter 9, it emphasises the intersections between different forms of inequality. SRA affords particular attention to institutions (including, for example, the household, the state, the army or the school). Institutions are sites in which (amongst other things) the 'gender hierarchy' (or hierarchy of gender-based power relations) is learned and transmitted. Although every institution has its own purposes and its own rules, the institutions that exist within a given society are structurally linked. Like Millett, Kabeer believes that the family generates values which are reproduced elsewhere, since 'familial norms and values are constantly drawn on in constructing the terms women and men enter, and participate in, public life and in the market-place' (Kabeer, 1994, p. 281).

Kabeer identifies five interrelated elements needing analysis within institutions:

- *rules*, or 'the official and unofficial norms, values, traditions, laws and customs which constrain or enable what is done, how it is done, by whom, and who will benefit' (p. 281), with the contrast between the official and the unofficial often being a key variable

- *resources* used or deployed by the institution, and patterns of resource distribution internally. This refers not only to material resources such as funds and human capital, but also to intangible resources such as information, solidarity, skills or political influence

- *people*, or the way that institutions privilege certain categories of people and exclude others, patterns which often reflect gender and other social differences

- *activities*, or institutional practices, and the ways in which these practices reinforce or undermine gender and class inequalities; activities might well include non-activities

- *power structures*, in which individuals within the institution have authority and control in particular areas, enabling them to maintain their own positions of privilege.

These five elements together describe how decisions are made, or not made, in the institution (how they are made, in relation to what, by whom, following what practices, and by which controlling interests). To illustrate how such a framework might be used in a real situation, we can develop an analysis of the state in Uganda (summarised in Table 10.1), based on information provided by Dolan in his chapter on masculinities (Dolan, 2002).

Table 10.1 Step 1: describing the five elements

Rules	Democratic institutions exist but some ethnicities feel excluded. The Ugandan army (UPDF: Uganda People's Defence Force) has rules of conduct governing interactions between soldiers and civilians (e.g. banning the recruitment of underage soldiers, punishment of soldiers who rape civilians). However, in many cases these are not observed and not upheld by the military authorities. Government introduced Amnesty Bill but appears from statements of politicians to have little commitment in practice.
Resources	Financial – little investment in north, poor infrastructure, limited education facilities and hence jobs. Political influence – southern groups closer to centres of power than northerners. Trust – lack of mutual trust between civilians and military, between north and south (exacerbated by colonial and post-colonial history and by socialisation). State uses conflict to justify high military expenditure and diversion of resources from social services.
People	Few Acholi in positions of influence nationally. Few Acholi accessing tertiary education.
Activities	Colonial state identified Acholi as warriors. Increasing militarisation through protected villages but lack of protection against LRA. No serious peace negotiations. Army commits rape and other abuses with impunity. Army fails to combat everyday discrimination.
Power structures	Senior politicians control peace negotiations.

Step 1 of the analysis describes an institution in terms of these five elements, providing a picture of how power dynamics work within it. In the case of the Ugandan state as described in Dolan's work, we note that the state's decision making about the war in the north has lacked transparency. The rhetoric of the state protecting its citizens and defending their rights sits ill with the actual record: the creation of insecure 'protected villages', UPDF inaction against the LRA, and the immunity from prosecution of soldiers accused of rape and murder. Central government – and the central corridors of government – has retained control of decision making about peace negotiations, making ambiguous statements about its intentions of peace. Resources are not lacking for the prosecution of the war in the north, but investment in the north is low, and education, jobs and public services remain inadequate. The countrywide context is one of competition for state favour between different regions, and especially between north and south, with the south playing a dominant role in the national political culture. Historically the development of this state of affairs can be traced to policies of the colonial state and later to events which exacerbated tensions between northerners and southerners.

Step 2 traces the links between the institution being described and other institutions, identifying the ways in which institutions reinforce – and are reinforced by – prevailing ideologies. It is these factors which can be assumed to contribute most effectively to the breakdown of political and social relations, and which consequently require greatest attention by those seeking to reconstitute a viable society in a postwar context. In the Ugandan case, prejudicial stereotypes of the Acholi as backward and less than human exist in society at large and are reinforced through language and socialisation. At the same time, Uganda's international backers reinforce the state's impunity by failing to challenge its record or to demand accountability against international policy (on the treatment of internally displaced persons, for example).

In step 3, we can use the analysis of steps 1 and 2 to identify points in the system where action for change would have the maximum impact. In relation to Uganda, Dolan himself suggests 'interventions to work with men to develop alternative masculinities ... to break the connections with ethnicity and race that provide politicians with so much leverage over individuals and groups' (Dolan, 2002, p. 81). We might perhaps add, based on his material: the need for strategies (perhaps through the national press and media) to undermine discriminatory attitudes between different Ugandan communities; the need to record abuses by state organs (the UPDF, for example) and to hold them to account; and encouraging other governments to require accountability from Uganda for the upholding of international law, policy and good practice. We can also see that the task of rehabilitating the position of the Acholi within the state – the unfinished task of the 1986 civil war in which the present government took power – will most likely be a long process, given its historical roots.

The SRF attempts to show that power relations are an integral feature of institutional life. However, the fluctuating distribution of resources and responsibilities within the institution, and the interplay of official and unofficial rules, ensures that the privilege and authority enjoyed by those in power are always fluctuating. Institutions are not isolated from the rest of society; power fluctuations within, say, the state, will be influenced by changes within civil society institutions or at the household, and in society at large. Institutional power is subject to constant negotiation, and can be transformed when sufficient members are willing to raise a challenge to it. Indeed, institutions are not monolithic structures but are constantly being recreated through the struggles of women and men to define their own equalities and empowerment. These are the struggles which, if given support from elsewhere, can effect lasting transformations in the power relations of postwar societies.

10.4 Reconstructing power relations (2): the state, civil society, and the international community

Essentially, the goal for all parties in postwar reconstruction is to re-establish the relationship between the state and the people, ensuring that all sections of society have a stake in the success of the national project and see value in committing energy to it. The international community has a right and a duty to involve itself in this process – a right to the extent that it often foots the bill, and a duty because it is committed to upholding international law and its principles. It is worth remembering that the quality of the relationship between people and government is probably more important than the form it takes, but that discussions about what the form should be can take people a long way towards cementing the relationship. The challenge for the international community, then, is: how to promote national dialogue, with a view to building confidence, ensuring inclusive political participation, challenging long-standing inequalities, and ensuring transparent and accessible decision making? And how to achieve this at a time when other priorities are equally urgent and critical? In this last section we look at this question from the point of view of an intervener's relationship first with civil society organisations, and second with the state.

10.4.1 Civil society organisations

Civil society consists of organisations formed by people joining together to pursue common interests. By most definitions (see Pearce and Howell, 2001), civil society is distinct from government, from the business community and private sector, from the military, and from 'natural' family or kinship-based institutions. It is often expected to provide a counterweight and a challenge to government, since by being organised in a relatively formal way it is capable of holding government to account. However, the fact that civil society depends on government for the conditions of its existence generates tensions between the two in which the real power is generally held by government.

Civil society usually includes non-governmental development and solidarity organisations (NGOs), community-based organisations (CBOs) such as neighbourhood groups, as well as media organisations, church groups, and trades unions. Some of these categories have decades of experience behind them while others are recent: for example NGOs have experienced rapid growth since the mid twentieth century.

The international community focuses much of its work on collaboration with identifiable organisations. This is partly derived from a belief that organising is good: that people are able to achieve higher levels of satisfaction of their needs if they do so in solidarity with others. But it is partly because collaborative organisations are more convenient ways for donors and policy makers to communicate with large numbers of people. Unlike informal forms of organising (such as self-help education schemes, revolving credit groups, or cultural performance associations), civil society organisations (CSOs) have relatively high visibility, enabling international organisations to connect more easily to local ones, and are amenable to operating in a way that facilitates that connection (e.g. they take minutes of meetings, write annual reports, undertake strategic planning, etc). The search made by international interveners for local partners is now such an ingrained reflex that it is sometimes hard to remember that not everyone chooses – or should necessarily choose – to join a formal organisation, nor does civil society necessarily represent the whole spectrum of interests or identities within the nation as a whole.

A civil society which is not yet well established, and which represents a society weakened by war, is likely to have difficulty withstanding government attempts to control or marginalise it. The international community does not have an unblemished record of support to CSOs. For example in El Salvador, despite plans for a broad-based and inclusive consultation regarding the national reconstruction programme, the NGO community was largely excluded. Donors such as USAID and the World Bank chose to develop partnerships with government bodies rather than NGOs or social organisations. NGO networks that did participate in the design and implementation of the national reconstruction plan noted that these international agencies ignored local organisations and expertise, reducing potential partners to beneficiaries (Alvarez Solis and Martin, 1996).

The argument for developing partnerships with CSOs is strong: the question is, which ones should be supported, and how? CSOs have a number of common weaknesses. They come from a variety of traditions and philosophies and a variety of sectoral or regional interests, which are not always compatible. They are often in competition amongst each other for funds and political influence. Some are more willing to make compromises with government than others. Some have overt or hidden nationalist goals, and represent the continuation of war by other means. Some owe their emergence to the existence of donor support funds (Kumar, et al., 2000) while others are administratively weak and can easily be destroyed by overgenerous support. Some groups that are outside the reach of mainstream civil society, like the Ugandan *lukeme* groups mentioned above, are most likely better off staying well under the radar of the donors and policy makers. Even though their work would be made available to a wider audience if they were networked into civil society, they could easily lose their vitality and independence.

But taken as a whole, civil society has a unique potential for linking across previously violent political divides. This is especially true of organisations representing women and young people, which – theoretically at least – have identities and memberships which cross-cut these divides. Time and again women's peace groups maintain that their value lies precisely in this capacity to build bridges: where patriarchal ideologies exclude women from political decision making, their powerlessness becomes a major advantage since they are not tied into identity politics in the way that men are (Gardner and El-Bushra, 2004). It may be useful, when considering collaborating with a group, to look at what it is already doing which involves joint activities across divides, and to encourage all activities to be done in inclusive ways if possible. Many women's groups make a practice of bringing women from opposing camps together for simple everyday tasks – farming, cooking, eating, for example. As a Congolese woman put it once: 'In our experience, even drinking a cup of tea with our enemies was something we thought would be impossible, but we made ourselves do it, because we believed that sharing the necessities of life might be the beginning of reconciliation' (Gégé

Katana, personal communication). International organisations can take initiatives to bring together CSOs drawn from one-time enemy communities, with a view to building up collaborations between them. This can be a very long-term process, and full of pitfalls for the unwary but a decade or more of preparation and painstaking inch-by-inch work can be successful.

Intervention implications

Supporting CSOs is often a major policy requirement in postwar situations and much is expected of such organisations. Yet often they are new, inexperienced, and operating in a politically hostile environment. It is almost inevitable that providing them with external support will in some way lead to a stifling of their creativity. Interveners have attempted to overcome this by, for example, creating networks of CSOs in which they share experience amongst themselves, or by using a 'capacity-building' approach in which information and training for organisational functions (such as preparing funding applications) is provided. Nevertheless this still leads to a situation in which many CSOs are in effect the creation of external agencies.

Does this matter? It may be that the development of a strong and vibrant civil society is dependent on some degree of interventionism. By contrast, if we are only able to view the societies we work in through the prism of our own concept of how an organisation should be, we are in danger of suppressing smaller, more informal and less visible initiatives, and of producing a homogenised global civil society which will not ultimately be able to raise the difficult questions.

As indicated above in the case of women's organisations, CSOs are capable of identifying their own weaknesses and of communicating these to donors who might wish to develop support strategies with them. International Alert's network of women peace activists, for example, was clear that one of their main institutional aims was to be able to develop an analysis of the political context from their own perspective as women. They saw this as being important both as a basis for devising their strategies, and as a 'calling card' with which to develop alliances with other organisations. The international community might usefully support such processes of strategic reflection. The women were also very clear on another priority lesson for donors: the need for *long-term* commitment to reconstruction processes, which, as we have seen, require deep-seated changes of attitude and mutual understanding as well as the establishment of complex institutional and political structures (El-Bushra, 2003).

Power relations within and between civil society organisations are an important factor for interveners to be aware of. Internally, one would look for organisations which have a commitment to sharing power, information, skills, responsibilities and decision making within the group, and externally for groups interested in forming alliances on the basis of shared analysis and inspiration. Supporting such qualities emphasises the value of replacing the tired politics of 'power over' with the more inspirational search for other forms of collective and individual power.

> ## Intervention implications

Redirecting power relations: some practical strategies for intervention

CSOs and reconciliation

- Look for ways previously opposed groups are sharing practical, everyday activities.

- Look for connectors – people, groups, events, symbols that can provide balance and lead to stability – and support them.

- Expect reconciliation to be a long, slow and painful process.

Working with CSOs

- Don't expect CSOs to participate in political arenas until they have their own analysis and strategies worked out.

- Listen to the analysis that groups have made of their own weaknesses and support the needs they identify.

- Aim to 'speak the institutional language' of local groups, rather than ignore those that don't speak yours.

- Help people reflect and strategise by engaging in dialogue with them (i.e. listen and learn, and share your experience as one resource among many).

- Support but don't overwhelm.

- Think with rather than for.

Enhancing the transformative capacity of civil society

- Look out for the people and groups who aren't obviously represented in civil society – why aren't they? What are the processes that are responsible for their marginalisation?

- Seek out youth organisations which are 'owned' by young people; take their views and contributions seriously and encourage others to do so. Likewise, seek out groups representing marginalised regions/ethnic groups/occupational categories.

- Look for people moving forward as a result of collective effort, spiritual inspiration, or enabling leadership, and use their power creatively.

10.4.2 The state

In postwar transition contexts, the main requirements in the medium to long term are the restoration of mutual confidence between previously warring parties, and the restructuring of political representation. In the short term, reconciliation and a justice process capable of delivering it, a stable economy and equitable investment are vital to prevent grievances erupting. These functions are normally provided by the state: as Cramer and Goodhand (2002) argue for Afghanistan, there are significant advantages in having a strong state at this point if Afghanistan is to pull out of its vicious circle of poverty and violence. A minimum of stability is essential for economic development and poverty reduction, yet economic development means making contentious decisions about how resources are controlled. For 'the credibility of the state-building project ... the state must monopolise the means of violence' (Cramer and Goodhand, 2002, p. 20), while also developing political legitimacy. Afghanistan may be one of the more extreme examples, but most countries pulling out of a long and destructive war are likely to face a similar discrepancy between the magnitude of the task at hand and the small degree of political cohesion available.

Taking political representation as an example, what are the challenges faced by the state and how can the international community best support the process? Creating a new political culture in the face of longstanding mistrust is a key challenge for any transition government. As we learned through the analysis of social exclusion, the lack of participation by discriminated minorities may well have become habitual through a long historical process, and may be accepted as right and reasonable by everyone, including the discriminated themselves. Those who are unaccustomed to participation in decision making may be excluded not only from the process itself but from the intellectual and social resources which participation requires, such as information sources, organising skills and social networks. For those groups to recover these resources will need government to invest time, money and political will.

Political representation is a broad issue which goes beyond the mere form of decision making. There is also a need to consider the whole functioning of the government machinery, local and national, to identify ways in which these can be opened up for popular accountability. Decentralisation may be a good strategy to engage local commitment to the political process, if there is genuine control placed in local hands, and if the knowledge and skills exist to exercise it. Initiating political processes which are open to genuine participation is not just a matter of restructuring institutions but also of changing the political culture. Those who previously held powerful positions will have to be prepared to hold themselves accountable, while those previously excluded from political fora will have to acquire knowledge, skills and civic engagement in what may be an untried process.

Elections are often considered to be a key element of democratisation and there are often calls for early elections, to remove any outstanding doubts about the legitimacy of the government. However, there are a number of problems to be resolved first if elections are to be carried out fairly. Firstly, if there is little experience of managing elections in the country, if there are practical problems of communication and transport, and if demographic record-keeping is poor, these weaknesses will hit hardest in the most discriminated or aggrieved regions.

Secondly, the electorate will not be able to exercise their vote freely if old inequalities still apply, and powerful individuals will still be able to exert influence to prevent people from making independent choices. For example, women who are unaccustomed to having a political identity can be influenced by that of their husbands, indebted peasants may follow the exhortations of landowners, and so on. Civic education and rights education are key prerequisites for open elections. Social movements defending the political rights of excluded groups often lack confidence that they have the necessary skills and knowledge to participate, and require time to develop their analysis and their organisations.

Elections provide many varied opportunities for blocking the true expression of people's political will, and indeed for exacerbating existing levels of abuse. They may, in effect, consolidate previous unequal power relations, rather than help dismantle them. It is worth asking what alternatives to elections might be more appropriate. Other forms of representation which may be equally acceptable and efficient include public discussion forums – through community radio, for example – and 'traditional' leadership councils. However, the same caveats about power relations apply here too – democracy requires people to have access to channels whereby they can voice their opinions in order to overcome inequalities, but at the same time these inequalities may prevent them from making use of these opportunities.

The process of elections provides just one example of an activity which offers opportunities for government and civil society to collaborate. Clearly, there are a number of points in the process where CSOs might have an important role to play. Yet if they are themselves lacking in experience it will be more difficult for them to exercise scrutiny over the process. This is perhaps a further reason for not wanting to push for elections too quickly. If the civil society can be given time to grow into an effective force, its growth will itself provide the context for Habermas' 'deliberative democracy' to

A woman demonstrates in Northern Ireland.

emerge. Civil society, if it works well, can provide platforms for debate by bringing people together within their own self-defined groups and across these; it can scale up the voice of marginalised groups, and it can mobilise popular opinion and popular action. If these things happen, the lack of elections may be less critical than it seems.

Ottaway (2002), reviewing the evidence for international intervention in postwar state formation, raises important questions about the commitment of the international community to support the reconstruction process. She begins by making a crucial distinction between reconstruction processes initiated by external actors (such as those in Bosnia or Afghanistan) and those initiated by internal forces, including, for example, Somaliland, Uganda, Eritrea and Ethiopia. Externally driven processes have tended not to work because they push for an overwhelming number of political and economic reforms to be put in place quickly and all at once, even though the evidence is that a slower approach is more effective in the long run; she cites the example of postwar Mozambique in the 1990s, where she argues that elections were – eventually – successfully held after prerequisite institutions had been put in place. Internally driven rebuilding processes have often succeeded in establishing stability and viable institutions at small cost, even though the results have not always been open and transparent democracy.

The external model, in which new and democratic institutions are implanted by outside interveners, is an attractive one in that it holds out the prospect of sidestepping attempts by power-holders to preserve their control. However, it overlooks the need for external actors to maintain security long enough for the institutions to grow effective roots, since 'in the short run, power trumps institutions' (Ottaway, 2002, p. 15). The costs of such a commitment are prohibitive. The international community has rarely shown willingness to maintain a long-term commitment to this process. Instead, it has gone for the 'bargain basement imperial option' (Ottaway, 2002, p. 21) in which it initiates rebuilding processes from the outside, but using minimal resources which fail to see the job through to its conclusion. This is a recipe for renewed violence.

Intervention implication

Early elections seem an easy way to produce a government with legitimacy, but equally they can reinforce traditional power relations by excluding people not accustomed to participation in decision making. Rather than rushing to elections, interveners should look for more inclusiveness. Civic education and support for social movements are essential prerequisites for inclusive elections; this requires a long-term commitment from interveners. Rapid elections and a quick exit by interveners is likely to leave grievances and horizontal inequalities unresolved, which can lead to renewed violence.

10.5 Conclusion

In this chapter we have tried to explore how the dynamics of power in post-conflict reconstruction influence the sort of transformations that may emerge. We have examined the part that women and youth can play in conflict transformation, i.e. in turning vicious circles of violence and mistrust into virtuous spirals of reconciliation and the co-creation of a new society. We have explored how external interventions can support the processes of reconstruction in which civil society and governments are engaged, noting that postwar is a period in which everyone has to dismantle their own prejudices in order to open up the way for restructuring of social and political institutions. We saw that people who are marginalised from the political process may be politically and organisationally 'invisible' and easy to maintain in their marginalisation: solving this problem means going to look for them and identifying frameworks for communication which suit them, rather than expecting them to fall in with the mainstream.

Child soldier (Kamajor) checking passes at a road block, Sierra Leone.

Those who intervene have a duty to ensure that they understand as much as possible about the situation they are working in and recognise how their understanding can improve prospects for peace. They need to understand that they cannot reverse long-standing injustices overnight. Developing policies that reflect international experience helps, but only if there is at the same time a recognition of the centrality of 'context, culture and empowerment', meaning that policies and tools work when they fit the context, resound with the culture, and provide opportunities for people to take control of their own lives.

For external agencies, knowledge is at a premium. They need information and knowledge about the background to the situation they are working in, including knowledge about the role of external forces. They also need to make their own analysis of the web of factors that have generated and perpetuated the war, so that they can understand how they might inadvertently contribute to prolonging it through naive (and sometimes not naive) misuse of the power they possess. They need knowledge of policy and practice in reconstruction work, and of its implications and consequences. They need to know when applying policy is useful and when it is better to trust to human nature. Crucially, they need to understand the limits of their knowledge, and hence the limits of their capacity to operate in a sovereign environment. Otherwise they are in danger of becoming part of the problem rather than part of the solution.

10.6 Chapter summary

A goal of postwar peacebuilding is to re-establish the relationship between the state and the people, reconstructing the social contract in a way that ensures all sections of society have a stake. That means not only dealing with the **obvious power holders** – governments, military factions, warlords and business interests – but also creating institutional frameworks for **those without a voice**. Divisions, tension and conflict always exist, and war happens when these become destructive. Mediation and 'conflict resolution' proved less effective because they often only involve elites so there has been a move to **conflict transformation** involving a broader range of actors and activities aimed at changing power relationships between groups.

The **social relations framework** is one way to analyse tensions and conflicts within institutions. It looks at **rules**, **resource distribution**, privileged and **excluded people**, institutional **practices**, and **power structures** within institutions.

Women and young people are often sidelined and subordinated to male elders; they may be politically 'invisible' and this is often seen as 'normal'. Particular ethnic, occupational or regional groups may also be disadvantaged. Postwar reconstruction requires redressing horizontal inequalities in power, to bring these groups into the process of creating the new social contract. This inevitably **challenges existing power relations**, which means transforming attitudes. **Civil society organisations** (defined as voluntary associations which are not government, military, business or family) can play an important role because of their ability to cross violent political divides. Women and youth may need **different kinds of institutional structures** to gain a voice, and may have difficulty fitting into formal civil society organisations or into structures established by donors, politicians and male elders.

Restructuring the state and creating a new political culture in the face of long-standing mistrust is a key task. Elections and democratisation are important, but should take place only when genuine participation is possible.

Interveners need to look at their own power relations with civil society organisations, and understand their own limitations and lack of knowledge. **Externally driven processes** rarely work, especially when they push for many reforms at the same time and fail to take into account the local context. Slower is often more effective, because long-standing injustices cannot be reversed overnight, and interveners need to make a **long-term commitment**.

References

Alvarez Solis, F. and Martin, P. (1996) 'The role of Salvadorean NGOs in postwar reconstruction' in Commins, S. (ed.) *Development in States of War*, Oxford, Oxfam.

Anderlini, S. (2001) 'Women, peace and security: a policy audit – from the Beijing Platform for Action to UN Security Council Resolution 1325 and beyond'. London, International Alert.

Anderson, M. (1999) *Do No Harm: How Aid Can Support Peace – or War*, Boulder CO, Lynne Rienner.

Cockburn, C. (2002) 'Women's organisation in the rebuilding of postwar Bosnia-Herzegovina' in Cockburn, C. and Zarkov, D. (eds) *The Postwar Moment: Militaries, Masculinities and International Peacekeeping*, London, Lawrence and Wishart.

Cramer, C. and Goodhand, J. (2002) 'Try again, fail again, fail again better? War, the state, and the 'post-conflict' challenge in Afghanistan', *Development and Change*, vol. 33, no. 5, pp 885-910.

Date-Bah, E. (1996) *Sustainable Peace After War: Arguing the Need for Major Integration of Gender Perspectives in Post-Conflict Programming*, Geneva, ILO.

Dolan, C. (1999) 'Bending the spears': Notes on Denis Pain's report to International Alert – 'The bending of the spears: producing consensus for peace and development in Northern Uganda', *COPE Working Paper* No. 31, ACORD/COPE.

Dolan, C. (2002) 'Collapsing masculinities and weak states – a case study of Northern Uganda' in Cleaver, F. (ed.) *Masculinities Matter! Men, Gender and Development*, London, Zed Books.

El-Bushra, J. (2003) *Women Building Peace: Sharing Know-how*, London, International Alert.

El-Bushra, J. (2005 forthcoming) *Monitoring and Evaluating Women's Peace Activism*, London, International Alert.

El-Bushra, J. and Dolan, C. (2002) 'Don't touch, just listen! Popular performance from Uganda', *Review of African Political Economy*, vol. 29 no. 91, pp. 37–52.

El-Bushra, J. and Kerr, D. (2005 forthcoming) 'NGOs, performance and conflict transformation', *LUCAS Bulletin*, Leeds, Leeds University Centre for African Studies.

Galtung, J. (1995) 'Twenty-five years of peace research: ten challenges and responses', *Journal of Peace Research*, vol. 22.

Gardner, J. and El-Bushra, J. (eds) (2004) *Somalia, the Untold Story: the War Through the Eyes of Women*, London, Pluto Press.

International Crisis Group (2003) 'Youth in Central Asia: losing the new generation', Asia Reports No. 66, Brussels, International Crisis Group.

Kabeer, N. (1994) *Reversed Realities: Gender Hierarchies in Development Thought*, London, Verso.

Kumar, K., Baldwin, K. and Benjamin, J. (2000) *Aftermath: Women and Women's Organisations in Post-conflict Cambodia*, Working Paper No. 307, Washington, Centre for Development Information and Evaluation, USAID.

Lederach, J. P. (1995) 'Conflict transformation in protracted internal conflicts: the case for a comprehensive framework' in Rupesinghe, K. (ed.) *Conflict Transformation*, Basingstoke, Macmillan.

Lederach, J. P. (2000) 'Journey from resolution to transformative peacebuilding' in Sampson, C. and Lederach, J. P. (eds) *From the Ground Up: Mennonite Contributions to International Peacebuilding*, Oxford, Oxford University Press.

Ottaway, M. (2002) 'Rebuilding state institutions in collapsed states', *Development and Change*, vol. 33, no. 5. pp. 1001–24.

Pearce, J. and Howell, J. (2001) *Civil Society and Development: a Critical Exploration*, Boulder CO, Lynne Rienner.

Rupesinghe, K. (ed.) (1995) *Conflict Transformation*, Basingstoke, Macmillan.

Sampson, C. and Lederach, J. P. (eds.) (2000) *From the Ground Up: Mennonite Contributions to International Peacebuilding*, Oxford, Oxford University Press.

UNIFEM (2003) Report of the Learning Oriented Assessment of Gender Mainstreaming and Women's Empowerment Strategies in Rwanda, 2–12 September 2002, UNIFEM.

Verhey, B. (2003) *Going Home: Demobilising and Reintegrating Child Soldiers in the Democratic Republic of Congo*, London, Save the Children UK.

Preparing to intervene

Jonathan Goodhand

11.1 Introduction

This chapter is concerned with the analytical tools that practitioners may use when intervening in wars and violent conflicts. It aims to focus on the 'real world' problems faced by practitioners whether their objectives are to end the violence, mitigate its effects or build peace. How can the analytical tools and frameworks introduced earlier in this book be used by practitioners? How can they contribute to improved development or peacebuilding practice? In order to answer these questions it is important to clarify what is meant by the terms 'practitioner' and 'practice'.

Firstly, for the purpose of this chapter 'practitioners' are understood to be people working within the international aid regime. This covers a broad range of actors, from the NGO field worker or UN peacekeeper working at the operational level to the World Bank official working at the policy level. Though their level of engagement is quite different, in this chapter we argue that violent conflict poses common challenges to practitioners wherever they are located within the aid system. Secondly, we take 'practice' to mean more than simply the implementation and management of projects. Development and peacebuilding outcomes can be achieved in many ways and projects are only one of them. This may be illustrated with reference to Figure 11.1.

Conventionally, practitioners have tended to focus on the innermost circle, i.e. what they can control. Most efforts to improve practice tend to home in on this area – from codes of conduct to monitoring and evaluation systems

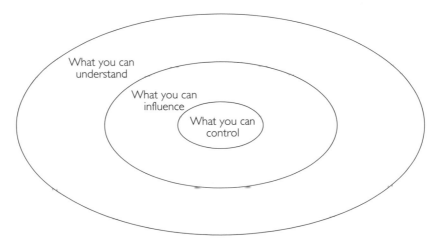

What you can understand

What you can influence

What you can control

Figure 11.1 The world of the aid practitioner

to organisational restructuring. These initiatives are important, but they are not the only way to increase effectiveness and impacts. And paradoxically, they may undermine an organisation's capacity to operate responsively in violent conflict if they lead to rigidity and a growing focus on internal processes rather than the external environment. It is an understandable practitioner reflex to attempt to create certainty in an environment of rapid change and uncertainty. Introducing logical framework planning (the 'log frame' planning tool now almost universally used by development practitioners and donors) and other new management, monitoring and evaluation systems may create an illusion of control. They assume a 'well-structured world of unambiguous objectives, mutually exclusive choices, authoritative decision-makers, and willing decision-endurers'(Johnston and Clark, 1982, p. 11). But if they are prioritised at the expense of the outer two circles – influencing and understanding – they may do little other than provide a false sense of security to the practitioner. Therefore in this chapter we argue that practitioners need to look beyond the traditional project-based approach. In essence this is about making a strategic shift from what Edwards et al. (1999) describe as 'development as delivery' to 'development as leverage'.

Intervention implications

Practitioners need to think of themselves less as managers of projects and more as change agents, capacity-builders and advocates. For them to take on such a role requires new skills, new relationships and new levels of analysis.

11.1.1 Creating room for manoeuvre

At the risk of stating the obvious, development practice is about making tough decisions. It is about engaging in a messy world – as Porter et al. (1991, p. 197) state, 'Development projects are not the products of immaculate conception ... Projects are born of an amalgam of international diplomacy and vested interests, humanitarian concern and optimistic good intentions.' Often it involves choosing between 'least worst' options in highly politicised (and compromising) environments. Although the same applies to more stable development settings, violent conflict tends to bring into sharp relief the dilemmas associated with making difficult choices. As emphasised in previous chapters, there is no such thing as 'best practice'. There are no 'uniquely best' solutions as every context is different and circumstances change over time. It is about matching responses to contexts rather than trying to apply a 'best practice' template from one place to another. This takes us towards a pluralist orientation, since 'the greater the uncertainty the greater the desirability of having the largest possible number of options available' (Porter et al., 1991, p. 202). Good practice is about increasing probabilities rather than creating certainties. However, merely to say that everything depends on context and timing is not very helpful. There is sufficient accumulated experience to suggest that applying certain principles of good practice may support the conditions that make success more likely. Whilst previous chapters have stressed the dangers of poorly designed interventions – in other words the dark side of aid – this and the next chapter highlight some of the success stories – what has worked in practice, why it has worked and how it might be replicated elsewhere.

If practice is about making decisions, these decisions are never made in a vacuum. They are shaped by a range of interconnected factors. Broadly there are three types of 'filters' that shape decision-making processes, which span the macro, meso and micro levels – these are the political context, the organisational environment and individual values and preferences.

The political context

Violent conflict is a game of high stakes. Intervention inevitably affects the calculus of those involved in conflict. There is no such thing as a 'non impact'. War may be the product of previous interventions or intervention may have contributed to new forms of contention. The idea of a neutral, third party intervention that stands 'above the fray' should be discarded. Practitioners intervene in highly political contexts and will be seen as political actors themselves. Even the International Committee of the Red Cross (ICRC), perceived by many as the archetypal neutral humanitarian organisation, are acutely aware of this – as one ICRC field worker commented to me once, 'to be neutral you have to be extremely political'. Decision making is shaped by both the politics of the emergency and the politics of the response. The intrinsic links between Northern politics and economics on the one hand and Overseas Development Assistance (ODA) and humanitarian action on the other is not new. But Kosovo, Afghanistan and Iraq signify a growing politicisation of international assistance, leading some to argue that the 'quality of mercy is now strained to breaking point' (Donini, 2003). In increasingly polarised contexts where one is forced to choose sides – 'you are either for us or against us' – practitioners must consider where they position themselves and the extent to which they can create political space or room for manoeuvre.

The organisational environment

Whilst a great deal has been written about political constraints, organisational questions have been a blind spot in the literature on intervention in what is often called complex political emergencies (CPEs). As the Brahimi Report (Brahimi, 2000) highlights, political will is crucial, but so too is institutional performance. Practitioners work within organisations – from small 'niche' NGOs to large UN specialist agencies to military peacekeeping units. These organisations and the wider institutional environment in which they are situated influence (and constrain) practitioners' choices. Good practice involves a constant tension between what is desirable and what is possible. Frequently, organisational and operational matters such as funding, capacity or management, force practitioners to make pragmatic choices based on what's possible rather than what is necessarily the most desirable course of action.

Organisational *capacities* may be one bottleneck, organisational *interests* are another. Practitioners work in 'messy' organisational environments in which they have to balance competing interests and forms of accountability. On the one hand there are the 'soft' interests in terms of declared mission and primary constituency; on the other there are the 'hard' interests related to funding, profile and market share. Within organisations there may be competing constituencies, for example between the relief and development sections or the Africa and Asia desks. Competitive relationships between organisations are also likely, particularly in high-profile, multi-mandate peace operations.

Therefore, how problems are framed and responded to is influenced by a range of organisational factors that are independent of the problem itself. For instance, two NGOs – one with a human rights mandate and another with a relief focus – working in the same context are likely to define the problem and respond to it in very different ways – one focusing on the denial of rights and the other on the lack of basic needs.

Practitioners almost never have a free hand in deciding what is to be done – organisational mandates and biases limit the range of options and approaches. But whilst organisations may be limiting (and using Chambers' 1997 phrase, 'self deceiving') they can also be empowering. This and the next chapter will highlight some of the positive examples of organisational learning and adaptation by agencies that have worked effectively in and on war and violent conflict.

Individual choices

Finally, the personal dimension tends to be another blind spot in debates on intervention in CPEs. Practitioners are often viewed as the unwilling agents of wider political and institutional interests. Structures are seen to operate in a deterministic way so that there is no space for individual agency. Yet personal experience suggests otherwise. Individuals do have agency and for better or for worse, they can make a difference. Although we operate within the limitations of structural constraints, such constraints operate through people. To take an actor-oriented approach as we do in this chapter is not to deny the importance of structures. Practitioners' room for manoeuvre is clearly limited by the wider political environment and this must be part of their frame of reference – in effect the outer circle in our diagram above. But, the biases, values and capacities of practitioners also have an impact on how problems are framed and responded to. Organisations vary from country to country and policies play themselves out differently in different contexts. Often this is because of the individuals involved on the ground. An overly structuralist analysis misses the diversity of 'actually existing' practice. Research highlights the importance of human agency and particular policies, which in a sense is good news for those seeking to influence violent conflict in a positive direction. While this does not mean that situations and events can be socially engineered by outsiders, it does indicate that the probabilities of peace or violent conflict can be influenced through particular policies and interventions.

Practitioners can and do create room for manoeuvre, leading to alternative discourses, practices and development outcomes. This leads us to an analysis of questions related to values, ideas, relationships, leadership and 'social energy'. These are not easy issues since they involve practitioners asking questions about themselves. As Tony Vaux (2001) argues in his book *The Selfish Altruist*, relief workers often have mixed and sometimes contradictory motives, which may get in the way of good practice. An honest engagement with these questions is a prerequisite for improved practice.

Therefore, we argue that development (and peacebuilding) practice involves making difficult choices in a messy, conflict-ridden and constantly changing world. Choices are shaped by the wider socio-political environment, the organisational context and individual biases and values.

11.1.2 Towards conflict-sensitive approaches

Whilst there is no such thing as best practice, it is relatively easy to identify what represents bad practice and what represents better practice. One can broadly identify three different approaches to war and violent conflict that have been adopted by relief and development agencies – working around conflict, working in conflict, working on conflict. The first approach represents bad practice and practitioners should aim for either the second or third depending on their mandate and the context.

Working '*around*' war and violent conflict. This treats war as an impediment or negative externality that is to be avoided, and is still the predominant approach of the major donors. Violent conflict is viewed as a constraint on development, and if any form of linkage is recognised it is the lack of development which contributes to conflict. It is a common reflex action of many policy makers and practitioners to argue that development by definition promotes peace (Uvin, 2002). In other words all that is needed is more of the same – but faster, since war may be seen as an opportunity for the application of 'shock therapy' reforms.

Although donors increasingly recognise the importance of conflict in policy statements, there appears to have been little change in practice. This may be partly due to the donors' rather narrow conceptualisation of security which is still largely viewed in terms of security of investments and reliability of commercial contracts rather than human security and structural stability.

World Bank and IMF conditionalities tend to be blind to horizontal inequities and war issues (Klugman, 1999). The Bank and the IMF are limited by their mandates to addressing issues of economic governance. The narrow interpretation of this mandate has inhibited approaches to conflict and governance.

In some cases donors may continue to work around war because of institutional interests. While part of the reluctance to categorise countries as having wars may involve political sensitivities, it may also be partly due to a reluctance to bring in humanitarian actors, who are in a sense viewed as competing with development actors for resources and profile.

Working *'in'* war and violent conflict. Agencies working in areas of active violence have attempted to mitigate war-related risks and also to minimise the potential for programmes to fuel or prolong violence. Attempts have been made to 'conflict-proof' programmes by avoiding large-scale infrastructural projects and focusing on low-profile, quick impact initiatives.

Development actors could learn much from the practices introduced by humanitarian agencies working in war zones, which have experimented with codes of conduct, operating standards, aid ombudsmen and robust coordination mechanisms. One of the main concerns, however, is maintaining the principles of neutrality and impartiality.

Working *'on'* war and violent conflict. Few agencies have an explicit focus of working *on* war – that is, policy and programmes with a primary focus on violence prevention and conflict management or resolution.

The few that do work *on* war tend to support work on reconciliation and human rights issues, primarily through civil society groups. They also provide support for political reform processes and education reform to provide a greater focus on reconciliation. Most steer clear of working on war, largely because they do not wish to entangle themselves in issues of sovereignty.

It therefore tends to be the smaller bilateral donor agencies who are leading these debates and experiments in conflict-sensitive policy and programming. These donors may be better adapted to working *on* war in that they have the potential to utilise a range of policy instruments from diplomacy to trade to development assistance. Also, they appear more willing to take risks and invest in sensitive areas like the judiciary, security sector and human rights.

Although some multilaterals such as the World Bank have supported programmes which attempt to work *on* war – for example the Rehabilitation, Reconstruction and Reconciliation programme in Sri Lanka – they have not mainstreamed conflict analysis into their wider portfolio of programmes. This is perhaps because multilaterals in general appear to have more restrictive modalities and mandates that are focused on economic issues.

The most successful examples of working on war appear to be where an NGO has either established a close and supportive relationship with an enlightened donor, or has enough of their own free money to pay for experimentation and learning. However, from an NGO point of view, the overall pot of money is dwindling, while the conditions placed on that money are increasing. In this kind of environment, practitioners tend to be on the defensive and experimentation is difficult.

Table 11.1 summarises the key features, assumptions and strategies associated with these different approaches of donors to war.

Table 11.1 Approaches to war

Approach	Working around war	Working in war	Working on war
Assumptions	War is a 'disruptive factor' over which little influence can be exercised Development programmes can continue without being negatively affected by violence	Development programmes can be negatively affected by, and have a negative impact on, the dynamics of violent conflict	Development programmes can exploit opportunities to affect the dynamics of conflict in a positive way
Strategy	Withdraw from or keep out of war-affected areas Continue to work in low risk areas on mainstream development activities	Reactive adjustments are made to programmes in medium and high risk areas Improve security management Greater focus on 'positioning', i.e. neutrality and impartiality Cut back on high input programmes	Refocus programmes onto the root causes of the war, e.g. governance, poverty alleviation, social exclusion Attempt to influence the incentives for peace and disincentives for violence Support for mediation efforts Focus on protection and human rights

It is recognised that the reality is more complicated than the taxonomy suggests since firstly agencies employ a combination of different approaches and secondly there are often disjunctures between what agencies say they are doing and what they actually do. Although the policy rhetoric has moved on to working 'in' or 'on' war and violent conflict, there remains a significant gap between the principles outlined in the OECD/DAC guidelines (1997) on conflict-sensitive aid and the prevailing practice. In the main, rhetorical 'feel good' changes have occurred at the expense of a fundamental reappraisal of strategy and approach.

Not everyone can work on war and incorporate an explicit focus on peacebuilding into all activities. As explored in the following chapter this requires a much more substantive shift in mandate, policies and capacities. It is not something that should be done lightly and it depends on the context, the timing, the agency's mandate and its capacities.

Intervention implication

'Conflict sensitivity' and working in war represents the minimum standard that should be expected of practitioners – they must have the basic awareness to 'conflict proof' what they do and to minimise the negative effects of their activities on conflict dynamics. Being conflict blind is simply not good enough, just as it is no longer acceptable for development agencies to be gender blind.

11.2 Preparing to intervene: understanding the context

As highlighted in earlier chapters, good practice has to be based on a foundation of strong analysis. Emergencies are frequently treated as an excuse for the absence of pause for thought (Jackson and Walker, 1999). Many of the standard maxims of good development practice such as contextual analysis, consultative appraisal and planning are viewed as expensive luxuries in CPEs. This is a mistake and will probably lead to badly designed interventions with the wrong incentives built in. The maxim of 'don't just do something, stand there!' (UNDP, 1994) is in most cases a wise one.

Practitioners, however, cannot be all knowing and all seeing. In a rapidly changing environment understanding will always be partial. Two points can be emphasised here. First, analysis should be tailored to the needs of the end user. What kind of information and analysis do you need in each particular context to optimise your chances of success? Using Chambers' (1983) phrase, what is 'optimal ignorance'? You do not need to know everything, so what

A worker from the Chadian Red Cross.

kind of information is essential and what is non-essential? The practitioner should aim for 'good enough' analysis, which is calibrated to the context and policy or programming needs. Second, violent conflict situations are constantly changing and so analysis must be similarly dynamic – the danger of in-depth, one-off conflict assessments is that they represent only a 'snapshot' of a war, which soon becomes outdated. Practitioners therefore need to develop mechanisms for constantly updating their analysis. In practice this means selecting a few key indicators which tell them about violence trends and dynamics.

In Box 11.1 some of the key stages of developing an analytical foundation for intervention are outlined. In reality the division between analysis and action is likely to be less clear than the box implies. Good practice tends to involve an incremental and iterative process in which policies and programmes are constantly adjusted in response to ongoing analysis.

Box 11.1   Preparing to intervene

1   Looking at the context

- Type of war, prior interventions, dynamics and phase (Fieldon and Goodhand 2001).
- Proximate causes, critical thresholds or turning points
- Are opportunities opening or closing?

2   Looking at yourself

- What are your mandate, vision and values?
- Where is your authority and legitimacy derived from? Who are you accountable to?
- What are your capacities? (and weaknesses)
- Where are you positioned in relation to other stakeholders?
- What changes are you trying to effect? – Which types of war and which levels are you attempting to influence?
- What is your level of commitment? What are your resources?

3   Looking at others

- Mapping conflict stakeholders
- What are the incentives/disincentives for war/peace?
- Who are the key spoilers?
- Who are your potential partners?

4   Looking at options

- Triggers for action
- Risks–opportunities/benefit–harm analysis
- Prioritisation
- Choose strategies

Before examining in more detail the stages highlighted in Box 11.1, it is important to make the point that the quality of the analysis depends on who is doing it and their sources of information. Understanding the tools and techniques of conflict assessment is one thing, but there is no substitute for deep in-country experience. This is partly an organisational issue, since practitioners who constantly move from crisis to crisis have little opportunity to develop the requisite depth of experience. The quality is also related to whom you talk to. Where do you get your information from? Who are your key informants? Based on my own field experience, I believe that practitioners often cultivate far too narrow a circle of key informants. Diplomats may be too heavily dependent on the capital city cocktail party circuit, while the 'compound culture' of aid workers means they rely too heavily on the views of other aid workers – leading to an extremely 'aid-centric' view of the world.

The best-informed practitioners tend to be those who have developed a diverse network of relationships and constantly 'ground truth' or test their assumptions by talking to as wide a group of conflict stakeholders as possible. For an operational NGO, for example, it is clearly important to have close links to the partners and communities one is working with. Often, strong community-based relationships are the best source of security for an NGO. But it is also important to be aware of what the 'unlike-minded' are thinking – what are the incentive systems of war entrepreneurs? What is the vernacular press saying? How are the spoilers likely to influence events? This means venturing out of the 'charmed circle' of the project system and examining the outer two circles in Figure 11.1 and how they impact upon what can be done in practice.

11.2.1 Looking at the context

Conflict analysis is not covered in depth here since it is dealt with elsewhere. In Box 11.2 some of the different analytical tools used by practitioners are summarised. Most methodologies or tools can be expected to cover some of the following areas: the structural roots or sources of war – security, political, economic and social – proximate causes, war stakeholders and dynamics and conflict–aid interactions.

To an extent, 'looking at the context' is shaped by 'looking at yourself' – the mandate, priorities, activities and capacities of your organisation provide the overall framework for your analysis. If you are involved in third party mediation, for instance, your analysis will focus to a much greater extent on war stakeholders and dynamics and the incentive systems of the various actors. By contrast, a development donor may concentrate on the wider socio-economic context of the war and how assistance impacts upon the roots of war. Whatever one's organisational remit, however, there is a need to think about the following:

1   *'Place' matters*: Too much of the analysis and consequent prescriptions are based on generalised lessons, stripped away from time and context. There is a need for practitioners to resist the temptation unthinkingly to apply lessons learned from elsewhere. One of the most important things

a practitioner needs to do when arriving in a new war zone is to 'unlearn' the lessons generated from other contexts. 'Place' matters and there is a need for policy and practice to be degeneralised and consequently more contextualised.

2   *Long-term and short-term approaches*: Firstly, as emphasised in earlier chapters, war is the product of historic processes of development and underdevelopment. It is something of a truism to state that practitioners aiming to support peacebuilding processes must think long term. But in practice it is still relatively rare for organisations to think beyond their one- or two-year project cycles. Secondly, wars are dynamic and changing. This suggests the need for agencies to combine a long-term time frame, with the capacity to gear up opportunistically when windows of opportunity present themselves. Analytically this means being able to scan the horizon for turning points, critical thresholds or war triggers and then respond accordingly. Paul Richards' (1996) idea of 'smart aid' is based on the assumption that strategic interventions at the right moment in time can have disproportionate impacts. It is like an acupuncture model – if you hit the right 'pressure point' you can have a system-wide effect. Another example is the media, which for good or for ill may have a massive effect on war dynamics, whether used by war or peace entrepreneurs.

3   *'Orderly eclecticism'*: Successful practitioners tend to 'pick and mix' theoretical approaches and tools according to their particular needs. A pluralist approach can be characterised as one of 'orderly eclecticism'. In situations of constant flux and uncertainty, this appears to be the most appropriate way to make choices about analytical tools and intervention strategies. For example, a political economy approach generates important insights into the functionality of war and the incentive systems of the various actors. It helps interveners understand the underlying rationality of violent conflict. It also helps establish a sense of proportion about the potential and limitations of external intervention in affecting the dynamics of violent conflict. By contrast, it may only provide a partial 'road map' for interveners. For example, it tells us little about the 'emotional' economy that violence generates. Socio-anthropological approaches may be more helpful here in generating insights about the 'passions' as well as the 'interests' which underpin war. Aid interacts with this emotional economy – it may have symbolic or cultural value as well as being an economic asset. The key point here, from a practitioner's perspective, is not to rely on only one theoretical framework or model. There is a need to use a different analytical 'lens' in order to understand the war environment. This suggests using an inductive rather than a deductive approach. In other words, select analytical tools and frameworks according to the requirements of the context, rather than rigidly applying the same analytical template to every conflict. For example, a political economy-resource war model may be extremely helpful in relation to the Afghan war, but have more limited explanatory powers in relation to Sri Lanka.

4   *Levels and linkages*: Given the multi-levelled and dynamic nature of contemporary wars, where should agencies intervene when their

purchase on the economic and political processes at work may be quite limited? It is important to develop an analysis of the different levels of conflict, how they are related to one another and where one's intervention 'fits' in relation to these different levels. Rather than asking simply how interventions interact with the dynamics of violence and peace, a more nuanced analysis leads us towards an examination of which particular types of interventions, at which particular times, impact on the different levels and dimensions of a conflict system.

New arrivals stand waiting as a UNHCR truck unloads provisions in the Benaco camp, Tanzania, for Rwandan Hutu refugees fleeing the aftermath of the genocide.

Earlier chapters have emphasised the international, regional, national and local dimensions of contemporary wars. In most wars today we are not talking about localised introverted wars. We see simultaneously processes of globalisation and of localisation. In Somalia, for instance, there has been globalisation of economic relations with the emergence of the trans-shipment and remittance economy, while there has been a localisation of politics with new forms of governance emerging at the local level (Bradbury, 2003). Local considerations may often trump national ones. Developing an analysis of these local considerations to complement an appreciation of the broad regional and global processes is therefore important.

For NGOs this means that even though they may act locally they need also to think regionally and globally. Perhaps the biggest gap in current analysis is an understanding of the linkages between the different levels of contemporary conflict systems. For instance, although we have some knowledge about the economics of drug production in Afghanistan, we know much less about the commodity chain which links Afghan farmers with warlords and ultimately drug dealers in the UK. Current work on diamonds from civil war zones has been innovative in this respect and has helped fill in some of the knowledge gaps about the political economy of trade and war. (Smillie et al., 2000). NGOs have played an important role in this process and it is a challenge that they are increasingly taking up. In many respects they have a comparative advantage in advancing understanding of the vertical linkages within conflict systems because of their multiple relationships and activities at the local, national and international levels.

There are a number of models and analytical tools that aid agencies can use to develop a better understanding of the context in which they are working and their role within it. It is beyond the scope of this chapter to go into any of these in detail, but Box 11.2 provides a list of some of them divided into: tools that focus on war analysis; tools developed in relation to livelihoods analysis that may also be useful in war situations; and tools that focus on the interaction between aid and war.

Box 11.2   Tools for contextual analysis

War analysis

Early warning: monitoring and analysis of early signals of potential war, with a view to anticipating trouble spots in time to respond effectively. Tools and indicators developed in early warning frameworks might be used by researchers analysing the patterns and dynamics of conflict.

Conflict mapping: usually a group-based, PRA-type activity (Participatory Rural Appraisal) involving the diagramming of a conflict which identifies the main actors, their relationships and the dynamics of the conflict and escalation into violence and war.

Stakeholder analysis: developing a matrix to identify the main actors and their underlying interests and incentives – in either peace or war.

Armed group analysis: analyses armed groups, including their aims and ideology, strategy, leadership, constituency, military command and structure, etc.

War timelines: a PRA tool used to highlight the main phases and events in a war.

War trees: map out the roots and effects of violent conflict, according to the perspectives of people living in war zones. The 'roots', for instance, might be long-term poverty and the 'fruits' could be displacement or increased crime.

Responses

Peace and war impact assessment (PCIA): evaluation frameworks which can be used to anticipate or assess the impact of programmes in war-torn or conflict-prone areas (see below).

Do no harm framework: used in order to minimise the unintended negative impacts of aid on war environments. It involves an identification of the factors

---

which divide or connect people ('dividers' and 'connectors') and mapping out how relief aid has a positive or negative impact on such 'dividers' and 'connectors' (see below).

Relief access analysis: an analysis of the strategies used by actors to access or manipulate relief resources, their impact and the reaction of aid agencies.

11.2.2 Looking at yourself

War analysis does not happen in a vacuum. Why and how it is done and what it focuses on depend in large measure on who does it. There is a risk that one's organisational mandate skews the analysis: whereas in the same context a human rights NGO may only see the denial of rights, a UN peacekeeper may focus only on ceasefire violations. Both suffer from 'functional ignorance' in the sense that they filter out information which does not immediately concern them or clashes with their world view.

However, in the real world parameters have to be set for the scope of contextual analysis. Conflict assessments (CAs) must be closely linked to an assessment of you as a practitioner, your organisation and its capacity to intervene in violent conflict or war. A CA helps disaggregate a conflict in terms of its different manifestations, levels and linkages, its causal mechanisms and dynamics. Looking at yourself – your mandate, capacities, resources etc. – is the next step towards developing an intervention strategy. The following is a selective list of some of the questions and issues to be considered.

1   As already highlighted, development practice is about making choices. One of these choices is about whether, where and how to intervene. For agencies with a 'pure' humanitarian focus, the question may be one of 'how can I achieve my objectives, while minimising the potential for negative side effects?' For a multi-mandate organisation with broader objectives the question may become 'how can I maximise the peacebuilding effects of my current portfolio of activities?' There is a whole range of subquestions related to the level of intervention (macro, meso or micro), the sector (e.g. governance, humanitarian, security sector), the type of conflict targeted (war or micro conflicts over water, land, etc.) and the geographical spread of activities. Different options will engender different levels of conflict-related risks and peacebuilding opportunities which need to be systematically weighed up before coming to a decision (see below).

2   These 'first order' questions cannot be answered without reference to an organisation's mandate. For example, Médecins Sans Frontières (MSF) and ICRC have clear mandates which prevent them from getting involved in areas like peace mediation or grassroots peacebuilding. In the past, the mandates of the World Bank and IMF have limited their involvement in 'political' activities such as peacebuilding (Boyce, 2002). Where mandates leave more scope for interpretation, there may be

internal disagreements about which kinds of activities fall within or outside the mandate. For example, within multi-mandate NGOs there may be internal tensions about whether the organisation should work more explicitly 'on' war. The emergencies section may argue for a narrow humanitarian focus, whereas country programmes may advocate a more maximalist approach involving an explicit focus on peacebuilding. These debates go to the heart of an organisation as it asks which values are privileged over others – for instance, does humanitarianism trump social justice or peace? Practitioners must take these internal conversations into account, as a critical mass of support within the organisation is crucial if a particular policy or programme is to succeed.

3   Decision making is influenced by organisational capacities, experience and commitment. A CA may reveal all sorts of needs and gaps, and these must be narrowed down by practitioners to a limited number of areas in which their organisation has the expertise and capacities to make a difference. This must involve an honest assessment of organisational strengths and weaknesses. For an NGO with a track record in small-scale rural development, it may make sense to incorporate a conflict transformation dimension into its work. But initiating a mediation process between warring groups would be more questionable. Similarly in Afghanistan (and elsewhere) soldiers are increasingly getting involved in reconstruction activities, leading to questions from aid agencies about whether the military have a comparative advantage in this area. It has also led to a blurring of the lines between humanitarians and the military. As discussed in the next chapter, working 'on' war may require different skills and capacities to working 'in' war and it is important to consider whether these skills can be developed and brought into the organisation or whether this is something best left to others better qualified. There is also the question of whether there is sufficient commitment to pursue a certain course of action. Internal commitment from the staff is one thing, but having the requisite resources is another. Is there funding available to develop new streams of activity and is it the right kind of funding? Peacebuilding activities can rarely be funded through six-month contracts. Short-term funding is the wrong instrument to address long-term problems.

4   It is important to consider an agency's positioning in relation to the war and to other actors. Does it have the political space to pursue a high-risk activity, say third party mediation between conflicting parties? Is it seen as a legitimate interlocutor? Does it have relationships with actors on all sides of the war divide? Do new strategic partnerships need to be forged? Are there other actors who could better play this role?

Box 11.3 Intervention strategies in a turbulent environment: case study of Afghanaid (AAD)

AAD began as a UK-based solidarity organisation that started work in Afghanistan in 1984. AAD's trajectory followed a similar path to many of the cross-border solidarity NGOs, who were at the time entangled with wider anti-Soviet political objectives. By the late 1980s, with the decline of superpower interest and the beginning of a new phase in the war, AAD emerged as a professionalised international NGO with a focus on rural rehabilitation and development. This has continued until the present day. For AAD it has been a constant challenge to make informed choices about implementation strategies, as the war and operating environment have evolved. In Afghanistan, like many other war zones, this has been made more difficult by the lack of data and research. In the early 1990s AAD made the strategic decision to focus on community development activities in remote rural areas. This decision was based on a number of factors including:

- an analysis of the war environment – remote rural areas at the time were more stable and less badly affected by fighting;

- an analysis of the needs – few other agencies were working in such areas and most donor funding was allocated to short-term relief activities;

- an analysis of internal capacities and commitments – AAD had built up a strong body of expertise in the areas of rural development and there was a great deal of support from the staff for such an approach.

However, there were also risks attached to this decision. Firstly, by working in a small number of areas in greater depth AAD was vulnerable to the ebbing and flowing of war – more so than an agency which could spread risk by working in a larger number of areas at a more superficial level. In a sense it was harder to 'violence proof' such a strategy. Secondly, it was higher risk in terms of funding. Few donors were willing to make the multi-year commitments that such an approach required. Moreover, delivering aid to remote areas is inevitably more costly, leading to higher administrative costs.

On the whole, however, AAD has been able to grapple successfully with these problems. The post-Taliban environment is posing new challenges for the organisation, which will demand different strategies. One challenge is whether in this 'postwar' environment the organisation should place a strong focus on peacebuilding to help consolidate the fragile war to peace transition. Another is the problem being faced by all NGOs in the country as a result of the changing organisational environment. With new organisations like the World Bank and private consultancy firms and the expansion of existing ones like the UN, there has been a haemorrhaging of NGO staff who have joined the better paying organisations – though they are not necessarily more efficient and effective. NGOs most importantly have now to learn to interact with an emergent Afghan state. To continue to be relevant and effective, AAD and other NGOs will need to continue adjusting their strategies in relation to the context, their own mandate and capacities and the activities of other actors.

11.2.3 Looking at others

Whether 'complex political emergency' (CPE) is a helpful label or not can be debated. Wars have certainly always been 'complex' and 'political'. However, the complex tag may be appropriate in relation to the international response to contemporary wars. There has been a trend in recent years towards more multi-faceted, multi-agency, system-wide approaches to war. Aid is becoming, as Duffield (2001) notes, increasingly complex and technical. NGOs are only one set of actors in a complex system involving different contracting arrangements and partnerships with a range of state and non-state, commercial and non-commercial actors. Capturing some of the key aspects of this response, and positioning oneself within it, are key analytical challenges for the practitioner. It is important not to see these responses as somehow separate from the war – they are an inherent part of the conflict context.

To a great extent the analytical challenge is one of mapping the various actors responding to the war and their spheres of work – both horizontally in terms of sectors and vertically in terms of levels of engagement. This can be done in different ways. In terms of functional areas it might be divided into: official diplomacy; non-official conflict transformation; military measures; economic and social measures; political development and governance; judicial and legal; communications and education (Lund, 2001). In terms of levels it could be divided into macro (international, regional, national), meso (provincial/region) and micro (district, village). This should provide a systematic analysis of where the main nodes or clusters of engagement are and where there are gaps.

(**Intervention implications**)

 As a practitioner you should be thinking about how your existing activities mesh with the wider response and whether any gaps identified represent opportunities for your organisation to influence the dynamics of the violent conflict or war. Are there particular pressure points that you regard as important and can be reinforced by your organisation? Are there likely to be spoilers who will undermine certain areas of work? Are there potential partners to build alliances with to increase impacts? Are there coordination groups and policy influencing subgroups that you should build links with? The key point here is that you should be thinking about the second circle in Figure 11.1 – 'what you can influence' – as well as the inner circle of 'what you can control'.

11.2.4 Looking at options

As argued so far, analysis should be action oriented, tailored to the needs of the end user. The main problem with CA tools is how they are used to convert the analysis into practical policies and programmes. Analytical frameworks tend to be either too generalised, taking a 'one size fits all' approach, or too complex and unusable in practice. The most useful frameworks occupy the middle ground, being neither too prescriptive nor too open ended.

Responses may be seen as the result of the interplay between four variables, as illustrated in Figure 11.2.

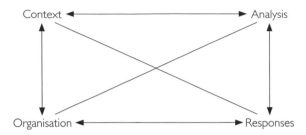

Figure 11.2   Factors influencing intervention in violent conflict

In practice there is an ongoing mutual adjustment and calibration between these four variables. The context determines what range of options is possible – in the height of a CPE the programming options are more limited than in the emerging war or emerging peace phases. Analysis is also calibrated to the context – a more in-depth and rigorous CA is likely to be necessary in an unstable environment than a relatively peaceful one. As argued above, the organisation's mandate and capacities play a role in shaping the analysis and responses. Responses in turn impact upon the context, feed into ongoing analysis and affect organisational capacities.

The Mary Anderson (1999) 'do no harm' framework introduced in Chapter 1 is one tool which aims to convert analysis into practical programming initiatives. It has value in sensitising practitioners to aid-war dynamics and helping them prioritise strategies which minimise harm and support constituencies for peace. Another tool developed by CARE International is *benefit–harm analysis*. This shifts the stress away from attempting to 'do no harm', towards consciously balancing the positive and negative effects of interventions. The relationship between intervention and conflict is likely to be two-directional and mixed. It is more useful to think about mitigating harm and strengthening the benefits. We should also keep in mind that peace and conflict are not necessarily binary opposites. As highlighted in earlier chapters, conflict is not necessarily a negative phenomenon, and the presence of conflict in a given context does not exclude peace on a wider level. Inevitably one cannot reduce such a complex problem to the question of whether intervention *either* does harm *or* builds peace.

Another tool for converting analysis into practice is the risk-opportunities framework. Table 11.2 illustrates the kinds of analysis and responses that may be appropriate for different types of contexts – defined in terms of a risk-opportunity calculus, meaning the war-related risks for the organisation/programme and peacebuilding opportunities. A matrix of four different risks–opportunities environments leads to different options in terms of the depth of CA and whether an agency works 'in' or 'on' conflict.

Table 11.2 Opportunities and risks analysis

War-related risks	Peacebuilding opportunities	
	Low	High
Low	**Box 1** Preliminary CA Continue with existing programme portfolio Ongoing monitoring of war-related impacts	**Box 2** Detailed CA Strengthen/scale up peacebuilding activities Re-orientate existing programmes and create new ones Look for multiplier effects e.g. media, awareness raising
High	**Box 3** Detailed CA Adapt strategies to mitigate war-related risks Focus on 'do no harm'	**Box 4** Detailed CA Careful analysis of risks and risk mitigation strategies Mainstream low-key peacebuilding approaches

Box 1: *Low risk, low opportunity.* Context may be relatively stable or in a postwar phase, and donor policies are unlikely to have any significant impacts on the war and peace environment. Therefore only a preliminary CA is appropriate.

Box 2: *Low risk, high opportunity.* Context may be a postwar setting where levels of open and latent conflict are declining, but opportunities exist to build relationships between different groups. Donor policies in, for instance, health and education may have the potential to build bridges between groups. A CA would provide guidance for how strategies and policies could be developed which exploit peacebuilding opportunities.

Box 3: *High risk, low opportunity.* There is a high level of latent or open conflict which the project could exacerbate, particularly if it involves significant physical resources in a resource-scarce environment. It is at a phase of the conflict where positions are entrenched and peacebuilding opportunities are limited. A detailed CA is appropriate with a view to minimising conflict-related risks.

Box 4: *High risk, high opportunity.* The environment is highly conflictual and very fluid. However, it may be at a phase when the opportunity structures are opening up and 'critical thresholds' could be exploited to build peace. A detailed CA would be appropriate, to mitigate risks and maximise peacebuilding opportunities.

Note: the 'do nothing' option

In environmental impact assessment, the 'do nothing' option is always retained and assessed. The same option should be considered within the CA framework, particularly in the high risk, low opportunity scenario where the harm–benefit ratio may be high. It also needs to borne in mind that certain types of activity may be inherently 'high risk' – advocacy on peace and conflict issues, for instance – thus increasing the war-related risks to other programming activities.

Intervention implications

Whatever analytical framework the practitioner uses, the key issue is whether they have systematically asked the right questions and gone through a process similar to the one outlined in Box 11.1. Many of the problems associated with poorly designed interventions could have been avoided through a more systematic process of analysis and diagnosis. This should be done jointly by programme stakeholders so that analysis is systematic, shared and transparent. Too often the analysis is hurriedly put together by a harassed project manager. This means that questions related to the nature of the problem, the causality chain, the underlying assumptions, the potential and negative externalities are often left implicit. Although improved analysis does not guarantee better outcomes, it is a basic precondition for those aiming to work 'in' or 'on' war and violent conflict.

11.3 Chapter summary

Interveners cannot stand outside the war, because their **decisions have an impact on the war**. They need to think of themselves less as managers of projects and more as **change agents** who understand and influence the conflicts that escalate to civil war. There are three approaches to war and violent conflict – **working around war** is being 'conflict blind' and treating war as an impediment to be avoided or ignored; **working in war** acknowledges the war and tries to be 'conflict sensitive', avoiding exacerbating conflict and being concerned with staff and project security; and **working on war** actively attempts to incorporate peacebuilding and conflict transformation in all activities.

Interveners need to take into account the **political** context and the roots of the war, the capacities and interests of their own **organisation**, their own **individual agency** – their capacity to make a difference despite organisational and political constraints, and the other **stakeholders** including other interveners. They should then list the possible **options** and their potential **harm and benefit.**

Questions must be asked **systematically**, and this is best done in collaboration with other stakeholders. Detailed conflict analysis and a **risk-opportunities matrix** can help. Each war is different and it is important to **unlearn the lessons** of other wars and consider the local context. **No single approach** will work, and successful practitioners **pick and mix**. The **do nothing option** must always be retained and assessed.

References

Anderson, M. B. (1999) *Do No Harm: How Aid Can Support Peace – Or War*, Boulder Co, Lynne Rienner.

Boyce, J. (2002) 'Investing in peace: aid and conditionality after civil wars', Adelphi Paper 353, IISS, September.

Bradbury, M. (2003) 'Living with statelessness: the Somali road to development', *Journal of Conflict, Security and Development*, vol. 3, no. 1, pp. 7–25.

Brahimi, L. (2000) *Report of the Panel of United Nations Peace Operations*, 21 August, New York, United Nations.

Chambers, R. (1983) *Rural Development: Putting the Last First*, Harlow, Longman Scientific and Technical.

Chambers, R. (1997) '*Whose Reality Counts? Putting the First Last*', London, Intermediate Technology Publications.

Donini, A (2003) 'The future of humanitarian action: implications of Iraq and other crises', Issues Note, Brainstorming Workshop organised by the Feinstein International Famine Centre, Boston, October 9, 2003.

Duffield, M. (2001), *Global Governance and the New Wars: the Merging of Development and Security*, London, Zed Books.

Edwards, M., Hulme, D. and Wallace, T. (1999) 'NGOs in a global future: marrying local delivery to worldwide leverage', *Public Administration and Development*, vol. 19, pp. 117–36.

Fieldon, M. and Goodhand, J. (2001) Peace Making in New World Disorder, The Case of Afghanistan.

Jackson, S. and Walker, P. (1999) 'Depolarising the "broadened" and "back-to-basics" relief models', *Disasters*, vol. 23, no. 2, pp. 93–114.

Johnston, B. F. and Clark, W. C. (1982) *Redesigning Rural Development. A Strategic Perspective*, Baltimore, Johns Hopkins University.

Klugman, J. (1999) *Social and Economic Policies to Prevent Complex Humanitarian Emergencies. Lessons from Experience*, Finland, UNU/WIDER.

Lund, M. (2001) 'A toolbox for responding to conflicts and building peace', in Reychler, L. and Paffenholz, T. *Peacebuilding. A Field Guide*, London, Lynne Rienner.

OECD (1997) *DAC Guidelines on Conflict, Peace and Development Cooperation*, Paris, Organisation for Economic Cooperation and Development.

Porter, D., Allen, B. and Thompson, G. (1991) *Development in Practice: Paved with Good Intentions*, London, Routledge.

Richards, P. (1996) *Fighting for the Rainforest: War, Youth and Resources in Sierra Leone*, Oxford, James Currey.

Smillie, I., Gberie, L. and Hazleton, R. (2000) *The Heart of the Matter, Sierra Leone, Diamonds and Human Security*, Ottawa, Partnership Africa Canada.

UNDP (1994) *Humanitarian Principles and Operational Dilemmas in War Zones*, New York, United Nations Development Programme.

Uvin, P. (2002) 'The development/peacebuilding nexus: a typology and history of changing paradigms', *Journal of Peacebuilding and Development*, vol. 1, no.1, p. 6.

Vaux, T. (2001) *The Selfish Altruist: Relief Work in Famine and War*, London, Earthscan.

12 Working 'in' and 'on' war

Jonathan Goodhand

12.1 Introduction

> The more critical an analyst is of what took place in a past emergency, the more numerous the verbs in the final paragraphs fall into the future imperative: 'have to', 'must', 'should'. Frequently missing, however, is an answer to the essential question 'how?'

> (Smillie, 1998, p. 55)

This chapter is concerned with the practical question of 'how?' As Smillie (1998) notes, although practitioners are regularly implored to 'do better', they are rarely given useful guidelines about how to do things differently. Conflict sensitivity should represent a minimum standard for practitioners intervening in areas affected by open or latent conflict. This means not attempting to avoid or work 'around' war but being sufficiently attuned to the context to work 'in' or 'on' war. What this means in practice depends to a great extent on individual contexts. However, one can identify some general principles of good practice drawn from empirical evidence of what does and does not work in particular types of contexts. In this chapter we examine some of the practical examples of good practice. As already noted, what one actually does is closely related to how one organises and relates to others. Therefore we will move from programming into a brief analysis of organisational and relationship-building challenges.

12.2 Programming challenges

12.2.1 Approaches to programming

Broadly, practitioners working in the international sphere are likely to operate in one of, or a combination of, four different areas of work:

- pursuit of peace and security through support for peacekeeping, conflict transformation, security sector reform, etc.
- support for political measures and the promulgation and monitoring of human rights
- the promotion of long-term social and economic development
- the provision of humanitarian relief in emergencies.

Some agencies may specialise in only one of these areas, for instance Amnesty International with their focus on human rights or specialist UN agencies, whereas multi-mandate organisations such as Oxfam work simultaneously in several areas. Agencies also employ different modalities of work to implement their programmes. These can broadly be categorised as:

- direct intervention, i.e. delivery of assistance, implementation of projects without working through intermediary organisations
- capacity building, i.e. working with and developing the capacity of intermediary organisations to sustain the effects of projects or programmes
- advocacy, i.e. influencing policy makers or decision makers to engender changes at the macro level.

While some agencies may favour one particular way of working, many pursue different combinations of all three depending on activity and context. Table 12.1 provides a typology for mapping agency interventions in terms of their areas of work and ways of working.

Table 12.1   Areas and modalities of intervention

	1 Security/conflict transformation/ peacekeeping	2 Political measures/ human rights	3 Socio- economic development	4 Relief
Direct intervention				
Capacity building				
Advocacy				

In practice the dividing lines between the different columns are likely to be blurred and categories merge into one another. For instance, 'relief' and 'development' are not clearly bounded categories. Development donors are frequently involved in a range of activities which span columns 2 and 3, from support for 'good governance' to 'poverty alleviation'.

While the table is not meant to denote a hierarchy, as one moves from the right to the left, the focus on peace and conflict dynamics becomes more direct and explicit. Furthermore, as one moves in this direction, the more one becomes involved in sensitive areas such as the judiciary and the security sector which directly impinge upon questions of sovereignty. Conversely, as one goes from left to right the peacebuilding impacts are likely to be more indirect and to be perceived as less politically sensitive. Activities in the first two columns are, to a great extent, high risk, high opportunity. They include mediation, peacekeeping and security sector reform, all of which have a direct focus on peace and conflict dynamics.

Peacebuilding can be conceived as both a separate area of activity falling within the first column – for instance a set of activities designed to develop linkages between civil society groups on different sides of a conflict – and an approach that can be applied to any intervention. In this sense it is a 'lens' to examine and shape existing work so that it is more sensitive to conflict dynamics and seeks to exploit peacebuilding opportunities.

If one accepts the idea of the 'peacebuilding lens' then one of the key challenges for practitioners is to mainstream peacebuilding approaches into everything they do. In the next section we will explore how this might be done in practice. However, a word of caution is required. Experience shows that without robust support for activities in the first column which explicitly aim to build peace and security, other activities are likely to have only small-scale and transitory effects. Development or humanitarian activities by themselves are unlikely to gain sufficient purchase on the forces driving violent conflict to be a leading edge in peacebuilding. International experience of peace operations demonstrates that there is no substitute for political will and the use of robust force.

The focus and balance of different activities within the matrix is likely to be constantly shifting, in response to the changing context and the evolving priorities and capacities of the actors involved. For instance, at the height of a complex political emergency (CPE) the focus is likely to be on direct intervention, involving quick impact activities particularly in columns 1 and 4 of Table 12.1. In an 'emerging peace' context the focus will shift towards capacity building particularly in columns 2 and 3. As levels of open violence decrease, the opportunities to exploit horizontal and vertical synergies will grow – for instance political reform linked to socio-economic development and direct delivery linked to capacity building and advocacy. For agencies attempting to cover multiple roles in fragile and politicised environments there are likely to be tensions and trade-offs. For instance, an NGO involved in delivering humanitarian relief may endanger these activities through advocacy work on human rights or peacebuilding. Similarly, development donors with a core focus on socio-economic development may find it politically risky to get involved in direct peace work in column 1.

Intervention implications

 Whatever type of agency you work for, the key is to think through the war-related risks and adapt strategies and programmes accordingly. This does not mean avoiding risks, but learning to manage them more effectively. The challenge is to mitigate the negative impacts and to accentuate the positive effects.

As already highlighted, it is not good enough to work 'around' war. Being conflict blind represents bad practice. Therefore the onus is on practitioners to make decisions and take actions that respond to war-related risks and opportunities. The sequencing of these decisions and actions is important. As with environmental impact assessment, risks must be mitigated first – this represents a bottom line for all interventions in conflict-affected areas. The three types of conflict–programme interactions are illustrated in Figure 12.1.

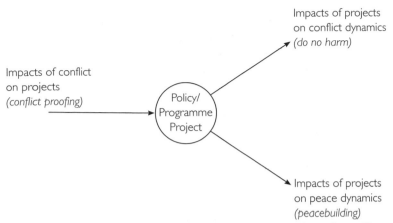

Figure 12.1 Project interactions with the dynamics of conflict and peace

12.2.2 Addressing conflict and peace dynamics

Conflict proofing

The aim of conflict proofing is to minimise the negative effects of violent conflict on your organisation, policies, programmes or projects. It relates primarily to the question of security. All organisations have a bottom line, implicit or explicit, which denotes the level of risk they are willing to take in pursuit of their mission. Once that organisational 'line in the sand' has been passed and the war-related risks are too great to justify your presence, withdrawal may be the only option.

Conflict proofing and 'do no harm' are two sides of the same coin. The former is concerned with the 'internal' environment, i.e. minimising security risks over the things you directly control, such as policies, programmes and projects. 'Do no harm' is concerned with the 'external' environment, i.e. minimising the negative impacts of the things you control on the wider conflict environment. In practice the two are closely connected. For example, relief projects which involve bulky assets are more likely to be affected by war, since they will attract the attention of warring groups. Because of this they may also fuel war dynamics through absorption into the war economy.

The foundation for effective risk mitigation is sound conflict analysis. This should involve an ongoing assessment of the threats to your organisation and activities. It also entails carefully monitoring what you are doing and how this may affect your positioning within the war environment. How you are positioned in a war is ultimately the result of the interplay between your proclaimed position (i.e. is it one of 'neutrality', 'impartiality' or 'solidarity'?), what you actually do, and how others perceive you. What you do and how you do it clearly affect the perception of your organisation and consequently the war-related risks. Going back to Table 12.1, certain activities are inherently high risk – for instance advocacy on war crimes or negotiating a ceasefire agreement. These kinds of activities are perhaps best left to non-operational, 'off site' agencies and individuals. 'On site' organisations, because of their operational presence, may have a lower risk threshold in terms of the type of activities they can engage in.

Risk-mitigation strategies must be calibrated to the level of perceived threat. It may involve tightening staff safety procedures, improving information sharing and coordination arrangements, and developing ground rules for engagement in war-affected areas. The content and style of programming may also change. In high-risk areas agencies may be forced to withdraw or go into 'hibernation'. In other words it may sometimes be necessary to 'do nothing' or 'do less'. Table 12.2 illustrates the range of impacts that war has had on aid programmes in Nepal and some of the mitigation strategies that have been adopted.

Table 12.2   The impacts of war on aid programmes in Nepal

Sector	Impacts of the war on aid programmes	Possible strategies to mitigate impacts
Security	Threats to staff from Maoists and police Targeting of NGO offices Threats to government implementing partners Inability of donors to conduct monitoring	Develop security guidelines Training for staff in security procedures Work through local partners
Political	Declining political and humanitarian space – agencies working in heartland areas seen as Maoist sympathisers	Negotiate ground rules with de facto authorities in war-affected areas
Economic	Retraction of government services and targeting of banks in war-affected areas, affecting sustainability of projects Maoist demands for percentage of staff salaries and project budgets	Avoid bulky assets Adapt banking and finance procedures
Social	Displacement of communities, migration of men and erosion of social capital, affecting social mobilisation activities	Adopt low-key approaches Focus on poverty alleviation and social support programmes

Aid agency responses in Nepal illustrate the difference between avoiding war-related risks and attempting to manage them. If the sole motivation of conflict proofing is to shield one's organisation and programmes from the effects of war, there may be perverse side effects. In Nepal, withdrawal from war-affected areas risks exacerbating war dynamics, since the decline of services in poor rural areas has contributed to growing grievances and increased Maoist recruitment. When aid is delivered only to the most secure areas it risks reinforcing the fault lines of the war. As Table 12.2 shows, many agencies have been able to adapt their approaches to ensure a continued presence in war-affected areas.

In a number of wars humanitarian actors have negotiated 'ground rules' or 'terms of engagement' with warring factions to ensure they can gain access to vulnerable communities and to protect 'humanitarian space'. In the case of Operational Lifeline Sudan, this involved the development of a joint agreement between aid actors and the warring parties. In other countries such as Sri Lanka, aid agencies tended to negotiate individual, bilateral agreements with the respective parties to the war. The danger of such an approach is that warring groups often may play one aid actor off against another, each one having different and often movable 'bottom lines'. This happened, for instance, in Taliban-controlled Afghanistan with different agencies adopting different policies related to gender equity. Clearly, the nature of the conflict and the warring factions themselves have an important influence on negotiations. The more decentralised and random the violence, the less easy it is to develop predictable relations with local power holders and thus ensure a 'framework of respect' for humanitarian actors. For the practitioner it may be useful to know what has or has not worked in different contexts, but simply transferring ground rules from one context to another has limited value.

Wheat from Tajikistan arrives in Zaat Kamaar, Afghanistan. The local population are beginning to return to their village, which had been the Northern Alliance frontier until the Taliban forces fled 12 days earlier. The land is heavily mined, and as winter sets in, the fields remain barren.

Ultimately, making decisions about war-related risks is not an exact science. It is an art that involves making informed judgements based on a systematic assessment of the information and on-the-ground experience. Whether to engage or whether to withdraw is a moral dilemma and requires some kind of an ethical framework to guide decision making. Examples of the kinds of questions to consider in conflict proofing are outlined in Box 12.1.

> # Box 12.1   Conflict proofing questions
>
> - What are the war-related risks: to my organisation, to my staff and to my programmes/projects?
> - Are the monitoring and information systems in place to update our threat assessment?
> - Can the risks be prioritised in terms of level of threat?
> - To what extent can the risks be mitigated?
> - To what extent do the risks prevent us from pursuing our organisational mandate?
> - Does the level of threat differ between different categories of staff – e.g. local and international; field-based and HQ-based; one region compared with another?
> - Are the conflict stakeholders aware of our role, mandate and activities?
> - Do conflict stakeholders respect our positions and provide us with 'space' or 'room for manoeuvre'?
> - Do we have a communications strategy with the various parties?
> - Are there contingencies for a sudden increase in war-related risks?
> - Do we have security guidelines and are staff conversant with them?
> - Are evacuation plans in place?
> - Are programming activities being adapted to war risks?

Do no harm (working in war)

Interventions in a war-ridden environment inevitably interact with the dynamics of war and peace. As previously mentioned, there is no such thing as a non-impact, though the magnitude and nature of the impact will vary. Recognition of this by the practitioner should bring both a sense of responsibility and a sense of proportion. First, it is self-deluding to think that one can somehow stand above the fray, hiding behind a banner of neutrality. An honest recognition of the potential for intervention to do harm as well as do good is needed. Second, practitioners should keep their role and impact in perspective. Good conflict assessment should help. It positions you in relation to the war and identifies the areas where you may potentially do harm or do good. Too 'aid-centric' a perspective can lead to an exaggerated view of one's own importance.

Interventions are unlikely to have unambiguously negative or positive impacts. Doing no harm may not be practically possible – unless one does nothing – and in the real world it is about minimising the potentially negative side effects of intervention. As already emphasised in this course, it is not about stopping conflict per se, but about minimising the potential for intervention to exacerbate or catalyse destructive, violent conflict. In order to do this, one needs an analytical framework, which pinpoints the types and levels of conflict that particular interventions interact with. For instance, while a local irrigation project and a national land privatisation programme may both do 'harm' by exacerbating war dynamics, the magnitude and nature of their impacts are quite different.

Intervention implication

 To minimise potential negative effects, practitioners should develop the skills to predict, categorise and quantify the kinds of harms that they may cause.

As mentioned in earlier chapters, it is often misleading to talk about 'the war'. In practice, unstable environments tend to be a complex mixture of different types and levels which become entwined with one another and are the roots of the war. Actors at different levels in this conflict system have different motivations and incentives for war or peace. The key point for the practitioners is that interventions interact with 'messes' where incentive systems, structures and relationships are complex, changing and ambiguous. What represents a 'harm' and what represents a 'good' can and will be contested. Simplistic divisions between constituencies for peace and constituencies for war or between war economies and peace economies have limited value. Calculating and mitigating the type and level of harm must therefore be done on a case-by-case basis. It also involves a value judgement on the part of the interveners. This requires a level of honesty, consistency and transparency on their part, concerning their own values and standards.

Impacts may be either direct or indirect: for example, humanitarian aid can be directly absorbed into the war economy or it may free up resources that can be used to wage war. They may affect the political economy of war, but may also have an impact on the 'emotional' economy of war. As well as their material effects, interventions are likely to have symbolic or legitimising effects. Impacts vary according to the magnitude and scope of intervention. Broadly, the level of impact can range from the individual (values, attitudes, behaviours, relationships, incentives, etc.), to the institutional (organisational culture, structures and processes, incentive systems, etc.) to the structural (background socio-political conditions). The effects of an individual relief project, for example, may be limited to the micro, community level. But a sectoral programme, focusing for instance on 'good governance', may for better or worse have an influence on the institutional environment and the decision making of political elites. Development policies and programmes over a number of years may have cumulative effects, and thus influence wider structural conditions. For instance, it has been argued that aid played a significant role in contributing to the background conditions that led to the Rwandan genocide (Uvin, 1998). Similarly in Sri Lanka, donor-funded projects such as the Mahawelli dam project have tended to follow the fault lines of the war, exacerbating underlying grievances that subsequently became ethnicised.

The practitioner therefore must be sensitive to the potential for 'negative externalities' and to adapt projects, policies and programmes accordingly.

But how does being conflict sensitive translate into changed programming? There is no universal answer to this question as every situation is unique. But the empirical evidence shows there are common patterns of project–conflict interactions, and knowledge of this can help the practitioner to achieve a better 'fit' between interventions and individual contexts.

Going back to Table 12.1 again, interventions in the areas of peace/security, political reform, socio-economic development and relief are commonly associated with different types of negative effect. Once this is recognised and to an extent predicted, practitioners can mitigate these harmful side effects.

Relief aid

The 'dark side' of aid has been mentioned elsewhere in this course. Basically, four types of negative effects can be identified. First, humanitarian aid can be 'taxed' by warring parties to help finance conflict. Second, aid is 'fungible' in the sense that it can free up domestic resources for war making. Third, relief can instil a false sense of security among the victims of war. Fourth, aid relief operations can serve as a smokescreen for inaction on other fronts by donor governments.

Aid agencies rarely face an either/or choice of whether or not to provide aid. They have to choose how much to provide, what types, to whom and with what conditions attached. As James Boyce (2002) argues, in the face of trade-offs between the positive and negative consequences of aid, a sensible decision-making rule is to weigh the good against the harm and then choose the best (or least bad) option. In Liberia in the mid 1990s during the height of the civil war, aid agencies had to reassess their role following the widespread looting of humanitarian relief. Box 12.2 outlines how aid agencies adapted to this situation.

Box 12.2   Questions about 'minimising harm'

- What types and levels of conflict will my intervention impinge upon?
- What types of 'harm' are my interventions likely to cause – e.g. distributional, substitution, symbolic/legitimation effects?
- How are spoilers likely to benefit from my intervention?
- What are the short-term and long-term costs of intervention?
- Who will bear the main costs of my intervention?
- Are the costs likely to outweigh the benefits of intervention?
- What strategies can be employed to minimise harm?
- Should war-related conditionalities be applied?

Development assistance

While much has been written about the negative effects of humanitarian aid, there has been less of a focus on the conflict-fuelling potential of development assistance. This is surprising since in global terms, much more is spent on overseas development assistance (ODA) than relief aid. Also, development policy impinges upon areas such as macro economic policy and state welfare provision that may become significant sources of conflict. Therefore, development aid tends to involve more resources and go much deeper than relief assistance. The distributional tensions are likely to be of a different magnitude and the potential for doing harm to be more significant. This is particularly the case in 'postwar' contexts which can involve 'conflict blind' donors injecting relatively large amounts of funding into fragile contexts. In such a situation the problem may be one of 'over-aiding' rather than a lack of funds. By injecting large amounts of assistance into war-torn countries donors unwittingly but inevitably distort local systems of production and exchange (Boyce, 2002).

Development practitioners have tended to treat war as a temporary aberration – a diversion from the road to development. The role of development assistance in contributing to a certain type of development that is conflict worsening has until recently largely been ignored. A range of negative political, economic and social effects can be identified which have contributed to the emergence of violent conflict. This particularly applies in transitional contexts, in which periods of accelerated change raise the political and economic stakes. Introducing resources into such an environment may both create opportunities for 'greed' and accentuate underlying 'grievances'. For example, land privatisation programmes in central Asia have caused tensions that have become increasingly ethnicised (Vaux and Goodhand, 2001). Donor-supported poverty reduction programmes in Sri Lanka have been used as a form of patronage by political elites, leading to a growing sense of frustration among the educated youth. In the same country, the education system, again supported by Western donors, has reinforced divisions based on ethnicity and language.

The current donor predilection for sectoral approaches may promote greater coherence. But since the impact is likely to be at the structural or institutional levels, there is also the risk that the magnitude of harm will be greater than for project-focused approaches. Relatively limited thought has been given so far as to how Poverty Reduction Strategy Papers (PRSPs) and sector-wide initiatives can become more conflict sensitive. Conflict-sensitive development may not involve wholesale changes to what you do, but it may involve fine-tuning how you do things. Of particular importance is sensitivity to the distributional impacts of aid. As James Boyce (2000, p. 367) notes:

> External assistance has political as well as economic impacts: aid affects not only the size of the economic pie and how it is sliced, but also the balance of power among competing actors and the rules of the game by which they compete.

In Afghanistan the lion's share of funding since the Bonn agreement has gone to the north, leading to growing dissatisfaction in the Pashtun south over the lack of a 'peace dividend'. If this situation is allowed to continue, it risks endangering the fragile war-to-peace transition.

Intervention implications

The practitioner must always ask 'who is likely to benefit and who is likely to lose as a result of this policy or programme?' Does an intervention have the potential to reinforce horizontal inequalities?

Conflict-sensitive policy and practice means looking at interventions through a human security lens rather than a narrow economic lens. This may involve compromises and trade-offs, with the emphasis shifting towards mitigating or reducing vulnerability, rather than simply boosting growth and production. Targets and time frames may have to be adjusted. Reducing risks and vulnerability to external shocks may take precedence over efficiency and production targets.

The institutionalised division between 'relief' and 'development' modalities is singularly unhelpful. Practitioners are often constrained by the lack of funding for transitional activities which occupy the 'grey' area between relief and development. The US Office for Transition Initiatives represents one attempt to bridge this gap. Quick Impact Projects are another, though they may have serious deficiencies in practice (Smillie, 1998). However, the principle of developing synergies between relief and development activities is a good one, to which policy makers and practitioners should at least aspire. Programming approaches that lack flexibility and are unable to adapt to the context are most likely to do harm inadvertently.

As Macrae (2001) argues, what distinguishes development assistance from relief is that the former involves a relationship with a recognised, legitimate government. War may force practitioners to rethink the nature of their relationship with the state. The government in power may be one of the parties to the war and partnership, or the keystone of development cooperation may no longer be possible or desirable. By contrast, as Stewart and Fitzgerald (2000) have pointed out, if countries at war do not qualify for development assistance they are in effect being 'twice punished' – turning off the aid tap on countries already vulnerable as a result of war risks pushing them further into a 'no exit' cycle of war.

Intervention implications

The practitioner needs to think creatively about the potential synergies between relief and development, whereby relief may represent an investment in longer-term development, while conflict-sensitive development helps reduce the risk of future war.

Finally, development practitioners may need to think about war-related conditionalities. The criteria for success may shift. For instance, an education programme that may be successful in its own terms – in enrolment, pass rates, etc. – can increase tensions between groups. Adjustments may need to be made and monitoring criteria introduced which could lead to a 'lowering of standards' but minimise the risks of increased tensions.

Political measures

There is no clear line between political measures (column 2 of Table 12.2) and socio-economic development (column 3), especially as aid has become more explicitly political in recent times. During the 1990s development donors added political conditions to their assistance, to complement the economic conditionalities applied in the 1980s. If this means a greater focus on the politics of the state, this could be seen as a positive development in relation to war prevention and peacebuilding – given the roots of contemporary wars in processes of state crisis and failure. However, in practice, donor policies directed towards state reform have often been conflict blind. This may inadvertently fuel war. (Cliffe and Luckham 1999, p. 29)

Intervention implications

'Normal' governance policies need to be scrutinised for their possible blindness to the war-promoting implications of accepted practices.

Aid policy may contribute to 'bad governance' in a number of ways. Badly planned reform programmes may contribute to the replication of authoritarian regimes. They may weaken social contracts between states and citizens (de Waal, 1997). The competitive individualism of the aid community can have a fragmenting effect on state authority (Moore and Putzel, 1999). In the 'postwar' moment, the gap between donor aspirations and the needs on the ground may be greatest, as Ottaway (2002, p. 1017) notes.

> the international community devises a model, builds its component parts and hopes that after being forced to adhere to the model for long enough it will be accepted without supervision... . It is a procrustean approach as the model is given and the country is pushed and pulled to conform to it.

The 'big bang' approach to institution building leads to unrealistic targets – and may place too great a burden on fragile structures and so become self-defeating. A veritable cottage industry has developed around the question of institutional design in postwar contexts. The intention is to create institutions which curb raw power and open up the political spaces for more representative and accountable forms of governance. But as Ottaway (2002) argues, the 'bargain basement' model usually employed by the international community simply does not work because of the mismatch between donor objectives and the resources they put on the table.

Many of the implications outlined above for conflict-sensitive development practice apply to political measures, i.e. the need for better analysis, sensitivity to distributional impacts, introducing war-related criteria to monitor and evaluate activities, etc. There is a need to think carefully about matching responses to individual contexts. For example, on the question of decentralisation, a 'one size fits all' approach will not work. In Afghanistan on the one hand, decentralisation implemented at the time of writing would simply strengthen the power of the warlords, contributing to the fragmentation of the country. In Sri Lanka on the other hand, there is a need for asymmetrical decentralisation, leading to greater autonomy for the north east. These two examples show there can never be a standard model of good governance – reforms must be sensitive to the dynamics of war and this may involve a trade-off between what is desirable in the long term with what is practicable in the short term.

Peace and security

As already mentioned, interventions in these areas are the most sensitive and have the most direct effects on war and peace dynamics. It is also an area in which development donors are increasingly involved, with peace conditionalities recently being added to the earlier generation of political and economic conditionalities. Failures in this sphere of activity can do the most harm. As Stedman (2001) has noted, more people died following flawed peace implementation processes in Angola and Rwanda than were killed in fighting before the settlements. Therefore, poorly conceived attempts to 'do good' may end up doing harm. At the micro level this applies to naive attempts at community reconciliation in Sri Lanka. At the macro level, the Bonn Agreement, which attempted to set out a road map for peace in Afghanistan, arguably had the effect of entrenching power.

The first problem for practitioners, whatever their sphere of involvement, is knowing *whether* and *when* to act. It may sometimes be important to exercise restraint and the 'do nothing' option on certain occasions may be the best one. Conversely, failure to act can sometimes do more harm than good. In Afghanistan, for example, the failure to deliver a visible peace dividend in the form of reconstruction activities in rural areas has been a major failing of the international community.

Understanding the intervention context and how one's actions or inaction may affect incentive systems is critical. What are the incentives or disincentives for war or peace? As examined in the following section, the choice is not just between continuing with business as usual or applying negative conditions to intervention. Interventions can be consciously fashioned to 'do good'.

Intervention implication

'The problem is we tend to conceptualise our choices as between negative conditionality and the continuation of business as usual. The former is clearly an action fraught with risks and uncertainties, while the latter is perceived to be neutral – amounting to no action at all. That is wrong: the continuation of business as usual is a form of action, it does send signals, and it has an impact on local political and social processes'

Uvin, 1998, p. 237

Peacebuilding (working on war)

In the last two sections we have examined war–intervention dynamics and how practitioners can minimise negative effects. In this section we explore the potential for interventions to have a positive effect, directly or indirectly, on peacebuilding processes and how practitioners can maximise this potential. We define peacebuilding here rather broadly, to include: 'Local or structural efforts that foster or support those social, political and institutional structures and processes which strengthen the prospects for peaceful coexistence and decrease the likelihood of the outbreak, reoccurrence or continuation of violence' (Goodhand, 2002, p. 839). On the basis of research on the role of NGOs in complex political emergencies, a range of indirect and direct approaches to peacebuilding can be identified. These are outlined in Box 12.3.

Box 12.3   Indirect and direct approaches to peacebuilding

Indirect approaches

Conflict-sensitive relief: Oxfam resettlement projects, eastern Sri Lanka.

Supporting local leadership: Christian Aid, eastern Sri Lanka.

Human rights monitoring/protection: e.g. ICRC, Afghanistan.

Governance: Constitutional reform, International Centre for Ethnic Studies, Sri Lanka; judicial reform, Liberian NGOs; election monitoring, Sri Lanka.

Local capacity building/civil society strengthening: e.g. Christian Aid, eastern Sri Lanka.

Socio-economic development/alternative livelihoods: Afghanaid, north east Afghanistan; Mercy Corps International, micro credit, Ferghana Valley.

Direct approaches

War prevention: conflict monitoring, Tolerance International, Kyrgyzstan.

Mediation/conflict resolution: between warring parties, e.g. ICRC in northern Sri Lanka; between and within communities: Afghan Development Association in Uruzgen, Afghanistan, human rights NGOs in Nepal.

Building peace constituencies: e.g. National Peace Council in southern Sri Lanka.

Reconciliation: Afghan Development Association community development and reconciliation in Afghanistan; Lutheran World Service trauma counselling, Liberia; Quaker Peace and Services community mediation programme, eastern Sri Lanka.

Security sector: Save the Children (SCF) programme with child soldiers, Liberia; de-mining NGOs, Afghanistan.

Advocacy/education: ICRC, international humanitarian law dissemination; Oxfam, cut conflict campaign; Oxfam, SCF, listening to the returned and displaced, Sri Lanka; SCF, children zones of peace, Sri Lanka; BBC New Home, New Life, Afghanistan.

Indirect approaches tend to mainstream peacebuilding into their ongoing activities, it being one of a number of objectives. Direct approaches tend to have a primary focus on peacebuilding or on influencing more broadly the security environment. This definition of peacebuilding distinguishes between micro or local level approaches and wider structural approaches. An example of the former is examined in Box 12.4.

Box 12.4   Peacebuilding from below? ADA in Khas Uruzgen, Afghanistan

In 1992 a local NGO, the Afghan Development Association (ADA), started working in Khas Uruzgen. It selected this area because of its geographical isolation, the lack of other NGOs working in the area and the fact that it is situated on an ethnic fault line and has on occasion experienced open conflict between the Hazara and Pashtun ethnic groups.

ADA has made a conscious decision to work with both Hazaras and Pashtuns in the district, bringing them together on issues of common interest. Though they have no illusions that they can solve the wider conflict, there is a conscious policy of building relationships at the local level to reduce the likelihood of mobilisation along ethnic lines in the future. Afghan communities are very sensitive about attempts at social engineering, and programmes with social objectives have to be extremely low key and sensitive. Communities are brought together on concrete issues that affect them both. Their programmes include building and support for schools, construction of micro hydro power stations, the provision of improved seeds and the development of fruit tree nurseries. In terms of their rehabilitation and development objectives these programmes have been extremely successful. There are tangible signs of recovery and improvement in the district; a number of villages now have electricity, schools have (until recently) been up and running for the first time for several years, there are many new orchards and agricultural production in the region has increased. Less visible and less easy to evaluate is the broader goal of peacebuilding. ADA point to the fact that Hazaras and Pashtun students and teachers go to the same school as each other and both communities continue to work together on common projects. They claim that this in itself is an achievement when in some other parts of the country the two communities are in open conflict with one another. To get to this stage has taken a long-term commitment on the part of ADA, combined with quite a sophisticated and fine-grained analysis of community structures and relations. Project staff have an extremely nuanced understanding of local leadership, tribal and ethnic structures and the incentives systems for cooperative (and non-cooperative) action.

ADA never talk openly to the communities about building relationships between Hazaras and Pashtuns. However, both groups work together on concrete tasks, for example constructing a school, maintaining a hydro power station or cleaning an irrigation ditch. The primary motivation for working together is economic need and the common ownership of resources. People recognise the need to cooperate out of basic self interest: 'We have seen the costs of war and it has made us poorer'.

Perhaps ADA have decreased the probability of war in the future since both communities have made investments in that future. The people themselves recognise that relationships have improved in recent years: 'When ADA came to the area relations between the two communities became "softer"'.

However, it is also important to see the limitations of such an approach. It is about building *probabilities* rather than certainties. If wider political and military events take a turn for the worse, then the low-key micro-level work done by ADA could get swept away very quickly. One staff member compared it with planting tree saplings in a nursery which could be swept away at any minute by a flood. However one could argue that because of the work done by ADA it will be more difficult for outside events to trigger such a war in the future.

The key to ADA's approach was sensitivity to and long-term support for local capacities – defined by staff in terms of institutions, norms and values. Protracted war at the national level had undermined local capacities to resolve internal disputes. Trust between Hazaras and Pashtuns was rebuilt by addressing material needs and by working through local institutions, the *shura* or council. However, as stated at the end of the case study in Box 12.4, the effects of such interventions may be limited. They are restricted to the local level and may be swept aside by wider events. By themselves they are unlikely to contribute to peace 'writ large'.

To what extent can interventions have an impact at the structural level? The case study in Box 12.5 explores the impact of peace conditionalities on the peace consolidation process in Bosnia. In this case it was the explicit intention of those who designed the intervention to have an impact on wider conflict and peace dynamics.

Box 12.5   Aid for peace bargains in Bosnia

In Bosnia donors experimented by using aid as a lever to support the right of refugees and internally displaced persons to return to their homes. Municipal authorities vary greatly in their commitment to the principles of the Dayton agreement. Some protected their minority residents during the war and others profited personally from ethnic cleansing and block minority residents' return. Donors allocated aid selectively so as to reward those seeking to implement the peace accord, penalise those who are obstructing its implementation and encourage vacillators to get off the fence. UNHCR pioneered this conditional aid strategy in its 'Open Cities' programme, targeting aid to municipalities whose officials publicly declared their willingness to welcome minority returns. UNHCR tailored the conditions for qualifying as an open city to local circumstances – in one city the key may be processing the paperwork to return apartments to their former occupants, in another it may be school enrolment for minority children. If local authorities renege on their commitments, open-city status and its attendant rewards can be rescinded.

In Bosnia a Peace Implementation Committee drafted guidelines for the application of peace conditionality. A selective approach was adopted which included exemptions for 'projects of a humanitarian nature, for example food, basic medical care, sanitation and a minimum supply of power'. However, the delineation of humanitarian aid that should be exempted from peace conditionality is not a straightforward matter. As James Boyce argues, 'In deciding whether or not to apply peace conditionality, and if so, to what types of aid, donors make choices that can mean the difference between life and death. But the fact that decisions are difficult does not mean that they can be avoided.' (Boyce, 2002, p. 60)

Whether and how to work 'on' war is not a decision to take lightly. As noted in the previous section, attempts to 'do good' may have the greatest potential to 'do harm'. A whole range of issues and questions need to be considered in relation to context, timing, organisational mission, programming activities, skills and capacities. Choices are unlikely to be cost free – the decision to shift towards a more explicit focus on peacebuilding is more likely to involve a careful consideration of the costs and benefits of doing so in relation to agency mandates and capacities and individual contexts. Applied to specific cases it may involve questions ranging from the more fundamental one of whether to intervene, to the specifics of time frames and the trade-off between urgency and participation, the particular programming mix, targeting of interventions, the sequencing of activities, and modalities of intervention, i.e. direct delivery, capacity building or advocacy.

In the following section I will take a necessarily selective look at some of the issues involved.

The context and wider response

As already mentioned, there can be no such thing as 'best practice' because every context is different. What is possible and desirable in one context will not be in another. The skilful practitioner is able to match responses to contexts. A maximalist approach may be appropriate in some situations – for instance when there is a legitimate peace settlement and an agreed strategy for 'postwar' reconstruction – but in others a minimalist approach may be the only reasonable option. For example, many aid agencies in Iraq have resisted pressures to align themselves behind the 'peacebuilding' strategies of the occupying forces. Clearly, working 'on' war must involve a political analysis of the kind of peace that one is trying to build. It may be decided that in certain contexts it is not possible to build peace with justice and consequently a minimalist approach will be adopted.

Practitioners should also keep their role in perspective. In Afghanistan for example, the intensity of the aid effort waxed and waned with no discernible impact on the war. Research points to the modest impacts of outsider efforts to engineer change on a social level. At best, one is creating probabilities rather than certainties. Moreover, without a robust government-led peace process, it is unlikely that civil society-led approaches can have anything more than a transitory effect on peacebuilding processes. By contrast, in many of today's wars top-down peace enforcement (i.e. Chapter VII of the UN Charter) is not enough. There may therefore be a need to apply top-down and bottom-up approaches simultaneously – a Cambodia model and a Somalia model respectively.

Timing

Firstly, war is rooted in long-term historic processes, and external actors need to adapt their time frames accordingly. For example, peace is not going to suddenly occur in Afghanistan as a result of lots of six-month projects. One needs to think, plan and act with a long-term time frame in mind if one is aiming at 'deep' rather than 'shallow' peacebuilding – structural and institutional change takes time. Secondly, war, as already mentioned, often brings windows of opportunity or critical thresholds when interventions can have disproportionate impacts. Being able to respond to these 'moments of change' is critical. Grasmci distinguishes between 'wars of position' and 'wars of movement' (cited in Fox, 2003). The former is analogous to trench warfare in which your aim is to hold on to your position, sometimes in the face of more powerful forces. In certain contexts – for instance 'frozen' conflicts such as Nagorno-Karabakh and Moldova – peacebuilding efforts may represent a 'holding operation'; interventions keep dialogue going and support civic structures that could break down altogether without external support. These may be stabilising points in civil society that may re-emerge once the fighting is over. By contrast, 'wars of movement' involve sudden shifts in position. For practitioners it is important to be able to recognise 'windows of opportunity' and to scale up efforts accordingly. In Sri Lanka for instance during the peace talks of 1994, NGOs played an important role in mobilising support for the peace process within civil society. Although talks eventually broke down, NGOs were able to gain useful experience that was put to good effect in the 2002 peace process.

Programming mix

Programming decisions and day-to-day project work are delimited by a combination of factors including organisational mission and risk threshold, the war context and individual staff members' own values. As already argued, good practice involves a contingent approach grounded in situational analysis. To what extent is good peacebuilding practice about doing different things or doing things differently? In our view, more important than stand alone or 'bolt on' peace projects is the need to examine everything you do through a peace and war lens – just as development agencies now do as a matter of course with regard to gender. For multi-mandate organisations this is certainly the main challenge. However, it is important to recognise the tensions and trade-offs involved in juggling multiple objectives. We have already highlighted the tensions between focusing on human rights and advocacy versus direct delivery or peace stabilisation. Often we see the triumph of operationalism to the detriment of protection. Roche (1996) and White and Cliffe (2000) argue that for those living in areas affected by war, aid agency divisions between relief, development, human rights and peacebuilding are meaningless. Communities employ a range of short-term and long-term strategies to cope and survive. It may be more useful to think in terms of adapting one's programming mix according to the context and phase of war, with the balance and emphasis constantly changing. A range of different programming approaches may be pursued simultaneously in relation to the same country. For example, the provision of relief in Kabul, community development programmes in the countryside and lobbying on the arms trade and land mines in London.

Intervention implications

Examine everything you do through a war and peacebuilding lens. Instead of stand-alone peace projects, constantly change your ongoing programme to reflect the peacebuilding possibilities of the current phase of the war. Look for windows of opportunity where interventions can be most effective. Provide support to keep peacebuilding civil society structures functioning during periods when intervention is not practical.

Punching above your weight?

To what extent are Paul Richards' (1996) ideas about 'smart' aid practicable and programmable? Is it possible to punch above your weight by identifying multiplier effects? All the examples of good practice that we have looked at have a capacity-building or influencing/advocacy component – agencies have focused not only on the inner circle of what they can control, but also have thought carefully about the outer two circles of influencing and understanding.

Peacebuilding is a capacity-expanding exercise. It involves support for individuals and for formal and informal institutions that play a role in managing or transforming conflict. The importance of individual 'peace entrepreneurs' is often missed in overly structuralist analyses. The sources of change in society are often highly motivated, atypical individuals who 'break the mould'. Aid agencies may play an important role (which they do not sufficiently recognise) in either supporting community level leadership or protection and holding in 'cold storage' civic leadership within their own organisations. For instance, before 9/11 (2001) in Afghanistan there were around 25,000 Afghans employed with aid agencies and the Swedish Committee for Afghanistan was the largest single employer in the country. NGOs prevented 'human capital flight' and nurtured a cadre of workers who then played a central role in the reconstruction and reconciliation process. In 2003 there were at least three Ministers and many others in senior positions in the Afghan Transitional Administration who came from an NGO background. The ADA and Bosnian examples show how interveners can work with and strategically support local actors and institutions. Both cases were based upon a nuanced analysis of institutions, incentive systems and individuals, allied to a long-term commitment to capacity development. This is clearly political work and in many respects involves moving away from the classic humanitarian position of neutrality towards one of solidarity.

Advocacy is another way of moving 'upstream' in order to scale up impacts. Working with the media is one way of achieving a multiplier effect. War generates its own 'information economy' and interveners must try to understand and engage with the battle for hearts and minds. Humanitarian and peace propaganda are increasingly deployed by the aid and peacebuilding community in war zones. War entrepreneurs have used the media, particularly the radio, to terrible effect. Aid agencies have become increasingly shrewd about working with local media, including the radio and vernacular press, to disseminate peacebuilding messages. Star Radio in Liberia and the BBC New Home New Life programme in Afghanistan are both positive examples of peace broadcasting. Advocacy may involve a diffuse or a concentrated strategy – one aiming to reach 'more people' and the other to influence 'important people' (Anderson and Olson, 2003). In practice the two strategies are often combined, with public campaigning and awareness raising being pursued alongside concerted lobbying of particular decision makers or institutions. For example, NGOs have been extremely vocal lobbyists and campaigners on the question of diamonds from war zones. They have been strong proponents (and critics) of the Kimberley process, which aims to bring greater controls on an extremely untransparent and unregulated diamond industry. This has involved a combination of public awareness raising and behind the scenes lobbying of the likes of De Beers and governments in the North and South. Particularly for those attempting to bring war to an end, advocacy and influencing necessarily involves dealing with the 'unlike-minded', in other words the 'spoilers' who may have little or no interest in peace. Different strategies may be required for different categories of spoilers – for instance, coercive measures may be

A man walks through the streets of Monrovia, Liberia, listening to radio reports of a ceasefire signed earlier that day.

the only option for 'extreme spoilers', whereas a combination of material and political co-option or benign neglect may be appropriate for others.

Attempting to co-opt rebel leader Foday Sankoh in Sierra Leone by including him in the government (and giving him virtual control of the diamond mines) clearly failed. But perhaps General Dostam, the Uzbek warlord of northern Afghanistan, can be co-opted politically into the new government with the right combination of (dis)incentives.

It is not only about advocacy once the war has started. NGOs may play a vital role in preventative humanitarian advocacy by warning of impeding crises. This is a risky form of intervention as it involves putting your credibility and reputation on the line. For example, a Disasters Emergency Committee (DEC) report found that aid agencies had overstated the magnitude of the food crisis in southern Africa in 2002 (VALID, 2003). This inevitably leads to questions about the motives for raising the alarm – do the 'hard' organisational interests of funding and profile have precedence over the 'soft' interests of mandate and the 'person in need'? As Alan Whaites (2000, p. 51) argues, a fundamental obligation of due diligence is owed by every humanitarian worker to the people they aim to assist. Credibility may be risked strategically but not negligently.

Combining advocacy with operationality is clearly difficult and often risky. There is a danger that by trying to be all things to all people you do nothing very well. Multi-mandate agencies have the potential to build synergies between their projects and their policy and advocacy work. But there is also a case for thinking carefully about the optimum division of labour and where you can best 'add value' to the overall response. Niche, 'off-site' campaigning NGOs such as Human Rights Watch or Global Witness may be much better positioned to lead on certain high profile advocacy interventions than generalist, operational agencies.

> ## Intervention implication
>
>
>
> Media and advocacy are important. Use local media, especially radio, to support peacebuilding and explain your role. Use media and advocacy to change policy and to warn of potential problems. Where there is a need to protect local operational staff, channel information through media at home or through independent campaigning NGOs.

12.3 Organisational challenges

Organisational questions have been a blind spot in the literature on war and intervention. Research has tended to focus on what aid agencies actually do and much less has been written about the internal workings of such agencies. The organisation is treated as a 'black box'. Yet institutional performance is often one of the main determinants of success. Practitioners work within organisations that can provide either an enabling or disabling environment for working 'in' or 'on' war. Can one identify certain generic factors – these might be termed 'peaceabilities' – which enable organisations to remain effective in conflictual environments? This is a huge area of study that has yet to be fully explored and a thorough examination is beyond the scope of this chapter. However, several key points can highlighted.

12.3.1 'Hearts and minds'

Successful organisations appear to have developed the right combination of 'heart' and 'mind'. By 'heart' we mean having a clear normative and ethical position and being able to communicate it clearly. By 'mind' we mean having the intelligence to analyse and learn from situations, to know one's own capacity and how to deploy that capacity to good effect.

Aid agencies are made up of people with strong personalities and egos and different backgrounds and world views. As a result aid organisations often have strong fragmentary tendencies and competing subcultures. When harnessed around a common vision, set of values and ethical framework, this dissonance can be a positive thing which keeps the organisation alive to alternative views and different possibilities. If just left to itself, these competing tendencies – say between a relief department and country desk or between the operations and marketing sections – may become dysfunctional and destructive. Successful organisations are 'self conscious' organisations that continually invest in and keep 'alive' common values, principles and ethical frameworks. ADA in Afghanistan, for instance, made a point of holding regular reflection workshops with field and head office staff to ensure that common goals and approaches were maintained. Although in some ways quite intangible, having a clear mission and set of values appears to be extremely important for the morale of staff working in challenging circumstances. After Rwanda this was recognised more explicitly by aid agencies and some have invested in the development of ethical frameworks to help guide agency decision making (Slim, 1997). As noted in Chapter 1, there has been a shift from absolute morality and duty-based ethics – in which merely attempting to 'do good' is enough – to utilitarian or consequentialist ethics – in which one must be held accountable for the consequences of one's actions. Such frameworks may go some way towards helping agencies negotiate the dilemmas of intervention and to an extent insulate themselves from political pressures that come with a blurring of the lines between humanitarian and non-humanitarian actors.

As well as having political and moral sensibilities, successful organisations have highly developed 'minds'. They stress the importance of learning by embracing error and developing feedback loops between field realities, practice and policy. They tend to be flat and responsive and place a premium on listening and participation. As already mentioned, in war situations many of these basic precepts of good development practice often 'go out of the window'. Finally, effective organisations tend to value and hold on to their staff. Rather than rotate them from one context to another every six months, they nurture expertise and invest in internal capacity building. As highlighted earlier, good conflict analysis depends on strong regional experience and expertise – this can only be developed by encouraging country or regional specialisation rather than rotating people from one emergency to the next. As Hugo Slim (1996) notes: 'Today's international relief professional is like the multinational executive who feels able to operate in any part of the world because she knows the way the firm works. However, she seldom knows how the country works'. Promoting national staff to positions of seniority would partly address the problem of shallow knowledge. But in many cases a 'glass ceiling' still appears to exist for nationals within international agencies.

12.3.2 Management and control

During the 1990s many humanitarian, development and peacebuilding organisations began processes of internal reform in recognition of the new challenges presented by contemporary wars. A number of initiatives focused on putting the humanitarian house in order. These included: a 10 point Code of Conduct, a Humanitarian Charter, the SPHERE Minimum Standards in Disaster Response and the Humanitarian Accountability Project. These are essentially concerned with reaffirming the humanitarian ethic and, as Slim (2002) argues, have come to operate as a 'soft law' in the NGO community. Whether such initiatives are a positive development has been debated – some argue that their 'back to basics' approach represents a new 'humanitarian fundamentalism' which is likely to stifle creativity and innovation within the humanitarian sector – but it appears that in practice the codes themselves have only been embraced lightly.

Another set of institutional reforms, introduced across the board, has been results-based management. Almost all aid agencies now employ log-frame analysis (LFA) and strategic planning techniques. The growth of managerialism has induced what Smillie (1998) refers to as the 'crisis of conformity' as aid agencies increasingly become more like one another under donor pressure to conform to reporting and accountability standards. Somewhat ironically, as the operating climate becomes increasingly messy and conflict ridden, aid agencies and donors seek security in mirror image by going to great lengths to codify, quantify and plan what is going to happen in the field (Edwards, 1999, p. 206). This in many respects is an understandable reflex – it is an attempt to create certainty in a climate of uncertainty. But this is unlikely to be an effective organisational solution to the problems posed by chronic insecurity. Consider how organisations and institutions best function in areas of war, taking for instance a guerrilla organisation – it is less likely to be a formal, rule-bound entity than a 'virtual' organisation or loose network lacking a clear hierarchy with the ability to mutate and constantly adapt to changing conditions. It is likely to be composed of small teams of individuals who are highly motivated, have a clear sense of mission, considerable room for manoeuvre and place a high value on local knowledge and intelligence. While not arguing that aid agencies should model themselves on guerrilla movements, they could perhaps learn to become more 'guerrilla like' by becoming more decentralised, flexible and responsive. Though such organisations have been called 'ad hocracies' or chaordic organisations, they are not chaotic messes – they combine order with disorder, having clear values, strategies and principles combined with free-flowing and decentralised structures and decision-making processes.

Clearly there is no uniquely best solution to the question of organisational design – what is appropriate for a relief agency is likely to be different for a conflict transformation organisation or a military peacekeeping force. But all need to consider the relative focus and organisational energies devoted to controlling, influencing and understanding. Too much organisational introspection with a focus on 'control' can be counterproductive. There is a need to get rid of the illusion of control since external control can never create certainty of outcomes – the greater the level of uncertainty the greater the desirability of having the largest possible number of options available (Porter et al., 1991. This takes us back to the idea of a pluralist approach towards organisations as well as towards individual practice. The practitioner needs to think carefully about the best organisational fit for each individual context and the task in hand.

12.3.3 The human factor

As argued at the beginning, individuals do make a difference. The same aid agencies can vary radically from country to country according to the quality and experience of their staff. This is a sign of a bad organisation in the sense that those lacking proper systems and structures become completely dependent on the qualities of the individuals concerned. However, there is no getting away from the fact that individuals do stamp their personalities on organisations and for the practitioner it is often as much about developing relationships with individuals as with organisations. The leaders of aid agencies may have a profound impact upon their own organisation and the wider environment. If you want to understand why aid agencies do what they do and if you want to get things done then you have to understand the individuals concerned.

12.4 Relationship-building challenges

Working effectively in and on war therefore involves *doing* things differently and *organising* differently. It also involves *relating* differently. Contemporary wars, as Mark Duffield (2001) notes, are 'networked' wars involving multiple actors in polyarchical and mutating relationships. The international response to war is similarly complex, involving a web of subcontracting arrangements between state and non-state, military and civilian, commercial and voluntary organisations.

Building the right kinds of relationship with the right kinds of people can literally be a matter of life and death. Working in war zones involves building up structured and ad hoc patterns of alliance and cooperation. This requires networking, negotiation and brokering skills. Good practitioners tend to be excellent networkers – they know the right people. This does not only mean 'people in high places' – it also involves keeping your feet on the ground by developing relationships with community members – the decision takers as well as the decision makers.

Good relationships are vital for a range of reasons: the quality of your analysis; your accountability and legitimacy as an external agent in someone else's war; your personal and organisational security; your access to primary stakeholders; the overall impact of your interventions. All of these are to varying degrees dependent on the quality of your interorganisational and interpersonal relationships.

Unfortunately the aid system often creates perverse incentives which prevent aid agencies from developing strong linkages. Firstly, funding processes tend to encourage interagency competition rather than collaboration and sharing. Secondly, the reward systems within aid agencies are such that there is a tendency to worship internal audiences – practitioners' energies are focused inwards at 'feeding the beast' of head office with log frames, reports, appraisals and evaluations. Careers are built more by keeping head office happy than by developing strong relationships with people in the field. Though these are not mutually exclusive, the balance in my view has shifted too far towards the internal rather than the external environment. One of the costs of the focus in recent years on professionalisation and standards has been the lack of time devoted to relationship building in the field.

> **Intervention implication**

Centralisation, ever more complex management systems and a stress on head office and organisational goals can make aid agencies less well suited for peacebuilding. Increasingly the focus is on a managerial approach, with people moving posts frequently and limitation on promotion of national staff. But conflict analysis requires staff with local experience and expertise. Local offices need to be loose and flexible so they can respond quickly to opportunities, rather than tightly controlled from the centre. Staff need to feel more responsibility to the war-affected country than to the agency head office.

Practitioners working in war zones operate in a crowded field, organisationally speaking. They interact with multiple organisations and forge different types of working relationships, characterised by varying degrees of coordination, collaboration, competition and sometimes confrontation. It is not possible to map out and analyse each category of relationships here, so we have picked out three for illustrative purposes.

First, one of the principal differences between working in war zones and working in development settings is the imperative to work with the 'unlike-minded'. For instance, it is simply not possible for an agency to function in Nepal or Sri Lanka without talking to the Maoists or the LTTE (Liberation Tigers of Tamil Eelman) respectively. In Afghanistan in the 1980s just to move from one part of the country to another involved negotiating safe passage with a chain of different commanders. It is a fine balance between talking to rebel groups (or rogue governments) without legitimising or being co-opted by them. Attempts by aid agencies to establish a 'framework of respect' with warring groups were mentioned earlier. These can play a role in protecting humanitarian space, but how they play out on the ground depends in large part on the careful humanitarian diplomacy of field workers.

Second, a defining characteristic of the international response to war at the turn of the century has been the growing relationship between aid actors and the military. Some see this as a logical and positive development involving the pooling of comparative advantages, leading to better protection and the delivery of aid. Others worry about the blurring of the lines between the military/political and the humanitarian – referred to by Duffield (2001) as the securitisation of aid. In Afghanistan and Iraq there are concerns that the traditional distinctions between the two have been strained to breaking point. To an extent these issues and questions are beyond the influence of the individual practitioner. But whether you are from the aid or the military side of the equation it is clearly important to be aware of the concerns of the other side and to look for ways of creating room for manoeuvre. So in Afghanistan the debate on Provincial Reconstruction Teams (PRTs), became in my view an unnecessarily polarised one between the humanitarians and the military. In practice there was a great deal of variation between the different PRTs and how they were implemented in different parts of the country. Some, such as the Mazar PRT, had involved a much clearer distinction between the role of the military and aid agencies than others (Box 12.6). This takes us back to the need to think carefully about each individual context and how to respond to individual actors rather than blanket categories.

Box 12.6   Responding to insecurity: Mazar PRT and the Security Committee for the North

There has been a long and complex history of intergroup politico-military competition in the north of Afghanistan. In 2004 the principal combatants were the militias of General Abdul Rashid Dostum and General Atta Muhammad. Although sometimes portrayed as ethnic or ideological, sporadic outbreaks of fighting often involve struggles for control of economic resources such as Kud-o-Barq fertiliser factory and power plant, lucrative opium trafficking routes and customs posts. There had previously been no mechanism in place to arbitrate disputes between the leadership of the militias. In 2002 discussions were held between UNAMA, the police and factions, leading to the establishment of the Security Committee for the North. This body subsequently played an arbitration role, responding to outbreaks of violence by bringing together faction leaders to broker agreements. While the Committee was relatively successful as a responsive mechanism for de-escalating inter-factional violence, it lacked the capacity to monitor and enforce agreements.

The initiation of the Mazar PRT complemented and built upon existing security arrangements. For instance, conflict escalation in October 2004 between Dostum and Atta led to a quick joint response from the Security Committee and PRT. In the end, high-level negotiations involving UNAMA, Jalali, the Minster of the Interior, the UK Ambassador and Colonel Dickie Davis, Commander of PRT, were able to defuse the conflict. Continued pressure induced the protagonists to agree to give up their heavy weapons and begin a demobilisation, disarmament and reintegration (DDR) process. This was seen as an opportunity to neutralise the factions.

The PRT has adopted a low-key, low-profile approach with a primary, though not exclusive, focus on security. Its success was based upon foundations of strong political analysis and a long-term strategic approach. It maintained a light presence, with roughly 90 troops patrolling an area the size of Scotland. The strategy was to negotiate with the factions rather than act as a combat force. As one long-term aid worker commented: 'The mere sight of uniforms helps provide security.' The ultimate goal is to create a stable environment which will attract further funding into the region, creating a virtuous spiral of increased security leading to more reconstruction, and consequently to growing confidence in the government and the wider peace process.

A small amount of British global conflict prevention pool (GCPP) funds was used on police uniforms, materials and equipment. But it was planned to scale up the reconstruction component of the GCPP. A possible GCPP project, for example, was to renovate all the police stations for the north. A DFID PRT adviser and a USAID official were 'embedded' within PRT, and were tasked with identifying reconstruction projects that would help consolidate the peace process. (Goodhand and Bergne, 2004)

Third, the key issue for Western aid agencies, particularly after Iraq and Afghanistan, is how they relate to their governments. While aid has always been politicised, some argue that Afghanistan and Iraq represent a steep change in this respect. Within the war on terror there is a strong tendency to distort humanitarianism towards Western security concerns. It is perhaps too early to assess whether Iraq is part of a trend or whether it is an extreme case and unrepresentative of the kinds of challenges practitioners will face in the future. However, one can be fairly confident that practitioners will continue to face external pressures from political actors and this will affect their relationships with local partners and with the 'unlike-minded'. The space for independent action, particularly in high-profile emergencies, is likely to get smaller. Practitioners may need to reassess how they manage and prioritise their multiple relationships. Perhaps the war on terror is a 'wake up' call for many aid agencies who, because they are too close to the powerful, have lost their room for independent action. Learning to say no to official donors (at the cost of staying small) and strengthening relationships with local partners, may be one way to create room for manoeuvre and revitalise flagging legitimacy.

12.5 How well am I doing?

12.5.1 Evaluating impacts

How do you measure success? What criteria do you use? 'Success' depends partly on how high you raise the bar. For instance, is an intervention 'successful' if it leads to an end to fighting? Or is success dependent on the holding of elections and establishing accountable democratic institutions? As this example demonstrates, it also depends on when you measure it – for instance, what appears to be a successful peace settlement now may look like a failure five years down the line if it leads to renewed fighting. There are also problems related to attribution. As mentioned at the beginning of this chapter, we are not dealing with linear cause–effect chains – processes of change are complex, unpredictable and contingent. The further one goes down the impact chain the more difficult it becomes to attribute impacts. For example how do you know whether 'behind the scenes' track two diplomacy is having any effect on peace 'writ large'? Do small-scale community reconciliation programmes have a cumulative impact at a societal level?

To an extent the monitoring and evaluation and impact assessment tools of development practitioners are much further advanced than those of their peacebuilding/conflict-transformation counterparts. It is only relatively recently that practitioners and academics have started to examine the impact of aid on war and on peacebuilding processes. However, there is a range of tools for examining how well you are doing in relation to war and peacebuilding which have already been mentioned: do no harm framework, peace and conflict impact assessment (PCIA) and benefit–harm analysis. Practitioners use and adapt a range of tools and frameworks according to the context and their particular needs. Usually it is possible to boil things down to a few key principles and questions (Box 12.7).

Box 12.7   Peace and conflict impact assessment in the Wanni, northern Sri Lanka

One might speculate that NGOs are in a number of minor ways either fuelling or prolonging conflict in the Wanni, including:

- relief distributions that cause tensions between the displaced and resident communities
- relief activities that may cut against the grain of existing social structures and undermine coping strategies
- siting of wells which cause intercaste, religious or gender conflict
- sending pro-war ethical messages by collaborating too closely with the LTTE
- repairing roads which might be used for military purposes
- providing resources which, somewhere down the chain, are tapped into by the LTTE (this seems to be partially unavoidable given the taxation system, but does not appear to happen on a significant scale)
- NGO programmes, by mitigating the impact of the war, may also be prolonging it – if people were 'hurting more' there might be more of an impetus to end the war. This is a difficult argument to sustain in the north, since the LTTE do not appear to be at all susceptible to pressure from civil society
- capacity building with NGOs that are closely aligned to the LTTE.

Given the constraints on NGOs in the Wanni, the holding operation scenario is probably the best that NGOs can achieve. It is a case of minimising incidents where aid fuels underlying tensions, and looking for spaces and opportunities to build peace when they present themselves. Most of the time, however, the focus is on supporting existing capacities and structures, protecting civic leadership and playing a bridging role with organisations in the south. Peacebuilding in these terms is not about having a separate programme, focusing for example on education or mediation. It is more about using a peace and war lens to look at ongoing work and programmes. What tends to happen in practice is that NGOs' preoccupation with humanitarian mandates and access causes questions about peace and war to get elbowed out of the analysis. The 'listening to the returned and displaced' campaign was a timely reminder that peace is very much on the minds of ordinary people.

A starting point for introducing a 'peacebuilding lens' might be a series of questions used by staff to appraise or evaluate programmes. For example:

- Do we have an analysis of the sources of tension and conflict in the area?
- Do we have an understanding of the current dynamics and phases of the war?
- Which people/groups are gaining and which people/groups are losing as a result of the war?

- What is the likely impact of the project on underlying conflicts?
- Is the project likely to improve relationships between different groups in the area?
- How can we assess the impact of the project on social relations between different groups?
- Who is likely to gain and who is likely to lose as a result of the project?
- To what extent are people involved and likely to have a sense of ownership over the project?
- How is the project likely to increase people's capacity to make decisions and resolve disputes in an inclusive way?

To an extent these questions represent nothing more than good development practice, allied to a more nuanced understanding of peace and war issues.

12.5.2 Peace auditing

An avenue that could perhaps be further explored is the development of 'peace auditing' methodologies to assess the capacities or 'peace-abilities' of organisations to work effectively in or on war. A peace audit like the 'social audit' would involve multiple stakeholders setting the criteria and then helping assess the agency in relation to these criteria. The framework could be structured as follows around 'doing', 'organising' and 'relating' – the questions are illustrative rather than exhaustive:

Programming

What is the programming mix and how has it adapted to the changing context? To what extent are strategies focused towards working 'in' or 'on' war? What are the ways of working – direct intervention, capacity building or advocacy – and how do they relate to one another? Which types of activities at which time and in which particular context have had positive or negative impacts? How have interventions affected the political, moral and emotional economies of war?

Organisation

What is the organisation's understanding of peace and how does this compare with primary stakeholders' perceptions? Does it hold and operationalise a concept of neutrality, impartiality or solidarity? Does the organisation have an ethical position or 'organisational conscience'? Do staff receive training in conflict analysis and peacebuilding approaches? To what extent is conflict analysis fed into ongoing programming? Are their flexible systems in place to facilitate learning from the field?

Relationships and linkages

What is the nature and quality of linkages with key stakeholders? How are organisational identity and values explained and transmitted to stakeholders? How does the organisation position itself in relation to its various constituencies? How are conflicting pressures and demands managed? How reactive or proactive is the organisation in influencing key stakeholders?

12.6 Conclusion

In this chapter we have outlined some of the challenges faced by practitioners working in war zones. In a sense it is as difficult to write generically about 'practitioners' as it is to write about 'war' – given the range of different actors, working for different types of organisations in different kinds of contexts. Each has their own unique sets of challenges and ways of responding to them. As emphasised at the beginning, there can be no such thing as 'best practice' because of the variegated nature of the context and the differing objectives of the interveners. However, we have attempted to identify some common sets of questions and dilemmas faced by practitioners working 'in' or 'on' war whether they are operating at the 'coal face' or sitting in head office.

The previous chapter examined the challenge of improving analysis, arguing that this must be the precondition for 'smarter' and more effective interventions. This chapter explored the challenge of intervening, focusing initially on what one actually does and then looking at the implications for how one organises and how one relates to others. An underlying theme of both chapters has been that better practice is likely to be based on a strong foundation of reflection and action – in other words moving towards Chambers' (1997) ideal type of the 'scholar–practitioner'.

As other writers in this book have emphasised, violent conflict is less about breakdown than about reordering and transformation. This observation might be applied not only to the societies and polities in which wars take place but also to the international organisations that respond to them. Contemporary wars have exposed profound weaknesses in the way international agencies conceptualise and respond, which in turn has led to a process of 'reordering' within the international response system.

For analytical purposes, three broad categories of response can be identified: leaving things as they are (Loyalty), modifying the existing approach (Voice) or rejecting the orthodox approach and proposing an alternative (Exit). This terminology is drawn from Albert Hirschmann's (1970) famous essay, *Exit, Voice, Loyalty*.

- *Loyalty*: This involves keeping quiet and getting on with your job. In other words, continue with 'business as usual'. Many practitioners (perhaps the majority) take this position, believing that they can do little to change the wider institutional environment and so just concentrate on doing their job to the best of their ability. While there may be a case sometimes for just keeping your head down and getting on with the job, we have argued that improvements are required and they are not going to happen by adopting a 'loyalty' position.

- *Voice*: This represents an attempt to modify the way things are. It involves a mixture of pragmatism and idealism – it is about recognising the wider political and institutional constraints but trying to create 'room for manoeuvre' to generate positive changes. This is a pluralist position in that it is about widening the range of choices open to practitioners. It is also basically a reformist position and a range of current initiatives fall into this category, from SPHERE to the Code of Conduct to more ambitious plans at institutional reform of the UN. Some would argue that the aid system has become adept at absorbing its critiques and blithely carrying on as before. Certainly many of the attempts to improve the way we do business have been little more than window dressing.

- *Exit*: This involves rejecting the current orthodoxy. Many feel a deep sense of unease about international interventions in Afghanistan and Iraq and their implications for independent humanitarian intervention. The room for manoeuvre appears to be shrinking. Some aid agencies have taken the 'exit' option in the past – for instance MSF's withdrawal from Rwanda and others who have refused to get involved in Iraq. Those choosing 'exit' feel that the only way to get meaningful change is through working outside the system, by metaphorically or literally taking to the barricades!

These are ideal type categories and in the real world it is much greyer than this typology indicates. For a practitioner any one of these responses may be appropriate at a certain time in a certain context. But overall we have argued in this chapter that existing practice needs to change and this is unlikely to happen if one adopts a 'loyalty' position. 'Voice' and 'exit' offer the best hopes for rethinking how we respond to war and, perhaps more importantly, why we respond.

12.7 Chapter summary

Interveners need to adopt a **peacebuilding lens**; working around war or being 'conflict blind' does not work. Working in war means a mix of '**do no harm**' – minimising negative impacts of intervention – and '**conflict-proofing**' an agency's operations – reducing the level of risk and deciding on when the risks are too great and the agency should withdraw. Practitioners need the skills to analyse risk and possible harm and benefit; they also need to work out who gains and who loses from their actions. **Development assistance** can have more peacebuilding potential, but it can also do harm. Donors can impose **conditions** but need to analyse the possible positive and negative impacts of them. **Continuing** with the same policies is not neutral and must always be analysed. **Do nothing** must always be an option.

Working on war, or peacebuilding, can do both more good and more harm, and demands greater commitment and analysis; many agencies have **inappropriate management** systems for peacebuilding and there is a need for the right balance of **heart and mind**. Peacebuilding requires doing things differently – **organising differently** and relating differently to people in war zones. **Timing** and the proper **mix** in the programme, **knowledge**, **flexibility** and **networking** are essential. Peacebuilding requires **support for local actors** as well as **advocacy** and work with local and international **media**. **Clear goals** and regular **impact assessment** are imperative.

References

Anderson, M. B. and Olson, L. (2003) *Confronting War: Critical Lessons for Peace Practitioners*, Cambridge MA, The Collaborative for Development Action, Inc. http://www.cdainc.com/rpp/publications/confrontingwar/ ConfrontingWar.pdf (accessed July 2005).

Boyce, J. (2000) 'Beyond good intentions: external assistance and peacebuilding', pp. 367–82 in Forman, S. and Patrick, S. *Pledges of Aid for Post-Conflict Recovery*, Boulder CO, Lynne Rienner.

Boyce, J. (2002) 'Investing in peace: aid and conditionality after civil wars', Adelphi Paper 351.

Chambers, R. (1997) '*Whose Reality Counts? Putting the First Last*', London, Intermediate Technology Publications.

Cliffe, L. and Luckham, R. (1999) 'Complex political emergencies and the state: failure and the fate of the state', *Third World Quarterly*, vol. 20, no. 1, pp. 51–68.

Duffield, M. (2001) *Global Governance and the New Wars: the Merging of Development and Security* London: Zed Books.

Edwards, M. (1999) *Further Positive: International Co-operation in the 21st Century*, London, Earthscan.

Fox, A. (2003) 'Advocacy research and the World Bank: propositions for discussion', *Development in Practice*, vol. 13, no. 5, pp. 519–26.

Goodhand, J. (2002) 'Aiding violence or building peace? The role of international aid in Afghanistan', *Third World Quarterly*, vol. 23, no. 5, pp. 837–59.

Goodhand, J. and Bergne, P. (2004) 'Evaluation of the UK Government Conflict Prevention Pools: Afghanistan case study', Country Case Study 2, Bradford University/Channel Consultants, June.

Hirschmann, A. O. (1970) *Exit, Voice, and Loyalty: Responses to Decline in Firms, Organizations and States*, Cambridge MA, Harvard University Press.

Macrae, J. (2001) *Aiding Recovery. The Crisis of Aid in Chronic Political Emergencies*, London, Zed Books.

Moore, M. and Putzel, J. (1999) 'Politics and poverty: a background paper for the World Development Report 2000/1', Brighton, UK, IDS, University of Sussex.

Ottaway, M. (2002) 'Rebuilding state institutions in collapsed states', *Development and Change*, vol. 33, no. 5, pp. 1001–23.

Porter, D. Allen, B. and Thompson, G. (1991) *Development in Practice: Paved with Good Intentions*, London, Routledge.

Richards, P (1996) *Fighting for the Rain Forest: War, Youth & Resources in Sierra Leone*, Oxford, James Currey.

Roche, C. (1996) 'Operationality in turbulence: the need for change', *Development in Practice*, vol. 4, no. 3, pp. 15–25.

Slim, H. (1996) 'The continuing metamorphosis of the humanitarian practitioner: some new colours for an endangered chameleon', *Disasters*, vol. 19, no. 2.

Slim, H. (1997) 'Doing the right thing: relief agencies, moral dilemmas and moral responsibility in political emergencies and war', *Studies on Emergencies and Disaster Relief*, No. 6, Uppsala.

Slim, H. (2002) 'Claiming a humanitarian imperative: NGOs and the cultivation of humanitarian duty', paper presented at the Seventh Annual Conference of Webster University on Humanitarian Values for the Twenty-First Century, Geneva 21–22 February, 2002.

Smillie, I. (1998) 'Relief and development: the struggle for synergy', Occasional Paper No. 33, Watson Institute, USA.

Stedman, S. (2001) 'Implementing Peace Agreements in Civil Wars. Lessons and Recommendations for Policy Makers', New York, IPA Policy Paper Series on Peace Implementation.

Stewart, F. and Fitzgerald, V. (2000) *War and Underdevelopment*, Vol. 1 *The Economic and Social Consequences of Conflict*, Oxford, Oxford University Press.

Uvin, P. (1998) *Aiding Violence: The Development Enterprise in Rwanda*, West Hartford, CT, Kumarian Press.

VALID (2003) 'A stitch in time? An independent evaluation of the Disasters Emergency Committee Southern Africa crisis appeal July 2002–June 2003', www.dec.org.uk/uploads/documents/ A_Stitch_in_Time_v103_Executive_Summary.pdf (accessed November 2004).

Vaux, T. and Goodhand, J. (2001) *Disturbing Connections: Aid and Conflict in Kyrgyzstan*, Conflict Assessments 3, Centre for Defence Studies, Kings College London, July.

de Waal, A. (1997) *Famine Crimes: Politics and the Disaster Relief Industry*, London, James Currey.

Whaites, A. (2000) 'NGOs, disasters and advocacy: caught between the Prophet and the Shepherd Boy', *Development in Practice*, vol. 10, nos. 3-4, pp. 506–16.

White, P. and Cliffe, C. (2000) 'Matching response to context in complex political emergencies: relief, development, peacebuilding or something in-between?', *Disasters*, vol. 24, no. 4, pp. 314–42.

Conclusion: understanding as a guide to action

Joseph Hanlon and Helen Yanacopulos

Trusted outsiders play a special role in ending civil wars and in peacebuilding. When people who live together start to kill each other, the 'security dilemma' is real – can you afford to trust someone who might use the space to take advantage and even try again to kill you? Often it is only trusted outsiders, who do not have a vested interest in the civil war, who can secure the peace and begin a truly fair and balanced peacebuilding process. Outsiders do not need to be foreigners, the local Red Cross, or local religious leaders (in wars where faith was not a factor), and local peace and development groups can all play a role. But most civil wars are in poor countries, so external resources are often needed, and foreigners are often deemed to be more independent. UN troops and police in their traditional blue hats or European or African Union peace forces are often essential in the trust-building process. A host of UN and bilateral agencies and NGOs are needed to support reconstruction – both physical and social.

But the burden on outsiders is heavy. As we have seen in this book, it is all too easy to make matters much worse. Outsiders may be independent and not have a vested interest (or they may), but they may not fully understand the war. It is easy to make a misstep, and charging in with nothing more than a desire to help can be catastrophic. In this book we picked up a UNDP slogan: 'Don't just do something, stand there.' This is not, as Mary Anderson stresses, a command to do nothing; rather it is an injunction to look before you leap, and not to assume you know what the problem is simply because you have worked in other wars. Because the other key point of this book is that every war is different, often fundamentally so. This leads, almost directly, to the third theme of this book: there are no right answers, only better or worse ones.

Not acting is not a choice, but acting incorrectly can be costly. Mistakes can be reduced only through analysis and understanding, which often runs in parallel with action as interveners try to correct mistakes on the fly. This book aims to provide some of the tools and ways of thinking that can be used by ordinary interveners caught up in real wars. And it is based on peeling away the superficial and simplistic interpretations that are given to wars both by outsiders and insiders. It is about listening creatively and looking sceptically at the received wisdom; donor misperceptions about Rwanda, for example, provide a salutary lesson. Perhaps the key reason to look back at the real roots of a war is that we cannot go back to the *status quo anti* – precisely because that caused the war. But we must understand the relations of power and access to resources that underlay the war because outside interveners need to support a change in those relations as part of building a new and more equitable social contract.

The Tree of Life, Mozambique is a product of the Transforming Arms into Tools project, supported by Christian Aid, and is made from decommissioned weapons.

Thus the first step is to go behind the simplistic explanations, often given by participants and media alike, about age-old hatreds or greedy warlords. This first step is to peel away the identities which people took on during the war and the corrupting influences of the war itself. In order to effectively fight a civil war, the sides have to develop clear identities to organise around – these are often language, ethnicity or religion. It is necessary to keep in mind that the war itself will have strengthened those identities and the antagonisms towards competing identities because each group will, inevitably, have committed atrocities against the other group. Interveners need to remember that the vast majority of identity groups do not go to war against each other, and that the groups in the civil war previously lived side by side in peace. Similarly, leaders who are now seen as corrupt warlords often did not start out that way. Resources such as diamonds or oil were necessary to fund the war, but the war itself has a corrupting influence on leaders who find they have unlimited access to funds and on followers who must steal and kill to survive. Thus the first step of peacebuilding is often to unpick the distortions caused by the war itself – to ensure that the two sides feel secure and that they do not need to fear the other side, to ensure that ordinary people can survive without murder and mayhem, and to undercut the power and wealth of unrepresentative leaders and allow space for alternatives.

But as the first half of this book showed, people do not go to war simply because they are misled or because of battles which took place centuries ago. They go to war because they can see no other way to redress underlying inequalities in power, rights, income and access to resources. At the extreme end of the spectrum, most readers will understand and accept the motivations of those who fought against colonialism and against dictatorships, such as the black majority fighting against the white minority 'apartheid' state in South Africa in the 1970s and 1980s. Other civil wars may seem less obviously justified to outsiders.

So the next step is to look at those inequalities which underlay the war and which seem impossible to resolve. Addison and Murshed in Chapter 6 discussed horizontal or group inequalities, which provide a useful framework to think about the explanations set out earlier in the book. Everyone is a member of multiple groups defined by age, gender, class, ethnicity, language, occupation, location, and so on. Judy El-Bushra looks at issues of power and the various and subtle ways in which power is manifested. She returns to the original definition of patriarchy, which is the way some older men have power both over women and over younger men. That is particularly important because it is mostly young men who fight wars; sometimes they are fighting for their elders, but increasingly they are fighting against them. Supporting positive changes to the power relations that caused the war is one of the key roles of outside interveners. But this is far from easy – clearly, people who hold power over others are reluctant to give up that power, even if it was the cause of the war. Here the distinctions of kinds of power becomes important – simple power over other people needs to be replaced, at least in part, by a power to build a better future. After the horrors of a civil war, people are looking for an alternative vision of the future. Outside interveners are particularly important in making this a more inclusive vision, in part because they have a certain distance which gives them some perspective that allows them in subtle ways to bring in new actors and new ideas. This is development as peacebuilding.

But outside interveners also represent an alternative power structure; their wealth and standing in the postwar period gives them immense power over central and local government and over the projects they support. The conditions they impose, the changes they demand, and most importantly the choices over whom to support and whom to reject mean that outsiders play a key role in shaping the postwar period. At its best, previously disadvantaged groups, including youth, women, marginalised regions and so on, are able to bypass the old power structures which caused the war. At its best, this can be genuinely empowering and can lead over several years to the negotiation of a new social contract which is more inclusive. At its worst it can lead to the promotion of old leaders who were partly the cause of the war, or precisely the opposite, the disempowering of traditional institutions which still have some status and legitimacy. As Judy El-Bushra notes, there is a real danger, for example, that simply empowering women leaves young men feeling even more marginalised. The use by outsiders of their power is one of those places where 'Don't just do something, stand there' becomes a key warning. Outsiders are under pressure to move quickly, both from the obvious internal needs and from their own headquarters which have agendas and priorities and a critical need to see results before the next funding cycle.

But rushing in to fund a target group because head office needs a project on the ground in the next six weeks, as often happens, can create waves which spread for years rather than weeks. Doing nothing is rarely the right choice, but thinking about 'do no harm' is essential – no decision should be taken without first asking: 'Who will be harmed? Who will be disadvantaged? Who will not be helped?' It is too easy to say 'Oh, we are only helping the poorest of the poor' or 'We are only making essential changes in the ministry to make it more efficient'. But outside agencies have huge impacts and make immense social and institutional changes; making a ministry more efficient disadvantages a lot of people and if they have been given jobs as an implicit part of a peace settlement, the impact could be grave. This leads directly to Jonathan Goodhand's division of working around, in and on war – which applies equally well to postwar peacebuilding. Not looking at the ripples that spread from any action is a classic part of working around war; working on war means trying to ensure that the ripples have a positive effect and that negative effects are mitigated – or where negative effects are large, rethinking the whole intervention to make it more transformative for everyone. In part, this is a function of listening to people about their real priorities.

Of course there is anger and bitterness about what the other side did in the war, and demands for justice and retribution, but beyond that priorities are usually developmental, about creating jobs and wells and school places, and especially about access to the often small amounts of money needed by people to rebuild their lives and livelihoods. Here, imagination is required – how to bend agency priorities to meet people's felt needs and how to respond to people's felt needs in ways that are peacebuilding and transformational. That is working *on* war.

The power of outsider interveners postwar is an important reminder of the role of outsiders in the war itself. Oil, diamonds, drugs and other resources help to fuel the wars. Neighbours, regional powers, and former Cold War and colonial powers continue to play a role. And globalisation, international financial institutions and trade also have a role. At one level it means that outside interveners need to act at an entirely different level, outside the postwar country itself. That can mean international campaigns for transparency in oil and diamond trading, to reduce the funding that fuels the war. It can mean pressure on the United Nations, regional bodies and individual governments (from both inside and out) to try to stop particular countries from intervening in ways which make things worse – both physical interventions and the support of compliant dictators. Support for human rights can play a key role because it makes it harder for parts of the international community to support oppressive governments – precisely those governments which in the past have collapsed into civil war. The role of the international financial institutions remains intensely debated, but too often they still seem to be working around war; changing this requires pressure in Washington on the institutions themselves, and pressure on the big powers with controlling votes to try to force changes in those policies.

Fair trade could play an important role because of the economic squeezes caused by globalisation; we have seen how falling coffee and cocoa prices were roots of wars, while pressure on land caused by the demand for exports has played a role elsewhere. Of course there is a necessary division of labour; it is difficult for people on the ground in a postwar country to lobby the UN or the IMF directly. But it is important to understand the global links and to support the campaigning being done internationally, with information, by joining campaign coalitions, and for the organisations which are intervening to understand the importance of campaigns to the peacebuilding mission.

As we saw in Chapter 5, the colonial and Cold War heritages have played a key role in creating the roots of war. Interveners need to understand the way colonists and 'Cold Warriors' radically changed social relations within countries. Frequently, they gave priorities to elites and particular ethnic and regional groups, created government systems based on patronage and lack of democracy, and distorted development priorities to extract the resources they needed. New elites have found it all too easy to continue in the same pattern and the international community often found it easy to support the new elites. Frequently, civil war was the result. Thus the horizontal inequalities are often deeply rooted in a society and government is shaped by outsiders who intervened over decades before the war. Peacebuilding interveners during and after the war have to support the dismantling of these distorted institutions and the construction of new institutions and a new social contract, but they have to do it in a careful way because power relations are complex, subtle and often deeply internalised. But if these relations had been acceptable, there would not have been a war, so, at some level at least, most people will realise the need for change and appreciate outsiders as change agents.

Finally, the state plays a key role both in the war and in the peace. Civil wars are often fought, directly or indirectly, over state power – parties want to defend their hold on power or gain access to it. Civil wars often come about because of state weakness or state failure. When a group challenges a felt horizontal inequality, an effective state with a strong social contract can respond, mediating the dispute and redirecting resources to respond to the inequality, thus preventing violence and war. But a weak state cannot do that, and the social contract crumbles. A group in a civil war may not actually want to destroy the state, but when attacked, the weak state's facade crumbles.

Rebuilding the state thus becomes a key part of peacebuilding. It is the state which provides security and basic services, and the social contract, in large measure, is between a state and the people of that state. When the war occurred because the state was too weak to keep its side of the social contract, rebuilding and reinforcing the state becomes an essential peacebuilding task. But, as with so much else in the postwar period, it is not rebuilding the same state; the goal must be to help to build a state whose focus is developmental. There is much rhetoric about the need to build civil society and the need for decentralisation, but you cannot have 'non-government organisations' without a government. Indeed, national and international NGOs all assume a government to relate to, to put pressure on, and to supplement the services of. We cannot expect religious bodies to maintain roads, NGOs to operate the entire school system, or the private sector to run the courts. Perhaps most importantly, government and especially parliaments are essential for the evolving development vision which is needed for real peacebuilding.

There are historical issues here too. We looked at civil wars in the context of the state-building process and noted that most civil wars are in countries which were only created or only came out of colonialism in the twentieth century. Here again the damaging impact of colonialism and the Cold War comes through. Thus building the state is not simply about redressing the heritage of the war; it is also about completing a process which was not finished before the war. In the late twentieth century, the concept of the small, or 'lean' state became fashionable, but it seems particularly inappropriate in the post-civil war context. The state must create the umbrella under which peacebuilding is done.

What does that mean for interveners? On the 'Do no harm' side, it means not undermining the fledgling state with autonomous projects; even if it is faster and more efficient for outsiders to do something, capacity building and state building means taking a bit more time and developing local ways of carrying out actions. At the next level, working on war, it means concrete support for government ministries and agencies to have a real peacebuilding agenda – to make sure that schools and health posts and the police serve all parts of the country, with special stress on the most disadvantaged groups.

The international financial institutions and many donors stress 'efficiency', but peacebuilding is only about long-term 'efficiency', and may require doing things in the short term in ways that may not be the most efficient, but may be more effective. Investment in the capital city may bring the most rapid economic growth, but investment in remote and formerly rebel-held areas may possibly provide a 'peace dividend' that is much more useful in peacebuilding. Here again, government plays a role. The private sector will be happy to work in areas with good roads near the capital, but it may only be the government and a few NGOs who are willing to work in more remote areas, which are the areas that may need the most support.

Individuals matter

- *Place*. The best interveners do not think in generalities, but root their interventions clearly in the place and in the specific needs of local people.
- *Links*. Linkages may be the most important thing an outside intervener leaves behind; projects often collapse without the foreign input, but if people have become accustomed to working together to build something new then those links will live after the project.

- *Time*. Peacebuilding can take decades, yet most interveners stay for a year or two and most agencies need 'results' in a year and are gone in three. As well as links in space, there is a need for links in time – finding ways to create a longer-term commitment. This may be the hardest part; if an outsider carefully building bridges between distrusting groups leaves before the links are cemented, the subsequent collapse of relations can do more harm than if nothing had been done in the first place. But even here, individuals can be key. They can pressure their organisation to make a longer-term commitment and they can move quickly to bring in local organisations which will not leave. Here, time, place and links come together.

After a bitter civil war, livelihoods and a new social contract must be constructed, bit by bit, over time. This requires a developmental vision of a different society in which the inequities which led to the war are changed. It is not just shifting power from one group to another, but creating new ways of doing things, from national government down to local schools and community groups. Outside interveners with patience and an understanding of the war, sympathy but a certain distance and independence, and resources in terms of money and skills can make a big difference in the social and physical reconstruction and in peacebuilding. It will never be easy; mistakes will be plentiful. But we hope this book is one small contribution to improving the skills of those who want to intervene and help and who want to learn to be more effective.

Acknowledgements

Grateful acknowledgement is made to the following sources for permission to reproduce material within this book.

Text

Synopsis, International Development Research Centre (Department of Foreign Affairs and International Trade) 2001. Reproduced with the permission of Her Majesty the Queen in Right of Canada, represented by the Minister of Foreign Affairs, 2005.

Illustrations

1899 © Corbis. Illustrated by Hatherall W., Illustrated London News (1904) © Mary Evans Picture Library. Dennis Lee Royle © EMPICS. Pep Bon © Panos Pictures. Sven Torfinn © Panos Pictures. © Panos Pictures. Fredrik Naumann © Panos Pictures. Fredrik Naumann © Panos Pictures. Jeroen Oerlemans © Panos Pictures. Crispin Hughes © Panos Pictures. © EMPICS. Sven Torfinn © Panos Pictures. Yola Monakhov © Panos Pictures. Michael Dwyer © Alamy Images. Mark Henley © Panos Pictures. Ujir Magar © EMPICS. Martin Adler © Panos Pictures. Tony Morrison/South American Pictures. Giacomo Pirozzi © Panos Pictures. Patrick Brown © Panos Pictures. Jacob Silberberg © Panos Pictures. Heidi Bradner © Panos Pictures. Giacomo Pirozzi © Panos Pictures. Giacomo Pirozzi © Panos Pictures. Fernando Moleres © Panos Pictures. Teun Voeten © Panos Pictures. Peter Morrison © EMPICS. Sven Torfinn © Panos Pictures. Heldur Netocny © Panos Pictures. Clive Shirley © Panos Pictures. Jacob Silberberg © Panos Pictures. © David Rose.

Index

by Margaret Binns